# Web Programming with the
# SAP® Web Application Server

 **PRESS**

SAP PRESS is issued by
Bernhard Hochlehnert, SAP AG

SAP PRESS is a joint initiative of SAP and Galileo Press. The know-how offered by SAP specialists combined with the expertise of the publishing house Galileo Press offers the reader expert books in the field. SAP PRESS features first-hand information and expert advice, and provides useful skills for professional decision-making.

SAP PRESS offers a variety of books on technical and business related topics for the SAP user. For further information, please also visit our website: *www.sap-press.com*.

Horst Keller, Joachim Jacobitz
ABAP Objects
The Official Reference
2003, 1094 pp., hardcover, 2 CDs, ISBN 1-59229-011-6

Sigrid Hagemann, Liane Will
SAP R/3 System Administration
2003, approx. 450 pp., hardcover, ISBN 1-59229-014-4

Liane Will
SAP APO System Administration
Principles for effective APO System Management
2003, 240 pp., hardcover, CD, ISBN 1-59229-012-4

Werner Hertleif, Christoph Wachter
SAP Smart Forms
Creating forms quickly and easily
2003, 454 pp., hardcover, ISBN 1-59229-010-8

Helmut Stefani
Archiving Your SAP Data
A comprehensive Guide to plan and execute archiving projects
2003, 334 pp., hardcover, ISBN 1-59229-008-6

Frédéric Heinemann, Christian Rau

# Web Programming with the SAP® Web Application Server

 PRESS

**Translation:** Lemoine International, Inc. Salt
Lake City, UT
**Copy Editor:** Nancy Etscovitz
**Cover Design:** department, Cologne, Germany

Printed in Germany
ISBN 1-59229-013-2

# Contents

# Preface

Today, companies are confronted with ever-changing demands. Global markets, increasing competition between companies, and a growing list of customer requirements are forcing businesses to adopt new practices to remain competitive. These constantly changing demands have had a significant impact on the IT infrastructure that is being used by companies. Data-processing systems, in particular, have become increasingly important in the struggle to compete in the worldwide marketplace of electronic business.

A few years ago, an important goal was to gain cost advantages by introducing ERP systems and thus provide a greater degree of business-process integration. The next trend was toward collaboration with companies along the logistics chain—that is, Supply Chain Management. In the age of the Internet, the focus has been on *E-Community Collaboration* with complex business processes between companies, systems, and customers on an almost unlimited virtual network.

This E-Community Collaboration has had a rippling effect, resulting in technological consequences for the data-processing systems being used. SAP has met this challenge with its R/3 ERP system. With the strength of the R/3 system (namely, its security and stability), SAP has provided the ideal complement to the Internet technologies that are critical in this new age. The SAP Web Application Server (SAP Web AS) provides an open, scalable, and highly available infrastructure for developing dynamic and company-wide Internet applications. Building upon the tried-and-tested architecture of the SAP Application Server (AS), this new server with its enhanced Web functionality is the new technological foundation for all mySAP Business Suite solutions. As an independent server, SAP Web AS also functions as a development platform outside existing SAP applications.

The use of the SAP Web AS and the standards implemented for creating Internet-compatible applications are the subject of this book. Readers will not only gain detailed insights into the basic principles and architecture of the SAP Web AS, they will also learn all the relevant techniques for developing complex Web applications through numerous examples and a business scenario.

The authors who contributed to this book drew upon their many years of experience as developers and consultants at Novasoft AG. With the support of other Novasoft colleagues, they developed one of the first application systems based on the SAP Web AS to be used in a real business solution. Since then, the authors have helped customers to develop numerous Web projects. The experience gained in this process has been distilled in this book.

I am pleased that with this book, a detailed introduction to the SAP Web Application Server is finally available to the ever-growing ranks of the developer community.

Rüsselsheim, Germany, July 2003

**Bernd Herth**
Managing Director of the Center of Technology at Novasoft AG in Rüsselsheim

# 1 Introduction

This book is intended primarily for developers who want to create and implement Web-based applications in the R/3 environment. Readers of this book need not be R/3 developers; however, they should be prepared to tackle the new concepts and technologies presented in this book, which was written for IT decision-makers, project managers, and interested parties alike.

Target group

Because of the complexity of the subject and the varied needs of the audience, the difficult task of explaining the interrelationships and the relevant knowledge of the SAP Web Application Server (SAP Web AS) becomes even more difficult. Providing practical ways of looking at the concepts inherent in this topic is one of the most important goals we strove for when we wrote this book. For this reason, methods and technologies have been presented and utilized using an actual development project and numerous examples.

However, the book goes beyond this presentation of methods and technologies. Today, more than ever before, IT decision-makers and project managers are faced with the difficult problem of selecting a technology platform; once they have made that decision, they must choose which of the available concrete technologies they will use to reach their corporate goals. This book provides a more in-depth look at the architecture of and the potential applications that can be implemented with the SAP Web AS, thereby combining theory with practice and supporting you in the decision-making process.

In order to understand the exercises, as well as the diagrams in the practical section (Chapter 5), you will require a properly installed SAP Web AS. For the majority of examples in this book, Release 6.10 will suffice; however, some exercises relating to Business Server Pages (BSP) extensions and the Model View Controller (MVC) design pattern will function only with Release 6.20 and higher. You will also require the necessary development authorization for the practice system.

Requirements

Knowledge of DHTML and JavaScript would certainly be helpful, and we recommend basic skills in ABAP programming for a thorough understanding of the examples. Newcomers to the subject will not be abandoned, however. We will also explain the basic principles of ABAP programming.

**Contents** The contents of the book are divided into chapters, each focusing on a particular theme:

▶ **Chapter 2—Overview: SAP Web Application Server**
Chapter 2 describes the architecture as a whole, new enhancements such as the Internet Communication Manager (ICM), the Internet Communication Framework (ICF), J2EE integration, the SAP Web Dispatcher, and many more topics relating to the use of the term "Web" in the name of the new basis system. Security issues, which are central to these developments, are also covered. The differences between the ABAP and Java personalities are also described, along with the Internet Transaction Server (ITS). The chapter ends with a look at upcoming versions and the new developments they will include.

▶ **Chapter 3—Basic Principles: BSP Applications**
Chapter 3 presents the basic principles required for development work using BSPs. After a brief look at the example scenario, beginners, in particular, will be given the opportunity to familiarize themselves with the necessary language and standards. Readers already familiar with ABAP, HTML, JavaScript, CSS, XML, and Internet protocols and cookies can skip this section.

The second part of Chapter 3 is dedicated to the actual components of BSP applications, the processing work, and the MVC design pattern.

The final section is an introduction to including mobile clients.

▶ **Chapter 4—Development: Tools**
Chapter 4 focuses on the tools, which represent the developer's interface to the system and are therefore an important factor in a developer's daily work. The development environment of the SAP Web AS is powerful, because it can be used to realize both BSP applications and all other development tasks arising in the R/3 environment. This broad range can seem daunting at first. Therefore, the first section describes the whole of the development environment concisely.

In the next section, we concentrate in more depth on the tools and concepts that are particularly relevant for developing BSP applications. These tools include the Editor, the MIME Repository, and the WebDAV interface, as well as several additional tools, such as version management and the translation tools that provide developers with considerable assistance in their work.

▶ **Chapter 5—Practical Exercise: Creating BSP Applications**
Chapter 5 is dedicated to creating Web applications with the SAP Web AS. Many of the tools and concepts that have been presented in theory

are explained and demonstrated here. The advantages and disadvantages are demonstrated using practical examples, and are accompanied by discussions based on the authors' professional experience.

Here, an initial concept is converted into a Web application step-by-step. This process has not only been documented; it also explains the necessary basics of navigation, design, performance, and security.

▶ **Appendices**
Appendix A provides information about the classes and interfaces required, logging, BSP extensions, and many more topics, which are arranged for quick and easy reference. An SAP glossary is included in Appendix B. The bibliography and information about the authors are included in Appendix C and Appendix D respectively.

You will find more information on this book, updates, and any necessary corrections on the Internet at *www.sap-press.com*. The complete change request for the sample application can be found for download at *www.sap-press.com*.

**More information on the book**

## Credits

The path from the conception of a book to its actual completion is long and complicated. Many people have helped us in this process. If, in the following credits, we have omitted anyone who has contributed to the success of this book, please forgive the oversight.

We would like to thank our colleagues and managers, without whom this book would not have been produced. We would like to give our very special thanks in particular to Bernd Herth and Dr. Gangolf Haub, who were immensely supportive in providing us with suggestions and comments. Special thanks go to Heinz Jörg Göbert, without whose assistance we would never have found enough time to produce this book. We would also like to thank all our colleagues for their understanding, as they often helped us in small ways, sometimes even without their knowledge.

A book such as this always requires technical support. On behalf of SAP AG, we would like to thank Dirk Feeken, in particular, for providing resources, and Rüdiger Kretschmer, Steffen Knöller, and Jürgen Opgenorth for reviewing the manuscript and answering our technical queries.

However much a book of this type needs authors and technical support, it also needs a publishing house and its support. Otherwise, all prior efforts are for naught. Therefore, our thanks go to our editor Florian Zimniak, who made his contribution to this book with particular patience, perseverance, and understanding as well as to Regina Brautlacht for the English edition. We would also like to thank our American copy editor, Nancy Etscovitz.

Finally, we give our thanks to all of those, especially our friends and family, who supported us in creating this book and who are too numerous to mention.

# 2 Overview: SAP Web Application Server

*This chapter describes the individual components of the SAP Web Application Server. Understanding the architecture of the SAP Web Application Server is essential for creating future-proof, stable, and successful Web applications. Recognizing the opportunities afforded by this e-business infrastructure enables companies to make the right decisions for their particular needs.*

Growing customer requirements and increasing competition between businesses are forcing companies to optimize business processes, reduce costs, and strengthen relationships with customers, suppliers, and partners. Globalization, increasingly shorter product cycles, and new technologies are affecting business in a way never before experienced, regardless of the market sector. In the age of the Internet, company-wide integration—also known as *C-Business* (*Collaborative Business*)—is becoming the decisive competitive factor in the worldwide marketplace. However, C-Business does not mean that companies need to be redesigned from the ground up; rather, it means that business processes need to be optimized and the World Wide Web needs to be gradually integrated into existing structures.

**Making the grade**

The "electronization" of business processes based on Internet technology has established itself as a tool for overcoming these challenges. This network infrastructure must be in place in order for the internetworking processes and systems to run cost-effectively, thereby saving time, money, and resources. The goal here is cost-optimized, company-wide business processes, realized in heterogeneous system landscapes and based on open Internet standards. Developing easy-to-use Web applications for operating these business processes is therefore a critical success factor for companies—in theory, at least. In practice, however, a successful implementation of Internet-based solutions depends on a variety of factors. Web-based solutions require more than an attractive design and a powerful user interface. In addition to requirements such as reliability, scalability, integration compatibility, internationalization, and security, there are organizational challenges to consider, such as redesigning existing process workflows and fostering acceptance and trust within and between companies. A successful, flexible, and competitive IT solution package must address all these requirements right from the start.

Today, Web applications are designed to meet the many different demands of a growing population of end users. Critical business Web applications demand an ever-increasing complexity just to stay current, and provide the speed and high availability tailored to meet individual needs. A complex program logic often accompanies the traditional contents displayed, such as text and graphics. This logic retrieves data from many different kinds of systems and processes it to generate a dynamic response. In addition to an easy-to-use development environment, scaling and deployment are fast becoming the main topics of interest. These technical requirements make developing Web applications a challenging task—one that necessitates support from the relevant development platforms.

**Web Application Server** The market has responded to these requirements and delivered a software solution known as the *Web Application Server (SAP Web AS)*.[1] Web application servers provide an IT infrastructure that accelerates the development of powerful Web applications and simplifies their operation. Web application servers are used as a platform for publishing and managing corporate applications on the Internet and are regarded as a key technology for information processing in the e-business age. SAP offers its own solution, the *SAP Web Application Server*.

## 2.1 The SAP Web Application Server

The SAP Web Application Server (SAP Web AS) is SAP's answer to the demands of collaborative e-business scenarios. This chapter covers the architecture, functionality, and strategic presentation of this development platform, and concludes with a look at future developments.

### 2.1.1 What Is the SAP Web Application Server?

The SAP Web AS is an open, scalable, and high-availability infrastructure for developing dynamic and company-wide Internet applications. It is a server based on the well-known SAP Application Server (SAP AS) technology, with the additional enhancement of Web functionality.

---

1  In addition to SAP, other companies supplying this market include IBM (with WebSphere) and BEA (with the WebLogic Platform).

The SAP Web AS is the new technological basis of all mySAP Business Suite solutions. It is also the core element of the SAP R/3 Enterprise system—the successor to the classic SAP R/3. In the first official release of SAP Web AS, Release 6.10, SAP Web AS was available both as a standalone component and as the foundation layer for such mySAP Business Suite solutions as CRM 3.0. The version of SAP Web AS used in this book is the current release, Release 6.20.

**SAP Web AS as the new basis**

Before we discuss the SAP Web AS in detail, we'll describe the architecture of Web application servers in general.

### 2.1.2 The Architecture of Web Application Servers

Web-based applications are designed as a three-tier architecture, which means that the application is divided into three layers. The frontend—the client computer—contains the user interface. The data is stored in the backend. Between the frontend and the backend layers is a *middle tier* (also known as an *application server*), which is responsible for controlling and processing applications. Each of these layers carries out very specific tasks and thereby promotes abstraction, scalability, reliability, and simple expandability. Each layer of the Web AS uses services in the layer below it and makes services available to the layer above it (*client/server principle*). This three-tier architecture is illustrated in Figure 2.1.

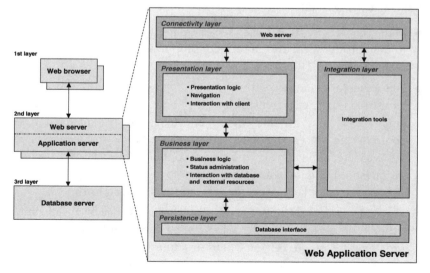

**Figure 2.1** The three-tier architecture of the Web Application Server

The three-tier architecture contains the following layers:

- ▶ Client layer (frontend)
- ▶ Application layer (middle tier)
- ▶ Database layer (backend)

**Client layer** The *client layer* contains a *graphical user interface* (*GUI*) that runs on PCs, workstations, and mobile terminals. In the Web environment, a Web browser is typically installed on this client.

**Application layer** An application server represents the middle layer and provides the necessary business logic and the system-oriented services. It also ensures connectivity via software programs required to run the business logic. In general, these programs provide services for other programs located either on the same computer or within the connected network.

For Web applications, a Web server is required for communication via the Web, in addition to a scalable application server. Using a TCP/IP connection, the HTTP protocol receives queries (*requests*) from a client, processes them, and responds (*responses*). The term "Web application server" is derived from the combining of Web servers and application servers, which means that Web applications that can be opened externally (using a Web browser) will run on a Web application server.

**Subcomponents of the application layer** As shown in Figure 2.1, the *application layer* contains other subcomponents (layers) with different tasks:

- ▶ In the *connectivity layer*, a Web server creates the necessary connection to the outside world using a series of supported protocols and Internet technologies (HTTP, HTTPS, SOAP, etc.).
- ▶ The *presentation layer* creates the GUI, for example, in the form of a generated HTML page, which consists of both static components (text, graphics, etc.) and dynamic components (e.g., display of read database contents). To process dynamic content, various tools and technologies are available (depending on the kind of support offered from the server in question). These tools and technologies include CGI/FastCGI, server-side script languages, servlets, add-ons, and so forth.
- ▶ The *business layer* provides the necessary business logic of a Web application. Complex business processes can be implemented based on the programming language(s) and infrastructure supported by the server environment. Up to this point, the process of building the architecture is virtually indistinguishable from traditional software development. Database accesses are facilitated, programs are invoked, calculations are carried out, the user status is managed, and so on.

► The *integration layer* ensures access to business functionalities from external resources. This is done using various interfaces, connectors (middleware), communication protocols, and support for general data exchange formats (e.g., XML).

► The *persistence layer* uses a general valid abstracted database interface to ensure a maximum level of database-independence and efficiency of access to datasets.

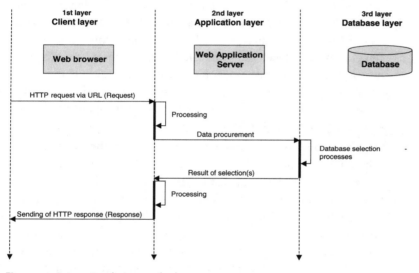

Developing complex Web applications without the dynamic generation of Web pages with links to a database is inconceivable. Data often needs to be accessed, temporarily stored, and written to a database. The *database layer* (the third layer) ensures the persistent (permanent) storage of data by means of a database server.

**Database layer**

**Figure 2.2** Interaction between the layers

The following steps illustrate the interaction between the various layers in the three-tier model (see Figure 2.2). Access to a Web application is via a URL using a Web browser running on a client PC (first layer). The Web AS (second layer) receives this request and starts the processing using the subcomponents described (i.e., the connectivity, presentation, business, integration, and persistence layers). The URL is used to detect which page and therefore which part of the application should be called. The required business logic is processed within the Web AS and the resulting page is created using the presentation subcomponent. When processing the business logic, external components are accessed or data is retrieved from

**Interaction between the layers**

the underlying database (third layer) via a database interface. The result of these interactions between the Web AS layers is an HTML page with both static and dynamic contents. The Web AS returns this page to the requesting Web browser as an HTTP data stream.

Requirements Web application servers must meet high demands:

▶ **Professional development environment**
A Web application server should provide a professional development environment specially tailored to the development needs of Web applications. High-scalability Web applications are typically developed on two levels.

▶ Developers are involved in creating the application layout on the presentation layer (which corresponds to the presentation layer subcomponent of the Web application server). Developers use primarily HTML, JavaScript, and Cascading Style Sheets (CSS) to create a user-friendly and standardized application interface (*Corporate Design*). Ideally, developers can select their preferred development tool and are not constrained by specifications. Often the server environment also offers templates to reduce the amount of coding work. For example, dynamic components of the layout can be created using server-side script languages.

▶ The actual business logic, which corresponds to the business layer subcomponent of the Web application server, is implemented on the second level. Here, application developers use the programming language(s) provided by the server environment via an integrated object framework. These business modules ultimately realize database accesses, make calculations, call remote methods, and provide the layout data for display. Integrated version management and control are also indispensable for team-based development.

▶ **High-scalability server architecture**
Numerous demands are placed on a Web application server. A page request must be processed just as quickly as a simple static HTML file. Nothing is more annoying than losing a potential customer because of an excessively long wait. Therefore, the prerequisite for increasing processing speed is the scalability of the Web application server. Separating the process of pure Web development from the productive operation is critical. All aspects relating to capacity, availability, scalability, and system monitoring, that is, tasks that generally fall to system administrators, must be viewed independently of the actual develop-

ment task.[2] A sudden rise in the number of users on Web application servers and the resulting higher load are indicative of this scenario. How does the system react if access to the Web application increases tenfold? Can stability and response time still be guaranteed?

The scalability of this type of system is a basic requirement for coping with bottlenecks and ensuring a smooth operation. Web application servers support this requirement using methods such as load balancing, fault tolerance, caching strategies, and system monitoring. In load balancing, performance problems are resolved using additional hardware (other servers). Here, the Web application is physically available on multiple parallel servers and a mechanism distributes the requests between the available servers. Examples of possible mechanisms include round robin DNS distribution (a method of managing server congestion by distributing connection loads across multiple servers), hardware/software distribution, and the use of reverse proxies. One positive side effect of load balancing across multiple servers (with the relevant configuration) is increased security against failure, resulting in increased fault tolerance of the entire system.

In addition to purely hardware-based solutions to increase availability (RAID, high-availability servers, recovery strategies, etc.), Web application servers also facilitate increased fault tolerance. Typically, a single server has multiple processes running on it. The server can be configured so that if one process fails, another process takes its place. This principle can also be applied to multiple servers functioning in a server cluster. If one server fails, another server can take over the first server's tasks. Another way to increase application performance is by temporarily storing frequently occurring responses (*caching*). Static contents are especially suited to caching. Using a monitor to continually check the system status can identify weak points (servers) early on. For example, you can evaluate system database accessibility via recorded log files, which can then be used for further system optimization.

► **Transaction security**
A Web application server's infrastructure must offer an environment for secure transaction applications. A *transaction* is the smallest logically related unit of commands or instructions. Transaction security means that in a successful case, the result of a transaction is secured; in

---

2   In reality, however, an entirely separate assessment is not possible. Developers also need to observe the performance of their solutions at all times, and work in close collaboration with system administrators in the event of bottlenecks.

the case of a fault, the result of the transaction can be reversed. This type of security ensures that the data is consistent.

▶ **Integration and connectivity**
You cannot connect to Web applications without having access to existing external systems. Access is provided via interfaces to other applications in many different types of systems. Web application servers typically function as an integration platform—that is, they need to support different systems via interfaces already provided, or via native support of recognized standards (e.g., various Internet protocols). Company-wide Web applications often combine different data formats from many different sources. To deal with the many formats, support for standardized and flexible data formats (e.g., XML) is provided. However, additional integrated or external tools are required to work with these data formats.

▶ **Security**
Web application servers need to provide a wide range of security mechanisms, which should ideally include central user management (registration and authorization), authentication procedures (e.g., passwords and certificates), and encryption of transferred data on the application level (e.g., Secure Sockets Layer [SSL]).

### 2.1.3 The Architecture of the SAP Web Application Server

The SAP Web AS is not a new system; rather, it builds on the proven traditional three-tier client/server architecture of the R/3 system.

**The traditional SAP Web Application Server**

The tried and trusted R/3 architecture (see Figure 2.3) is divided into presentation, application, and database layers.

Presentation layer
The *presentation layer* is the interface between the application and the user. Its task is to receive data and commands selected from the application layer and to prepare them for output. Using the *SAP Graphical User Interface (SAP GUI)*, which is the GUI used to operate SAP R/3, data is exchanged between the SAP GUI and the application layer. This exchange is carried out via SAP's own *DIAG* protocol *(Dynamic Information and Action Gateway)*.

Application layer
The *application layer* forms the central component of an R/3 system. This component is also known as the *system core* or *basis system*. The basis system covers a variety of programs, some of which facilitate business appli-

cations on the operating-system level as processes, as tasks, or as a whole. Upon starting, the R/3 application server generates a complete range of processes that provide various services.

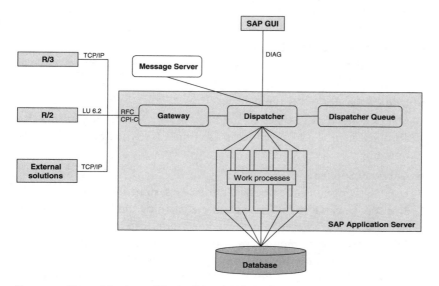

**Figure 2.3** The architecture of the traditional SAP Application Server

One of the most important operating-system processes is the *Dispatcher*, which can generate its own specialized subprocesses (*work processes*). The number of work processes generated and the tasks they complete are specified in a profile file. Incoming requests from the presentation layer or from other application servers and tasks for print and background management are distributed across these work processes. The services managed by the Dispatcher include:

▶ **Dialog Service (DIA type)**
Processes the user dialogs with the presentation layer. After processing a task, the work process is released and is available to other users. A different work process may be instructed to process further requests from the same user. In this case, all (previously saved) environmental conditions specific to that user (user context) are loaded back into the main storage so that the work process can access them. This process of transferring the user context into and out of storage is called *roll-in* and *roll-out*. The corresponding memory area is called a *roll area*[3].

---

3  The *roll area* is a memory area to which a work process belongs. If the context of the work process is changed, the data from the roll area is copied to a common resource—the roll file. To avoid the frequent copying of processes, there is an additional roll buffer in between, which is part of the shared memory.

- **Spool Service (SPO type)**
  Prepares and distributes the print jobs for the operating system printers.

- **Batch Service (BTC type)**
  Processes programs in the background.

- **Enqueue Service (ENQ type)**
  Ensures data consistency by maintaining and managing a block table in the main storage.

- **Update Service (UPD type)**
  Makes consistent changes to the database by transferring changes to an updater process. The process used here is asynchronous database updating.

- **Gateway Service**
  Used for communication between the SAP system and other programs. This service can also be started and managed by the Dispatcher. Alternatively, it can represent a process family similar to the Dispatcher. The *CPI-C protocol* (*Common Program Interface for Communication*) is used for communication between programs. The *RFC protocol* (*Remote Function Call*) is based on the CPI-C protocol and remote-capable ABAP function modules, and makes it simple to call functions on a remote computer.

**Dispatcher Queue**    In the *Dispatcher Queue*, the requests for the various work-process types are collected in separate queues. The Dispatcher also manages the system's memory resources and organizes the communication between the processes.

One process that is independent on the Dispatcher is the *message service*, which plays an important role in distributed R/3 systems. All application servers log their available services on a specifically named server (message server) on which the message service is running. The message service recognizes all services so that it can distribute all the tasks to the integrated server's available services. Using the information available, the message service can also perform a load-balancing process, such as forwarding logons to the server with the lowest load.

**Database layer**    On the *database layer* is the *R/3 database,* which provides the necessary data for the applications. There is just one database in each R/3 system. For each declared work process, an associated database process or database thread is started on the database side. This database process or thread is then responsible for running the SQL commands. A separate persistence layer (Open SQL) abstracts access to different database systems.

This architecture provides an R/3 system with good scalability on the presentation and application layers. It also offers the necessary resources to serve many users simultaneously and to meet increasing demands in real time.

### Expansion of SAP AS into the SAP Web Application Server

The SAP Web AS has been enhanced at the application level via the native opening of the system onto an intranet or the Internet. For this purpose, a process has been added to the SAP core enabling it to receive and process these requests directly. This process is known as the *Internet Communication Manager (ICM)* (see Figure 2.4). The ICM can be started automatically when the system is booted; it then acts as the Web server for the system. The ICM realizes the connection to the Internet and provides the environment for TCP/IP-based network connections. The secure variant HTTPS and SMTP for e-mail are supported in addition to the HTTP protocol. The ICM is based on a scalable multithread architecture[4], which means that it can process requests from the Internet in parallel.

**SAP Basis plus Internet using ICM**

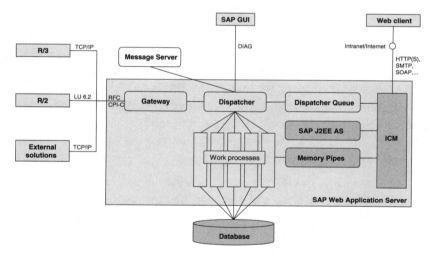

**Figure 2.4** The technical architecture of the SAP Web Application Server

The SAP Web AS can do more than simply function as a server; it can also function as a client. As a server, an HTTP request from any Web client (e.g., Web browser) is received directly by the ICM and processed. An HTTP response is then returned to that client. In this case, SAP Web AS

---

4  Threads are activities that run in parallel within a program and provide a better utilization of resources.

can function in both *stateful* mode (context is kept for an entire session) and *stateless* mode (context is lost after the page is changed).

"Stateful" versus "stateless" mode In stateful mode, a Web application is comparable to a traditional SAP R/3 transaction—that is, the application context is retained for each request/response cycle. In stateless mode, the SAP Web AS forgets everything after a request/response cycle—that is, the application context is lost. The stateful and stateless principles in the SAP Web AS are explained in more detail in Section 3.3.3.

When using the SAP Web AS as a client, HTTP requests can be generated from an ABAP program, for example, and sent to a remote Web server to receive and process the response.

**SAP Web AS in the server role** In the server role, the ICM responds to requests containing a server/port combination in the URL registered to it. Assigned methods (*Handlers*[5]) are then called to process these requests. This type of request can be addressed to a Web application created using the SAP Web AS programming model—the *Business Server Pages* (*BSP*). BSP pages may contain server-side scripting along with a page description language (e.g., HTML). The scripting consists of ABAP instructions requiring processing. To process the ABAP instructions, a work process provided by the Dispatcher is called, and it constructs a user context. The SAP system's entire ABAP functionality can then be accessed. The result of the processing (e.g., an HTML page) is then sent back to the ICM. This is carried out via memory-based communication objects called *Memory Pipes* (*MPI*), which facilitate the communication and data exchange between the work processes and the ICM. The result is returned to the client as a response. The steps of this process are as follows:

**Example request— Processing**
1. The ICM receives an HTTP request, because the URL contains the combination of server name and port that the ICM is "listening" to.

2. The ICM determines that a BSP application is the destination for the request, and selects the required handler.

3. The ICM stores the received data in an MPI (located in the shared memory) and informs the Dispatcher, because an ABAP context is required.

4. The Dispatcher places the ICM request in the Dispatcher Queue, creates a new context (if there is not already a context and the stateful condition is being used), and selects a work process for editing.

---

5  In general, handlers are specific methods that respond to certain events, initiate a process, and then return the control to the runtime environment.

5. The work process Taskhandler reads the data from the MPI, edits the request, and writes the response back to the MPI. It then signals to the ICM that the editing of the request is complete.

6. The ICM returns the response data to the client.

When the SAP Web AS is acting as a client, HTTP requests can be created from an ABAP program and the responses can be evaluated. When a work process wants to send a request via Internet protocol, the process proceeds as follows:

The SAP Web AS in the client role

1. The work process writes the data to be processed to the MPIs and calls the ICM directly via a TCP/IP connection.

2. This request passes the required information to an MPI handle, which allows the ICM to function in response to the relevant MPI sectors.

3. The ICM edits the data from the MPIs and, after receiving the response, returns the result to the MPIs.

4. If the work process waits for a response, it uses the status of the MPIs to detect whether the response has already been received.

5. If the work process has been rolled out, the ICM places a request in the Dispatcher Queue. This request contains a login session ID to roll back the work process that has been released into the correct context.

Since Release 6.20, it has been possible to install a J2EE-compatible application server as an additional component. This means that Web applications based on the Java language (to be precise, Enterprise Java-Beans [EJBs] and Java Server Pages [JSPs]) can be created. Therefore, depending on the installation, the SAP Web AS can support both the ABAP world and the Java world in one single system.

Java support

In addition, the SAP Web AS uses SAPConnect to support the sending and receiving of e-mail by supporting the SMTP protocol.

E-mail

The system's scalability permits the parallel use of multiple SAP Web AS instances. The load balancing this facilitates is carried out using the message server. The requests from the Web are then forwarded to the application server with the lowest load via a redirect.

So far, we have introduced both the overall architecture of Web application servers and the basic SAP Web AS features (see Section 2.1.2). The SAP Web AS architecture is shown in Figure 2.5.

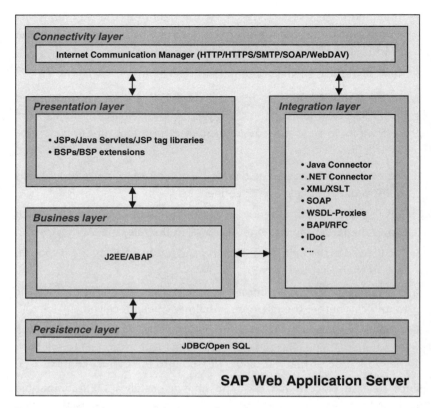

**Figure 2.5** The architecture of the SAP Web Application Server

The connectivity layer is represented by the ICM. A variety of standardized protocols, such as HTTP and SMTP, are supported for communication with the outside world.

**Two "persona-lities"** The SAP Web AS contains two different personalities: ABAP and Java. These complementary environments produce the options available for developing user interfaces (see the presentation layer in Figure 2.5). On the ABAP side, Web applications can be developed using BSPs; however, development is supplemented by a toolset, *BSP Extensions*. The J2EE-compatible Java personality can be used to display JSPs, Java servlets, and JSP tag libraries. Depending on the personality, the business logic is implemented in either the ABAP world or the J2EE world (JavaBeans).

The integration layer ensures the communication with a variety of systems and applications. The SAP Web AS provides all the necessary mechanisms for connecting the SAP world (e.g., RFC, BAPI[6], IDoc[7]) and the non-SAP world via a variety of connectors (e.g., Java- and .NET-connectors).

The SAP Web AS supports Web service technology (via a separate SOAP framework) and multitude of document standards, most notably XML. The persistence layer is an abstraction layer for integration with different database systems. On the ABAP side is a powerful concept for integrating various databases licensed by SAP: the Open SQL interface. The Java side provides database-specific links to different databases using JDBC.

## 2.1.4  Features of the SAP Web Application Server

The SAP Web AS makes the possibilities of the Internet available for all enterprise systems. The SAP Web AS builds on the known reliability and high scalability of the SAP R/3 application server architecture; however, it is more than a simple e-business platform for Internet projects. It provides the necessary infrastructure for meeting the many complex demands of e-business projects. The most important features are summarized below:

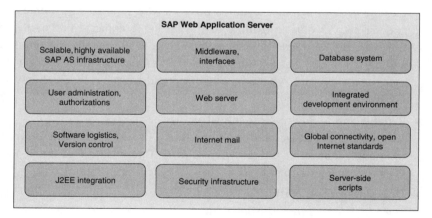

**Figure 2.6** Overview of the most important components in the SAP Web Application Server

---

6  BAPI stands for *Business Application Programming Interface* and provides an open, stable, and object-oriented interface for accessing business objects in an SAP system.

7  IDoc stands for *Intermediate Document* and is an SAP format for the electronic data exchange between systems.

▶ **Open Internet standards**

These standards include HTTP, HTTPS, SMTP, HTML, WML, SOAP, and XML with native support in the SAP Web AS. Any high-level XML transformations can be accomplished with an Extensible Style Language Transformation (XSLT) engine. The server also acts as a client and can therefore communicate reciprocally with other Web application servers.

▶ **Server-side scripts**

SAP's own language, ABAP, provides Web developers with an "in-house" programming language as well as a server-side script language. As previously mentioned, this programming model is known as *BSPs* in the SAP Web AS. When developing dynamic BSP applications, developers have the familiar and trusted workbench of the SAP environment available to them. This supports developers in the work of versioning, debugging, release, and data transport. BSP application development has been fully integrated into the SAP system's native development environment. With Release 6.20 of the SAP Web AS, an SAP J2EE Application Server (Sun Microsystems Java 2 Enterprise Edition) can also be installed. Therefore, you can now generate dynamic page content using JSPs.

▶ **Flexible Web design and layout**

Flexible Web design and layout is possible with style sheets, themes, and scripts. All objects relating to the layout (graphics, multimedia, CSS files, etc.) are held in a separate section in the database. Layout and design can be created both within the SAP development environment and with external professional frontend tools via the WebDAV interface.

▶ **Reliable and highly scalable infrastructure**

This feature, which was already part of the SAP Server, combines with the multilanguage functionality typical of SAP to ensure that the SAP Web AS provides a solid basis for cross-language applications.

▶ **Open integration platform**

The SAP Web AS uses existing communication technologies and supports the integration of standard middleware components and common communication standards. Because the SAP Web AS is a native SAP system, it provides the best possible support for integrating SAP components. Existing Internet applications can be integrated because the SAP Web AS can also act as a client. The SAP Web AS supports the Unicode standard, which is recognized worldwide and which allows characters to be used in all kinds of applications, regardless of the platform, program, or language. These applications can be used for many systems, languages, and countries directly and without any loss of information. No further modification is required.

▶ **Security**
Security is fundamental in implementing critical business Internet applications. The SAP Web AS supports the familiar authentication and secure communication options, as well as the most important Internet security standards. To ensure that data is transmitted securely, Secure Sockets Layer (SSL) is supported on the basis of HTTP (HTTPS). Certificates (X.509), tickets, and cookies are used for authentication purposes. The SAP Web AS can therefore be fully integrated into single-sign-on (SSO) environments, or can itself create SSO environments.[8] The authorization checks known from the R/3 environment are also available.

▶ **Support for platforms**
The support for platforms (operating systems, databases, middleware, etc.) corresponds to the familiar standards of SAP technology. The operating systems supported include Windows 2000 Server, AIX, Linux, Z/OS, HP-UX, and Solaris/Sparc.[9] On the database side, the systems from Oracle, Microsoft SQL Server, Informix, SAP DB, DB2/UDB, DB2/390, and DB2/400 are supported.

▶ **Java support**
Support for all Java-based components of the mySAP Business Suite is provided by an *SAP Java 2 Enterprise Edition Standard (J2EE) Engine* integrated into Release 6.20 of SAP Web AS (to be fully integrated in the future). The *SAP Java Connector (JCo)* guarantees the link between the ABAP and Java worlds. This means that two different runtime environments, or personalities—the Java personality and the ABAP personality—are integrated into the SAP Web AS and share a common infrastructure. The Java engine conforms to the J2EE Engine. An integrated development environment (IDE) is not supplied as standard. Java applications can generally be developed using any Java IDE. SAP explicit support offered by the SAP IDE JBuilder5 is now replaced by the development environment of the open-source platform *Eclipse* from IBM. SAP Web AS 6.30 version provides the IDE specific SAP development environment, which ist named 'SAP Net Weaver Developer Studio'.

---

8 The SAP Web Application Server can also issue tickets for SSO accesses itself.
9 Both 32-Bit and 64-bit versions are available. Not all of the OS/DB-combinations are currently released.

▶ **Minimizing overall system costs**

The SAP Web AS features low overall implementation, maintenance, and infrastructure costs because a single system unites all the necessary components—the BSP development environment, database, application server, Web server, interfaces, software logistics, authorizations, and so on. Standardization allows the number of interfaces to be reduced. For companies, this means a protection of investment, because standardization facilitates simpler and faster integration with a variety of existing systems. The link to traditional SAP systems, in particular, is inherently very well supported.

The SAP Web AS provides comprehensive support of open Internet standards for creating an integration platform, especially in heterogeneous environments. However, this type of server does not necessarily herald the end of existing Internet-based SAP solutions such as the Internet Transaction Server (ITS) or the SAP Business Connector[10]. The development of the SAP Web AS is the logical progression of SAP's goal of full integration of the R/3 system into the Internet environment.

### 2.1.5 SAP NetWeaver and the SAP Web Application Server

Behind the name *SAP NetWeaver* is a new infrastructure concept, which can be used for all existing and future SAP solutions. The new SAP NetWeaver infrastructure builds on the existing R/3 system architecture primarily in the areas of the interface, applications, and links to external systems. The purpose of this concept is to integrate the following directives for the e-business applications running on it:

▶ Architecture founded on security, scalability, reliability, and internationalization

▶ Openness in the use of platforms

▶ Support for open and standardized Internet technologies

▶ Bundling of information, applications, and processes on a common user interface

▶ Complete integration for achieving in-house and company-wide collaboration in business applications

SAP NetWeaver is an evolutionary development of mySAP Technology, which has been expanded with a *Composite Application Framework* and the *Master Data Management Service* (MDM).

---

10 The SAP BC is replaced by the SAP Exchange Infrastructure (XI).

The Composite Application Framework permits the cross-functional reproduction of business processes across different application, system, and organizational levels. The applications facilitated by this process view are known as *SAP xApps*. They allow existing systems to be flexibly integrated and new functional components to be included in the business processes.

**Composite Application Framework**

The MDM is a standardized concept for solving the challenge of integrating data from a variety of sources and heterogeneous system landscapes. Ensuring data integrity in a company network is the MDM's foremost goal. This is achieved by collecting all master data in one controlled system and then distributed to other systems.

**MDM**

SAP NetWeaver is predicated on a kind of technological integration that provides the openness, security, and infrastructure necessary for developing e-business applications. It also provides various solutions, tools, and services for establishing Internet-based business processes for company-wide collaboration across heterogeneous components. Because SAP NetWeaver is an Enterprise Application Integration (EAI) platform, the focus is on process integration as well as a purely technological solution. SAP NetWeaver consists of three central components, SAP Web Application Server, the SAP Enterprise Portal, and the SAP Exchange Infrastructure, which form the basis for this new technology platform (see Figure 2.7):

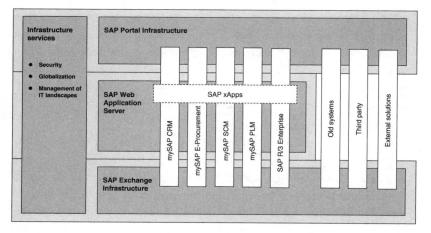

**Figure 2.7** Overview of SAP NetWeaver

► **Portal infrastructure**
The SAP Enterprise Portal functions as a superordinate system that combines the information content and the underlying systems and displays them on an efficiently operated user interface. The role-based

combination of information and applications ensures an efficient method of working for each user. Ideally, users should be able to "Drag & Relate" between applications, without having to exit the portal.

Preparing Information

The flood of information and the associated range of applications that users face on a daily basis increase the complexity of both business decisions and the underlying software systems. To avoid jeopardizing productivity, an architecture solution is required that allows information to be prepared and compiled automatically. To avoid overloading the employee with irrelevant information, the information needs to be tailored to the particular needs of the employee. The prepared information could be both unstructured information from many sources (e.g., Web pages, text files, documents, etc.) and structured information (e.g., orders) from databases on connected systems.

Because all too often much of the workday is misspent in the search for information, an efficient classification and search system is essential. The multitude of retrieved and associated information is then displayed on a standardized user interface. Ideally, access to relevant applications, as well as information, should be provided.

The portal solution from SAP meets these requirements. SAP Enterprise Portal provides uniform access to all applications such as business intelligence systems, documents, Web content, and Web services, both inside and outside the company. Employees gain an entirely new insight into the company and its processes. They can organize their work more efficiently, because the information they require for their respective responsibilities can be compiled and customized. The portal ensures the integration and bundling of all kinds of information, applications, and services from the user's point of view.

► **SAP Web Application Server**
The technological basis of all mySAP Business Suite applications is the SAP Web AS. This e-business development platform is used to provide a reliable, future-proof, infrastructure for critical business (Web) applications and (Web) services, both within and outside the company. To ensure this infrastructure, Internet functionality is integrated directly into the basis system. An expanded programming environment is also provided for developing Internet applications. Web applications can be developed using either ABAP or Java.

► **SAP Exchange Infrastructure**
The technological basis of the SAP Exchange Infrastructure (XI) is the SAP Web AS. It ensures the application integration of in-house and

company-wide business processes between software solutions from many different providers. This foundation forms an open, standardized infrastructure based on XML and Java. Technological integration is achieved with support for various standards, protocols, and connectors such as HTTP, XML, SOAP, and the Java Connector. In addition, the SAP XI meets the challenge of recording the different priorities of exchanged information in the business context of the relevant company and system, and allocating them appropriately. This principle of *Shared Collaboration Knowledge* is the basis for storing knowledge and is exemplified via the SAP XI for exchanging information with other systems.

## Extra note: Web services

Understanding Web services and the roles they can play in your SAP environment is critical to thriving in a heterogeneous system landscape. Web services and the standards involved are the interface technology of the future for integration both within a company and between companies. Web services are modular software components that can be published, searched, and made accessible via a network (e.g., the Internet) founded on open standards. A Web service is based on the following standards:

▶ SOAP (Simple Object Access Protocol)

▶ UDDI (Universal Description, Discovery, and Integration)

▶ WSDL (Web Services Description Language)

▶ XML (eXtensible Markup Language)

SOAP describes a protocol for calling Web services in distributed landscapes. The functionality is comparable to a Remote Procedure Call (RPC). SOAP uses HTTP as the transport protocol. One of SOAP's significant advantages is that it can be easily integrated into infrastructures with high-security requirements (firewalls).

**SOAP for calling Web services**

Web services are searched and published using public-directory services. UDDI has been used to define a standard of this type. UDDI is different from other directory services because no actual documents or specifications are stored; only references to the documents or specifications are stored.

**Search and publish with UDDI**

A Web service is described using WSDL. WSDL is defined as XML-documented and has a specific appearance, which is described in a *Document Type Definition* (*DTD*) or XML scheme. DTD specifies the structure of an XML document. All elements that may occur in the XML document are entered in the DTD. Specific rules, such as how often an element occurs

**Describe with WSDL**

and the content it might contain, are stored for each element of the DTD. A parser can be used to check whether an XML document conforms to a DTD. The XML scheme is used to define and describe a class of XML documents using scheme components. The scheme components limit the significance, use, and relationships of the components (data types, elements, and their contents, attributes, and their values) of the scheme (XML) documents and document them. Schemes can also provide the specifications for additional document information, such as normalization and the specification of attribute and element values. Schemes have options for self-documentation. Therefore, XML schemes can be used to define, describe, and categorize XML vocabulary for classes of XML documents.

A WSDL description of a Web service is characterized by a number of *Web service EndPoints* or *Ports*. A port contains a port type and the operations defined for this port type. A port is generally expressed as a URL and points to the Web service implementing the operations. The binding—that is, the definition of the protocol to be used—also depends on this port, which makes it possible to define a service and to address it via different ports using different protocols.

XML as the foundation
XML is a formatting language that allows document structures to be defined. The data is delimited with tags. The sequence of the tags can be precisely specified with DTDs or XML schemes. XML plays a special role in the Web service environment. Much like the messaging format SOAP, the WSDL description of a Web service, like the interchange data itself, is represented in XML format.

Web service support in the SAP Web AS
Since Release 6.20 of the SAP Web AS, components that can be developed in both the ABAP and the Java personality can be called as a Web service.

In the ABAP personality, each remote-compatible function module or BAPI can be released as a Web service. The required WSDL description can be generated automatically by activating the integrated Web service browser. This browser can be accessed via *http://www.my-domain[11].de/ sap/bc/bsp/sap/webservicebrowser*. After entering the URL, the R/3 Webservice Browser is displayed as shown in Figure 2.8. All function modules and BAPIs released as Web services can be found here.

---

11 The domain *http://www.my-webas.de* does not directly lead to a real SAP Web AS but to a "normal" domain. You should replace the links in this book with the domain of your choice when you install SAP Web AS 6.10/6.20.

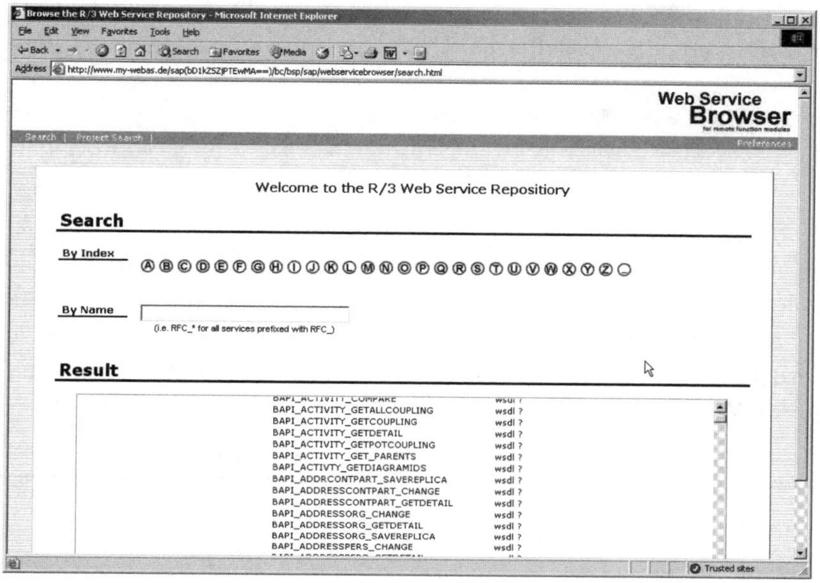

**Figure 2.8** The Web service browser

Behind each function module is a link, which generates a WSDL description when activated and displays it in another window. The WSDL description can be saved locally for further processing.

If the service needs to be used from a Java-based environment, for example, proxy generators can be used to generate the required `class` files. The result is a source text prototype, whose classes ultimately need to be completed with the necessary application logic. In principle, any available proxy generator can be used; however, SAP also supplies a proxy generator as part of the SAP Web Service Toolkit.

In the Java personality, all methods of a stateless Java SessionBean can be made available as a Web service. The *Java Web Services Pack* from the Java community standardizes the procedure. SAP supplies a Web service toolkit based on this procedure. This toolkit can be used to view all deployed beans via *http://your_Java_host/soapdispatcher*, to release them as a Web service (in Release 6.20, all stateless SessionBeans are released as a Web service by default), and to generate the required WSDL descriptions.

Access to external Web services is also supported for both ABAP and Java personalities. A uniform SOAP framework and a proxy generator are available for this purpose. The proxy generator is started in ABAP using Trans-

**Access to external Web services**

action SPROXY and in Java from the *Integration Builder* context menu. You must enter the URL for the WSDL description for the required Web service. The proxy generator then generates an ABAP or Java class, whose methods create a framework for the Web service functionality. The proxy class generated in this way can be linked into separate applications and its methods can be used.

**Integration Engine**  The proxy classes use the SOAP framework for communication via Web services. Here the SOAP framework provides an object-oriented framework for the *Integration Engine*, which is a fixed component of the SAP Web AS and the SAP Exchange Infrastructure (XI). The Integration Engine carries out the actual low-level communication via the Internet Communication Manager (ICM) and provides a uniform API for both personalities.

Searching and publishing in accordance with the UDDI standard is also supported by SAP XI. The architecture described for Web service support in the SAP Web AS is displayed once more in Figure 2.9.

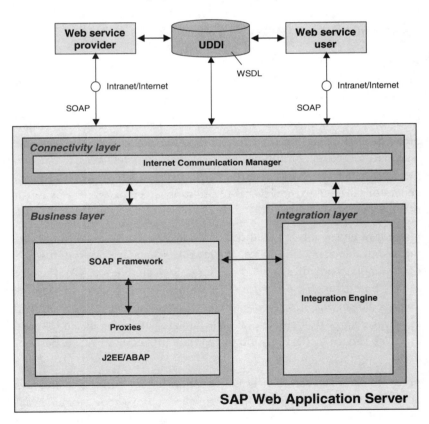

**Figure 2.9** The Web service architecture

Web services will play an important role as a promising interface technology in the integration between companies. The importance of Web services is reflected in SAP NetWeaver. All three components of SAP NetWeaver have different tasks. The SAP Enterprise Portal makes the Web services visible for the end user via a Web-based interface. Web services are developed and run with the help of the SAP Web AS. Finally, the communication and integration via Web services between applications is accomplished with the SAP XI.

Infrastructure services that are integral to SAP NetWeaver are available across all components. These services include indispensable security mechanisms and tools for monitoring and maintaining IT system landscapes in a globally distributed corporate IT structure.

**Infrastructure services**

Without the necessary security mechanisms, even the most cleverly thought-out infrastructure cannot succeed in the marketplace. Application-level security plays a critical role, as well as network-level security. Clear authentication of the communication partners and effective encryption of all transmitted information are of vital importance. In complex system landscapes, it is also useful to manage users' roles and access rights centrally. You can achieve this centralized management by using directory services based on the LDAP standard. SAP NetWeaver provides support for this standard as well as its own user management and rights management functions. The SSL protocol and Virtual Private Networks (VPN) are supported for encrypting the information flowing between applications, using procedures such as RSA. The system also incorporates digital signature management and an interface (GSS-API) for other security services.

**No business without security**

SAP NetWeaver provides an overall technological concept for reproducing and integrating Web-based business processes, which is ensured using direct support for XML and Internet standards. In the current release, the SAP Web AS, which functions as the basis for this infrastructure, already supports several of these standards (see Section 2.1.4). SAP NetWeaver is making SAP technologies available in both the frontend and the backend areas. SAP Enterprise Portal provides a central and uniform entry point for a large range of business tasks. The SAP Web AS is a powerful e-business development platform. The SAP XI integrates internal and company-wide business applications on the basis of standardized Internet technologies. Security mechanisms are an integral part of this infrastructure, and ensure secure business processes. This overarching concept also permits the complete life cycle of an IT landscape to be managed in a global and heterogeneous environment.

**Conclusion**

### 2.1.6   Uses of the SAP Web Application Server

The SAP Web AS provides the necessary infrastructure for bringing together business applications and the Web. As we described earlier, the server unites all components on one platform for developing and using scalable, dynamic, and collaborative Web applications. All the necessary Internet technologies are integrated into this basis system to realize correspondingly integrated SAP Internet applications. Professional enterprise applications can be implemented from the ABAP development environment without additional Web and application servers. The additional Java support meets the requirement for modern Internet applications and provides the necessary connectivity into the non-SAP world. The Web applications created are fully integrated into the SAP system, ensuring a high level of protection of investment.

Although the SAP Web AS is recommended primarily for Web applications, with a focus on integrating SAP systems, this application server's possible uses are exceptionally varied. The main uses of the SAP Web AS are:

▶ Developing personalized Web frontends for (all) existing SAP applications

▶ Developing new Web applications with access to existing SAP and non-SAP systems

▶ Developing new separate Web applications

▶ Providing a Web service development platform

All of these objectives make the server best suited for Internet projects focusing on integration with SAP and other systems. However, user departments in the company itself can develop separate Web applications quickly with a good knowledge of ABAP and HTML. Applications displaying and integrating collaborative information from multiple companies in the frontend are also feasible—for example, a supply chain management portal abstracted and personalized for the customer. If a customer configures a computer online, the various components' delivery times and the choice of components are evaluated based on various criteria. The availability check could be accomplished by using a Web service for the components based on information on supplier stocks.

## 2.2    The Internet Communication Manager

The *Internet Communication Manager* (ICM) ensures TCP/IP communication between the SAP Web AS and the outside world by providing basic TCP/IP functions for the SAP Web AS. The Internet protocols supported are provided as plug-ins and can be loaded and removed during operation. Currently, plug-ins for the HTTP and SMTP protocols are supplied as standard, and the SAP Web AS can also be configured to use HTTPS. Each plug-in is assigned to one or more TCP/IP ports, with no overlaps permitted (e.g., port number 80 for HTTP and port number 25 for SMTP). These settings are maintained with system profile parameters.

In the server role, the ICM can process requests from the Internet that are received with URLs with the server/port combination that the ICM is listening to. The ICM then invokes the local handler responsible for processing these requests, based on the URL. BSP applications need an ABAP context and are transferred to a work process. Java requests are transferred to the J2EE engine for processing.

### The architecture of the Internet Communication Manager

The Internet Communication Manager (ICM) is a part of the SAP Web AS that is required to communicate with the Internet via HTTP(S) or SMTP. It is implemented as a separate process that is started and monitored by the Dispatcher.

Figure 2.10 provides a detailed overview of the architecture and functional principle of the ICM. The ICM contains various threads for parallelizing the triggered activities.

**Multithreaded architecture**

The ICM control center is implemented by the *thread control*, which receives the incoming requests and forwards them to the thread pool for processing. The thread control can create new threads or reactivate sleeping threads.

**Thread control**

The actual processing of requests and responses is carried out by *worker threads*. To ensure parallelization, multiple worker threads are available in a thread pool. The number of worker threads can be specified with system profile parameters. Each worker thread contains an I/O handler, which creates the network connections and plug-ins for the protocols being supported. Plug-ins for HTTP and SMTP protocols are currently implemented. There is a separate encryption and decryption component for the HTTPS protocol (if this protocol is set up). Requests may contain a session ID for establishing sessions with context. These session IDs are

**Worker thread**

then transferred to the Dispatcher to restore the corresponding user context for the session in question. Each worker thread can write requests directly to a free work process in the Dispatcher Queue.

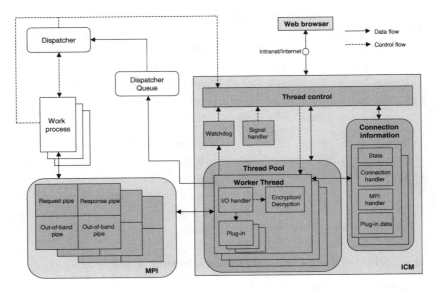

**Figure 2.10** Architecture and functional principle (ABAP requests) of the Internet Communication Manager (ICM)

**Watchdog**  A worker thread typically waits for the response to the request that has been placed. If the response takes too long, a time-out mechanism is triggered for the worker thread. This timeout also occurs if not all of the response's network packets have been received. In this case, the waiting process for full completion of the response is transferred to a separate thread, the *watchdog*. If the watchdog receives the response, thread control is informed, and the relevant worker thread is activated. The watchdog also initializes threads and connections if a work process is terminated and leaves an inconsistent status.

**Signal handler**  The *Signal handler* processes signals generated by other processes (e.g., the Dispatcher) or the operating system. This processing of signals means that the ICM can be started and stopped, via the Dispatcher, for example, and the ICM trace level can be changed.

**Memory pipes**  The *memory pipes* (*MPI*) are responsible for data exchange between the work process and the ICM, and are located in the shared memory. An MPI consists of four pipes, with two pipes available for the requests and two pipes available for the responses. Each of these pairs of pipes contains one pipe for normal data and one pipe for control information (*out-*

*of-band pipe*). Their main task is to signal whether a work process has been rolled out due to an excessive waiting time, and whether a work process has finished writing the request or response data to the MPIs.

Each link contains required information that needs to be stored temporarily. This information includes data on the status and condition of a link,
data across memory sectors of the MPIs, and reserved data sectors for the
plug-ins.

**Link information**

The ICM console is accessed via Transaction SMICM (see Figure 2.11). The ICM status (traffic light) and the condition of the threads are displayed in this transaction's start screen.

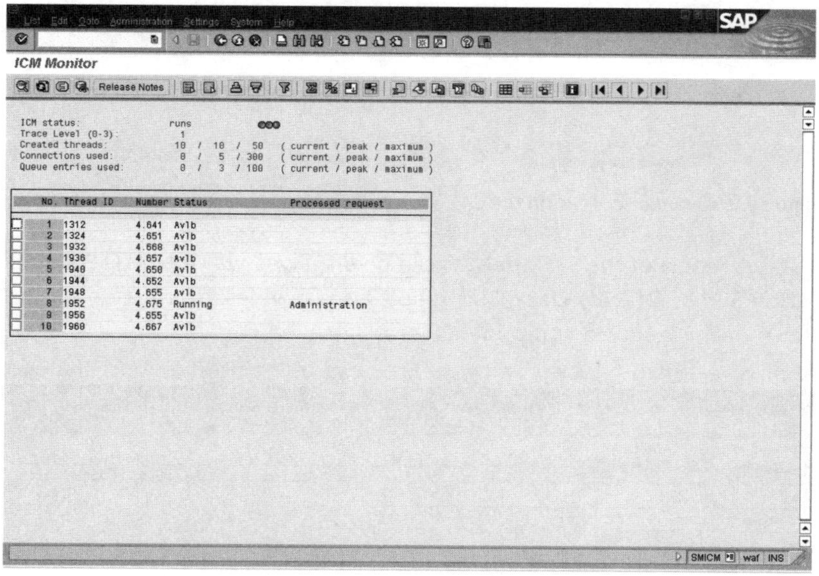

**Figure 2.11** The Internet Communication Manager (ICM)

The **Administration** menu can be used to control and manage the ICM, the Dispatcher, and the J2EE application server.

The **Goto** menu provides a clear overview of the various settings and configuration options. The most important settings are summarized below.

An overview of the protocols (services) available on the SAP Web AS can be found via **Goto Services** (see Figure 2.12). The available protocols, assigned port numbers, and set time-out parameters can be viewed here.

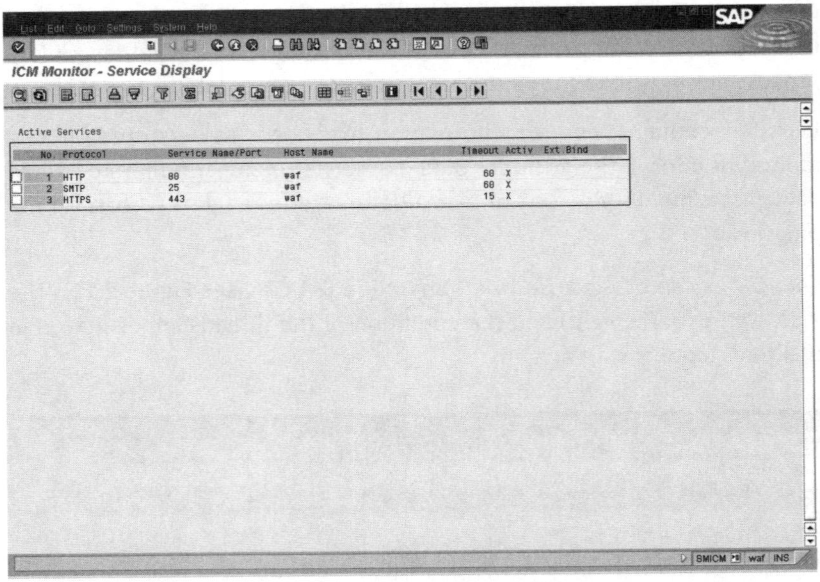

**Figure 2.12** Defined services on the SAP Web Application Server

A status report of the SAP Web AS can be displayed via **Goto HTTP Application Server Display Data**. This report also provides information on the status of the installed components (see Figure 2.13).

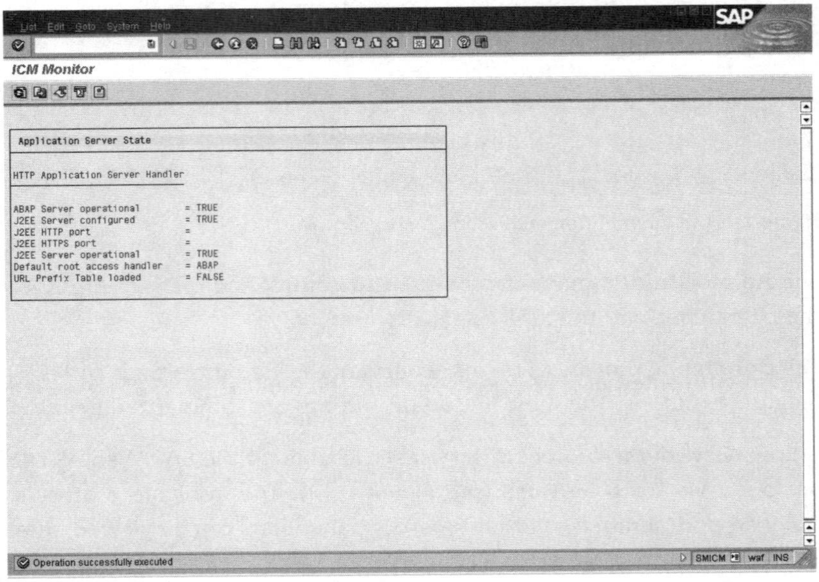

**Figure 2.13** The status of the SAP Web Application Server

Following changes to the ICM configuration, only the ICM needs to be restarted via the Administration menu; not the entire application server.

## The HTTP plug-in for the ICM

The HTTP plug-in (see Figure 2.14) provides the basic functionality for processing HTTP requests and responses. The plug-in consists of a variety of subhandlers performing specific tasks.

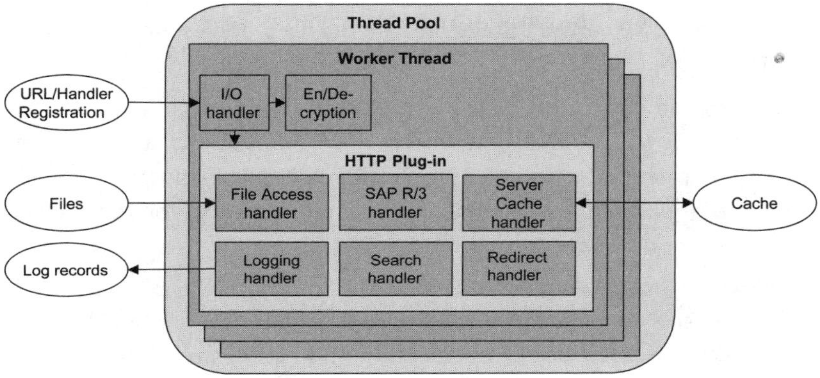

**Subhandlers**

**Figure 2.14** The HTTP plug-in

This breakdown is used to increase performance, because it isn't necessary to create a user context in the work process for each request (e.g., for an HTTP redirect). You can use system profile parameters (HTTP subhandler parameters) to maintain the URL prefixes to which the various handlers should correspond. The handlers are called and can edit the request themselves or forward it to the next handler. An incoming request is then assigned to the most appropriate subhandler according to the settings from the I/O handler based on the URL prefix. This assignment is derived from the I/O handler of the URL Subscription List. The handlers are entered in this configuration list according to priority. In addition, the *call type* determines whether a subhandler is run in the current thread context (internal), or whether a new process needs to be generated for integration with external products (external). The handler that is then called either edits the request, signals a fault, or indicates that it is not responsible for this request. In the latter case, the request is forwarded to the next suitable handler. If multiple subhandlers are entered for a URL prefix, the subhandlers are accessed in the order in which they were entered.

Given below is a more detailed description of the available subhandlers:

▶ **Redirect handler**

The *Redirect handler* forwards an incoming HTTP request to a different HTTP server. For each HTTP redirect (301), a URL prefix for the incoming requests and a destination URL should be entered. Up to 100 redirects can be maintained.

▶ **File Access handler**

The *File Access handler* returns static files from the file system to the incoming HTTP request. Static files are mainly graphics, documents, or HTML pages.

▶ **Logging handler**

The *Logging handler* does not answer the HTTP request; rather, it saves metainformation (metadata) (e.g., a URL with timestamps) in a text file on the application server. The configuration options for the logging process are described in Appendix A.3.

▶ **Server Cache handler**

The *Server Cache handler* reads and writes data from the ICM server cache (this is described in detail later). This cache is used for the temporary storage of frequently used non-dynamic data. For frequent requests (for the temporary storage of objects), this cache can prove very helpful in returning the requests to the initiator in a much more timely fashion. Each cache entry receives a timestamp specifying the validity of an object. If an object expires, it is deleted from the cache and needs to be read in again. If a request can be operated from the cache, no user context is created. If the data is not available in the cache, the request is transferred to the SAP R/3 handler.

▶ **SAP R/3 handler**

The *SAP R/3 handler* is the default handler. It comes into play if no other suitable handler can be found for the incoming HTTP request. The request is forwarded to the SAP system and the response is returned. A user context is created in a work process.

The subhandlers can be called multiple times in succession during a request/response cycle. For example, it would be useful to log a request in the first step (Logging handler), and then try to fulfill the request from the cache (Server Cache handler). If the cache access is unsuccessful, the SAP R/3 handler is called. The response is then written to the cache (Server Cache handler) and can be logged once more (Logging handler).

## The SMTP plug-in

The SAP Web AS supports the sending and receiving of e-mail using SMTP (Simple Mail Transfer Protocol). Therefore, e-mail can be exchanged between the SAP Web AS and any SMTP-compatible mail server, without additional external components. The SAP Web AS transfers the outgoing e-mail to a single mail server. Incoming e-mail can be received by any number of mail servers. SMTP works primarily according to the store-and-forward mechanism. Here, a mail client forwards the message to a linked MTA (Mail Transfer Agent). The MTA saves the message and forwards it to the next MTA, until a destination MTA can resolve the message for a local user. The link between the different communication partners is created via a handshake procedure. Just as it can with the HTTP protocol, the SAP Web AS can assume the role of either an SMTP client or an SMTP server (see Figure 2.15).

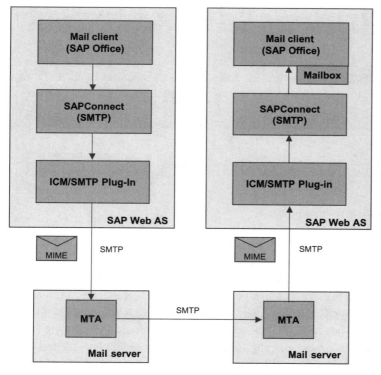

**Figure 2.15** Sending and receiving e-mail

The actual creation and processing of e-mail is carried out via the SAP-Connect interface.

**SMTP client**    Sending an e-mail using SAPConnect via SMTP is carried out as follows (see Figure 2.16). SAPConnect generates the message being sent in a MIME-compatible[12] Format. This message is transferred to the SMTP processor as a data stream. The processor sends the stream to the ICM. Any error messages or delivery confirmations are returned to the SMTP processor. For outgoing e-mail, the work process sends a request for SMTP communication to the ICM. A free worker thread is then selected within the ICM via the thread control. The SMTP plug-in is called via the I/O handler. This plug-in receives the message stream and forwards it to the next MTA.

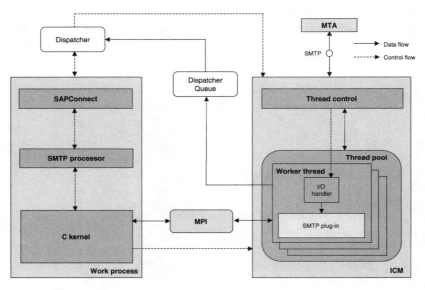

**Figure 2.16** SMTP implementation

**SMTP server**    When the ICM receives an e-mail, the SMTP plug-in (see Figure 2.16) is called to create the connection. The plug-in receives the message and saves all recipients and the message itself in the MPIs. After a successful save, the I/O handler is informed. This handler then generates a request in the Dispatcher Queue, because an ABAP context is required for further processing. The Dispatcher selects a free work process and calls the SMTP processor. The processor calls SAPConnect and the data is extracted from the MPIs. SAPConnect then attempts to deliver the message. If errors occur during the delivery, the SMTP plug-in is informed, and the sender is

---

12  MIME stands for *Multipurpose Internet Mail Extensions* and is the expansion of the SMTP protocol. MIME can be used to attach and send binary files (images, videos, applications, etc.) through text-based e-mail.

informed in a new message. If all recipients have been successfully reached, the plug-in sends a confirmation message to the sender and closes down the connection. The associated ABAP context is then deleted.

## The ICM Server Cache

Short response times are essential in increasing acceptance from end users and making a Web application successful. It is advisable to keep frequently occurring and relatively constant parts of an application available in order to permit especially fast access. This task is carried out by the *ICM Server Cache (ISC)*, also known as the *Internet Server Cache*. This server cache is part of the ICM and provides temporary storage of requested HTTP objects. Repeated client requests for the same temporarily stored objects can be provided immediately from this cache.

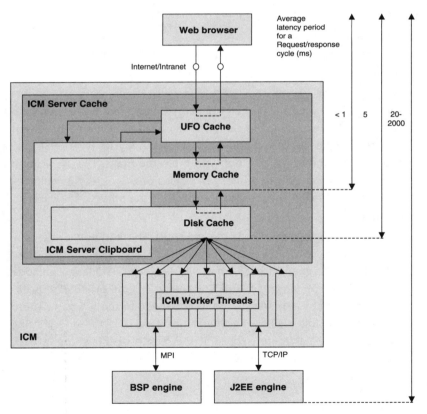

**Figure 2.17** The ICM Server Cache

Because these requests are served directly by the ICM without having to request a work process to process a BSP page, the ICM Server Cache can provide significant performance advantages. Whether an object is included in the cache can be controlled using the HTTP Request handler, which is used because it can access the ICM Server Cache. Figure 2.17 shows the structure of the ICM Server Cache.

A requested object passes through several stations in the ICM Server Cache. If the request cannot be served by that cache (*cache miss*), the object needs to be collected from the server (i.e., from the database). In the following section, we will investigate the various components and concepts of the ICM Server Cache in more detail.

The first requirement for a caching operation is a unique identification of the objects to be placed, manipulated, or invalidated in the cache. The following three options are available for identifying objects:

▶ **URL prefix**
Search pattern `<pref>*` can be used to address all objects in the ICM Server Cache matching `<pref>`.

▶ **Etag**
The ETag is a unique *key* (*GUID—Globally Unique Identifier*) assigned to an object. It is saved at the time of the object's creation. This key is required if logically identical objects have been physically stored in the cache under different URLs, but with the same ETags. The application then needs to be able to address all copies of the objects simultaneously via the ETag at the invalidation point of the object.

▶ **Cache Key**
A *cache key* is generated from the request URI[13] and contains a fully translated URL path. To generate a cache key, encrypted information, in the form of a query string such as SAP language (ISO language code for the SAP logon language) and SAP theme (theme of a BSP application) separated by ampersands (&), is appended to the ICF path. These characters are followed by another ampersand and the query string with the query parameters. To limit the length of this string, a hash procedure is applied to the query string beforehand. An example of a cache key follows:

---

13 You specify a location or target address via a URL. The more exact term would be URI (*Universal Resource Identifier*). A Request URI is a URI that identifies and requests a resource on a server (e.g., a Web page). URLs are special instances of URIs that are designated for network usage (especially on the Internet).

▶ The request URL is:

```
http://www.my-webas.de/sap(bD1kZQ==)/bc/bsp/
sap/xyz/default.htm?name=misterx&year=2002
```

▶ The cache key entry may then look as follows:

```
sap/bc/bsp/sap/xyz/default.htm&de&SAP_
DEFAULT&BD12AF6689
```

The following section describes the individual parts of the ISC.

The *UFO* (*unfound objects*) *cache* supports the temporary storage of invalid requests that would result in errors on the SAP Web AS or the database backend. The UFO cache is best described as a large list of invalid request entries (negative list). The UFO list is kept in the main memory and addressed using an access index. Using this type of list ensures that all HTTP requests that have been rejected by the system will, in turn, be rejected from the cache in future. This process is particularly advantageous for invalid requests because no unnecessary application context is created, resources are conserved, and the backend can be protected against overload situations and malicious attacks, such as denial-of-service attacks.

**The UFO cache**

The *memory cache* uses the main memory as temporary storage. These accesses are very fast, so you will need to pay particular attention to the appropriate dimensioning and setting. The latency time for successful access to entries in the UFO cache or objects in the memory cache is less than 1 ms.

**Memory cache**

Because the main memory is a limited resource, other objects need to be moved to the hard disk memory. The *disk cache* is not as fast as main memory access; however, it does offer sufficient storage options; and, with an average of 5 ms, access is still gratifyingly fast.

**Disk cache**

The *ICM Server Clipboard* is a special range in the ICM Server Cache that is used for the temporary storage of special objects. These objects are what are known as *Data BLOBs* (*Binary Large Objects*). BLOBs may be memory-intensive graphics, for example. The goal of the ICM Server Clipboard is to make data available even before the first request in the cache. Unlike typical cache entries, the object must be found in the clipboard. If you encounter a failed cache access, you will note that the object cannot be collected from the server. The ICM Server Clipboard avoids extra loading on the backend.

**ICM Server Clipboard**

The ICM Server Cache uses both the main memory and the hard disk for temporary storage, an arrangement known as a *two-level cache hierarchy*.

The settings for the different caches can be specified with system profile parameters.

One difference between the ICM Server Cache and conventional HTTP standard cache procedures, such as HTTP proxies, is the ICM Server Cache's support for the temporary storage of dynamic contents. Primarily static contents, such as pictures, are traditionally stored. However, thanks to technologies such as server-side script languages, the proportion of dynamic pages is growing continually, so *dynamic caching* is becoming increasingly important for reducing response times. A significant advantage for developers of Web-based applications (e.g., BSP) is the integration of cache functionalities into the Internet Communication Framework (ICF) via classes and methods. Therefore, the application has full control over the objects located in the cache. This procedure is known as *active caching*.

**Figure 2.18** The HTTP cache of the Internet Communication Manager (ICM)

During the development process, caching should be deactivated to permit access to current datasets (e.g., CSS files). To deactivate caching, set the maximum usability period of the cache entries, using the system profile parameter

```
icm/HTTP/server_cache_<xx>/expiration
```

on a lower value (e.g., 2 seconds). Of course, this reduces system performance. It is possible to delete cache entries manually using Transaction SMICM, via **Goto HTTP Server Cache Display**. From here, you can view the objects stored in the cache and delete entries. Alternatively, you can invalidate the entire cache (see Figure 2.18).

The SAP Web AS's caching or caching attributes can also be changed on the application side by calling methods of the ICF. An overview of these options can be found in Appendix A.1.

## 2.3 The Internet Communication Framework

The Internet Communication Framework (ICF) provides the environment for handling HTTP requests/responses in the work process of an SAP system. It is also known as an *HTTP framework*. However, only parts of the ICF are specific to HTTP; it also includes general and SMTP-specific components. As already stated, the SAP Web AS can act as the server or the client.

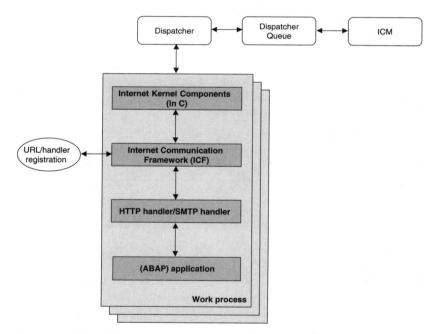

**Figure 2.19** The Internet Communication Framework (ICF) architecture

The ICF provides an object-oriented framework for working with the requests and responses in the ABAP personality. This framework consists of a variety of classes and interfaces for HTTP or SMTP communication. You can envision the ICF as a bridge between the core Internet components written in the language C and in direct connection with the ICM, and the actual ABAP application. The architecture of this framework is displayed in Figure 2.19.

The ICF can handle both the server and the client sides for HTTP processing using the same interfaces (see Figure 2.20). For the server, there is the interface IF_HTTP_SERVER, and for the client, the interface IF_HTTP_CLIENT. The interfaces IF_HTTP_RESPONSE and IF_HTTP_REQUEST are the same in both client and server roles.

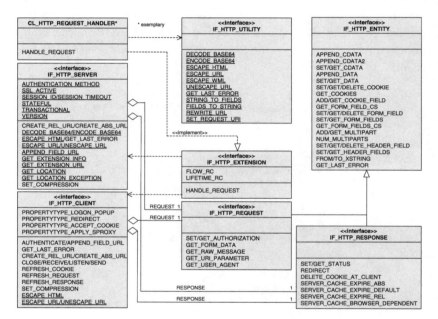

**Figure 2.20** The UML class diagram of the ICF for HTTP processing

**HTTP request handler**

In the server role of the SAP Web AS, the ICF can be used to process HTTP requests from the Internet. However, before the ICF can process requests, the interface IF_HTTP_EXTENSION needs to be implemented. The application logic called by this request is implemented by an HTTP request handler. The entire HTTP link is then modeled for the server role by the interface IF_HTTP_SERVER. This interface can then be used to access the request and the response. An HTTP request handler is an ABAP-OO class implementing the interface IF_HTTP_EXTENSION. This interface contains the method HANDLE-REQUEST called by the ICF. In order for this call to function, the handler and the URL need to be registered to activate the link between the handler and ICF, which occurs in Transaction SICF. The handler is then known to the system and can process the HTTP request directed to it under this URL. The handler can read the data from the request (e.g., coded in the URL as query string), process it, and generate a response. The ICF can be used flexibly for the required application because the separate HTTP request handlers can be designed individually.

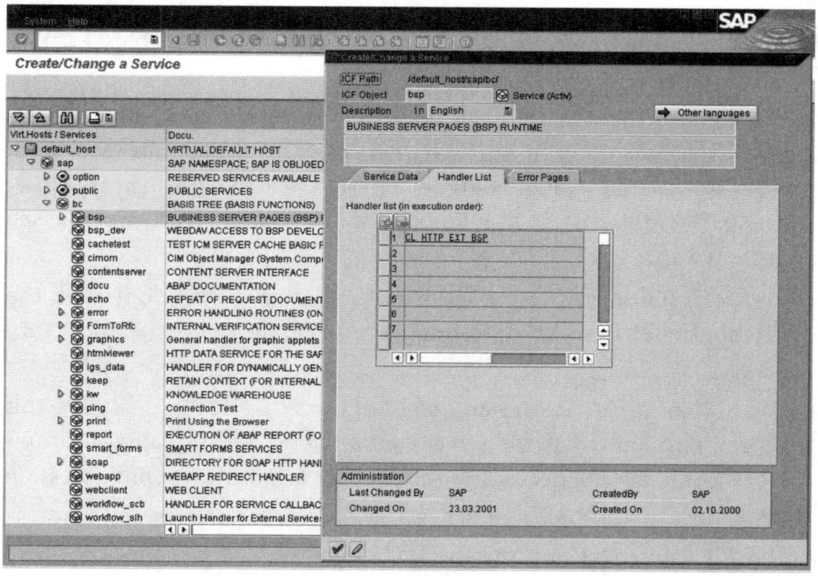

**Figure 2.21** The request handler for processing BSPs in the ICF service tree

An HTTP standard handler for processing BSPs is included in the SAP Web AS. This handler implements the interface IF_HTTP_EXTENSION using the class CL_HTTP_EXT_BSP (standard BSP handler). Figure 2.21 shows the registration of the request handler for BSP applications in the ICF service tree under the URL prefix http://default_host/sap/bc/bsp.

For all Web applications (i.e., BSP applications) created on the SAP Web AS, an ICF service is automatically created under the named URL prefix in the SAP namespace. This means that all of these applications use the BSP standard handler for BSP processing.[14]

---

14 A separate request handler can be stored for each ICF service. If no handler is found for the processing work, a suitable entry is searched for on the next highest level in the ICF service tree.

Other standard handlers that are or can be used as the template for in-house handlers include:

► CL_HTTP_EXT_PING
Realizes an HTTP ping

► CL_HTPP_SMARTFORMS
Provides SAP Smart Forms HTTP services

► CL_HTTP_EXT_SOAPHANDLER_RFC, CL_HTTP_EXT_SOAPIF and
CL_HTTP_EXT_SOAP_DOC
Available for SOAP processing

**The server role**  For a more detailed description of the behavior of the ICF in the server role, see Figure 2.22.

1. The initiator's HTTP request is first received by the ICM. Because the processing occurs in a work process, the Dispatcher makes a work process available. In this example, a BSP page is to be displayed. However, HTTP requests can also be processed without a work process (see Section 2.2).

2. Control is transferred to the Taskhandler starting the ICF controller. The ICF controller is realized as a function module (HTTP_DISPATCH_REQUEST).

3. The ICF controller creates an object of class CL_HTTP_SERVER. This object, also known as the *server control block*, encapsulates all of this HTTP connection's necessary information (request, response, session ID, etc.).

4. The ICF controller imports the HTTP request and fills the REQUEST attribute of the server control block with this data.

5. The ICF controller then uses the URL to determine which HTTP request handler should be called for processing. The URL is resolved (hostname, port, URL prefix) and the search for a suitable ICF service entry commences.

6. The Web browser now needs to be authenticated for this service. The logon data required for this authentication can be maintained in a service table assigned to the relevant HTTP request handler (Transaction SICF). Basic HTTP authentication is frequently used for logging on (see Section 2.5). To authenticate the Web browser, the ICF controller sends the return code 401 to the browser, which generates a pop-up window for the authentication process. The required data (username and password) is then transferred directly to the SAP system. The

default client and the default language of the application server (unless otherwise specified) are used for the client to log onto the SAP system.

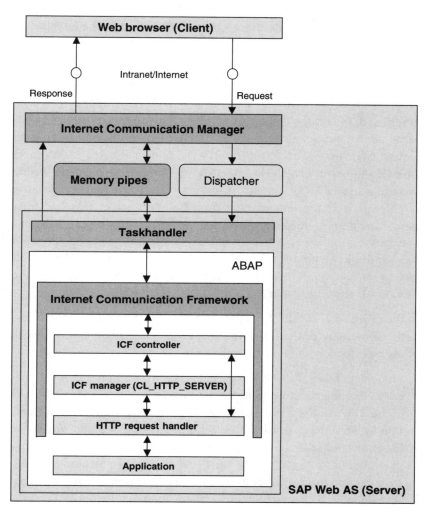

**Figure 2.22** The Internet Communication Framework (ICF) in the server role

7. The HTTP request handler then starts the processing work by calling the HANDLE_REQUEST method. The request data can then be read by the application and processed. For the response, the RESPONSE attribute of the server control block is filled. By terminating the method, control is returned to the ICF controller.

8. The ICF controller can then call other handlers stored in the service table for the ICF service. If no other handler is stored there, the server control block data is converted into an HTTP stream (serialization).

9. Finally, the ICF controller returns this HTTP stream to the initiator via the Taskhandler on the ICM.

**"Stateful" and "stateless"** In the server role, the ICF supports both stateful (with context) and stateless (without context) communication. The term *context* means the application context in the roll area of the SAP Web AS. Depending on the mode used, the system defines whether the application context (roll area) exists across individual requests (stateful) or is re-released after each request (stateless). The stateful and stateless principles in the SAP Web AS are explained in more detail in Section 3.3.3. The ICF can maintain the life cycle of a special HTTP request handler across a single request. Because HTTP requests[15] are independent from one another in terms of their design and do not provide any inherent support for session contexts, this application context needs to be artificially created. Session cookies called `sap-contextid` are used to create this application context. The default setting for communication is the *stateless* mode, which is set using the `STATEFUL` attribute of the `IF_HTTP_SERVER` interface.

In the client role, an ABAP program sends an HTTP request to the Internet. The behavior of the ICF in the client role is described in more detail in the next section and is also displayed in Figure 2.23.

**The client role** 1. An object of class `CL_HTTP_CLIENT` is generated from the ABAP program. This object, also known as the *client control block*, encapsulates all of the HTTP connection's necessary information (request, response, session ID, etc.). To generate this object, the `CREATE` method, which has the connection data of the interface transferred to it, is called. Alternatively, the `CREATE_BY_DESTINATION` method can be used to create a connection to an HTTP destination whose data is maintained in Transaction SM59. In Transaction SM59, there are two different HTTP destinations from which to choose: the *HTTP connection to the external server*, and the *HTTP connection to the R/3 system*. Both of these connections can be used; they differ only in the logon procedures supported.

2. The client control block (or more accurately, the `REQUEST` attribute) is filled with the required data. There are several options:

---

15  By definition, the HTTP protocol is stateless.

- Setting header fields for the request with `SET_HEADER_FIELD`
- Setting cookies using `SET_COOKIE(IF_HTTP_ENTITY)` to obtain a session
- Specifying the procedure for cookies, redirects, and logon screens for the HTTP server (`PROPERTYTYPE_*` attributes)

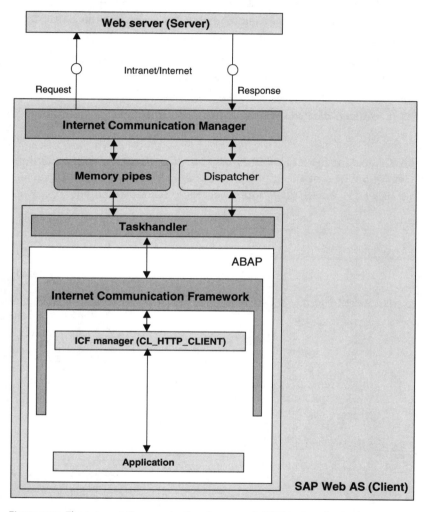

**Figure 2.23** The Internet Communication Framework (ICF) in the client role

3. The request is sent via the `SEND` method. It is converted into an HTTP stream (serialization) and forwarded to the requested HTTP server via the Taskhandler and ICM.

4. If the HTTP server addressed prompts you for authentication, the logon data should be transferred. For an SAP server, this occurs via an SAP logon pop-up window; otherwise, you are prompted via the standard browser pop-up window. Before sending the request, the AUTHENTI-CATE method can be used to transfer the necessary logon data.

5. The requested HTTP server generates and returns a response.

6. The RECEIVE method is used to read the response and the RESPONSE attribute of the client control block is filled.

   You can also send multiple parallel requests to different HTTP servers. Using the LISTEN method, the received responses can then be assigned to the requests that have been sent.

7. The received data can now be processed and issued.

8. Finally, the CLOSE method is used to close the HTTP connection.

**SMTP request handler**
The ICF, like for the HTTP framework, provides a set of classes and inter-faces for SMTP processing (see Figure 2.24). To include an SMTP server, the IF_SMTP_EXTENSION interface should be implemented.

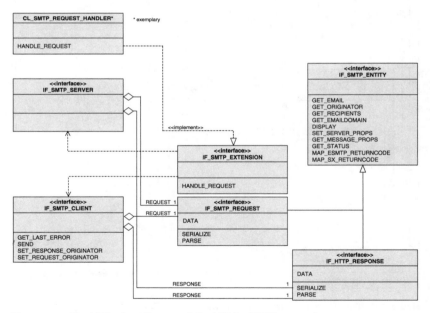

**Figure 2.24** The UML class diagram of the ICF for SMTP processing

The following SMTP request handlers are included as standard:

▶ CL_SMTP_EXT_EMAIL and CL_SMTP_EXT_SAPCONNECT
For editing e-mail

▶ CL_SMTP_EXT_PING
For creating an SMTP ping

To send Internet e-mail, you need to configure various settings on the
SAP Web AS, including configuring the SMTP plug-in, SMTP node, and an
SMTP service. More information can be found in the online documenta-
tion.

## 2.4 The J2EE Application Server

Release 6.20 of the SAP Web AS makes available the non-proprietary
object-oriented language Java (for platform-independent Web applications), in addition to ABAP. An integrated Java application server, the *SAP
J2EE Engine*, is now part of the SAP system, and is fully compatible with
the Java 2 Enterprise Edition (J2EE) standard. The J2EE standard specifies
all functionalities required for fulfilling complex tasks in the corporate
environment.

### 2.4.1 The J2EE Architecture

With Enterprise JavaBeans (EJB), the Enterprise Edition of the Java-2
technology (J2EE) provides the environment for a proven component
model. The EJB architecture defines roles responsible for separate aspects
of developing and installing the components. Developers can therefore
concentrate on their specific skills, and are freed from having to manually
implement security aspects, transaction security, and concurrency. An
overview of the SAP J2EE architecture is illustrated in Figure 2.25. This
architecture's components are described in the following section.

### 2.4.2 J2EE Support in the SAP J2EE Engine

The J2EE engine supports the HTTP/HTTPS protocols and has the following characteristics:

▶ **J2EE conformity**
The J2EE engine of the SAP Web AS provides full compatibility with
the J2EE 1.2 standard. Parts of the J2EE 1.3 standard have also been
integrated into the platform.

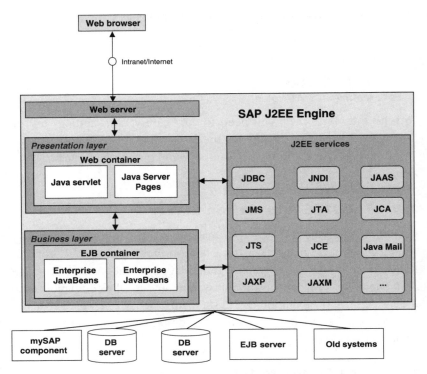

**Figure 2.25** The architecture of the SAP J2EE Application Server

▶ **Enterprise JavaBeans**

Enterprise JavaBeans (EJB) are part of J2EE. As component technology, they provide application-specific business logic and many different types of system services. The current version of SAP Web AS supports the specification of the EJB 1.1—that is, SessionBeans (stateful and stateless) and Entity Beans.

Release 6.20 does not support message-driven beans. The server does have an EJB 2.0 implementation, but this is not enabled for productive applications. Officially, Release 6.20 supports only EJB 1.1, which does not yet contain any message-driven beans.

▶ **Web and Internet support**

With Java Server Pages (JSP) and Java servlets, J2EE technologies are available for developing Web-based J2EE applications. JSP technology, whose basic principle is identical to BSP technology, permits contents to be dynamically generated for portable, cross-platform Web applications. *Java servlets* provide a mechanism for expanding a Web server's functionality; they are server components (in other words, instantiated classes) that can be executed from the client side using parameters. JSP 1.2, Java Servlets 2.3, and the standard Internet protocols HTTP/HTTPS are supported.

▶ **J2EE programming interfaces**

The J2EE platform provides a series of application programming interfaces (APIs) to support connectivity, transaction, and security functionalities[16]:

▶ The *Java Naming and Directory Interface (JNDI)* permits access to multiple and heterogeneous name and directory services within a company. Version 1.2 of the JNDI is currently supported.  **JNDI**

▶ *Java Database Connectivity (JDBC)* is an interface for relational database management systems. JDBC allows the connection to a database to be made in order to send a SQL instruction to the database and process the results. Version 2.0 of JDBC is currently supported.  **JDBC**

▶ The *J2EE Connector Architecture (JCA)* defines standards for connecting the J2EE platform and various application systems. These systems include ERP, mainframe, and database systems, for example. Version 1.0 of the JCA is currently supported.  **JCA**

▶ A range of special APIs, *Remote Invocation (RMI)*, are available for developing distributed applications based on the Java programming language. RMI permits methods for remote objects to be called. Communication is carried out via sockets and data streams. *RMI-IIOP* combines the use of RMI with CORBA's *Internet Inter-Object-Request-Broker Protocol (IIOP)*. Therefore, Java applications can communicate with CORBA objects, implemented in any language, and vice versa.  **RMI-IIOP**

▶ The *Java Transaction API (JTA)* is used as the interface for managing and coordinating transactions between various application systems. Version 1.0.1 of the JTA is currently supported.  **JTA**

▶ The *Java Transaction Service (JTS)* is a common programming interface for implementing a transaction manager that supports JTA. The JTS interface is a Java mapping based on the Object Management Group Object Transaction Service 1.1 Specification.  **JTS**

▶ The *Java Message Service (JMS)* provides a uniform programming interface for message-oriented middleware from various manufacturers. These services permit the asynchronous exchange of data and events via queues, publication, and subscription. Version 1.0.2 of the JMS is currently supported.  **JMS**

---

16 Supported versions may change with upcoming releases.

| | |
|---|---|
| **Java Mail** | ▶ *Java Mail* permits uniform access to various mail systems. Version 1.2 of Java Mail is currently supported. |
| **JCA** | ▶ The *Java Cryptography Architecture* (*JCA*) provides cryptographic functionalities. |
| **JCE** | ▶ The *Java Cryptography Extension* (*JCE*) expands the JCA with further security algorithms. |
| **JAAS** | ▶ The *Java Authentication and Authorization Service* (*JAAS*) combines functions for user-related authentication and access control. Version 1.0 of the JAAS is currently supported. |

▶ **XML support**

For XML support, the SAP Web AS has an XML toolkit, which contains or supports the following:

  ▶ XML parser

  ▶ *XML Scheme* support and validation

  ▶ *XSLT Processor* including XSLT-1.1 expansions

  ▶ *SOAP* support including attachments

  ▶ *Java API for Processing XML* (*JAXP*) in Version 1.1

  ▶ *Java API for XML Messaging* (*JAXM*) as part of the XML parser

### 2.4.3 The Combination of ABAP and Java in the SAP Web Application Server

The SAP Web AS allows Java and ABAP environments to be integrated on a single server. Both personalities can therefore be administered and maintained within a common infrastructure. This reduces the total costs (*total cost of ownership or TCO*) considerably, as it enables centralized and uniform installation, configuration, monitoring, and load balancing on a single system.

**Configuration options**

The installation and configuration process for both ABAP and Java personalities is fully integrated and permits the following configuration options on a single server:

▶ **ABAP personality only installed**

With this SAP Web AS configuration, only HTTP requests that can be handled by the ICF or the HTTP plug-in of the ICM can be processed. Communication and data exchange between the ICM and any work process required is carried out via the MPI. This principle was already supported in SAP Web AS Release 6.10.

▶ **Combined installation of the ABAP and Java personalities**
With this SAP Web AS configuration, ABAP requests can be processed by the ICF, and J2EE requests can be processed by the relevant SAP J2EE Engine. The ICM then uses the URL prefix to decide which component is responsible for processing. These URL prefixes are maintained in the HTTP service tree (Transaction SICF). Here it is possible to specify, for example, that all requests containing the `/myportal/Java/` prefix are processed by the SAP J2EE Engine. In order to do this, the `/sap/public/icman` service must have been activated; the ICM uses this service to forward requests to the J2EE server. Communication between the SAP J2EE Engine and the ICM is carried out via a TCP/IP-based network connection.

▶ **Java personality only installed**
With this configuration, only the SAP J2EE Engine is installed without the SAP Web AS—the (ABAP) functionalities of the SAP Web AS are intentionally omitted. As a standalone, the SAP J2EE Engine includes a separate Dispatcher as well as the server itself, which are run together in a virtual machine. The Dispatcher (*dpj2ee*) starts all the required processes (ICM and J2EE server) and can connect to a message server to exchange information (logon data for HTTP[S] and J2EE[S]). The Dispatcher does not need a database, work processes, or a gateway. To provide secure operation of the Dispatcher, set the profile parameter `icm/dpj2ee` to `TRUE`. The SAP J2EE Engine also includes a Web server. However, you can operate other Web servers (e.g., Apache) with the SAP J2EE Engine. This configuration option is suitable primarily for small solutions with a small number of client requests.

In a system landscape with more than one SAP Web AS, you can combine several of these options. An overview of three SAP Web AS instances is provided in Figure 2.26. The SAP Web Dispatcher shown functions as a Web switch, establishes load balancing between the different systems. The Dispatcher knows the options (ABAP/Java) and capacities of the connected SAP Web Application Servers. A detailed description of the SAP Web Dispatcher is provided in Section 2.5.

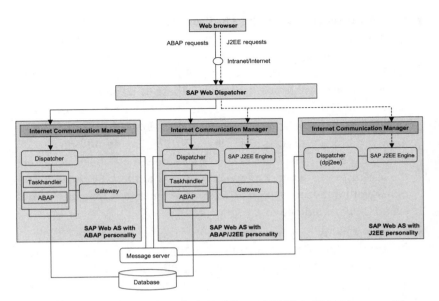

**Figure 2.26** A system landscape with three different SAP Web AS instances

## 2.4.4 Integrating ABAP and Java

From a developer's point of view, the *SAP Java Connector* (*JCo*) plays an important role in coupling servers. It is available automatically and functions as the communication bridge between the ABAP and the Java personalities (see Figure 2.27). Therefore, ABAP functionalities (e.g., BAPIs) can be called from the Java context and Java modules can be used from ABAP.

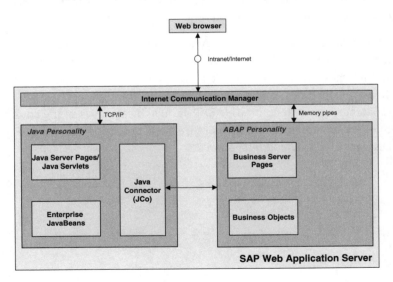

**Figure 2.27** Integrating Java and ABAP

## 2.5   Security

Like all other systems that use Internet technology and connect to the Internet, the SAP Web AS faces not only the advantages, but also the dangers and risks of the World Wide Web (WWW). The dangers for a system that is accessible via an intranet or the Internet include the following:

▶ Data and network sabotage

▶ Theft or espionage of sensitive data

▶ Unauthorized access from outside and inside

These activities have many and varied consequences, the worst of which is financial damage. Depending on the extent of the financial damage, a company's very survival could be placed in jeopardy. The security of Web-based applications and systems is therefore critical for achieving widespread acceptance for all kinds of Web applications. Security creates trust, and trust is the foundation of long-term business relationships. These are fundamental principles, especially for company-wide business processes. Web-based solutions that do not meet these requirements are destined to fail.

Security can be considered on several technical levels. Two levels are of particular interest: On the network level are technologies such as firewalls, virtual private networks (VPN), secure network communication (SNC), and SAProuter. On the next level are the applications themselves, whose interfaces protect one another and the users. All application systems and, in particular, systems with productive business data, should be in *demilitarized zones (DMZ)* with fixed, defined access rules.

**Security on many levels**

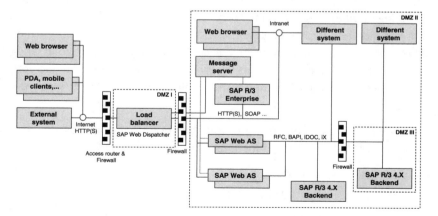

**Figure 2.28** Secure system landscapes

These zones are defined using firewalls that filter the permissible network traffic. Depending on the functionality of the component or the system, other DMZs can be defined within a DMZ (see Figure 2.28).

A comprehensive security concept should include all levels.

**Secure connections and authenticity** Security on the application level involves principally protecting personal user data or sensitive corporate data and applications against unauthorized access. The technologies required for this level of security must guarantee two primary requirements: secure communication links and the authenticity of the communication partners.

Unsecured connections are an unacceptable security gap for sensitive data. If a user accesses the SAP Web AS via an unsecured connection, security measures such as passwords or user IDs are relatively useless. A potential attacker can listen in (eavesdrop) on all the data traffic between users and the SAP Web AS without risk. Attacks from the company-wide network (LAN) are just as easy. Therefore, server/server connections need to be considered, as well as client/server connections. The data must be encrypted, even before it leaves the application, to prevent any unencrypted partial data streams from leaking through. This type of protective encryption is known as *application security*.

In addition, the communication partners must ensure that they can actually communicate with one another—there must be reciprocal authentication of both partners. If the partners do not recognize one another, the necessary authentication can take place only via a third trusted instance.

Effective encryption of transferred information and unequivocal authentication of the communication partner are therefore critical requirements. Meeting modern security standards without creating too much extra administrative work is a complex task. A directory service based on the LDAP protocol is useful here in the central management of roles and access rights. SSL (Secure Sockets Layer) is now established as an encryption process between Internet-based applications or between applications and users.

The SAP Web AS supports many security functions that can be used when running applications. These functions include:

▶ User authentication via
  ▶ Logon tickets (SAP Logon Tickets)
  ▶ X.509 client certificates
  ▶ Single Sign-On (SSO) and Smartcard authentication

- ▶ Traditional R/3 authorization concept with
  - ▶ Authorization check
  - ▶ Profile generator
  - ▶ Info system authorizations
- ▶ Secure network communication with
  - ▶ Secure Network Communication (SNC) and the standard Generic Security Services (GSS-API) interface
  - ▶ SAProuter
- ▶ Support for Secure-Store-&-Forward mechanisms (SSF) and digital signatures within a Public Key Infrastructure (PKI)
- ▶ Check and logging via
  - ▶ Audit Info System (AIS)
  - ▶ Security Audit Log
- ▶ Encryption of HTTP connections with SSL
- ▶ Support of the standardized directory service LDAP for central user and rights management

### 2.5.1 Logon Procedure

Several logon procedures are supported for authorized access to the SAP Web AS. When a Web client connects to the SAP Web AS via a URL, a logon to the SAP system is carried out. For this purpose, ICF services can be stored for a Web application retrieved via a URL. From Release 6.20 on, an ICF service will also be created automatically for each Web application. This will be carried out using Transaction SICF (see Figure 2.29), which stores the logon data. An ICF service can then be activated or deactivated.

The unproblematic activation and deactivation of ICF services allows Web applications to be rapidly removed from the network as required.

Activated ICF services represent a security risk insofar as they can be directly accessed from the Internet via HTTP. It is therefore essential to restrict access using suitable measures, such as verifying that the ICF service is accessed only via a user with the appropriate authorization. All automatically created ICF services should be deactivated by default.

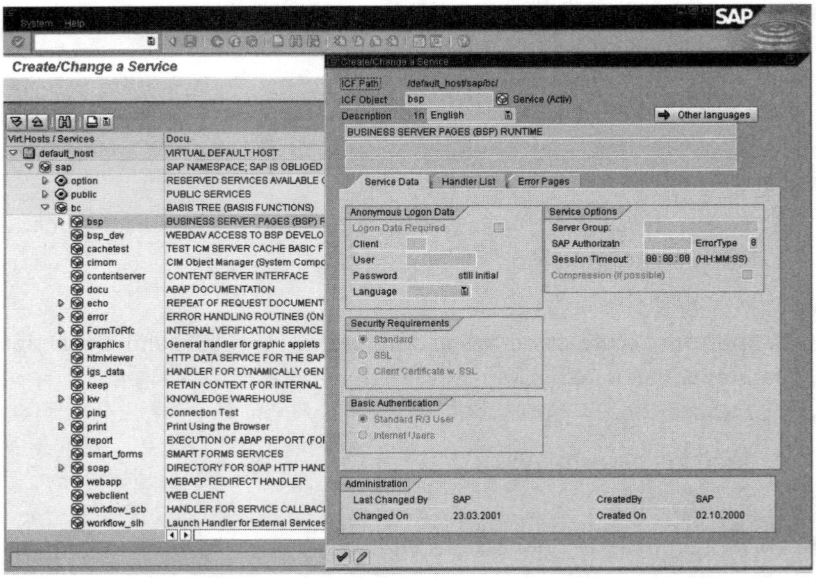

**Figure 2.29** Creating and maintaining ICF services

**Logon alternatives** The following logon alternatives are available:

▶ The user does not need to log on—that is, the Web application is freely accessible. For these public applications, a corresponding user should be maintained in the associated service. The logon is then carried out in the background via this user.

▶ The user is prompted to enter a User ID and password via a pop-up window in the Web browser. The logon is carried out via basic authentication, in which the language and client are preset. This procedure is the default logon procedure if no other procedure is used. The necessary settings need to be maintained in the service settings.

▶ During runtime, the required HTTP fields `sap-language`, `sap-client`, `sap-user`, or `sap-alias` and `sap-password` can be completed on a freely accessible page, such as an HTML form, and transferred to the server as logon data.

▶ Users are identified using Single Sign-On (SSO) logon tickets or X.509 client certificates. This is also set up in the service.

**Maintaining the ICF services** The ICF services are arranged hierarchically. For each service entry, settings can be made on the service data tab (Transaction SICF) in the sections **Anonymous Logon Data**, **Security Requirements**, **Basic Authentication,** and **Service Options** (see Figure 2.29). These parameters are explained briefly as follows:

▶ **Service Options**

▷ **Server Group**

In the server group, a group of application servers can be entered on which the ICF service is to be run. These server groups can be maintained using Transaction SMLG.

▷ **SAP Authorization**

The SAP Authorization parameter specifies the necessary authorization (authorization object S_ICF) for using the ICF service.

▷ **Error Type**

The Error Type parameter specifies the handling of authorization errors in the ICF using a numeric code. With 1, an A-Message (*program abort*) is sent; with 2, an X-Message (*program error*) is sent; and with all other values, an E-Message is sent.

▷ **Session Timeout**

The Session Timeout parameter is used to specify the session timeout for stateful connections. By default, the details are culled from the profile parameter `rdisp/plugin_auto_logout` (30 minutes).

▷ **Compression**

If the recipient page also supports the Compression option, the ICF service attempts to reduce the response page in size according to the gzip compression procedure.

▶ **Basic Authentication**

If the logon is made via basic authentication, this parameter is used to define whether the user is to be interpreted as an Internet user (alias user) or as a standard R/3 user.

▶ **Security Requirements**

The Security Requirements section is used to store the security requirements that the client must meet. The parameters include **Standard**, **SSL** (logon only via HTTPS), and **Client Certificate with SSL**.

▶ **Anonymous Logon Data**

An anonymous user can be entered for a service. Service users (Internet users) should be used. These users can be created in the Transaction SU01, and this user's required authorizations are assigned via a reference user. The service user should then be entered into the relevant field of the ICF service, and the client, language, and password added. Dialog users (standard SAP users) should not be used for anonymous access.

If the **Logon Data Required** parameter is set as the default, the anonymous user data is also used in all subservices; however, special fields, such as **Client**, can be overwritten in the subservices. When Logon Data Required is activated, all other logon procedures are overridden. If this parameter or option is not activated, the stored anonymous ICF logon data is used only if the other logon procedures are not available and no anonymous ICF logon data is stored in even more specialized ICF services.

If a logon attempt fails, an explicit response page can be stored on the **Error Pages** tab. In addition, with a logon error in the HTTP framework, the user can be redirected to a specified URL (see Figure 2.30).

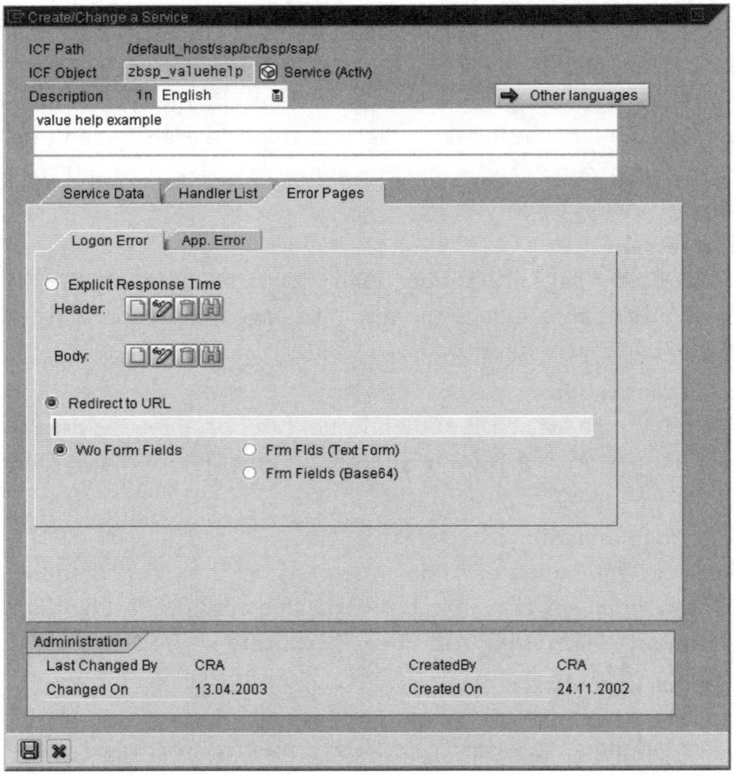

**Figure 2.30** Specifying error pages and redirects for failed logons in the ICF service tree

If the ICF services have been created as part of a package rather than as a local object, they can be transported according to the correction and transport group configuration.

Web applications can also be created using secured and public areas. There are several alternatives for such situations:

In the first alternative, a single application can be divided into two different applications: a first application for the public area that is accessible to all users, and a second application that is used to implement secured functionalities. For both applications, a service entry is created automatically to store anonymous logon data for the public application and one of the alternative logon procedures for the secured area.

The second alternative is similar to the first. However, instead of creating two separate applications, a single application is divided into two subtrees (e.g., a *public folder* for the public area and a *protected folder* for the secured areas). In the ICF service tree, different logon procedures can then be stored on the level of this subtree.

In the third alternative, the user can be changed from a separate logon dialog. The switch is then made from an Internet user to a dialog user. The function module SUSR_INTERNET_USERSWITCH makes this functionality available.

The best alternative will depend on the situation. It might be useful to provide external users with the option of creating an Internet user themselves. The function module SUSR_USER_INTERNET_CREATE makes the necessary functionality available. This method is fully integrated into the central user management system.

### 2.5.2 Load Balancing: The SAP Web Dispatcher

With distributed application servers, a component is required for controlling Internet access to the various SAP Web Application Servers. The following options are possible:

▶ Network Address Translators (NATs)
▶ Reverse proxies
▶ Physical Web switches
▶ Software Web switches

Each of these options has advantages and disadvantages. SAP recommends using an SAP-developed software Web switch called the *SAP Web Dispatcher*. The SAP Web Dispatcher is available in a system landscape between the Web client (browser) and the SAP system running the Web applications. Available since Release 6.20, the SAP Web Dispatcher can also be used for Release 6.10 of the SAP Web AS. The SAP Web Dispatcher is used as a "software Web switch" between the Internet and the SAP system, consisting of one or more SAP Web Application Servers, which means that there is only one point at which HTTP(S) requests can enter the system. The SAP Web Dispatcher also performs load balancing so that the request is always sent to the server with the most free capacity. The load can be easily distributed using this process. Software Web switches can be configured much more cheaply and simply than physical Web switches. Collaboration with the message server, in particular, has been optimized to consider existing SAP system configurations.

Because the SAP Web Dispatcher is a separate program run on the computer, which is directly connected to the Internet, the amount of configuration work required for operation is minimal. Only some of the SAP Web Dispatcher's profile parameters need to be set. At a minimum, these parameters must define the port to receive HTTP(S) requests, where the Dispatcher can find the SAP Message Server and the port receiving these HTTP requests. If the Web application then needs to be called from outside via the URL *www.my-webas.de,* for example, this hostname must be mapped internally to the SAP Web Dispatcher. The Dispatcher then forwards the HTTP(S) request to a suitable SAP Web AS.

### The principle of load balancing in the SAP Web Dispatcher

The SAP Web Dispatcher forwards the incoming requests (HTTP, HTTPS) to the SAP Web AS of the SAP system in sequence. The amount of requests that a server receives is determined by that server's capacity, which is based on the number of configured dialog work processes. If the application is stateful, the SAP Web Dispatcher ensures that on the user's next request, that request is returned to the server processing his or her application. For HTTP connections, the Dispatcher uses the session cookie, and with HTTPS connections (with SSL), the Dispatcher uses the client IP address to forward the incoming requests. The SAP Web Dispatcher also decides whether the incoming request is forwarded to an ABAP or a J2EE server.

 In the HTTP service tree (Transaction SICF), the service /sap/public/ icf_info must be activated. This service provides the SAP Web Dispatcher with information on logon groups, server load, and so on.

Unlike HTTP load balancing using the SAP Message Server, when using the SAP Web Dispatcher, no redirect is carried out. The disadvantages (multiple IP addresses need to be known, bookmarking is not possible, authentication after changing application server) are avoided in this case.

A series of profile parameters are set in the profile file for the proper running of the SAP Web Dispatcher. The defaults are generally suitable for normal operation.

In summary, the most important features of the SAP Web Dispatcher are as follows:

**Features in the SAP Web Dispatcher**

► Support for SSL connections (end-to-end)

  ► SSL connections end in the SAP Web Application Server

  ► All servers appear under a unique identity on the Web

  ► All servers use the same server certificate

► The SAP Web Dispatcher provides a central entry point—that is, an IP address, a port for HTTP requests, and a port for HTTPS requests

► Support for load balancing via communication with the Message Server

► Support for stateful sessions with the use of session cookies for HTTP connections and client IP addresses for HTTPS connections

► No manual configuration of servers, ports, and so forth, because the information is taken from the Message Server

Ensuring that the security concept satisfies Internet-based business processes' high demands and priorities on all security levels is essential. When these demands and priorities are considered, the SAP Web AS can be seamlessly integrated into the existing IT infrastructure. A successful security concept requires more than simply implementing technical options to secure the system landscape; the concept also needs to be actively used by all persons involved and therefore realized in its full capacity.

**Conclusion**

## 2.6 The Delimitation of the Internet Transaction Server

The rapid developments in the Internet environment in the mid-90s forced SAP to adapt its R/3 system to meet new challenges. At that time, the R/3 Basis system did not support the necessary Internet protocols (TCP/IP, HTTP, etc.), and therefore, an alternative was needed—the *Inter-*

*net Transaction Servers (ITS)*. The ITS has since functioned as the bridge linking the Internet and R/3 system, by fostering communication between the R/3 application server and the HTTP server.

**Inside-out versus outside-in** Many companies are already using the ITS, which raises the issue of how and whether to delimit the ITS from the SAP Web AS. When should the decision be made? In favor of which product? To answer these questions, we need to examine the philosophies behind both the ITS and the SAP Web AS systems. The systems' primary uses are very different. Both solutions typically facilitate a Web connection. In the Web link, a basic distinction is drawn between two approaches: *inside-out* and *outside-in*. To distinguish between the two methods, we need to examine where the actual application transaction logic can be found. First, we look at the architecture and the functional principle of the ITS.

SAP already included the SAP Internet Transaction Server (ITS) in Release 3.1H. To place R/3 applications on the Web, SAP added a component for Internet communication to the existing three-tier architecture. In comparison to the R/3 application server, ITS behaves like a standard SAP GUI client, facilitating the opening of the R/3 application server onto the Internet. The ITS is a gateway between the Web server and the R/3 application server, converting special transactions directly into HTML and JavaScript and forwarding these pages to the Web server.

**Internet Application Components** Special *Internet Application Components (IAC)* are available as dialog transactions in the R/3 system. These transactions are called via the ITS and they include a variety of *Easy Web Transactions*, as well as ITS-based Internet solutions, such as:

▶ SAP Internet Sales
▶ SAP Online Store
▶ mySAP Workplace
▶ SAP Employee Self-Service
▶ SAP Markets Enterprise Buyer

The ITS can also be used as an Internet frontend for accessing the R/3 system. This *Web GUI* allows access to most, though not all, of the features that would be available with an SAP GUI.

**WGate and AGate** The ITS consists of two components that can be installed on two different servers. These servers should be protected against unauthorized access attempts using firewalls (see Figure 2.31). The first component, the Web Gate (WGate), facilitates the communication with the Web server also requiring installation. The second component, the Application Gate (AGate), facilitates the communication with the R/3 system via the DIAG protocol and behaves like a typical client with the SAP GUI. The WGate and the AGate communicate via the TCP/IP protocol.

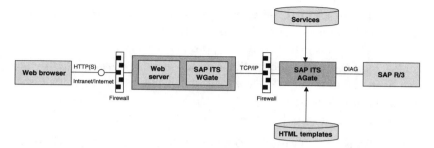

**Figure 2.31** The architecture of the Internet Transaction Server (ITS)

The procedure for an ITS session consists of the following steps:

**Procedure for an ITS session**

1. The user calls an ITS service (e.g., the IAC Online Store) in his or her Web browser via a link.

2. The Web server detects that this call is an ITS call and forwards the request to the AGate via WGate.

3. The AGate can identify the requested service with a service file. The service and the associated R/3 transaction are now started (a logon may be required). The data to be transferred is prepared and forwarded to the R/3 application server.

4. The R/3 application server processes the transaction call in exactly the same way as does the standard SAP GUI client.

5. The R/3 system sends the first Dynpro to the AGate. The AGate uses naming conventions to find the correct HTML templates for the Dynpro sent, and generates the finished HTML pages from the context data and the template.

6. The AGate sends the finished HTML page via WGate to the Web server, which sends the page directly to the user.

7. The user can then make further inputs. For example, the user could complete a screen mask and transfer the data to the SAP system by pressing a button. These inputs would then be processed and a new response page would be generated.

All other transactions are run similarly to this ITS session, until the user terminates the transaction, or the application is closed automatically following a timeout.

This approach, in which the business logic is implemented within the R/3 system, is also known as the *inside-out approach*. Here, the application logic remains in the R/3 application server and is therefore driven by the backend. For the R/3 application server, there is no difference between the inside-out approach and the transaction processing using an SAP GUI. The advantages are that the entire application logic remains in the R/3 system, and no reprogramming is necessary. The disadvantage, however, is that because this logic is very rigid, it does not allow the navigation or control logic to be changed on the Web server-side. *Flow logic* has therefore been added to the ITS. Flow logic allows the presentation logic and the application logic to be separated. Unfortunately, the concept of flow logic is not widespread, because it is difficult to manage.

Dynpro-based
model The SAP ITS is primarily used to convert existing Dynpro-based R/3 transactions into HTML code. This code is then sent to the client and displayed. The SAP ITS is ideally suited to the enabling of existing R/3 applications for the Web. This programming model is also known as *Dynpro-based*. There is a generic compilation of the Dynpro into HTML code. The Web application in the browser can therefore be regarded as a representation of a transaction started in the R/3, which means that for each user logged on, a new session is opened and maintained. With these typical stateful applications, you must ensure that the R/3 system knows at all times where the user is currently located on the Web page. The use of client-side browser interaction (such as clicking on the browser Back button) can lead to problems, because the server does not detect this action. In addition, resources are blocked for unnecessarily long periods if the user does not log off correctly.

The ITS is a tried and trusted system, known for its stability and good integration with the SAP system. However, ITS can prove difficult if a separate logic is to be represented, or another application is to be integrated. Therefore, we primarily recommend ITS for those applications where the existing Web transactions can be used. The Web GUI and simple Web reporting are also ideal operating directions. However, if interface and integration demands escalate, or the need for flexible and customized frontends increase, the ITS quickly reaches its limits.

The R/3 system's lack of native support for standard Internet technologies has been compensated for by using additional products (e.g., ITS, Java Connector, Business Connector). Each new development in the Internet environment requires an additional modification or development on SAP's side to integrate the new technology. Native support for standard

Internet technologies is absolutely necessary in the technological basis of R/3 systems. The result of this need is an open integration platform with integrated Web, XML, and Java support: the SAP Web Application Server.

The SAP Web AS, unlike ITS, takes a pure *outside-in approach*[17]. The *inside-out approach* and the *outside-in approach* are compared in Figure 2.32.

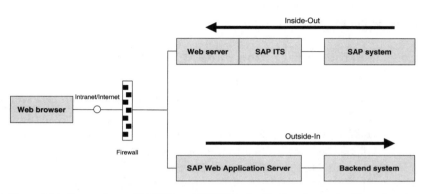

**Figure 2.32** Comparison of SAP ITS and SAP Web Application Server (inside-out and outside-in approach)

The application logic is requested on the SAP Web AS and is disconnected from Dynpro-based R/3 transactions. The established SAP communication interfaces (e.g., RFC/BAPI) or open, standardized Internet technologies (e.g., Java and SOAP) carry out access to required data and functionalities from back-end systems (SAP and non-SAP). With a page-based programming model (BSPs), Web applications can be redesigned from scratch. In this model, the requests from the Internet/intranet are received directly by the SAP Web AS, which makes the SAP Web AS the ideal tool for Internet applications that place high demands on the frontend and the integration with other systems. An overview of the uses of the SAP Web AS can be found in Section 2.1.6.

**Approach behind SAP Web AS**

In the future, it is planned to integrate ITS's functionality into the SAP Web AS. The entire ITS functionality will then be made available on all platforms supported by the SAP Web AS.

---

17 An outside-in approach can be realized using the Flow Logic concept of the ITS. However, this approach does not provide anything that parallels the flexibility and the magnitude of the integration options of an SAP Web Application Server.

## 2.7    The Outlook

As the development of the SAP Web AS is continuously enhanced, so with each new release, new features are added. Many areas will experience further technological enhancements and increased functionality. All new dimension products, as well as R/3 itself, will profit from these advances, as the SAP Web AS functions as the foundation layer technology. The most interesting developments in upcoming releases are described in the following sections.

### 2.7.1    Further Integration of ABAP and Java

**Equal access of ABAP and Java**  The integration of the J2EE engine into the SAP Web AS is being continually refined and extended. SAP's goal is to seamlessly integrate Java and ABAP into the SAP system as two equally supported languages. The primary goal of the continued integration of Java developments into the SAP system will be the integration into the tried and tested Change and Transportation System (CTS). In addition, for the next integration step, it is essential to ensure efficient access to the SAP database and all necessary development objects (e.g., repository objects and the ABAP Dictionary).

**Eclipse IDE**  As early as Release 6.30 of SAP Web AS, SAP will support the open-source tool platform Eclipse as a development and management interface for Java developments. Eclipse integrates a variety of features under a common interface. The functionality of this interface can be easily expanded with plug-ins. For example, the standard functionalities include project and task management, powerful search engines, and editors, and configuration options for the interfaces. When including a Java IDE in this platform, a variety of required development features are available via this interface. These features include deployment, Web services, source management, syntax highlighting, source code tools, debugging, hierarchical object browser, versioning, and much more. Using Web Dynpro technology (see Section 2.7.4), SAP will provide a plug-in for the graphical creation of user interfaces.

### 2.7.2    The Integration of the SAP Internet Transaction Server

In future versions of the SAP Web AS, the entire ITS package will be integrated into SAP Web AS, making it possible to run ITS applications without additional components and modifications to SAP Web AS. The required functionalities will be integrated into the Internet Communication Manager (ICM). This guarantees protection of investment for existing

ITS applications. Furthermore, the familiar Web GUI from the ITS package will be available. The Web GUI provides the functionality of the SAP GUI in the form of an HTML-based user interface, and permits access to all SAP functionalities via a Web browser.

### 2.7.3  SAP R/3 Enterprise

The SAP Web AS, in the mySAP Business Suite strategy from SAP, forms the technological basis of SAP R/3 Enterprise, which is the successor to the tried and trusted SAP R/3 4.6C system. SAP R/3 Enterprise consists of three components: the SAP Web Application Server as the basis system, the SAP R/3 Enterprise Core with an expanded and stable application pool, and the SAP R/3 Enterprise Extensions, providing additional extensions to the system's functionality. All three components have an independent release cycle.

### 2.7.4  The Web Dynpro Technology

The Web Dynpro Server will be introduced with the next release of the SAP Web AS (see Figure 2.33). This generic concept permits the platform-independent creation and execution of modern, Web-based interfaces using graphical tools (see Figure 2.7.1) and programming. The concept is particularly impressive thanks to its high general validity, platform-neutrality, and expandability. These attributes enable modifications to be made with a considerably lower level of implementation work. To ensure this, the description of interface contents is based on *metadata* (also referred to as *metainformation* in this book). The associated code can be generated from the compiled meta model of the user interface "at the touch of a button." This is the programming of previously defined events in the presentation logic requiring the addition of a separate application logic. Three different server code languages are supported: ABAP code for the ABAP personality, Java code for the Java personality, and C# for the .NET environment. SAP also provides a Dynpro converter that converts existing Dynpros (semi-)automatically into Web Dynpros. These generated applications all run in the stateful condition—that is, the session management is part of this concept. The modeling and development of the user interface is carried out according to the Model-View-Controller (MVC) concept, allowing for a strict separation between the presentation and application logics.

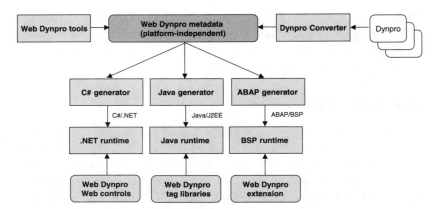

**Figure 2.33** The Web Dynpro technology

Until now, we have described the server-side framework (SSF) for the Web Dynpro technology. This framework runs on the SAP Web AS. On the client side, in modern browsers, a client-side framework (CSF) can also be used (see Figure 2.34).

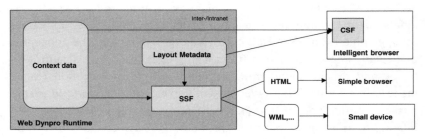

**Figure 2.34** Server-side and client-side frameworks

This framework runs in the Web browser and is based on HTML templates, enriched with JavaScript and Cascading Style Sheets (CSS). During runtime, the Web Dynpro checks whether the client being addressed (PDA, desktop, etc.) offers the necessary capabilities for using this framework and sends the required content to the recipients accordingly. The use of the client-side framework provides many advantages. Both the ease of operation and the performance of the application can be improved. Direct input checks and field and value tools can be achieved by the support for concepts such as drag and drop, and by the use of delta handling. In this process, only data that has actually been changed for screen updates is transferred between the server and the client, which considerably reduces the required bandwidth.

Web Dynpro will be an integral part of Release 6.30 of the SAP Web AS. The tools that will be available are part of the Java development environment from SAP, based on the *Eclipse Framework*, a registered open source project from IBM. The successor version, which will be published with SAP Web Application Server Release 6.40, contains an ABAP runtime, a converter that generates Web Dynpro pages semi-automatically from Dynpro pages (in other words, pages generated with the SAP Screen Painter) and support for User Interface Patterns.

# 3 Basic Principles: BSP Applications

*Now that you've read about architectures and systems of Web applications, you should be ready for more "developer material." However, you will still benefit from an overview of basic concepts and practices. This will make the practical section all the more interesting, and your theoretical excursions will be more meaningful.*

## 3.1 Introduction and a Look at the Web Scenario Being Developed

This chapter provides the basic principles for developing Web-based applications using the Web Application Server (SAP Web AS). Experienced Web developers will quite rightly point out that many of the various Web standards—such as Wireless Markup Language (WML), Flash (for complex, animated graphics, and menus)—are not covered here. Discussing these standards is beyond the scope of this book, and would not be useful in developing BSP pages. Instead, we will concentrate on the languages and concepts that you can put to use immediately to better understand the world of BSP applications.

Incidentally, readers who already know their way around the language jungle of the World Wide Web (WWW) are welcome to skip Section 3.2.

Because the flight-booking portal will be constructed step-by-step in Chapters 4 and 5 using numerous examples, we will not explain the examples in the same detail here.[1] The focus here is on understanding the basics and providing an overview of what is involved.

At this point in the chapter, you don't need to understand the following paragraphs on the flight model. You are welcome to refer to this section later on as a reference.

---

1 However, we have provided you with a few recommended sources in the bibliography, which is located in Appendix C. These references cover the relevant topics in considerably more detail.

**The practical example** Just a word on the example before we start. We have decided to use a Web-based flight booking portal as a scenario. Experienced users of ABAP and those users who have completed standard SAP training courses will already be familiar with this particular scenario.[2] Several reasons for using the familiar *flight model* are:

► It offers business processes that are varied enough to require the technologies and tools highlighted within the examples, without the subject becoming boring due to repetition.

When appropriate, we will also compare competing solutions, using their advantages and disadvantages in concrete examples.

► Much of the business logic and many of the structures and table types required as part of the examples are already provided in the Data Dictionary of the SAP Web AS. This provision makes it easier for you to concentrate on developing the Web application itself.

► Those of you who are already familiar with developing Web-based applications using SAP Web AS should feel right at home with this topic.

For those of you who are new to this topic and the flight-model scenario, don't worry. We'll keep the examples straightforward so that you won't need to have completed a "pilot's training course" to understand the basic, underlying business logic.

**A short excursion into the SAP data modeler** The flight model is based on the BC_TRAVEL data model, which can also be viewed as the system using the data modeler. The procedure for displaying the flight model in the SAP Web Application Server (SAP Web AS) is described in the following steps.

1. Go to the initial screen of the ABAP Workbench and select **Development Data Modeler** or enter the code SD11 in the entry field for the transaction code, as shown in Figure 3.1. The initial screen of the data modeler appears.

2. In the **Modeling object** field, enter "BC_TRAVEL" (see Figure 3.2) and click on **Display**. You can now view the description of the flight model.

3. Select **Utilities Graphic** to display the data model as a graphic.

---

2  The traditional IDES water pump is not mentioned here, although experienced ABAP developers will be more than familiar with it as standard material from the IDES training environment.

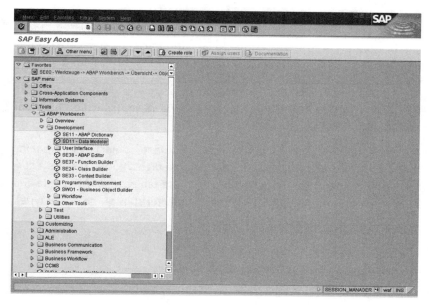

**Figure 3.1** Starting the SAP data modeler

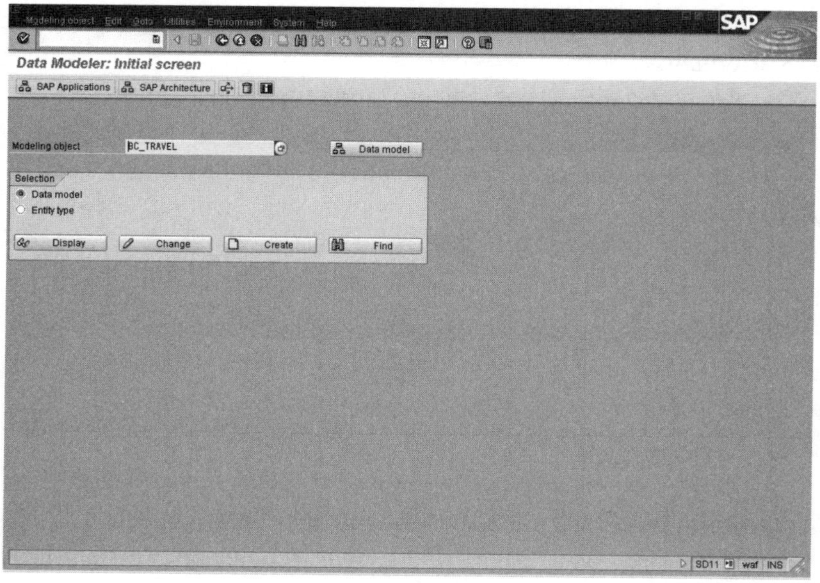

**Figure 3.2** Selecting the flight data model

The flight model provides a simple explanation of how customers can book flights on passenger planes. The booking process is carried out by an airline sales outlet, by a travel agency, or, as in our example, via the Internet.

Individual flight connections, described accurately in the flight plan, are what constitutes a flight-booking system. There are specific flights for each flight connection.

For each type of entity (common description of objects of the same type—the construction plan, as it were) in the flight model, there is a corresponding table in the Data Dictionary. These tables record the data and type definitions of the relevant entities (characteristics of the entity type).

The most important tables in the flight model are:

► **T000**
Client table

► **SCURX**
Currencies (key: currency key)

► **SBUSPART**
Business partners (key: client, partner number)

► **STRAVELAG**
Travel agencies (key: client, number of the travel agency)

► **SCUSTOM**
Customer (key: client, customer number)

► **SCARR**
Airlines (key: client, airline code)

► **SCOUNTER**
Sales outlets (key: client, airline code, sales outlet number)

► **SPFLI**
Flight plan (key: client, airline code, connection number)

► **SFLIGHT**
Flights (key: client, airline code, connection number, flight date)

► **SBOOK**
Flight bookings (key: client, airline code, connection number, flight date, booking number, customer number)

The table SBUSPART contains all the business partners of an airline; each business partner is assigned with and identified by a number. In addition, the data for the contact person (the representative for the business partner) is stored with the business partner. A business partner may be a travel agency or a customer (e.g., a company that frequently books flights directly with an airline); different data is required for each type of business partner. For example, a travel agency's data is stored in the table STRAVELAG, and a customer's data is stored in the table SCUSTOM, which means that for each entry in the SBUSPART table there is an entry with the same key in either the table STRAVELAG or the table SCUSTOM.

The table SCARR contains the airline codes and names. Every airline offers a range of flight connections, each of which is stored in the table SPFLI. The concrete flight data for each flight connection is provided in the table SPFLIGHT. Bookings can be made for each flight in the table SFLIGHT, and are recorded in the table SBOOK.

The airlines maintain sales counters at the airports; each counter is stored in the table SCOUNTER. For each booking, the number of the customer or the travel agency for whom the booking is made is stored in the table SBOOK. If a booking was made directly at a sales counter, the number of that sales counter is also entered in the table SBOOK along with the booking data.

## 3.2    Introduction to Languages and Standards

As we present the languages required for creating BSP applications, you will note that many of the terms and topics recur in several of the languages, not only in one language. For example, CSS and DTD files can affect and control both HTML and XML in the same way.

In addition, some standards are described that play an important role in the context of Web programming. Covered in brief are the HTTP protocol (HTTP) and HTTPS, which is essentially HTTP with extra security mechanisms. Also worth mentioning is the use of cookies—in particular, server-side cookies—which play an important role in *stateless Web applications* for the temporary storage of information and data. Stateless Web applications are Web applications without a context, which means that the server "forgets" the client between requests. We will cover this topic in more detail later.

Please note that this book is not intended to be a textbook for learning Internet languages. Rather, this book is intended to offer a brief introduction, a kind of "starter pack," to the concepts that underscore developing Web applications. A more in-depth description would be beyond the scope of this book. However, to provide you with an overview of the basic priniciples of BSP applications, it is certainly worth describing the concepts behind the individual languages to explain why they are actually used.

To avoid any misunderstandings, we will first define a few distinctions between the different uses of the languages.

**Differentiation of the languages in client- and server-side contexts**

*HTML* is required for displaying the Web application on the client. It is static—that is, each time an HTML page with the same parameters is called, the same HTML code is transferred by the server. The display and contents are therefore the same on each call.

*Client-side JavaScript* is run by the browser on the client while a page is being displayed. This behavior is generally referred to as *dynamic* because, when used appropriately, it can add dynamic capabilities to a static HTML page. For example, client-side JavaScript makes it possible to react to the user's actions and modify the contents accordingly. This, in turn, fosters client-side interaction between the user and the Web application.

*Server-side scripting*, however, is always run on the server before the page is sent to the client. From the server's point of view, therefore, the client-side JavaScript is not dynamic, because the Java code is sent unchanged to the client.

In the context of BSP, server-side scripting is typically referred to when speaking of dynamic page sections.

### 3.2.1 ABAP

**Development environment**

*ABAP* is the programming language of the enterprise resource planning (ERP) system *SAP R/3*. The *ABAP Workbench* is the associated development environment. It is a fixed, integrative part of the ERP system. However, the ABAP Workbench is also available as a standalone system via the SAP online shop.

Since the introduction of ABAP/4, virtually all of SAP R/3, including the development environment itself, has been written in ABAP. Therefore, every program developed by SAP can be easily understood and analyzed; only the system core is written in C.

**History**

The history of ABAP is as long as the history of SAP itself. In the 1970s, ABAP was created as a "reporting tool." Now ABAP provides the entire range of a $4^{th}$-generation language, including object-oriented concepts. When SAP R/2 was current, ABAP stood for *Allgemeiner Berichts- und Aufbereitungsprozessor* (English: General Reporting and Preparation Processor). Today, ABAP stands for *Advanced Business Application Programming*.

SAP R/1 (1972) and SAP R/2 (1979) were programmed in Assembler. At this time, ABAP was basically a sequence of Assembler macros and instructions. The process of generating analyses was highly complex. For this reason, SAP developed ABAP/3 in the mid-80s to create a full-scale interpreter language that could create business programs and dialog-controlled transactions easily. In 1992, SAP R/3 appeared and ABAP/4 was the developers' tool. The last step in ABAP's development to date is *ABAP Objects*. To this end, ABAP/4 was expanded with object-oriented functionalities such as encapsulation, inheritance, and polymorphism. Nevertheless, ABAP remains fully backward-compatible, and the programmer can even, with few exceptions, use procedural and object-oriented elements in parallel.

An important feature of ABAP is that the components of the programming language are subject to the concept of formatting programs in R/3 (e.g., the Dynpro concept). ABAP consists of instructions specially designed for a precisely defined program type with a specified functionality and structure. ABAP's scope is not based on any particular standard, but is entirely unrestricted and is being expanded continually. This means that many commands and their meanings can be exploited only with the relevant programming concept.

Here we have provided a simple code example intended to give you a first impression of the ABAP language. At this point, we are purposely omitting the steps in the development environment before the creation of the program. This is a fairly complex process and we don't want to introduce here what will later be covered in Chapter 5, especially since the creation of a pure ABAP program differs from that of a BSP page with integrated ABAP code. For a complete introduction to ABAP objects, we recommend *ABAP Objects* by Horst Keller and Sascha Krüger, also published by SAP PRESS.

**ABAP says "Hello World!"**

For the purpose of clarification, the ABAP keywords and their additional specifications are given in capital letters throughout this book.

**Listing 3.1** The first ABAP program

```
*************************************************************
*   PROGRAM HELLO WORLD                                    *
*************************************************************
REPORT Z_HELLO_WORLD.
*************************************************************
```

```
*  DECLARATIONS                                                    *
**********************************************************
DATA lv_user(12) TYPE c.    "character variable length 12
DATA lv_output   TYPE string. "string variable
**********************************************************
* PROCESSING BLOCKS                                               *
**********************************************************
lv_user = sy-uname.         "get name of R/3 user
CONCATENATE 'It''s me: '     "build output
            lv_user  INTO lv_output SEPARATED BY space.
WRITE: 'Hello World!',       "print output
       lv_output.
```

**Correct ABAP syntax**

The following conventions illustrate the correct syntax of ABAP programs:

▶ A program consists of at least one command and comments.

▶ A comment starts with an asterisk ( * ) in the first column or a quotation mark ( " ) after a command. The compiler ignores everything in the row of text after these indicators.

▶ Each command starts with a keyword and ends with a period. There may be operands, operators, and additions to keywords in between.

▶ The ABAP compiler does not make a distinction between uppercase and lowercase; however, in BSP development with JavaScript code, case-sensitivity is very important).

▶ There may be multiple commands in a program line.

▶ A command may be spread across multiple lines.

▶ Brackets and the characters for plus and minus signs count as ABAP words and are therefore separated from their operands by spaces.

Because of these conventions, Listing 3.1 (the first ABAP program) becomes much clearer and easier to read. It starts with a few comments. The first command is REPORT   Z_HELLO_WORLD. The keyword is REPORT,[3] and the operand is Z_HELLO_WORLD, which identifies the code that follows the operand as an executable program.

---

3  ABAP cannot hide its origins here. Previously, there were reports only, i.e., report lists. Later, these reports turned into full-scale programs. There is also the initial instruction PROGRAM, although this program is intended primarily for the "Module Pool" program type.

This is followed by the global data declaration. Here, two data objects (also known as *variables*), `lv_user` and `lv_output`, are declared using the keyword `DATA`. A variable's type is defined by the keyword addition `TYPE`, followed by the data type. The variables are assigned a value later on.

The actual procedural program flow takes place in the processing block. First, a system field containing the name of the user who is logged onto the system is assigned to the data object `lv_user`. System fields, also known as *system variables*, are also present during runtime. Typically, only read access is available to the user.

`CONCATENATE` is then used to write the static output text and the new value of the variable `lv_user` to the variable `lv_output`. The individual variables are each separated by a space in this process.

Finally, `lv_output` is output to the screen using the `WRITE` command. This also familiarizes you with the *chain rule*, identified by the colon. The chain rule enables you to clearly display consecutive commands using the same content and with less typing. To do this, ensure that the keyword is followed by a colon. The remaining commands are separated by commas without keywords.

The output of the ABAP program, Listing 3.1, is shown in Figure 3.3.

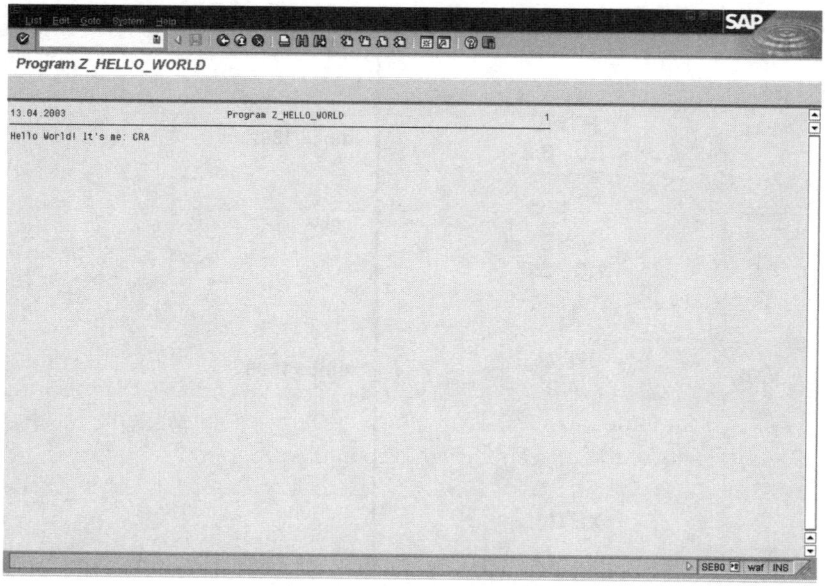

**Figure 3.3** The first program— "Hello World" in ABAP

### 3.2.2  DHTML

You may be asking yourself what the "D" in DHTML stands for. Most readers are familiar with HTML, but only Web disciples are likely to know that the "D" stands for "dynamic."

Dynamic HTML is a collective term for a combination of various languages (e.g., HTML, JavaScript) and tools (e.g., Macromedia Flash) that allow you to create Web pages that are more animated and more responsive to user actions than previous HTML, that is, change elements of a page dynamically (either automatically or via input from the user) while the page is currently being displayed.

**DHTML— A collective term**  Therefore, DHTML is basically a representation of the interaction between different languages and programs, the most important of which are HTML, JavaScript, and Cascading Style Sheets (CSS).

### HTML

**HTML: The mother of all Web languages?**  *HTML (HyperText Markup Language)*, the language that a Web browser uses, is an example of an *SGML*-based language (*Standard Generalized Markup Language*)—the metadata or standard for specifying a document markup language.

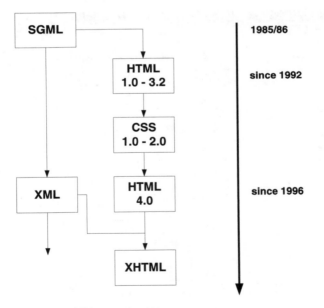

**Figure 3.4** Offshoots of SGML

HTML is continually being developed (see Figure 3.4). An offshoot of HTML has also appeared, known as *XHTML (Extensible Hypertext Markup Language)*. In version 1.0 of the language, XHTML is a redefinition of HTML using XML. It removes some of the untidy elements of HTML. An XHTML file looks like a somewhat more elaborate HTML file.

Developed by Web founder Tim Berners-Lee during the Web boom, HTML became the most successful and widely distributed file format in the world. HTML is easy to learn and is more than adequate for the majority of the data currently displayed on the Web. It is used primarily for formatting texts; however, multimedia data such as videos, graphics, and sound can also be included.

Using HTML, you can create headings, text paragraphs, lists, and tables as well as clickable links. These elements can be displayed on any other Web page or data source on the Internet. Forms can also be integrated into HTML pages, with contents that can be forwarded to a server for further processing. HTML provides interfaces for add-on languages such as CSS and JavaScript, which can be used to arrange and format HTML elements as required or to handle interactions with users.

As the "lingua franca" of the Internet, HTML is overextended with specialized demands. HTML alone can't satisfy graphic designers, who want to control every pixel on the screen, or data designers, who come from the world of relational databases and who want application-specific solutions. For this reason, there are now style sheets such as CSS and languages such as XML that enable and support data design and data integration.

All of this does not minimize the fact that, because HTML is standardized and universally available (thanks to the wide distribution of the Web browser), it is ideally suited to text and hypertext.

HTML is what is known as a *plain text format*. HTML files can be edited using any text editor that can save data as pure text files, so creating HTML files requires no specific piece of software. Numerous products in all price ranges allow simple editing and testing of HTML.

**HTML as a software-independent plain text format**

As HTML is a plain text format, it can also be easily generated by a program. The BSP pages of the SAP Web AS are starting to exploit this option. For example, if you want to display a database table in the browser, the HTML code for the table formats can be generated dynamically within the layout using ABAP scripting. It is therefore possible to automatically resize the table to fit any database.

**HTML as a mark-up language**

HTML is a *markup language*. It has the task of describing the logical components of a text-based document. As a markup language, HTML therefore enables you to identify typical elements of a text-oriented document, such as headings, text paragraphs, lists, tables, and graphic links.

HTML's markup schema is based on a hierarchical classification. HTML marks up the contents of documents. Documents have global properties such as header data; the actual content consists of elements such as headings, text paragraphs, tables, and graphics. Some of these elements have sub-elements. For example, a text paragraph contains a highlighted or bold text section; a list contains individual items with bullet points; and a table is divided into individual table cells or even sub-tables, with their own table cells.

Most of these elements have a fixed, defined range. For example, a heading extends from the first to the last character; a bulleted list extends from the first to the last item in the list; and a table extends from the first to the last cell. Markup flags identify the start and end of elements. To mark up a heading, for example, the schema is as follows:

```
[Head] Text of the heading [End head]
```

With an element that possesses sub-elements, such as a bulleted list, the same schema is used:

```
[List]
[List item] Text of the list item [End of list item]
[List item] Text of the list item [End of list item]
[End list]
```

 Not all elements of HTML have a closing element.

When a Web browser displays an HTML file on the screen, the browser resolves the markup flags, known as *tags*, and then displays the elements in the style of the form specified by the formatting tags. The screen display is not the only possible form of output. HTML can also be used on audio systems using synthetically generated voices, for example.

**HTML for hypertext**

One of the oldest and most important features of HTML is the ability to define links. Hyperlinks may take you to other points in the same application, but they can also point to any other addresses on the World Wide Web (WWW), and even to Internet addresses that are not part of the WWW.

Thus far, the discussion has been rather theoretical, so we will now illustrate the necessary principles of using HTML with a practical example (see

Listing 3.2). Enter the example into the text editor in the operating system environment and save it with the extension *.htm*. Then double-click on the file to check the result in your Internet browser. You can also use a convenient HTML editor, such as Macromedia's *HomeSite*, which will allow you to view the result directly in a window next to the editor itself.

**Listing 3.2** A first HTML example

**A practical example**

```
<!DOCTYPE html PUBLIC "-//W3C//DTD HTML 3.2//EN">
<HTML>
  <HEAD>
    <TITLE>
      My little Web site
    </TITLE>
  </HEAD>
  <BODY>
    <P>
      A couple of airlines
    </P>
    <TABLE
     border="1"
     cellpadding="5">
      <TR>
        <TD>
          Airline 1
        </TD>
        <TD>
          Lufthansa
        </TD>
      </TR>
      <TR>
        <TD>
          Airline 2
        </TD>
        <TD>
          American Airlines
        </TD>
      </TR>
    </TABLE>
  </BODY>
</HTML>
```

The first command line with the command !DOCTYPE is a document type specification. Behind each document type specification is a *document type definition* (DTD). A DTD controls which elements a document may contain, which elements may occur in which other documents, which attributes belong to an element, whether it is compulsory to specify these attributes, and so forth. For example, it is not absolutely necessary that you specify the document type, but it is recommended so that the browser can interpret and display it correctly. Based on these specifications, the browser detects how it should interpret the various attributes and commands. Many HTML tools also generate the document type specification automatically.

**The basic HTML framework** The basic framework always has the same structure: The root element ⟨HTML⟩...⟨/HTML⟩ encloses the remaining contents of each HTML file, which consist of the header ⟨HEAD⟩...⟨/HEAD⟩ and the output section ⟨BODY⟩...⟨/BODY⟩.

**The heading section** The heading section contains only the command ⟨TITLE⟩. It has multiple functions and should be included in all HTML pages:

▶ The title is displayed in the title bar of the display window. In our example, the output is displayed at the top left of the window frame.

▶ The Web browser uses the title when saving bookmarks (favorites).

▶ The Web browser displays the title in the list of sites visited.

▶ Many automated Web search programs use the title as an important input. If the file is one of the hits in a search, many search engines provide the title of the file as a clickable link.

**The body or output section** The output section is enclosed with ⟨BODY⟩. The actual output is given here. In the ⟨BODY⟩ tag, attributes affecting the overall appearance of the page can also be set.

The first element defined in our example is a text paragraph, which requires the paragraph tag ⟨P⟩. Paragraphs are used for the visual layout of a text. In this case, the paragraph is used as a heading for the table underneath.

The ⟨TABLE⟩ tag initiates a table. The table is one of the most important elements. If, in the starting ⟨TABLE⟩ tag, the attribute border= is assigned a value higher than "0," the table will be divided using visible gridlines of the corresponding thickness.

The <TR> (table row) tag initiates a new table row. The cells (columns) of the relevant row are then defined. The end of a table row is closed with the end tag </TR>.

A table can contain header cells and typical data cells. Text in header cells is emphasized, generally through bolding and centering. The <TH> (table header) tag initiates a header cell, and the <TD> (table data) tag creates a typical data cell. The contents of a cell are noted after the tag in each case. Although the corresponding end tags </TH> or </TD> are officially optional, we highly recommend that you always use them, because it makes the display in the code tidier, and also because if you don't use these tags, some browsers may have difficulty in displaying the page properly.

In addition to normal text, any elements can be placed in a table cell. Even other tables can be defined within a table cell.

Figure 3.5 shows the result of Listing 3.2. It's not spectacular, but not difficult to program.

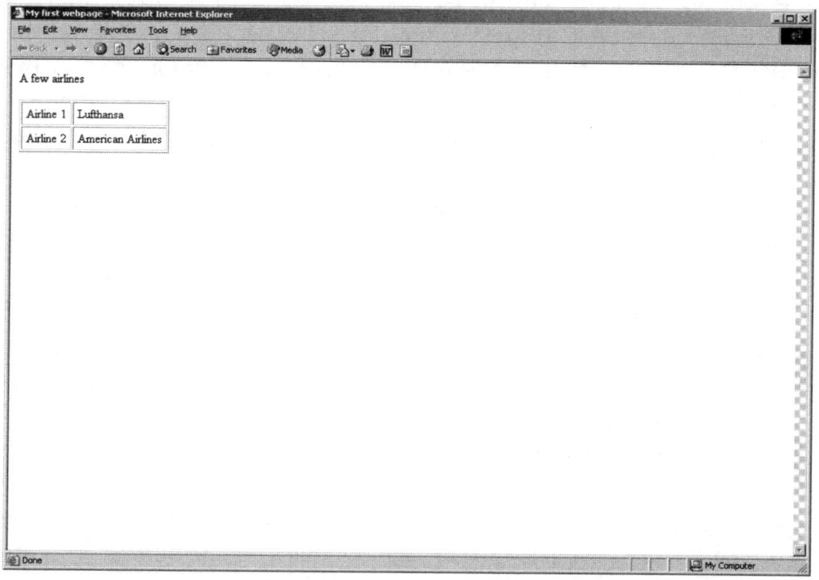

**Figure 3.5**  Output of Listing 3.2: A first HTML example

To give you a broader historical understanding of HTML, here is a brief overview of its development:

HTML versions

▶ *HTML 1.0* (1992) contained markups for standard elements such as headings, text paragraphs, graphic links, and text links.

▶ *HTML 2.0* became the official language standard in November 1995. The specification for HTML 2.0 is still available from the W3 Consortium, although today it is the lowest common denominator. However, HTML 2.0 does contain language elements that even today are not fully supported or are not supported by the big browsers, such as the `<LINK>` tag. When published, HTML 2.0 had already been surpassed by Netscape Navigator 2.0. Navigator caught on more quickly, thanks to the variety of proprietary display options that Netscape developed. Functions such as frames (multi-window technology) and multimedia references had already been implemented, and these technologies were far beyond the official HTML standard. Most Web site authors had little patience with the restrictions of HTML 2.0. This is how Netscape Navigator was able to establish itself as a pseudo-standard.

▶ *HTML 3.2* became the official language standard in 1997 after an extended debate. The specification for HTML 3.2 is available on the W3 Consortium Web site. The W3 Consortium, unimpressed by the successes of the Netscape browser, developed a version 3.0. The proposals for HTML 3.0 did contain some interesting components, but overall the suggestions did not meet the needs of the Web, and HTML 3.0 never actually became an official standard. HTML 3.2 is the result of a complete revision of HTML 3.0. Now tables were finally an official part of HTML, and language elements that allowed direct text formatting were integrated. This is why, from today's point of view, HTML 3.2 was a step backward in HTML's development. In HTML 3.2, the designers attempted to establish HTML as a language for graphical design. However, the nature of the language didn't measure up and graphical design features were therefore implemented only half-heartedly. Many parts of the language introduced in HTML 3.2 have now been classified as "deprecated"[4] These parts should therefore be removed from the HTML language standard in the future, because

---

4 This classification means that the function or the command are still implemented, but no longer should be used since later releases may no longer support them. The same applies to some ABAP commands that are still contained in the language modules only for compatibility reasons, but should no longer be used. These commands may even be forbidden in the ABAO-OO context (the so-called *obsolete* language elements).

HTML can be upgraded with other technologies, such as CSS. To ensure upward compatibility, we recommend using CSS for all graphic formatting options. We'll delve deeper into this subject later.

▶ *HTML 4.x* was approved as a language standard at the end of 1997. This language version was revised several times, and there is now a version 4.01. The current version of HTML 4.x can be found on the W3 Consortium Web site at *www.w3c.org*. HTML 4.0 is an attempt to return to the core tasks of HTML. The arsenal of language components in this version primarily controls the integration of CSS and script languages such as JavaScript in HTML. Another important issue that HTML 4.0 addresses is internationalization. Unlike its predecessors, HTML 4.0 is fully conversant with the Unicode system, which means that it allows texts in all conceivable languages to be marked up to conform to HTML. However, there are many confusing issues in HTML 4.0, which include the three language variants provided by the W3 Consortium: HTML Strict, HTML Transitional, and HTML Frameset. Furthermore, HTML was redefined in the form of XHTML in the process of establishing XML, complicating matters further.

## JavaScript

Introduction

Since its introduction in 1996, Netscape's JavaScript has become increasingly popular and widespread. On many Web sites, it is the preferred programming language for invoking dialog elements. JavaScript can be used for much more than this, however. What follows is a brief description of the commands in JavaScript and their applications.

### Embedding in HTML

JavaScript is fully integrated into HTML. Depending on the programming, JavaScript code can be run on either the client (the browser) or the Web server. This chapter uses the term JavaScript to refer to client-side JavaScript. Ideally, the JavaScript source code that is to be integrated into a page should be positioned in the HTML header. This makes the code available before the entire page is loaded, and therefore, it can be accessed from the first line of the HTML body, which is especially useful for calls made in the <BODY> tag.

When entering the printed code, you must ensure that the use of uppercase and lowercase is exactly the same for all commands and variable names within the <SCRIPT> tags. This convention must be adhered to because JavaScript is case-sensitive.

The HTML structure with the integrated JavaScript code looks like this:

**Listing 3.3** The first JavaScript example

```
<!DOCTYPE html PUBLIC "-//W3C//DTD HTML 3.2//EN">
<HTML>
  <HEAD>
    <TITLE>
      JavaScript—a brief overview
    </TITLE>
<SCRIPT type="text/javascript" language="JavaScript">
  document.write("Hello World");
</SCRIPT>
  </HEAD>
  <BODY>
    <P>
      The first example
    </P>
  </BODY>
</HTML>
```

The line `document.write("Hello World")` outputs the traditional "Hello World" in the active document ("document" is used here to mean the current browser output window).

### Conditions

Conditions are major elements of any programming and script language. JavaScript provides two commands for processing conditions. The first is the 'if' command, which is typically used to check a condition. If the variable can adopt multiple values, it's preferable to use the second command, the 'switch' command, because the layout is clearer than when using multiple nested 'if' commands. The syntax of the 'if' command permits a response to an actual value and the triggering of a counter-event if the condition does not occur.

'if' command    The syntax is as follows:

```
if (condition) {
    Command(s);
}
else {
    Command(s);
}
```

An HTML page with an input field and a button to send the result will be used to demonstrate this command:

**Listing 3.4** 'if' example

```
<!DOCTYPE html PUBLIC "-//W3C//DTD HTML 4.01 Transitio-
nal//EN">
<HTML>
  <HEAD>
    <TITLE>
      JavaScript training: 'if' example
    </TITLE>
<SCRIPT type="text/javascript" language="JavaScript">
        function check1(Name){
        if (Name != "")
            alert("Hallo, " + Name);
        else
            alert("Hallo");
        }
</SCRIPT>
  </HEAD>
  <BODY>
    <FORM name="Form1">
      <P>
        <INPUT type="text" name="t1" size="20">
      </P>
      <P>
        <INPUT type="button" value="Send"
        name="B1" onclick="check1(t1.value)">
      </P>
    </FORM>
  </BODY>
</HTML>
```

After the button is clicked, the function `check1` with the contents of the input field is called. If a value has been entered into the field, the program branches to the first command and the contents of the field are output together with the string "Hello, ". Otherwise, the 'alert' command is used to output a simpler "Hello" message. In this example, != (not-equals sign) is used as the operator (see Table 3.1).

| Operator | Meaning |
|----------|---------|
| + | Has different functions depending on the context: It is used both to add numbers and to consolidate two strings. For example, blue + white is bluewhite. |
| – | Subtraction |
| * | Multiplication |
| / | Division |
| % | Module operator. Rest of a division. |
| += | x+=10 is the short form of x=x+10. The operators –=, *=, and /= are defined in the same way. |
| ++ | Increases the value of the variable by 1. There are two variants: ++x increases the variable first and then returns the value, whereas x++ processes the variable before increasing it. |
| – – | Reduces the value of the variable by 1. Otherwise the same as ++. |
| == | Equal. Checks that the variables are the same. |
| != | Not equal. Checks whether the variables contain different values. |
| > | Greater than |
| < | Less than |
| >=, <= | Greater than or equal to / less than or equal to |
| && | Boolean AND operator. True if both operators are true. |
| \|\| | Boolean OR operator. True if one of the two operators is true. |
| &= | A&=B is the short form of the Boolean equation A=A&B. The operator \| is defined in the same way. |

**Table 3.1** JavaScript operators

If more than one command is used to respond to an event, the commands need to be grouped using curly brackets { . . . }, and each command must be concluded with a semicolon.

When using the 'switch' command, multiple values of a variable can be specified. Assigned commands are used to respond to them.

**'switch' command**  The syntax is as follows:

```
switch (Variable) {
case Value1: Command(s);
case Value2: Command(s);
```

```
...
default: Command(s);
}
```

The 'switch' command can be used to respond to events in different ways. Various messages are output depending on the input. As an example, in Listing 3.5, the 'check' function is given as a 'switch' command.

**Listing 3.5** 'switch' example

```
function check1(Value){
    switch (Value) {
    case "1":
        alert("Super");
        break;
    case "2","3":
        alert("OK");
        break;
    default:
        alert("Well");
        break;
    }
}
```

With the 'switch' command, you can link multiple possible values of a variable by using a command. The individual data items simply need to be separated by commas, as shown in Listing 3.5.

Unlike the 'if' command, command blocks are not grouped using brackets, but are ended directly with the 'break' command.

### Loops

Loops are another important part of every programming language. In JavaScript, there are two different types of loops: the 'while' and the 'for' loops. For both loops, a counter is initialized before the first pass.

With the 'for' loop, the initialization, check, and change of the counter **'for' command** is carried out in one line. In this process, multiple variables can be initialized at once and incremented or decremented independently of one another.

```
for (initialization; check; incrementation/
    decrementation of the variables)
Command(s)
```

The 'while' loop requires a variable to first be specified as a counter. It can be assigned using an initial value. This value is checked before every loop pass. The counter must be explicitly changed at the end of each loop pass.

```
Counter initialization;
while (check){
Command(s);
Adjust the counter value
}
```

Given below is a comparison of the loops using the same example. This provides a precise picture of the different structures of the loop types. You can select the familiar HTML frame from Listing 3.4 to run the example. The following check to the check1 function is required:

**Listing 3.6** 'while' loop

```
function check1(value){
    var icount = 0;
    while (icount < value){
        document.write("Current value of icount: ",
icount, "<BR>");
        icount++;
    }
}
```

The number of loop passes is specified in input field t1. The function check1() is then triggered by pressing the Send button.

To execute the loop, a counter variable is required. This is defined by the line var icount = 0; and is initialized with the value 0. At the start of the loop, a check is run on whether the specified conditions icount < value still applies. If this is the case, the loop is processed, the counter is increased, and the abort criterion is checked once more.

Things are a little different with the 'for' loop. In this case, the counter is automatically increased by one after each loop pass, so no further action needs to be taken. This minimizes the risk of producing an endless loop in which the abort criterion is never reached.

```
function check1(value){
    for(icount=0; icount<value;icount++){
        document.write("Current value of icount: ",
icount, "<BR>");
    }
}
```

With both loop types, the same consideration applies as for the 'if' loop: If there are multiple commands to be processed within a loop, they need to be grouped together using curly brackets. The strings are appended using `document.write()`.

## Variables

Variables are used to save values that are used multiple times and are changed during the running of the program. They can be accessed using a defined name. Variable names must start with either a letter, a number, or an underscore (_).

JavaScript is case-sensitive, so the variable names "Test" and "test" count as two different variables, for example.

When declaring a variable, you have two options: You can implement a new variable, including value assignment, in the program code, such as `test = 4711`. However, defining the variable using the keyword `var` at the start of a function or at the start of a script is a preferable. This option provides a clearer overview of the variables used and their values. For the declaration of a variable, the position where it is defined is very important to its validity. If a variable is specified within a function, you will only be able to access it within that function. Once the function is exited, the variable is no longer valid.

**Variable declaration**

Local variables must always be identified using the keyword `var`!

Using global variables is much easier than using local variables; however, in general, global variables should be avoided wherever possible. A global variable is always defined outside a function, and therefore it can be accessed from anywhere in the program code.

## Data types

Programming languages usually have a defined quantity of data types for numbers, strings of characters, and logical values. JavaScript is poorly equipped with just four characteristics:

▶ **Number**
Comprehensive data type grouping all possible numbers

▶ **String**
May contain letters, special characters, and numbers

▶ **Logical value (Boolean)**
Can be either `true` or `false`

▶ **Null**
Identifies a variable as undefined

When declaring a variable, only the variable name needs to be specified. It is not necessary to specify the data type. JavaScript will handle everything else, including the data-type conversion, which means that a variable defined using `var test` can be assigned different data types in a function:

```
var test;
test = "Hello World !";
test = 4711;
```

A variable can also be assigned numbers and strings in one step. JavaScript converts the numerical values into strings automatically:

```
test = "Another" + 4 + "weeks to Christmas";
```

### Literals/constants

Literals and constants are fixed values specified within a program. These fixed values can be numbers, strings, the Boolean values `true` and `false`, and the initial value `null`. In order to allow specific actions, such as a line break or a tab, to be integrated into strings, JavaScript contains what are known as *escape characters,* which consist of a backslash (\) and another character. Table 3.2 provides a summary of these escape characters.

| Sequence | Meaning |
|---|---|
| \b | Backspace—same effect as the backspace key |
| \f | Form feed—for printers |
| \n | New line—line is ended, cursor goes to a new line at position 1 |
| \r | Carriage return—inserts an empty line |
| \t | Tabulator |
| \" or \' | Inserts quotation marks within a string |
| \000 | Character with the octal code 000 is output |

**Table 3.2** Escape characters in JavaScript

With the following two listing lines, a string containing two line breaks and double quotation marks within the string is output:

```
var test = "Now for a new line \n and another one \n
\"This text has quotation marks\"";
alert(test);
```

Unfortunately, the escape characters that affect the alignment of the text can be used appropriately only in the `alert()` function, because these characters are not effective in pure HTML text output using `document.write()`. Only the standard HTML tags such as `<BR>` or `<P>` function in `document.write()`.

**Functions**

In the "sequential" programming method (from top to bottom), you quickly hit a wall using the previously described procedure. You can break through the wall by using functions that group a series of commands into one unit, which can be executed at any point within the program code.

As an example, we've used an HTML page with two text boxes and four buttons (see Listing 3.7). The values of the two text boxes are transferred by clicking on various functions. As an exercise, you can implement the functions "Multiply" and "Divide".

The first button is assigned using the function `add (a,b)`, the second button is assigned using the function `sub(a,b)`, the third button is assigned using the function `div(a,b)`, and the fourth button is assigned using the function `mul(a,b)`. Because the two transferred text-box values `T1.value` and `T2.value` are strings, they first need to be converted into figures within the function. A new number object is created to which the corresponding values are assigned. This produces two numbers that can be processed further. None of the four functions has a return value. A value can also be calculated within the function and returned to the calling point.

**Listing 3.7** Example of a function call

```
<!DOCTYPE html PUBLIC "-//W3C//DTD HTML 4.01 Transitio-
nal//EN">
<HTML>
  <HEAD>
    <TITLE>
      JavaScript training
    </TITLE>
<SCRIPT type="text/javascript" language="JavaScript">

function add(a,b){
  a = new Number(a);
  b = new Number(b);
```

```
      c = a+b;
      alert("The result is "+c);
   }
   function sub(a,b){
      a = new Number(a);
      b = new Number(b);
      c = a-b;
      alert("The result is "+c);
   }
   function div(a,b){
      a = new Number(a);
      b = new Number(b);
      c = a/b;
      alert("The result is "+c);
   }
   function mul(a,b){
      a = new Number(a);
      b = new Number(b);
      c = a*b;
      alert("The result is "+c);
   }

</SCRIPT>
   </HEAD>
   <BODY>
      <FORM name="Form1">
         <P>
            Number 1: <INPUT type="text" name="T1"
                        size="20">
         </P>
         <P>
            Number 2: <INPUT type="text" name="T2"
                        size="20">
         </P>
         <P>
            <INPUT type="button" value="Add"
            name="btnAdd" onclick="add(T1.value, T2.value)">
            <INPUT type="button" value="Subtract"
            name="btnSub" onclick="sub(T1.value, T2.value)">
```

```
        <INPUT type="button" value="Divide"
        name="btnDiv" onclick="div(T1.value, T2.value)">
        <INPUT type="button" value="Multiply"
        name="btnMul" onclick="mul(T1.value, T2.value)">
      </P>
    </FORM>
  </BODY>
</HTML>
```

Functions can also provide a return value. This is always used if the value determined is required for further processing following the call.

Using the example from Listing 3.7, you can show and integrate the additional options easily. Until now, the output of the result happened within the function, which meant that a new definition was required for each operator. In addition, the start of the calculation with four buttons is not particularly elegant. In their place, there should be a **Calculate!** button and the operator should be selected using a drop-down field. The HTML code now looks like the output in Listing 3.8.

**Listing 3.8** Function call with return value

```
<!DOCTYPE html PUBLIC "-//W3C//DTD HTML 4.01 Transitio-
nal//EN">
<HTML>
  <HEAD>
    <TITLE>
      JavaScript training
    </TITLE>
<SCRIPT type="text/javascript" language="JavaScript">
        function sub(a,b){
          a = new Number(a);
          b = new Number(b);
          return a-b;
        }
        function div(a,b){
          a = new Number(a);
          b = new Number(b);
          return a/b;
        }
        function mul(a,b){
          a = new Number(a);
```

```
                  b = new Number(b);
                  return a*b;
                }
              function add(a,b){
                a = new Number(a);
                b = new Number(b);
                return a+b;
              }
              function calculate(a,b,c){
                erg = new Number();
                switch(c){
                  case 0:
                  erg = add(a,b);
                  break;
                  case 1:
                  erg = sub(a,b);
                  break;
                  case 2:
                  erg = div(a,b);
                  break;
                  case 3:
                  erg = mul(a,b);
                  break;
                }
                output(erg);
              }
              function output(d){
                alert('The result is: ' + d);
              }
          </SCRIPT>
        </HEAD>
        <BODY>
          <FORM name="Form1">
            <P>
              Number 1: <INPUT type="text" name="T1"
                        size="20">
            </P>
            <P>
              Number 2: <INPUT type="text" name="T2"
                        size="20">
```

```
  </P>
  <P>
    Operator: <SELECT name="sell" size="1">
      <OPTION>
        +
      </OPTION>
      <OPTION>
        -
      </OPTION>
      <OPTION>
        /
      </OPTION>
      <OPTION>
        *
      </OPTION>
    </SELECT>
  </P>
  <P>
    <INPUT type="button" value="Calculate !"
    name="btnCalculate" onclick="calculate(T1.value,
    T2.value, sell.selectedIndex)">
  </P>
</FORM>
</BODY>
</HTML>
```

After clicking the Calculate! button, the values of both text boxes T1 and T2 and the index of the displayed operator are transferred from the `select object` to the `calculate()` function. In this case, the transferred index is used for further processing of the transferred number values. In other words, one of the functions (`add()`, `sub()`, `mult()`, or `div()`) is called and the calculated result is returned to the function to be called. The output is encapsulated in a separate `output()` function in this process. This ensures that the corresponding code does not occur more than once.

If the code from Listing 3.8 has been entered correctly, the result should look something like the screen displayed in Figure 3.6.

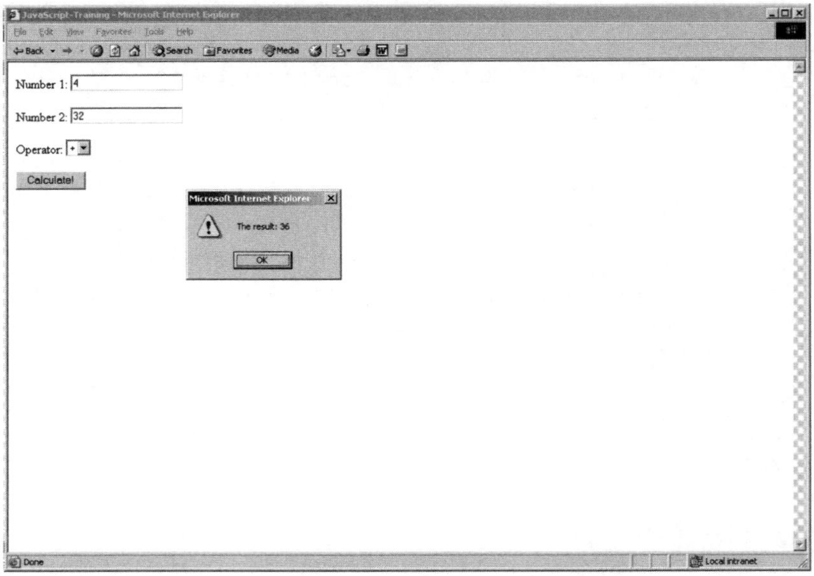

**Figure 3.6** Result of the coding from Listing 3.8

When transferring the parameters to a function, some extra information is saved in addition to the actual values. This information is useful later on. If a function does not have the correct number of parameters transferred to it, it cannot be run without errors, so the transferred values should be checked first to avoid the risk of an incorrect transfer quantity.

In the function `calculate(a,b,c)` in the example from Listing 3.8, the code may look something like this:

```
function calculate(a,b,c){
//The number of transferred values is being checked
if (calculate.arguments.length != 3){
alert("Not all the parameters have been correctly
      transferred!");
exit;
}
```

Each function saves the transferred values in an `arguments[]` array. The number of stored parameters can be queried using the `arguments.length` attribute.

In an `if`-query, there is a check as to whether three parameters have actually been transferred to the `calculate()` function.

With nested calls, it's easy to lose control of the point from which a function was called. The caller property was implemented in JavaScript for this reason. The caller property returns the function as a result, including all of the source code. Listing 3.9 demonstrates this functionality.

**Listing 3.9** Example of caller function

```
<!DOCTYPE html PUBLIC "-//W3C//DTD HTML 3.2//EN">
<HTML>
  <HEAD>
    <TITLE>
      JavaScript Training-Caller Example
    </TITLE>
<SCRIPT type="text/javascript" language="JavaScript">
function main_caller(){
alert(main_caller.caller);
}
function start_caller(){
main_caller();
}
</SCRIPT>
  </HEAD>
  <BODY>
    <A href="javascript:start_caller()">Caller Example
    - Please click</A>
  </BODY>
</HTML>
```

After clicking the text, `start_caller()` is used to call the `main_caller()` function that returns the function being called.

## Objects

Objects are special data types that store information. The special feature of this storage is the access to the data using the name or attributes. Each object may possess and group any number of attributes, which means that an object can be used to access information with different data types. In JavaScript, the period operator is typically used to carry out the value assignment and the reading of data. The attributes of an object can be accessed via `<object name>.<attribute>`. For example, `w=image.width` assigns the width of an image to the variable "w".

There are two options when using objects: Netscape implemented basic objects in its programming language. These objects can be used to cover a variety of functions. Microsoft included most of these objects in its implementation of JavaScript, as well as defining a few more. JavaScript also enables you to define separate objects with attributes and methods, based on the object-oriented approach to the language. This option is rarely used when developing BSP pages, however. For this reason, this chapter will simply explain how to use the most important objects.

### Methods

Objects are more than the sum of their attributes. Strictly speaking, the methods are more important because they can be used to edit an object's attributes. *Methods* are functions that execute actions. However, unlike the functions mentioned above, methods are linked to a specific object. Many predefined JavaScript objects have methods. For example, there is the predefined JavaScript object document that displays the actual Web page. The method write() outputs a text directly on the Web page.

```
document.write("Hello");
```

A complete overview of individual objects' methods and attributes can be found in the Netscape documentation, which is available for download from the Internet at *www.developer.netscape.com*.

Table 3.3 displays all the objects that JavaScript knows automatically. The most important objects are described in more detail below.

| Object | Description |
|--------|-------------|
| all | The object permits direct access to all elements of an HTML file. It is not included in the official JavaScript standard, but it is implemented in Internet Explorer from version 4.0 on. |
| anchor | The object contains all link anchors in an HTML file. |
| applet | The object contains all Java applets in an HTML file. |
| Array | This object is used to generate arrays. Its elements can be addressed via a common designation and an index. |
| Boolean | An object with logical values. |
| Date | The object contains information on the date and time. |
| document | This object represents the Web site itself. |
| event | An object that is generated in user events and that can be used for (central) event handling. |

**Table 3.3** JavaScript objects

| Object | Description |
| --- | --- |
| form | An object representing the forms in an HTML page. |
| frame | An object representing the framesets and frames in an HTML page. |
| Function | An object with JavaScript functions. |
| history | This object contains information on the URLs visited by a user. |
| image | An object that can be used to access graphics in an HTML file. |
| layer | The layers in an HTML file (Netscape-specific). |
| link | The object representing the links in the current HTML file. |
| location | This object triggers information via URL addresses. |
| Math | An object with numerous mathematical constants and methods. |
| mimeType | An object with MimeType information. |
| navigator | The object representation with information used on the WWW browser. |
| Number | An object with numerical values. |
| plugin | An object representing the existing plug-ins in a browser. |
| RegExp | An object with regular expressions. |
| screen | An object with information on the screen being used. |
| String | An object for manipulating characters and strings. |
| Style | The object representation of an element's style attributes. |
| window | This object contains status information on the entire browser window. Each window has a separate `window` object. The `window` object is the highest object in the object hierarchy of objects directly affecting the browser. |

**Table 3.3** JavaScript objects (Cont.)

JavaScript does not have a separate data type for managing strings; however, it does have a `String` object, which provides a variety of manipulation options.

**String object**

One of the most basic pieces of information in a string is its length. This is stored in the `length` property. The object's methods can be roughly divided into two classes:

▶ Information on the string
▶ HTML formatting

You can use the String object to check the information from input fields, for example. If you know that a material number must have nine digits, you can run a check when entering the number without sending the information to the server first.

The following example (see Listing 3.10) focuses on the information contained in a string and the way in which a string can be manipulated. The string can be checked for its length and displayed in uppercase and lowercase. The two methods charAt() and indexOf() are especially useful in the plausibility check for inputs, for example, to check a filename or path entered. The functions big() and small() convert the entered string into uppercase or lowercase and output it in the input window. For direct access to the text field, the addressing via the name (document.Form1.txtInput.value) is used. With the remaining functions—with the exception of the validity check—the direct call of the methods is used.

**Listing 3.10** Example of the string object

```
<!DOCTYPE html PUBLIC "-//W3C//DTD HTML 4.01 Transitio-
nal//EN">
<HTML>
  <HEAD>
    <TITLE>
      JavaScript Training—String Example
    </TITLE>
<SCRIPT type="text/javascript" language="JavaScript">
function new(wert){
  teststr = new String(value);
}
function count(){
  anz = teststr.length;
  alert("The length of the string entered is
      "+anz+" characters");
}
function big(){
  big = teststr.toLowerCase();
  document.Form1.txtInput.value = big;
}
function small(){
  big = teststr.toLowerCase();
  document.Form1.txtInput. value = small;
```

```
}
function pos(value){
  if (value != ""){
    if (value > teststr.length)
    alert("You have exceeded the total length of the
        string !");
    else {
    character = teststr.charAt(value-1);
    alert("The character at the entered position is
        "+characters);
  }
}
else
  alert("Please enter the position of the character
      !");
}
function indexof(value){
  if (value != ""){
    pos = teststr.indexOf(value)+1;
    if ((pos != -1) && (pos != 0))
    alert("The first position of the character found
        is "+pos);
    else
    alert("Characters or character string not present in
        string!");
  }
  else {
    alert("Please enter a search string!");
  }
}
</SCRIPT>
  </HEAD>
  <BODY>
    <FORM name="Form1">
      <P>
        Please enter a string: <INPUT
        type="text" name="txtInput" size="30">
      </P>
      <P>
        Position within string: <INPUT type="text"
```

```
                    name="txtPos" size="5"> Search string: <INPUT
                    type="text" name="txtStr" size="20">
                </P>
                <P>
                    <INPUT type="button" value="Transfer text for
                    analysis" name="btnNew" onclick=
                    "new(txtInput.value)">
                    <BR>
                    <INPUT type="button" value="Length" name=
                    "btnlength" onclick="count()">
                    <INPUT type="button" value="Upper;" name=
                    "btnBig" onclick="big()">
                    <INPUT type="button" value="Lower" name="
                    btnSmall" onclick="small()">
                    <INPUT type="button" value="Determine charac-
                    ters"
                    name="btnSymb" onclick="pos(txtPos.value)">
                    <INPUT type="button" value="Search characters"
                    name="btnIndex" onclick="indexof(txtStr.value)">
                    <INPUT type="reset" value="Delete" name=
                    "btnDelete">
                </P>
            </FORM>
        </BODY>
    </HTML>
```

**Date object**  Much like the string, there is no separate data type for the date. The only option is manipulation via a separate object. The date is expressed as a numerical value, starting with 01.01.1970, 00:00:00, in milliseconds. A similar procedure is used by Java and many spreadsheets. The methods set and get of the date objects can be used to set or read out different times, which makes direct access to all date variables possible (seconds, minutes, hours, day, date, months, and year).

 This object is an elegant way of checking date specifications without having to transfer the data to the server first.

The example below uses several of these commands to calculate the days remaining to the start of the year 2005.

**Listing 3.11** Example of the date object

```html
<!DOCTYPE html PUBLIC "-//W3C//DTD HTML 3.2//EN">
<HTML>
  <HEAD>
    <TITLE>
      JavaScript Training–Date Example
    </TITLE>
<SCRIPT type="text/javascript" language="JavaScript">
function timeremain(){
  today = new Date();
  tomorrow = new Date("January 1,2006");
  MSecperDay = 24 * 60 * 60 * 1000;
  remainTime = (tomorrow.getTime() - today.getTime())
  /MSecperDay;
  remainTime = Math.round(remainTime);
  document.write("Another " + remainTime + " days to the
            year 2005");
  }
</SCRIPT>
<SCRIPT type="text/javascript" language="JavaScript"
for="window" event="onload()">
  timeremain()
</SCRIPT>
  </HEAD>
  <BODY>
  </BODY>
</HTML>
```

Because the calculation is carried out in milliseconds, the difference is simply divided by the number of milliseconds per day. The value is then rounded and output.

Any Internet user will be more than familiar with the pop-up advertisements that appear automatically at the top of a Web page when you click on a site. JavaScript, in particular, is ideally suited to creating and displaying these windows, and not just for advertising purposes! In the example below, the control of an additional window is transferred from a normal page. Using three small functions, an additional window can be generated and closed again as necessary, and the main window itself can be eliminated.

**Window object**

You can use the open method of the window object to generate a new window. The transferred parameters of the method are divided into three parts:

▶ Page to be displayed in the new window

▶ Name of the new window

▶ Additional parameters to determine the appearance of the new window

```
newWindow=window.open("", "newWindow", "toolbar=no,
                      status=no, height=200");
```

In this example call, text information is output from JavaScript for display in the window, rather than calling an existing HTML page. Therefore, the first parameter is empty. Otherwise, the name and the path of the HTML page being displayed must be provided. Using the additional parameters, the status line and the browser toolbar are hidden and the window is assigned a fixed size. Thanks to the variety of options, you can format your window as you want.

**Access to a window via JavaScript**
In order to assign contents to or modify the appearance of the window via JavaScript, an object—in this case myWindow—is still required. This object can be used to access the window via the program. The rest is basic HTML programming.

Listing 3.12 is an ideal starting point for displaying additional information on your own pages, for example. Therefore, you can display detailed information, including an image, in an extra window.

**Listing 3.12** Example of the window object

```
Example of the window object
<!DOCTYPE html PUBLIC "-//W3C//DTD HTML 3.2//EN">
<HTML>
  <HEAD>
<SCRIPT type="text/javascript" language="JavaScript">
  var myWindow;
  function window_open() {
    myWindow = window.open("image1.htm", "This is
    not an empty window", "width=600, height=250, resiz-
    able=yes, directories=yes, menubar=yes, location=
    yes");
  }
  function window_close()  {
```

```
    myWindow.close();
  }
</SCRIPT>
  <TITLE>
  </TITLE>
</HEAD>
<BODY>
  <A href="JavaScript:window_open()">New window
  open</A>
  <BR>
   <A href="JavaScript:window_close()">New window
   close</A>
  <BR>
  <A href="JavaScript:self.close()">Active window
  close</A>
  <BR>
 </BODY>
</HTML>
```

The window[5] is accessed directly via the specified name (myWindow) and the method close(). Each window can be closed from JavaScript itself. The object self can be used in this process instead of a name. Each browser executes this command a little differently. Whereas Netscape's Navigator closes the window immediately, Microsoft's Internet Explorer uses a pop-up to confirm that the user does want to close the window.

If an event occurs on a Web page, in JavaScript 1.1 and beyond, a separate object is generated. This is the event object, a sub-object of window. The event object contains many different types of information on an event that has occurred on a Web page, including the marginal conditions involved.

**Event object**

On a Web page, a situation generating an event object could be a mouse click on any part of the Web page. A mouse click generates an event object containing the following information:

▶ The key used

▶ Any other keys pressed (**Ctrl, Alt, Alt-Gr, Shift**)

▶ The coordinates where the click was made

---

5 *image1.htm* probably doesn't exist in your example environment. Instead, simply save one of the previous examples as *image1.htm*.

Other `event` objects generated with other events contain information modified for the event. When a key is pressed, the pressed key is available as information that can be queried.

Because event objects exist permanently in the background of a Web page, they are available anywhere in the code. Various concepts can be addressed as an `event` object. For example, you can address the object by its name (`event`). In this process, you also need to specify the object from which the event object was generated. The syntax for specifying this object is the standard period notation from object-oriented programming:

```
[object].event
```

During an evaluation, you will want to use very specific information from an event. From the object-oriented point of view, this will include the attributes of the object. For example, a mouse click may look like this:

```
document.event.CLICK
```

Both Internet Explorer and Netscape Navigator understand the basic principle of this specification. Unfortunately, however, the browsers implement the command differently. The two browsers also differ in the syntax for monitoring events (as already in the support of the event handler).

The Microsoft object model allows the central handling of events using the following syntax:

```
<SCRIPT FOR=[object] EVENT=[event] language="Java-
Script">
...[actual commands]...
</SCRIPT>
```

For example:

**Listing 3.13** Example of an event linked to the document

```
<!DOCTYPE html PUBLIC "-//W3C//DTD HTML 3.2//EN">
<HTML>
 <HEAD>
<SCRIPT type="text/javascript" for="document"
event="onclick" language="JavaScript">
 alert("there's a click");
</SCRIPT>
   <TITLE>
```

```
    </TITLE>
  </HEAD>
  <BODY>
    <H2>
    Click here
    </H2>
    <H3>
    Click there
    </H3>
  </BODY>
</HTML>
```

It is more elegant to use the event handlers provided by HTML. These event handlers are an important link between HTML and JavaScript and are designated as attributes in HTML tags. There is a specification for which event handlers may occur in which HTML tags. However, older browsers, such as Netscape 4.x, do not implement this specification very neatly. Internet Explorer, on the other hand, has interpreted event handlers since version 4.x, as universally as intended by the W3 Consortium. In the final analysis, the only solution is to test each situation with different browsers.

Event handlers can be identified by the way in which the HTML attributes start—that is, always with on, as in onClick=. A JavaScript command is specified after the equals sign in quotation marks. If you want to run multiple commands, it is best to define a function in a JavaScript range and to call it after the equals sign—for example, onClick="Convert()".

Each event handler stands for a specific user event. For example, onClick= stands for the event "User has clicked the mouse." The display area of the HTML element where the event handler is noted is the trigger element. If the event handler onClick= is noted in a form button, for example, the JavaScript code linked to it is executed only if the mouse click is made in the display area of this element. This may sound obvious, and it is, as long as you are talking about form buttons. However, according to the expanded model of HTML 4.0, an HTML area defined using <DIV>...</DIV> may also contain an event handler such as onClick=.

In Listing 3.14 you can see an example of an event linked to a specific object:

**Listing 3.14** Example of an event handler call

```
<!DOCTYPE html PUBLIC "-//W3C//DTD HTML 4.01 Transitio-
nal//EN">
<HTML>
  <HEAD>
    <TITLE>
    </TITLE>
  </HEAD>
  <BODY>
    <FORM>
      Place the cursor in the first text box,
      then press any key and release.
      <BR>
      <INPUT type="text" name="text1" size="20"
      onkeydown="form.text2.value = 'key down'"
      onkeyup="form.text2.value ='key up'">
      <INPUT type="text" name="text2" size="20">
    </FORM>
  </BODY>
</HTML>
```

In addition to the objects described, there are a few more basic objects in JavaScript (see Table 3.3).

### Frames

JavaScript is useful for more than just managing windows. It can also make life much easier when addressing frames. With multisection pages in particular, where the contents of individual frames change depending on the context, JavaScript is an invaluable tool.

The following example shows the options for addressing frames from JavaScript. To avoid having an example with overly complicated code, we used just one page with two frames. The HTML page *frames.htm* for controlling the two frames has been deliberately kept simple and is used merely as an aid in this example:

**Listing 3.15** Example of using frames with two pages

**frame.htm**
```
<!DOCTYPE html PUBLIC "-//W3C//DTD HTML 4.01 Frameset//
EN">
<HTML>
  <HEAD>
    <TITLE>
      JavaScript Training - Frames
    </TITLE>
  </HEAD>
  <FRAMESET cols="*,*">
    <FRAME name="left" src="links.htm">
    <FRAME name="right" src="about:blank">
  </FRAMESET>
</HTML>
```

**links.htm**
```
<!DOCTYPE html PUBLIC "-//IETF//DTD HTML 2.0//EN">
<HTML>
  <HEAD>
    <TITLE>
      Left page
    </TITLE>
  </HEAD>
  <BODY>
    <P>
      Click on one of the following links and the
      page will be opened in the right-hand frame.
    </P>
    <P>
      <A href="#" onclick="top.frames[1].location
      ='test1.htm'">Test page 1</A>
      <BR>
      <A href="#" onclick="top.right.location
      ='test2.htm'">Test page 2</A>
      <BR>
      <A href="#" onclick="parent.right.location
      ='test3.htm'">Test page 3</A>
      <BR>
```

```
      <A href="#" onclick="parent.frames[1].location
      ='test4.htm'">Test page 4</A>
      <BR>
    </P>
  </BODY>
</HTML>
```

The left-hand frame *links.htm* contains an HTML page with multiple hyperlinks for controlling the right-hand frame. The example shows different access options for the four links. The addressing can be carried out via the frames array. All the frames are stored with consecutive numbering.

Alternatively, access can be made via the objects `top` and `parent`. Other methods include direct access via the name of the frame, again with the two different objects. From a hierarchical point of view, when you access another frame, it always takes you to the top common root of the frame, and from there back down via the name or the index of the frame.

However, there is a disadvantage that we should mention: Saving links is tricky for inexperienced users, because the frame border is usually saved as a link, which points to the start page when called. Therefore, there is no quick way to save a specific target page of the frame as a link.

Before programming, you need to decide in favor of one access variant. Otherwise, the code can become very confusing.

### Summary

In this chapter, you learned that although JavaScript is powerful, it does have some disadvantages—namely incompatibility, which is a recurring stumbling block. For this reason, when considering JavaScript, we advise you to take some time to think about the type and scope of its use.

For a Web application on an intranet, it may still be relatively convenient to use JavaScript. In this case, users often use a prescribed browser, and as a developer, you can concentrate on that particular browser. On the Internet, however, you need to reckon with all possible browser versions.

### Cascading Style Sheets

*Cascading Style Sheets* (CSS) is a style sheet language derived from SGML (see Figure 3.4). CSS is used in the same way as formatting templates, and defines the formatting properties of individual HTML commands. A CSS file is a file with layout instructions—that is, a file with specifications for the character, paragraph, and page formatting. Thanks to its various features, CSS can be used for the following purposes:

Advantages of CSS

► **Simple maintenance**
You can control the appearance of documents with one central file. You do not need to waste time updating every document individually if, for example, you want to change the corporate identity.

► **Uniformity**
By using a central CSS file for all Web applications, a corporate identity can be guaranteed across all applications.

► **Performance**
The performance is increased thanks to more streamlined code. The CSS file is loaded from the server only once and is then stored in the faster main memory or in the browser cache. Frequently occurring formatting instructions and attributes are called using short designations, similar to macros.

The specification was developed by the World Wide Web Consortium (W3C). CSS describes how the Web documents linked to a style sheet are displayed and printed. These style sheets contain information on the appearance of the page, such as the font and the line spacing. CSS allows both Web designers and Web site visitors to apply style sheets to pages. The advantage of CSS files lies in the fact that you specify formatting only once in a central location. The CSS specification determines how the formatting template for an HTML document is integrated with the template defined by the user. *Cascading* means overlapping levels, and CSS makes cascading possible. This means that the same document can be assigned multiple style sheets, which can be applied to documents according to the specified priorities.

Unlike XML, HTML makes no strict distinction between tags used for the logical structure of a document and tags specifying the appearance of the document. For example, tags marking a heading or a paragraph, and tags setting a text passage in bold or in a different font type, are both saved in the same HTML file, just like the text on the page. With CSS, the goal is to separate the structural tags from the layout (typographical) tags. Information on the format of the HTML document is therefore excluded from the HTML page itself and saved in a separate style sheet.

The development process

Cascading Style Sheets are available in several versions. The first official version, *Cascading Style Sheets Level 1* (CSS1), appeared in 1996. The most recent version, *Cascading Style Sheets Level 2* (CSS2), appeared in 1998. CSS2 is an enhancement that can be used to specify various document output formats, such as instructions for conversion to Braille or for adding audio. Unlike CSS1, CSS2 can be applied to XML. W3C is already working on the development of CSS3.

*eXtensible Style Sheet Language* (XSL) is also used for formatting XML pages. XSL offers additional functions, such as the display of consecutive page numbers. Whereas CSS assigns a display object to each XML element, XSL can assign a single XML element to a group of display objects.

CSS—Many options CSS lets you control the appearance of your Web page in many ways. We have listed a few of the categories here:

- ▶ Font face, size, and color
- ▶ Text markups (italics/bold/underline and others)
- ▶ Text alignment (left/right/centered/full justification)
- ▶ Line spacing
- ▶ Word spacing
- ▶ Hyperlink formatting (colors/underline/hover)
- ▶ Changing the input fields on the forms
- ▶ New mouse pointer shapes
- ▶ Frame
- ▶ Background color or background image (including backgrounds for text sections)
- ▶ Border spacing
- ▶ Positioning (relative and absolute for any object)

You can use style sheets in many ways. There are five options for including CSS on HTML pages:

1. **Directly in the source code** (inline `style` attribute)
   These commands affect only certain places on a page, such as within a heading or a paragraph.

   ```
   <H1 style="color : red">Heading</H1>
   <P  style="color : red">Text</P>
   ```

2. **For sections**
   Larger sections can be defined using the `<SPAN>` command. Everything located within the "span" is affected.

   ```
   <SPAN style="line-height : 150%">Text</SPAN>
   ```

3. **For a page** (embedded `<STYLE>` tag)

A complete HTML page can be formatted by placing the style instructions in the file header. In this case, the syntax is a little different:

```
<!DOCTYPE html PUBLIC "-//W3C//DTD HTML 3.2//EN">
<HTML>
  <HEAD>
    <TITLE>
      Page name
    </TITLE>
<STYLE type="text/css">
  P { line-height : 150%; text-align : justify ;
    color : red; font-weight : bold; font-size :
    110% ;}
</STYLE>
  </HEAD>
  <BODY>
    <P>
      Test
    </P>
  </BODY>
</HTML>
```

4. **Centrally for a Web application** (linked style sheet)

A major benefit of style sheets is revealed when they are stored as format templates in an external file. This means that the template can affect all the pages on a Web site. Because you don't have to code information in each document, the HTML pages are smaller and the time you save by not needing to retype information is greater. Changes can be applied to the entire Web site at lightning speed by making a single change to the external file. The external file is saved in a simple text format and contains the style instructions (CSS rules) in plain text. External CSS files can be applied to any HTML file with the `<link>` tag. Each HTML page must be able to import or link this external CSS file in order for the CSS rules it contains to take effect.

The external CSS file is linked to an HTML file using the following command line in the `<HEAD>` area of the HTML page:

```
<LINK rel="STYLESHEET" href="style.css"
type="text/css">
```

5. **Using the `Class` command**

This command can be used to assign your own formats. Use the following procedure: A flag is set within the HTML file at the point in the file where the formatting is to take effect. The name of the class can be freely chosen, as long as it is preceded by a period (for example, `.small`).

This flag is given in the CSS file, together with the formatting being defined:

```
.small { font-size : 9pt; text-align : left;
line-height : 150%;}
```

Anywhere a `class="small"` flag appears in the HTML file, the text is displayed in a size of 9pt, aligned left, and with double the spacing of the other lines used. This method of customizing specific styles is also useful when an external style sheet already has CSS rules applied to it, and you want to enhance the default format.

You can also combine these CSS options; however, the following rule of thumb applies when working with style sheets: The closer in the code the definition is to the object, the stronger its effect (i.e., it can override definitions that are farther away from the object). An inline `style` attribute always overrides a linked style sheet.

 Use CSS consistently right from the start. The extra work at the beginning will always pay off in the remaining development work.

### Summary

The options offered by Dynamic HTML (DHTML) appear to be very enticing. However, you must understand that everything relating to DHTML requires a considerable amount of programming work. Advanced programming knowledge of JavaScript is also required. On the Web, you can find plenty of example programs for all kinds of possible problem scenarios, but in most cases these examples will still require modification. If you want to get seriously involved with DHTML in order to develop your own solutions, there's no real way of avoiding this programming work. DHTML offers Web designers nearly unlimited options for controlling the appearance of the Web page, however complex it may be. Given the wide variety of options, particularly in graphical design, it's also a good idea to consider the target group.

Listing 3.16 is useful if, for example, you want to ensure that people with a red/green color blindness can customize the page to meet their needs.

**Listing 3.16** DHTML example—Replacing a CSS template during runtime via JavaScript **DHTML example**
in HTML

```
<!DOCTYPE HTML PUBLIC "-//W3C//DTD HTML 4.01 Transitio-
nal//EN">
<HTML>
  <HEAD>
    <TITLE>
      Replacing a style sheet
    </TITLE>
    <LINK type="text/css" rel="stylesheet" href=
    "stylesheet.css">
<SCRIPT type="text/javascript" language="javascript">
function replace() {
  if (document.styleSheets[0].href !=
     "newstylesheet.css">
    if (document.styleSheets[0].href !=
       "newstylesheet.css">
  }
  else {
    document.styleSheets[0].href = "stylesheet.css";
  }
}
</SCRIPT>
  </HEAD>
  <BODY>
    <BUTTON onclick="replace();">Click me to replace
    the CSS file</BUTTON>
    <P>
      A few Airlines
    </P>
      <TABLE border="1" cellpadding="5">
        <TR>
          <TD>
             Airline 1
          </TD>
          <TD>
             Lufthansa
          </TD>
        </TR>
        <TR>
          <TD>
```

```
                Airline 1
             </TD>
             <TD>
                American Airlines
             </TD>
          </TR>
       </TABLE>
    </BODY>
</HTML>
```

The example in Listing 3.16 shows how displayed contents can be replaced or changed, without having to load a completely new page each time. Users can choose the appearance of the page themselves. In the `<BODY>` section, the event `onClick` is used to call the JavaScript function `replace`. This evaluates the object `styleSheet` and assigns the result accordingly to the style sheet not currently loaded. The result is visible immediately (see Figure 3.7). Each click on the button toggles the display between the two display variants.

This is one of the characteristic features of DHTML. A Web page seems to behave like an application loaded into the working memory. Then, based on the user's actions, it determines or modifies what is displayed on the screen.

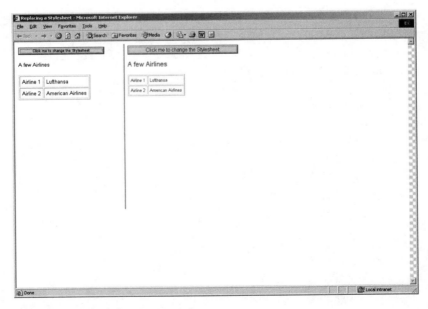

**Figure 3.7** The result from Listing 3.16

While HTML 4.0 is supported by both Netscape and Microsoft's Internet Explorer, DHTML has spawned a browser war between Microsoft and Netscape. In addition to this war of the predominant browsers, there are also other browsers on the market, some of which have implemented the standard for HTML in rather unconventional ways. This is why some attempts at standardization failed before they even got off the ground—the browsers implemented code in a fundamentally different way. Unfortunately, because Microsoft and Netscape have different ideas about which technologies should be used to make HTML more dynamic, browser and operating-system incompatibilities are rife. You still need to code separately for Microsoft-specific and Netscape-specific DHTML, provided you are willing and able to write the code for both browsers. Where does this leave you?

**Browser incompatibility**

Fortunately, a uniform standard has emerged—the *Document Object Model* (*DOM*), which, like HTML and CSS, was defined by the World Wide Web Consortium (W3C). The latest versions of Web browsers convert the DOM into JavaScript (with just a few minor variations in the details) so that in the foreseeable future it will become easier to program DHTML.

BSP developers have no reason to fear, however. The SAP Web AS has included the BSP extensions since Release 6.20. These extensions provide some help with the issue of browser incompatibility and also relieve the programmer of some of the layout development work. We will cover this in more detail later on.

**SAP Web AS— BSP extensions as a solution**

### 3.2.3 HTTP and HTTPS

The *HyperText Transfer Protocol* (HTTP) is the standardized protocol on which the World Wide Web (WWW) is based. HTTP is called during each Web transaction and is used to transfer Web pages written in HTML. HTTP can be used to transfer images and sounds as well as text according to the client/server principle. HTTP servers (Web servers) respond to the data call via HTTP clients (Web browsers) by sending the requested Web document to the browser in packages. On the HTTP server, a program known as *Daemon* (*Disk and Execution Monitor*) processes the client's data calls. The clients access the data stored on the server using HTTP.

Unlike other Internet addresses such as FTP addresses, Web addresses always start with the protocol code *http://*. Most Web browsers are now set up so that it isn't necessary to enter *http://*, because the client program adds this protocol code automatically.

HTTP is based on the TCP/IP data transfer protocol (*Transmission Control Protocol/Internet Protocol*), which is part of the application level of the OSI layer model[6]. The specification for HTTP is, like many other standards, managed by the W3C.

With HTTP no permanent connection ist created, which ist different than the File Transfer Protocol (FTP). Instead, a connection to the server is opened for each client request, the system waits for the server response, and the connection is then cancelled. This means that the connection between the client and the server is disconnected once the requested document has been delivered; the HTTP server's ports (network connections) are not permanently occupied.

HTTP is known as a "stateless" protocol because each command is executed without knowledge of and without reference to the commands that were previously executed. This is why a Web site cannot respond interactively to user inputs. However, the problem of HTTP's statelessness can be resolved using cookies and various script languages.

**HTTP 1.1**  The current version is HTTP 1.1. It includes the following capabilities that HTTP 1.0 does not have:

▶ **Virtual hosting**
  The server can manage more than one domain name for an IP address.

▶ **Permanent connections**
  The client always uses the same TCP/IP connection to the server for its requests and transfers these requests more efficiently using *pipelining*. Pipelining produces a lower network load and increases the network's speed.

▶ **Efficient caching**
  The caching of data on servers is defined in full by new specifications in the protocol. Efficient caching is also displayed by proxy servers explicitly intended for the intermediate storage of frequently required data.

HTTP is one of the most important Internet protocols, but by no means the only one. For example, there is also the *Simple Mail Transfer Protocol* (SMTP) and the *Post Office Protocol* (POP) for sending and receiving electronic mail (e-mail), and the *File Transfer Protocol* (FTP) for data exchange (uploading and downloading) between the server and client.

---

6  In the OSI reference model, the communication is established using service elements or work units that have a defined task. The service elements can be implemented as hardware, firmware, or software.

HTTP-NG (*HyperText Transfer Protocol—Next Generation*) is a standard currently being developed by the W3C to improve the performance of HTTP and to introduce other functions, such as protecting transferred data. Unlike the current "stateless" HTTP standard that establishes a connection for each request, HTTP-NG specifies a connection setup for the entire duration of a session between a specific client and a specific server.

**HTTP-NG**

S-HTTP (*Secure HyperText Transfer Protocol*) is a planned enhancement of the HTTP protocol supporting various encryption and authentication procedures to protect data on the transmission path against unauthorized viewing or modification.

**S-HTTP**

HTTPS is HTTP with the added security of the Secure Sockets Layer protocol (SSL protocol).

**SSL extension**

The SSL protocol offers the following options:

▶ **Encrypted connections**
SSL encryption protects the data channel(s) between the client and server against eavesdropping, and therefore offers a greater degree of confidentiality for communication. The data is protected against manipulation during the transfer, and the message integrity can be checked.

▶ **SSL server authentication**
SSL server authentication enables the client to check the identity of the server.

▶ **SSL client authentication**
SSL client authentication enables the server to check the identity of the client.

▶ **Reciprocal authentication with SSL**
Reciprocal authentication with the SSL protocol means that the client and server can check one another.

For accessing Internet sites protected with SSL, *https://* is used in the URL instead of *http://*.

### 3.2.4 XML

*eXtensible Markup Language* is a method for structuring data. As in HTML, the data is structured by marking the document with tags. XML can be used to structure tables, address books, configuration parameters, and data on financial transactions and technical drawings, for example.

Either binary files or text files can be used to save this data. By saving the data as text, you have the advantage that the data can still be accessed and displayed if the program used to create it is not (or is no longer) available. XML is a set of rules for creating this type of platform-independent text file. XML files therefore consist of text only, just like HTML files. They can be opened and edited in a simple text editor.

Because XML files can be created and read on any computer, data structured using XML can be exchanged regardless of technical platform limits. Files structured using XML have none of the wide-ranging disadvantages associated with the other file formats, such as platform-dependence, ambiguity, lack of expandability, and difficulties with internationalization and linguistic modification. This means that XML simplifies data management in (heterogeneous) computer networks.

**HTML vs. XML**  Like HTML, XML is derived from the *Standard Generalized Markup Language* (SGML). Therefore, XML has formal similarities with HTML. Just like HTML, XML uses tags and attributes enclosed in angle brackets (< >). However, while HTML tags specify how the text enclosed by the tags is displayed in the browser, XML tags are used to delimit different data elements. How the tags are interpreted and converted is left up to the XML application program processing the XML data, or is specified with style sheets.

HTML describes how text and graphics on a Web site are arranged and formatted, as well as providing visitors with interactive options. XML, on the other hand, describes the content of a document. Unlike HTML, XML can structure data not only according to formal criteria (such as body text or as a heading), but also according to content aspects, such as address, book title, bibliographical reference, or product.

In HTML, the meaning of each tag and attribute is preset; in XML, however, the user can define his or her own tags. This is why XML is known as "extensible." For example, the character string <P> in HTML always identifies the start of a paragraph; however, this tag in XML may be marking up a price, a parameter, or the name of a person, depending on the context. An XML element with the tag <TELEPHONE> could specify that the data it encloses represents a telephone number. Depending on the application processing the XML data, the telephone number can be displayed, saved, or selected.

The coding rules for XML are much stricter and more unforgiving than are the rules for coding in HTML. A forgotten tag or an attribute that is not placed in quotation marks makes an XML file unusable (keywords here are *correct form* and *validity*), where as most browsers tolerate these errors in an HTML file. The XML specifications state explicitly that application programs must not ignore missing tags or attributes, but must interrupt processing and issue an error message.

An XML document can be used to create many different output formats, such as HTML, Wireless Markup Language (WML), Rich Text Format (RTF), Portable Document Format (PDF), and LaTeX, as required. An XML document can therefore be transferred into other file formats.

Listing 3.17 shows an example of an XML file. The files belonging to the file **An example** *persons.xml* can all be entered using a text editor. Double-clicking on the XML file should start the browser and display the contents. The files can also be downloaded from the SAP PRESS Web site at www.sap-press.com.

**Listing 3.17** A person file in XML

```
<?xml version="1.0" encoding="ISO-8859-1"?>
<!-- edited with XML Spy v4.4 U (http://www.xmlspy.com)
by Frederic Heinemann (Private) -->
<?xml-stylesheet href="persons.css" type="text/css"?>
<!DOCTYPE PERSONEN SYSTEM "persons.dtd">
<PERSONS>
        <PERSON>
                <NAME> Santa Claus </NAME>
                <STREET> Ice Hall </STREET>
                <ZIP> 2412 </ZIP>
                <TOWN> North Pole </TOWN>
                <TEL> 012/241200 </TEL>
        <PERSON>
        <PERSON>
                <NAME> Edward Easter Bunny </NAME>
                <STREET> 28 Egg Road </STREET>
                <ZIP> 87654 </ZIP>
                <TOWN> Eggford </TOWN>
                <TEL> 034/678376 </TEL>
        </PERSON>
        <PERSON>
                <NAME> Captain Bluebeard </NAME>
                <STREET> 3 Swinders Court </STREET>
                <ZIP> 21211 </ZIP>
                <TOWN> Smugglers Cove </TOWN>
                <TEL> 08765/324553 </TEL>
        </PERSON>
</PERSONS>
```

A document type definition (DTD) file is used to define the structure of an XML file. This makes it possible for the *XML Interpreter* to check that the semantic content of the XML file is correct.

Listing 3.18 specifies the format of these tags. Here only the type PCDATA (*Parsed Character Data*—pure text, or in other words, a string) is used.

**Listing 3.18** The DTD persons.dtd for the persons file

```
<?xml version="1.0" encoding="UTF-8"?>
<!-- edited with XML Spy v4.4 U (http://www.xmlspy.com)
by Frederic Heinemann (Private) -->
<!--DTD generated by XML Spy v4.4 U (http://www.xml-
spy.com)-->
<!ELEMENT PERSONS (PERSON+)>
<!ELEMENT PERSON (NAME, STREET, ZIP, TOWN, TEL)>
<!ELEMENT NAME (#PCDATA)>
<!ELEMENT TOWN (#PCDATA)>
<!ELEMENT ZIP (#PCDATA)>
<!ELEMENT STREET (#PCDATA)>
<!ELEMENT TEL (#PCDATA)>
```

 The DTD being used should have the name of the root element. If the root is called "persons", the DTD should be called *persons.dtd*. You can also integrate the DTD declarations directly into the declaration range of the XML file. However, this is advisable only with small XML files that occur only once. Also, DTD definitions should be declared in separate files to make reusing and centrally maintaining them easier.

So far, the display in the Web browser looks rather simplistic. With the help of the CSS file from Listing 3.19, we will set up a few layout definitions. This file belongs in the same directory as the XML and the DTD files. Also, the line

```
<?xml-stylesheet href="persons.css" type="text/
css"?>
```

needs to be inserted into Listing 3.17.

**Listing 3.19** The CSS definition persons.css for the XML example

```
NAME,STREET,ZIP,TOWN,TEL
{
font family: Arial;
font size: 16pt;
```

```
text-align:left;
display:block;
}
NAME
{
font size: 20pt;
color: red
}
STREET
{
color: yellow
}
ZIP
{
color: green
}
TOWN
{
color: blue
}
TEL
{
font size: 12pt;
color: magenta
}
```

The development of XML began in 1996. In 1998, the W3C approved the XML 1.0 specification. Although XML is still a relatively new page description language, it has already overcome its "teething troubles." XML was developed by a workgroup acting under the patronage of the W3C, with the help of Adobe, Hewlett-Packard, Microsoft, Netscape, Sun, and other companies. XML is license-free and platform-independent, and has a whole range of tools.

**XML — The development**

### 3.2.5 Cookies

*Cookies* are snippets of data that can store information about a Web site visitor on his or her hard disk or on the server. For example, cookies can store the number of visitors to a site, a list of the products viewed, or data that the visitor entered via an order form. When that page is called again by the same user, the server reads the cookie and the Web site "knows" the visitor's preferences.

Cookies that are stored on the hard disk and are not deleted upon leaving the site are known as *persistent cookies*. In contrast, *non-persistent cookies* are stored in the client's main memory and are deleted when the browser is closed. For example, the session ID cookie procedure that the server stores on the client during initialization—that is, when first called—is used in this way.

### Client-side cookies

*Client-side cookies* are always stored in the client browser. They are addressed using the `document` object of the runtime instance of the HTML page. A *client-side cookie* is a small amount of text information written to a browser in a specified directory that can then be read out again. However, Internet Explorer and Netscape Navigator handle the actual files using slightly differently methods. Netscape Navigator typically saves all entries in a single file called *cookies.txt* in the directory provided by the browser. Internet Explorer, on the other hand, generally creates a separate file in the Windows cookies directory for each cookie. The index.dat file found there in the directory is responsible for managing these cookies. Just for a refreshing change, these different methods on the file level do not affect the procedure in JavaScript.

The following entries are made in the cookie:

1. **Domain name or IP number of the called page**

2. **Cookie availability across the entire domain**
   Yes/No

3. **Directory where the cookie has been placed**
   Used to specify directories within this domain. If this information is missing, the path for the current document is used. Cookies are typically available only in the folder used to create them; otherwise, this folder or directory needs to be defined separately.

4. **Permission to forward cookie via HTTPS connection (secure)**
   Yes/No

5. **Expiration date of the cookie**
   An important optional property is the `expires property`, which is used to set the validity date of a cookie. The format is:

   `Wdy, DD-Mon-YY HH:MM:SS GMT`

   `Wdy` is a string representation of a weekday, `DD` is two figures for the day of the month, `Mon` is a three-letter string representation of the month, and `YY` is two digits for the year. `HH`, `MM`, and `SS` are two-figure specifications for the hour, minute, and seconds (optional). The final variable, GMT, is the time zone.

An example:

```
expires=Wednesday, 09-Nov-01 20:15:40 GMT
```

6. **Cookie name**

The name is important for reading out, changing, and deleting the cookie.

7. **Value of the cookie**

The actual content of the cookie in the form of a string (e.g., the user name, the password, a date, the number of times the page has been called by a specific user, etc.).

Points 1 and 3 are set automatically.

In general, a cookie consists of at least the name and the value assignment. The name is used to identify a cookie again when reading it. The assigned value is the actual information to be saved.

A cookie can typically be set using `document.cookie`. In addition, string methods such as `substring()`, `charAt()`, `indexOf()`, or `lastIndexOf()` are used for different operations.

The character string to be transferred to the `cookie` property of document must contain the required information as values separated by parameters. An example of setting a cookie is:

**Properties**

```
document.cookie = "myCookie=123";
```

Or if you want to set a "validity date":

```
document.cookie = "myCookie=123; expires=Wednesday, 09-
Nov-01 20:15:40 GMT";
```

Unfortunately, it's not that easy if you want to store and read out more complex information in a cookie. JavaScript doesn't offer much help here.

Cookie values cannot contain spaces or special characters. For this reason, these characters are masked using the function `escape()` when written, and are unencrypted using `unescape()` when read out.

In addition, various actions need to be carried out, such as determining the length of a value or separating specific characters in the string.

A cookie can be deleted by setting the expiration date to January 1, 1970.

Here is another example extract:

```
function DeleteCookie (name) {
var exp = new Date();
exp.setTime (exp.getTime() - 1);   // This cookie is his-
tory
var cval = <Name of the cookie>
document.cookie = name + "=" + cval + "; expires=" +
exp.toGMTString();
```

A complete example can be found at sap-press.com in the extras for the book under *cookiecomplete.html*.

### Server-side cookies

Server-side cookies have the same basic structure as client-side cookies. However, they have several advantages over client-side cookies, as shown in Table 3.4:

| Feature | Client-side | Server-side |
|---|---|---|
| Cookie size | 4 KB | unlimited |
| Total number | 300 | unlimited |
| Number per server or domain | 20 | unlimited |
| Can be deactivated by browser (client) | yes | no |

**Table 3.4** Differences between client-side and server-side cookies

The last point in Table 3.4 is the critical one. All modern browsers can reject cookies or block them completely. Server-side cookies, however, are controlled only by the server or the application.

When using server-side cookies, developers have to be conscientious and sensitivite in handling the data on the tag. The data contents decide, for example, whether the user needs to explicitly give his or her permission for the data to be saved.

Due to the technical advantages, server-side cookies are ideal for developing BSP applications. For this reason, they are covered in much more detail in Chapter 5.

## 3.3  BSP Applications

*Business Server Page (BSP) applications* are standalone Web applications with presentation logic, workflow logic, and application logic that are functionally self-contained. In many ways, BSPs are similar to the server page technologies (*xSP*) from other software manufacturers, such as Active Server Pages (ASP) from Microsoft and Java Server Pages (JSP) from Sun Microsystems. Thanks to its many advantages, Server Page Technologies have become relatively widespread in the field of Web development.

BSP applications are developed on the SAP Web AS using the Web Application Builder, which is integrated into the SE80 development transaction. Like standard applications, BSP applications can access function modules, classes, BAPIs, and the database, which are linked to the Change and Transport System (CTS).

**Complete integration**

In this type of BSP application, the presentation level where the actual display takes place (in this case on the client browser) is formed from a sequence of Web pages, which consists of the following elements:

► **Static Web pages**
These Web pages do not contain any server-side scripting.

► **Dynamically generated Web pages**
These Web pages contain server-side scripting and are assembled to form a finished Web page only on request during the runtime of the application server.

► **MIME objects**
These objects include graphics, symbols, sound files, and style sheets, which can be included in Web pages.

In addition, client-side JavaScript for dynamic actions without server roundtrip[7] and client-side cookies for the temporary storage of information can play a role when required.

For the Web application to run on the client, a series of components and mechanisms is required. These mechanisms interact with one another on the application server and need to be applied.

---

7  *Server roundtrip* means that data is exchanged with the application server to process interactions. Depending on the browser and coding, this may not be absolutely essential.

This chapter describes the individual components, the management, and the processing sequence of these BSP applications. Also discussed is the *Model-View-Controller Design Pattern (MVC)*, which offers an interesting alternative to the BSP programming previously described.

### 3.3.1 Components

Underneath the presentation layer described above—that is, on the application server—are the individual parts of the BSP application. During runtime, these parts are processed and sent to the client in a format it can understand. Of course, the client's response can also be processed within the BSP application. A BSP application comprises several or all of the following components (see also Figure 3.8):

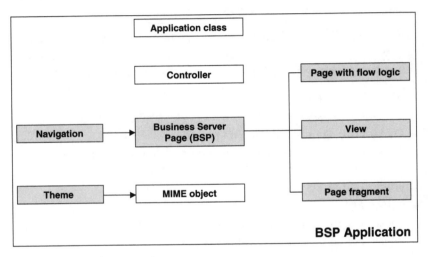

**Figure 3.8** Parts of a BSP application

Static HTML    You can use the development environment to link several static HTML pages via hyperlinks. These links can be invoked by the user in a more or less fixed sequence. However, this would be a very simple application that, with a little practice, could be created using a basic text editor. It isn't necessary to use the SAP Web AS for this, and a small amount of Web space with an Internet provider would be perfectly adequate. However, you would quickly find this limiting. As soon as it becomes necessary to write back data and to use dynamic content (such as that generated from databases), the separation of layout and data, as well as other dynamic elements (such as for input checks and selection help) is absolutely necessary.

For this reason, you must initially divide the logical unit of a BSP application into presentation components, screen sequence control, and application logics. A BSP application also contains a variety of management attributes.

In the actual conversion process, a clean division is not always possible, of course. For example, when using BSP pages, it is almost always necessary to integrate a flow logic into the layout. This one situation is avoided by using *MVC Design Pattern*. Because of the special nature of the MVC concept, a separate section is dedicated to this concept (see Section 3.3.4), so we will not cover the MVC components in any detail at this point.

As part of the BSP application, all the objects described below are integrated into the SAP Change and Transport System (CTS) and are handled as a logical unit, that is, all objects in a BSP application can be fully and consistently transported between SAP systems.

### Properties/management attributes

Every BSP application has a range of management attributes describing its general properties, such as assigning the package, theme and application class, the HTTPS flag, and so forth. These properties are defined on the Properties tab of the BSP application. Chapter 5 covers these points in detail.

### Presentation components

This section describes the components used to generate the graphical display on the screen.

### BSP pages

The *BSP pages* form the foundation for the contents ultimately displayed on the client browser. They may contain static Web code[8] and dynamic scripting code (ABAP). This scripting code is transformed into code that the browser can understand (e.g., HTML) at the time that it is generated or when processing on the server begins. This makes it possible to specify the final appearance of the page at the runtime stage, that is, at the time of the request.

---

8   Although HTML code is only used in the examples below, this does not mean that other standards such as XML, WML, and XHTML cannot be used.

A BSP page may have the following characteristics:

▶ **Pages with flow logic**
The *pages with flow logic* are those pages whose process flow is controlled by event handlers (event handler-based model). Usually, there should be little application logic in the pages; instead, a special construct, the application class, handles the application logic. The application class permits the required business logic to be encapsulated. In addition to the layout, a page with flow logic implements the flow logic via the event handlers and has page attributes and type definitions.

**Page attributes**    *Page attributes* are global variables available on a BSP page. They are available in the layout and in all event handlers, and can "remember" their value across the entire runtime of the request. The content of a page attribute filled in the event can therefore be output in the layout code easily. Page attributes in which the property `Auto` is activated are automatically filled with the value from the parameter of the same name after the page object is created, assuming that a parameter has been transferred to the page. Page attributes can adopt any elementary type (except for XSTRING), structure, or table type.

**Type definitions**    Any *type definitions* can be generated in the BSP page type definition. The page can access these definitions at any time. For example, the type of an internal table can be defined to specify the page attribute type.

The pages of type "page with flow logic" are executable and can be addressed via a URL or via navigation from another page. Chapter 5 covers the relevant programming in detail. A complete BSP application can also be constructed solely of pages with flow logic and the relevant event handlers, as required.

▶ **Page fragments**
*Page fragments* are created in the same way as BSP pages, however, they identify a fragment of a page. Page fragments differ from pages only in that they do not have separate event handling, separate attributes, or type definition. They are integrated by other BSP pages using the `include` directive as a simple text-include. Page fragments inherit the page attributes from these other BSP pages.

Page fragments can themselves include page fragments, but not pages with flow logic. Because page fragments enable the modular structure of the layout of BSP pages, they can make more program code reusable.

▶ **View (MVC)**

*Views* are used to visualize data that is made available as part of the *Model View Controller Design Pattern* (see Section 3.3.4). Views are called almost exclusively by controllers, which means that they do not have a separate URL. Like pages with flow logic, Views have page attributes. Unlike pages with flow logic, however, Views cannot be filled automatically via the Auto flag. The assigned controller is responsible for filling attributes, accepting the request, and managing the flow control.

## MIME objects

*MIME (Multipurpose Internet Mail Extensions)* is an extension of the original Internet e-mail protocol permitting the exchange of different data types on the Internet. These mail extensions include audio, video, and graphical data, Cascading Style Sheets, application programs, and ASCII files. Client browsers can process these object types using either plug-ins or integrated applications; therefore, ordinary Web browsers can display most graphics formats without external utilities. Other object types, such as Flash animations, require plug-ins.

With each newly created BSP application, a directory of the same name is created in the MIME repository and is used to store all the MIME objects specific to the application. The MIME repository is used to manage the MIME objects centrally.

## Themes

*Themes* are used to define replacements for MIME objects being used, which means that you can customize the page layout of BSP applications without first changing the layout source text. Therefore, each MIME object within a BSP application can be replaced by another object from the local file system.

A theme is created as a separate development object in the Web Application Builder (WAB) and acts as the container for all replacement definitions. For the changes to have an effect during runtime, the theme must be explicitly assigned to the relevant BSP application.

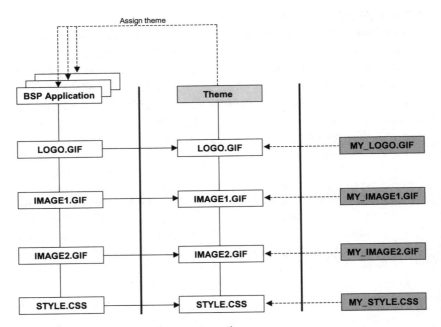

**Figure 3.9** Replacing MIME objects using a theme

**Replacement during runtime**
Once a page requests a MIME object, the BSP runtime environment determines whether the running BSP application is assigned a theme. If a theme has been assigned, the correct object is determined from the replacement definition. While the BSP application is running, this object is transferred to the client in place of the object entered in the BSP application. In Figure 3.9, the MIME object to be sent to the client (*LOGO.GIF*) would be replaced during the runtime by *MY_LOGO.GIF*, if the theme of the active BSP application was assigned. The *Themes Editor* is available for working with themes.

### BSP extensions
When creating a BSP application, ensuring the corporate design remains consistent is always an issue. Cascading Style Sheets (CSS) can be very useful; however, with larger projects involving more developers, there is a risk that the defined style instructions will not be used correctly or consistently. In the worst-case scenario, the appropriate CSS elements must be continually reassigned for each HTML element on each BSP page. This is a lengthy and error-prone process. The clarity of the HTML code also suffers, making changes even harder to implement. This is where BSP extensions can help. They function as an abstraction technique that can simplify both the syntax

and the semantics of HTML code blocks. This mechanism has an open structure and can be used in sections of XML and WML code, for example.

A *BSP extension* is a container for BSP elements. Each element is assigned an ABAP class in the BSP context. Embedded in this class is the functionality to create the code to be executed on the client-side and its functionalities. The elements' definitions and the mapping to the ABAP classes are flexible. This technology can be used to meet a variety of requirements not limited to graphical objects.

**Container for BSP elements**

The SAP Web AS provides an infrastructure for managing BSP extensions, allowing them to be used as part of BSP applications relatively easily. Release 6.20 of SAP Web AS includes many predefined extensions, such as *HTML Business for BSP (HTMLB)*, which can be modified, expanded, and customized. You can create and edit BSP extensions with the editor integrated into your development environment.

**Extension infrastructure**

By using HTMLB as a template for creating your own extensions, you can save yourself both time and effort.

BSP extensions can be used in BSP pages via the `extension` directive. Composite elements can also be created to unite multiple BSP elements into a subset. This makes it possible to affect all the BSP elements simultaneously when changing the layout, which reduces the amount of work involved in complicated BSP applications.

Every BSP extension consists of a collection of BSP elements, each of which has defined attributes and is assigned to an ABAP class. The attributes provided in the element function as the input parameters for the assigned ABAP class, and are used to determine the appearance, the input behavior, and other functionalities. BSP elements are inserted into BSP pages in XML notation.

In the outgoing HTML data flow, the element class writes the serialized HTML code on the basis of the functionality provided by the element. It is assumed here that all elements in an extension support a common output style.

Using BSP extensions has the following advantages:

**Advantages of BSP extensions**

▶ The HTML code needs to be developed only once. Changes have an immediate effect on all calls of the elements. Because of the flexibility of HTML code, it can be used across applications, increasing the reusability in terms of corporate design.

- The ABAP class (element class) assigned to the element may contain additional logic to generate browser-dependent HTML code, thus avoiding browser-dependent code in the layout.

- The style sheet assignments are also located in the element class. Because CSS assignments take place at one specific point, the generated HTML code places the correct references on the style sheets.

- The standard XML syntax can—unlike HTML code in the layout—be parsed and checked at the point of generation, thus ensuring accuracy.

In addition to a BSP extension for standard HTML elements such as buttons, input fields, drop-down lists, and so forth, highly specialized extensions can be implemented. An example of such an extension could contain a composite element to implement a complete news banner, including generation frame and application logic. The news banner can then be made available in any BSP applications via the directive `exten-sion` with all its attributes parameterized.

To truly reap the advantages of BSP extensions, you need an increased amount of programming to implement them. For this reason, this technology is best suited for larger projects. If, however, a standardized corporate design is very important, you should always use BSP extensions wherever possible.

### Components of the flow control

A program's flow control determines the temporal and logical flow of an application. The time when specific components of a program are executed is partly fixed in the case of BSP applications and can be partly controlled by the developer. The first group includes the event handlers that are part of BSP pages with flow logic. The second group includes the navigation structure and controller, for example.

### Event handlers

The *event handlers* are executed at specific points during the runtime of a BSP page in a fixed, defined sequence. They are filled with ABAP code and permit access during runtime to specific objects, such as the application class, or to specific runtime objects in order to provide access to request information. This topic is covered in detail in Section 3.3.3.

### Navigation structure

The *navigation structure* is used to define navigation requests, which describe the beginning and destination of a request—that is, the order of pages in the navigation process. Assigning the pages via navigation requests creates a purely formal description of the navigation scheme within a BSP application. This makes it possible, for example, to change the flow control of a BSP application without intervention in the coding.

### Controllers (MVC)

*Controllers* are another part of the MVC Design Pattern. From the data of an incoming request, Controllers evaluate a suitable View on the basis of a model. The View can then be rendered for the response. Controllers represent the link between the Model and the View.

## Components of the application logic

The *application logic* (*business logic*) handles the actual processing of the data. As is the norm in standard ABAP programming, the application logic can be addressed in the form of BAPIs, function modules, or class libraries from a BSP application, for instance from the event handlers.

The SAP Web AS also provides additional structuring aids—the BSP application class and the MVC—that can be used to encapsulate the required application logic.

It is even possible to house the application logic in the layout part of a BSP page; however, this is not recommended.

### Application class

The *application class* is used to encapsulate a BSP application's application logic via a standard, global ABAP class. It calls business data from backend systems via BAPI, for example, and writes this data back to the BSP application after processing. An application class of this type is assigned to the BSP application and is then directly available to each page of the BSP application with its components (attributes, methods, etc.) via the standardized object reference application. This all happens automatically. Neither "manual" declaration nor instantiation is required before use.

**Encapsulation of the application logic**

The tasks of a BSP application that are implemented in application classes can include the following:

▶ Cross-page saving of BSP application data in the form of attributes
▶ Encapsulation of the application logic in methods
▶ Framing of repetitive tasks (e.g., authorization checks, complex input checks, saving and restoring data using server-side cookies) in methods

An application class can be used in any number of applications as well as in typical ABAP programs. However, only one application class per BSP application can exist. The assignment is made on the Properties tab of the BSP application, as shown in Figure 3.10.

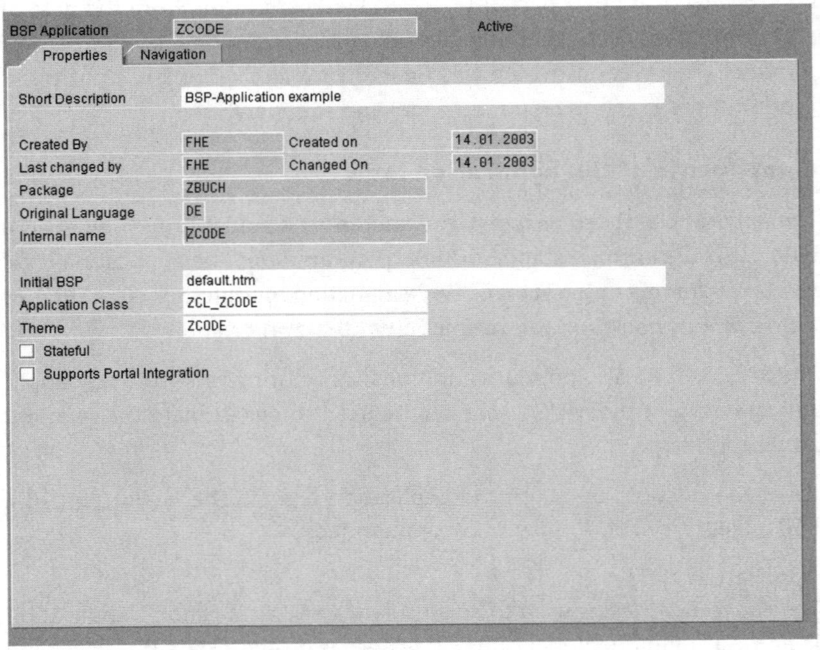

| BSP Application | ZCODE | | Active | |
|---|---|---|---|---|
| Properties | Navigation | | | |
| | | | | |
| Short Description | BSP-Application example | | | |
| | | | | |
| Created By | FHE | Created on | 14.01.2003 | |
| Last changed by | FHE | Changed On | 14.01.2003 | |
| Package | ZBUCH | | | |
| Original Language | DE | | | |
| Internal name | ZCODE | | | |
| | | | | |
| Initial BSP | default.htm | | | |
| Application Class | ZCL_ZCODE | | | |
| Theme | ZCODE | | | |
| ☐ Stateful | | | | |
| ☐ Supports Portal Integration | | | | |

**Figure 3.10** Assigning the application class

Other classes can be included in a BSP application in addition to the application class.

Existing application functionalities of the SAP Application Server (SAP AS) or the backend systems are generally framed within the application class, which makes the code easier to read and maintain.

When using application classes, please note the following:

▶ If the application class is assigned a *stateful* BSP application, its life cycle will be exactly as long as the BSP application, which makes it ideal for data storage.

▶ If the application class is assigned a *stateless* BSP application, its life cycle is exactly the length of a BSP page, from the receipt of the request to the completion of the response object. Because, like all objects, it is destroyed directly afterward, it is not suitable for data storage. In this case, server-side cookies are used for data storage.

▶ Application classes are singleton—that is, there can be only one instance per session.

▶ A BSP application can be assigned only one application class.

▶ The Constructor must be free of parameters.

You should carefully consider how you will implement data acquisition. For example, it is inefficient to acquire the complete material master of the backend system in the application class in a stateless BSP application. This process would repeat at each page change and the application's performance would be permanently slowed. In a stateful application, however, this method of data acquisition could be very useful because the data will load from the backend only when the application is first called—that is, when the application object is instantiated.

The interface IF_BSP_APPLICATION_EVENTS can be implemented in the application class. This interface makes a BSP application's other processing times accessible via methods that permit both flexible control and access to the processing logic. The interface's individual methods are presented in Appendix A.2.

**Application events**

It is useful to get the application class from the predefined base class CL_BSP_APPLICATION. This class provides methods that can be called or set: the session timeout, the current URL for the BSP application, the status mode, and so forth. The associated interface's individual methods are also presented in Appendix A.2.

**Application base class**

Figure 3.11 uses a simplified scenario to explain the process flow of a request with encapsulated application logic. The search for an address is triggered on HTML page 1. Using the event onInputProcessing, the request is directed to the BSP page HTML page 2. In this process, the name is transferred as an Auto page attribute. The event onInitialization calls the application class that, in turn, controls an RFC call for data acquisition in the backend. The result is returned to the application class, where it is made available from the event handler. The attributes now filled are output in the layout code and appear in this form in the client browser as HTML page 2.

**An example**

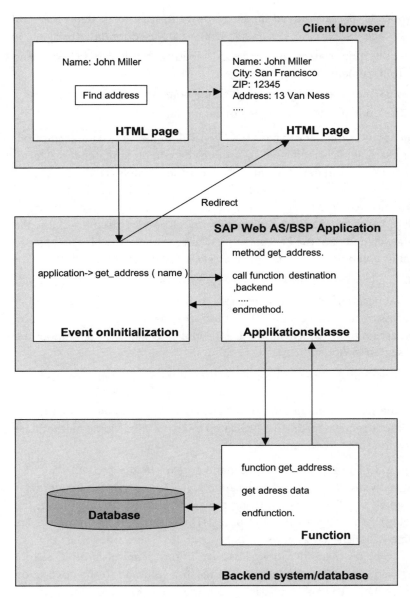

**Figure 3.11** Typical process flow for encapsulated application logic

### Model (MVC)

The *Model* is used as an application object to control the behavior and the application data. It answers both information requests via its status, which generally comes from the View, and instructions for status changes, which are usually sent by the Controller.

The Model recognizes neither its Views nor its Controller. This means that the model alone is used for internal data processing, without referring to the application with its user interface. In short, a Model is specified using a reference of the Controller to a class.

### 3.3.2 Access to a BSP Application

This section explains the special features of access to a BSP application. An overview of the standard error message is provided in the section following it. The system-specific URL parameters are then presented. You can use these parameters to configure the application call and can modify the parameters to your own requirements.

**Addressing**

A BSP application is executed by a *URL* (*Uniform Resource Locator*). The application can be called directly by entering the URL in the address line of the client browser.

You can also save the BSP application in your *favorites* or list of bookmarks and call it easily with the favorites management feature, or you can save the application to your desktop. In this process, name/value pairs (see below) can also be specified for parameterization, which means that the Web application can be called after being parameterized.

A BSP application's URL has the following general structure:

`<Protocol>://<Host>:<Port>/<Name Range>/<Application Name>/<Page>?<URL Parameters>`

**Parts of the URL**

▶ **Protocol**
BSP applications support the protocols HTTP and HTTPS. If HTTPS is to be used, this protocol must be present as a service in the ICM. Therefore, configuration via instance profile and the installation of the corresponding system files are required.[9]

---

9  We do not explain this procedure in this book. You can find the relevant installation instructions in the documentation for the SAP Web Application Server under "SAP Web Application Server—Using the Secure Sockets Layer Protocol" or on the Internet at *http://service.sap.com/instguides*.
The installation package is available to authorized customers in the SAP Service Marketplace at *http://service.sap.com/swcenter* for using the SAP Cryptographic Library.

▶ **Host**

The *host* is the name of the application server on which the application is to be executed. Either the IP address of the host or the DNS name, including network domain, should be specified.

▶ **Port**

The *port number* specifies the port on which the application is to be run if the default value is to be circumvented. The relevant protocols are assigned to the ports via the profile settings (profile parameter icm/server_port_<xx>).

▶ **Name range**

The *name range* is the BSP application's name range code. SAP applications are supplied in the name range **sap**. BSP applications can be created in a separate name range.

▶ **Application name**

The *application name* is the name of a BSP application as defined in the development environment.

▶ **Page**

The *page* is the name of the required destination page of the BSP application, which may be a BSP page, a static page, or a controller of the MVC. It's helpful to use the initial page to ensure that the application is also correctly initialized.

▶ **URL parameter**

The *URL parameter* can also be specified to the application as *name/value pairs* when called. These pairs may be specific to the system, or they may relate to the application (see further down in this section). These name/value pairs are separated from the actual URL with a question mark (?).

The last two parts can also be omitted. In this case, the entry point is the default page specified in the BSP application properties. Spaces are not permitted, but can be reproduced in the final URL with *escaped URLs*, in which case spaces are displayed as %20 .

A URL in the SAP name range may then look as follows:

*http://www.my-webas.de:8080/sap/bc/bsp/sap/zcode/start.html?var_1=init*

Because these URLs are long and unwieldy, you can define an external alias in the ICF. The alias then maps the address. The previous URL might look as follows:

*http://www.my-webas.de/zcode*

## Error messages

If the BSP application cannot be reached or executed, the system sends a standard error as a response in the form of an HTTP error code. The best-known error is probably the error code HTTP Error 404. This error is sent if the requested resource could not be found. The code `500 internal server` error is especially important during development. In Appendix A.1, you will find a list of the error codes generated by the SAP Web Application Server.

To obtain meaningful error messages from the server, especially during the development relating to error code `500`, the option **Show friendly HTTP error messages** should be deactivated in Internet Explorer (see Figure 3.12). Otherwise, "user-friendly" error messages, which have virtually no practical use during the development process, are displayed by Internet Explorer.

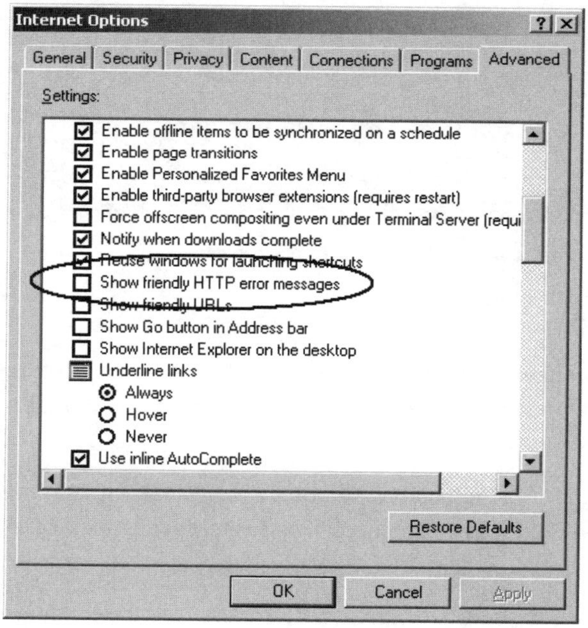

**Figure 3.12** Deactivate the option Show friendly HTTP error messages in Internet Explorer

The SAP Web AS also allows you to respond to logon and application errors. You have two alternatives. You can create your own error pages, which provide the user with comprehensive information about the error or suggested solutions. Or, you can use a redirect to forward the user to another URL. With a redirect, the form fields already passed to the desti-

**Response to logon and application errors**

nation page can also be transferred to the new address, so you get an immediate display of the parameters—namely, those parameters that caused the application to produce errors. This will save you time during long debugging sessions (see Figure 3.13).

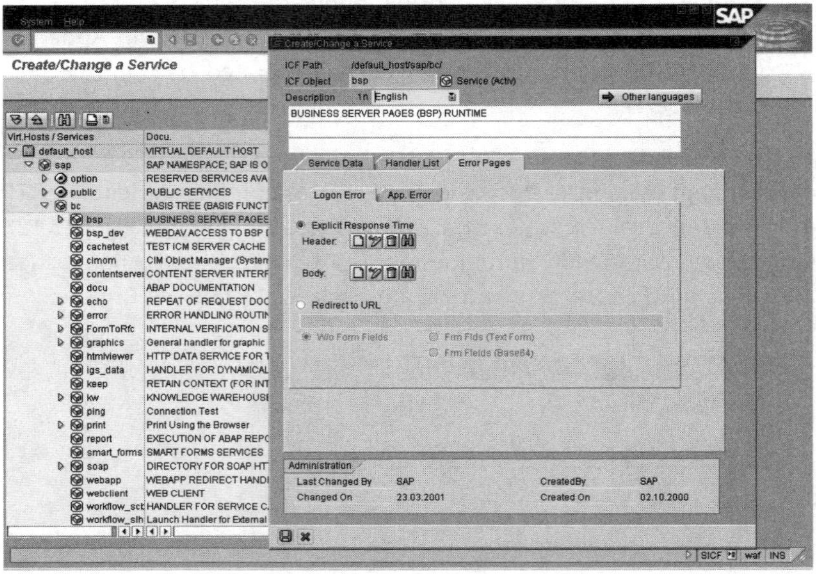

**Figure 3.13** Creating your own error pages or using a redirect to the URL

### URL parameter

A BSP application's behavior can be controlled via the URL. To do this, this URL is expanded by a query string, which is the part of a URL that is preceded by a question mark (?).

The parameter name and its associated values are case-insensitive. One exception is the parameter `sap-exiturl`, if the reference is to a case-sensitive server.

The query string has a sequence of name/value pairs, separated by an ampersand (&), such as:

*http://www.my-webas.de:8080/sap/bc/bsp/sap/zcode/start.htm?status=0&org=sap*

Here the address of the BSP application has two query string parameters added: `status` and `org` with the values "0" and "sap". This has an effect equivalent to the value assignment in the code using:

```
status  = '0'.
org     = 'sap'.
```

The SAP Web AS is familiar with a range of system-specific URL parameters. The server automatically checks these URL parameters on each call; some of the parameters have a decisive effect on the behavior of the application.

The possible system parameters have the following basic structure:

```
sap-<parameter-name>=<value>
```

Multiple system parameters can be combined.

A description of the individual parameters and their possible uses are given below:

▶ `sap-sessioncmd`
The parameter `sap-sessioncmd` is used to open and close a running BSP application.
The value "open" is used to restart a running BSP application or, if it is not yet running, to start it for the first time.

*http://www.my-webas.de:8080/sap/bc/bsp/sap/zcode/start.htm?sap-sessioncmd=open*

The value "close" is used to close a running BSP application. On closing, the browser is directed to an empty page. Closing the browser has the same effect as entering the transaction code /n in the SAP frontend.

*http://www.my-webas.de:8080/sap/bc/bsp/sap/zcode/start.htm?sap-sessioncmd=close*

▶ `sap-exiturl`
The parameter `sap-exiturl` is used to branch to the specified URL address.

Combining this parameter with the parameter `sap-sessioncmd` makes the application easier to close. If the current BSP application is explicitly ended in the Web browser and you want to branch to a destination page, the call might look something like this:

*http://www.my-webas.de:8080/sap/bc/bsp/sap/zcode/start.htm?sap-sessioncmd=close&sap-exiturl=logout_success.htm*

▶ `sap-theme`
The parameter `sap-theme` specifies the theme used for the called BSP page and therefore affects the overall appearance of the applica-

tion. A theme can be described as a collection of replacement definitions for MIME objects.

A theme defined as the default for a BSP application is therefore overridden. For example:

*http://www.my-webas.de:8080/sap/bc/bsp/sap/zcode/start.htm?sap-sessioncmd=open&sap-theme=vip_customer*

▶ `sap-syscmd`
The parameter `sap-syscmd` is used to specify the value `nocookie`, which indicates that the session cookie is transferred as part of the URL rather than being saved on the client. The session cookie is then concealed in the URL-mangling code.

*http://www.my-webas.de:8080/sap/bc/bsp/sap/zcode/start.htm?sap-syscmd=nocookie*

**Logon parameter**  The following system parameters are used to control the SAP Web Application Server's logon parameters:

▶ `sap-client`
The parameter `sap-client` defines the client on which a logon to the SAP Web AS takes place. A client specified here overrides the predefined default client. If the client does not exist in the system, an error message is issued.

▶ `sap-user`
The parameter `sap-user` ensures that the logon to the system is carried out under the specified name. If the user does not exist in the system, an error message is issued.

▶ `sap-password`
The parameter `sap-password` transfers the password for logging the user on. If the password is incorrect, an error message is issued.

The password should never be used in the query string of a URL for two reasons: First, there is a transfer in plain text (HTTP); and second, these URL strings are temporarily stored in the cache and would theoretically be accessible to third parties.

▶ `sap-language`
The parameter `sap-language` specifies the logon language of the system, which means, for example, that another available language version of the BSP application can be loaded onto the system. The default logon language is then overridden.

An example of the entire logon process for an English-speaking user might look something like this:

*http://www.my-webas.de:8080/sap/bc/bsp/sap/zcode/start.htm?sap-sessioncmd=open&sap-theme=vip_customer&sap-client=100&sap-language=en&sap-user=en_george*

Because the password is not part of the query string, this system parameter is missing from the URL for complete authentication. A corresponding pop-up window will open to prompt you to add the missing data.

Another part of the URL is what is known as *URL-mangling code*. This code is generated by the server and is specified in brackets. The coded values contain various logon, session, and theme settings for the called BSP application.

**URL-mangling code**

An example of mangling code might be:

*http://www.my-webas.de:8080/sap(bD1kZQ==)/bc/bsp/sap/zcode/start.htm*

### 3.3.3 Event Handler-Controlled Processing

A BSP application's basic processing flow follows a permanently defined scheme. The general flow logic is therefore always the same, regardless of whether it's for simple address management, or for a complex task-management process with integrated availability check via a backend system. A BSP application typically consists of multiple BSP pages (pages with flow logic). The user starts the application via an entry page and then navigates through the application to the various BSP pages. At some point, the user exits the application. The individual steps in this processing flow (see Figure 3.14) are:

▶ Start of the BSP application
▶ Creation and display of the requested BSP page
▶ Response to user inputs and navigation, as required
▶ Exiting the BSP application[10]

These steps are covered below in depth. However, first we need to explain two important aspects of BSP applications in more detail: the *event handler* and the *status model* of the BSP application or page. These two concepts have a significant impact on the application's processing

---

10 Exiting a BSP application is only of interest in the stateful model. This stateful model is explained in more detail below.

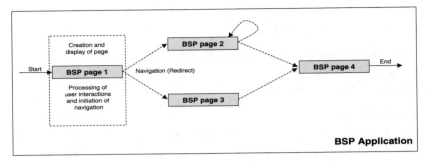

**Figure 3.14** The basic processing flow and navigation in BSP applications

flow. The event handlers have already been covered briefly in Section 3.3.1. These handlers are available at specific times to process a BSP page. During these processing times, separate program logic can be executed to implement specific tasks within the processing logic of a page. The processing flow—running through the various event handlers, in particular—is also affected by the status model currently active for the application in question. In the next section, we will explain the two status models supported in SAP Web AS.

### The status model for BSP applications

Stateful and state-less applications There are two status models available for use in BSP applications: stateful and stateless. This functionality is provided by the ICF supporting both operating modes in the server role. A running BSP application is known as a *BSP session*. In Section 3.3.2, we said that the start and end of a session can be influenced from outside by the user. The end of a BSP session can also be initiated by the application itself, or by the Web browser's being closed. The important thing to note is the separation of the BSP session and the browser session. A browser session can be ended only by closing the browser.

Stateful A *stateful* BSP application is—as with a traditional SAP transaction with SAP GUI screen changes—executed across all user interactions in a single context (roll area). The application context is therefore maintained throughout the response. As the application continues to run, the corresponding context is rolled into the work process. This means that data that is entered by the user while running the application, or data that has been determined by the application itself, is maintained for the duration of the session. With stateful applications, the data is stored via the application class. Figure 3.15 shows the stateful model. In this process, a separate session is provided in the SAP Web AS for each session of a Web browser. This session contains the application context and is available for multiple request/response cycles. Next to sessions 1, 2, and 3 are shaded boxes of different lengths, which represent user activities. These identified user activities are the points at which the resources of the servers are actually being used.

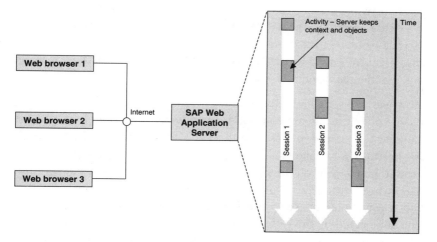

**Figure 3.15** The stateful model in the SAP Web Application Server

One problem in implementing this action is the statelessness of the HTTP protocol. There is no implicit mechanism for assigning independent requests from a common logical session to a context, for example. The BSP runtime environment solves this problem with session cookies. A multi-digit session ID is generated and a unique stamp is added to each request. The requests can then be identified as part of a specific session. The name of the session cookie stored on the client side is `sap-contextid` and is valid to the end of a session (the browser session ID corresponds to the BSP session ID here). The assignment is made via the URL of the BSP application, which means that a BSP application can be executed only once at a specific time within a browser. Another BSP application has a separate session cookie and can be operated in parallel in the same browser. The same BSP application can be executed by multiple users and browsers any number of times.

**Session cookies**

The stateful model has a range of advantages and disadvantages to be considered:

The programming of stateful BSP applications is relatively straightforward. Once data has been acquired at great cost, it can be stored in the attributes of the application class. On the next page, this data can simply be re-accessed. Costly database accesses can be kept to a minimum; therefore, it isn't necessary to reread large quantities of data, which could

**Fewer database accesses**

result in significant improvements in performance on the server side. In addition, the network load is minimized thanks to fewer requests to the backend systems.

However, you need to consider the fact that it's easy to distinguish between the state within the application and the state a user adopts on the basis of his or her user interface. The simplest example of this is the use of the Back button in the browser. These client-side actions are not necessarily forwarded to the server. You need to ensure that possible inconsistencies are captured, and that the client and server are "resynchronized."

**Memory resources**  However, the simplified programming means that each session of the relevant context needs to be saved. As the number of sessions is at least the same as the number of users (in the same way as the SAP GUI), a much greater load is usually generated on the SAP Web AS with the stateful model than with the stateless model. This places increased demands on the memory resources in order to execute various sessions in parallel. If the available memory space is exhausted, no other uses are accepted, and will be rejected by the system. If the user does not explicitly end the BSP application, system resources are also blocked for unnecessarily long periods of time. If the user simply goes to another page, for example, the session in the SAP Web AS is maintained. In these cases, the Web browser does not automatically log off of the system. The context is retained and then released only after a specific period of time.

The time period for an auto-logoff from the SAP Web AS is specified with a time-out parameter in the instance profile.

**Stateless**  Contrary to the stateful model, in the stateless model, resources on the SAP Web AS are not blocked for long. After processing a request, all occupied resources (application context) are immediately released. For each request, this means that a new application context (roll area) is generated and rejected after the response.[11] Resources are therefore directly used only during the processing of a request. This conservative use of resources makes the stateless model ideal for implementing Web applications with a number of parallel accesses, because it provides good scaling of the SAP Web AS. The stateless model, as it functions in the SAP Web AS, is illustrated in Figure 3.16. You can see that for each access to a Web browser, the resources for processing the request are used on the server for only a short time.

---

11 In stateless mode, the very first session ID is used to identify the associated browser session.

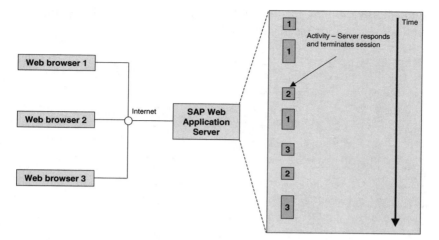

Figure 3.16 The stateless model in the SAP Web Application Server

The disadvantage of the stateless model is that in releasing the application context, data is read several times and needs to be prepared each time. Therefore, the memory advantage is unfortunately offset by runtime losses. Using different techniques allows data to still be recovered in the stateless mode via requests. These techniques and options include:

▶ **Hidden form fields**
These hidden fields are also transferred when sending a form, but are invisible to the user. These are input fields with the attribute `type=hidden`.

▶ **Client-side cookies**
The data on the client-side is temporarily stored in small text files; certain restrictions need to be considered (see Section 3.2.5).

▶ **Server-side cookies**
The data is not located on the client-side, but on the server. Unlike client-side cookies, there are no size restrictions (see Section 3.2.5).

▶ **DB tables**
Another option is to store the data in a DB table specifically created for this purpose. This allows you to customize the tables to your liking. The disadvantage is the increased amount of programming work.

Now that the two state models have been described, we'll explain how to set up your mode of preference. You can do the setup either during development or runtime. If nothing is set, the BSP application will always work in the stateless mode (default setting).

During development, the required mode can be set on the **Properties** tab of a BSP application (see Figure 3.17).

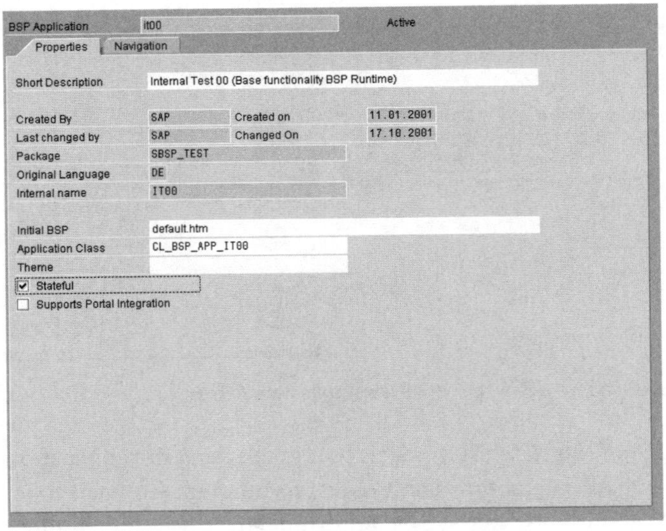

**Figure 3.17** Setting a BSP application to "stateful"

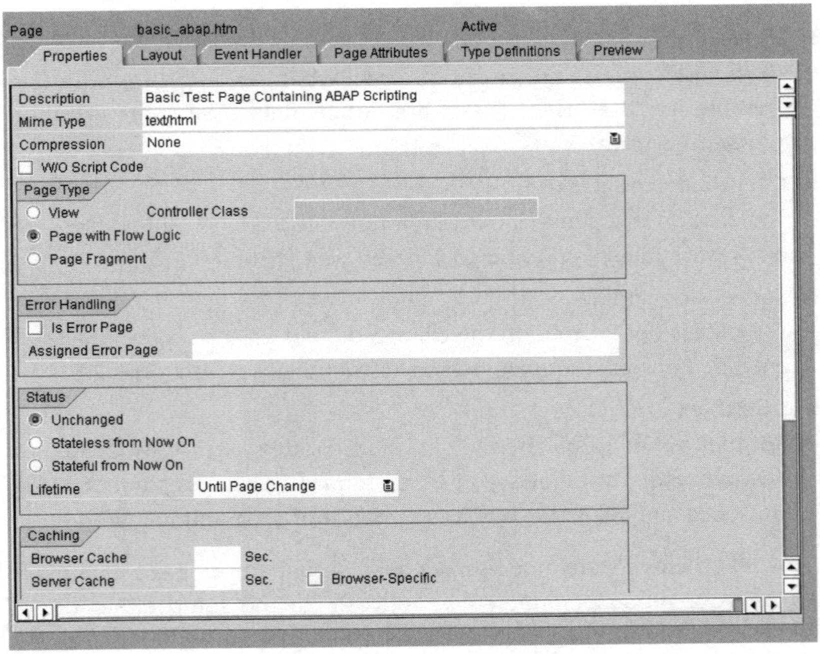

**Figure 3.18** Setting BSP pages to "stateful" or "stateless"

However, individual BSP pages of a BSP application can be set to "stateful" or "stateless," which is illustrated in Figure 3.18. As you can see, you can make various settings that relate to the life cycle (in stateful mode). These settings include:

▶ **Until Page Change**
The page is destroyed when another page is used.

▶ **Request**
The page is destroyed after each individual request. In other words, it exists only for the duration of a request.

▶ **Session**
The page is destroyed at the end of the session.

You can also switch between stateful and stateless during the runtime (dynamic). Use the runtime object `runtime`, which relates to the interface IF_BSP_RUNTIME. The setting is made by setting the value of the attribute KEEP_CONTEXT. This attribute can adopt the values "0" and "1". The following example sets the stateful and stateless modes:

```
runtime->keep_context = 1. " set application to stateful
runtime->keep_context = 0. " set application to stateless
```

These settings override any definitions made from the development environment.

Now that you have learned about the stateful and stateless models, we will describe the available event handlers.

## The event handlers

The event handlers are the event concept of BSP pages. A range of predefined handlers is passed through in a specified sequence when processing a page:

▶ `onCreate`
This handler is called when a page is first opened, and is used for the one-off initialization of objects and data required on the page. The handler is always called when a BSP page class is generated. In stateful mode, the handler is called precisely once when generating the page. In stateless mode, the page object is re-initialized each time—in other words, the handler is called anew each time. If you are using the stateful mode without explicit navigation and are simply running through the page once more, the page instance is retained and the handler is not passed through again.

▶ onRequest

This handler is called on each access (request) to a page. It is used to restore internal data structures from a request.

▶ onInitialization

This handler is used for data retrieval. Ideally, this data is saved in page attributes and is then available in the layout. In addition, any programs can be called. This handler is triggered after the onRequest handler.

▶ onLayout

This is a hidden event handler which renders the layout of the page and generates the HTTP data flow for the response. No code can be added.

▶ onManipulation

This event handler permits the subsequent manipulation of the HTTP data flow. It is processed once the layout elements of the page have been generated. This handler is rarely used.

▶ onInputProcessing

The task of this handler is to manage user inputs, input checks, and navigation (on the same page or to subsequent pages). Certain requirements need to be met for this handler to be triggered.

▶ onDestroy

In the future, this handler will be called immediately before deleting a page instance. Follow-on actions can then be carried out here for a page. It is the opposite of the onCreate handler. In stateless mode, onCreate and onDestroy are passed through for each request/ response cycle. In stateful mode this handler is not called for each cycle, but only if the system changes to stateless mode.

This event handler is intended for future use, and is not currently called when processing a page.

Certain global runtime objects are available within each event handler. These objects permit access to the request object and the response object or permit navigation between BSP pages via the navigation object, for example. An overview of these available objects and their meanings can be found in Table 3.5.

| Object | Meaning | Interface/class/type |
|---|---|---|
| runtime | BSP runtime information | IF_BSP_RUNTIME |
| application | Attributes and methods of the application class | separate class of derivative of CL_BSP_APPLICATION |
| page_context | Page context object[1] | IF_BSP_PAGE_CONTEXT |
| page | BSP page information | IF_BSP_PAGE |
| request | Access to the request object | IF_HTTP_REQUEST |
| response | Access to the response object | IF_HTTP_RESPONSE |
| navigation | Data transfer and navigation | IF_BSP_NAVIGATION |
| event_id | User interaction | STRING |
| messages | Treatment of error messages[2] | CL_BSP_MESSAGES |

**Table 3.5** Global runtime projects of a BSP application

1 The page_context object is a framework of a BSP and plays a role only in connection with the BSP extensions.

2 The message object is an attribute of the page object.

Table 3.6 provides a summary of which objects are available in which event handlers.

| Event handler | Available global objects |
|---|---|
| onCreate | runtime, application, page_context, page (messages) |
| onRequest | runtime, application, page_context, page (messages), request, navigation, event_id |
| onInitialization | runtime, application, page_context, page (messages), request, response, navigation |
| onManipulation | runtime, application, page_context, page (messages), request, response |
| onInputProcessing | runtime, application, page_context, page (messages), request, navigation, event_id |
| onDestroy (not available at present) | runtime, application, page_context, page (messages) |

**Table 3.6** Global runtime objects in event handlers

**The processing sequence**

To start the application, enter the relevant URL into the Web browser's address line. This URL identifies the BSP application to be started. The start characteristics of an application (BSP session) can be configured with various URL parameters, as already shown. Entering the URL results in an HTTP GET request that is sent to the BSP runtime. The BSP runtime then determines the appropriate BSP application and the requested BSP page. Depending on the setting, a logon to the SAP Web AS may be necessary (see Section 2.5.1).

Within the BSP runtime environment (BSP engine), the requested BSP page is processed, its components are passed through, and the corresponding processing steps are triggered according to the programmed logic. The result is a Web page that is sent to the initiator as a `response` object. The generation process takes place in phases. In this process, events are run through in a specific sequence, over which the programmer has limited influence. These events are represented by event handlers that carry out different tasks. The processing flow of a BSP application—running through the various event handlers, in particular—is also affected by which status model is currently active. An overview of the schematic process flow (both for stateful and for stateless) is provided in Figure 3.19.

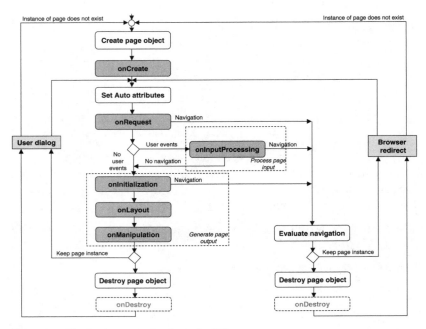

**Figure 3.19** The basic processing flow of a BSP page

When the page is called, the BSP runtime first determines whether there is already a page object for this BSP page. If this is not the case, the onCreate event handler is run. This handler generates the page object or an instantiation of the object. From the developer's point of view, this handler can be used to initialize data or to generate required objects.

**Processing flow in the stateless model**

In the next step, any existing auto page attributes are transferred.

The onRequest event handler is then called. This handler is called on each request to a page, and is used to restore internal data structures from the request.

A decision now needs to be made on whether a user interaction has taken place. If this is the case, the onInputProcessing event handler is called; otherwise, the onInitialization event handler is called. First, we'll take a look at the situation without user interaction.

The onInitialization event handler is used to acquire the necessary data. This data may originate from many different kinds of sources (from DB tables, via function modules, BAPIs, etc.).

The onLayout phase is processed once the necessary data has been acquired. The design and the presentation of the page that the user sees are specified here. In other words, this involves the preparation and formatting of the requested pages. A page consists of static (e.g., HTML) and dynamic (server-side scripting) parts. Whereas the client-side scripting (e.g., JavaScript) is returned unfiltered to the client, the server-side scripting (ABAP) is processed and transformed into code that the browser can understand. The result is a serialized HTTP data flow.

One option for manipulating the HTTP data flow is the onManipulation event handler. This event handler is called after the onLayout event handler.

In the stateless case, the generated page object is destroyed again. In the future, in order to carry out work afterward (e.g., to save the data in a server-side cookie), the onDestroy event handler will be available. As this event handler is not currently run through, it is identified in the graphic accordingly (striped box).

This HTTP data flow is then sent to the initiator, and the requested Web page appears in the user's browser.

Only displaying the page, however, is not sufficient. The user should be able to input data, make selections, or simply navigate to another page.

**Response to user inputs and navigation**

To make this possible, the relevant user interactions (e.g., mouse and keyboard inputs) should be accepted and processed accordingly. The result could be a new Web page, the updated output page, or even an error message, depending on the programmed logic. These user inputs are processed by the `onInputProcessing` event handler. If this type of user interaction has taken place, after `onRequest` the `onInputProcessing` event handler is called instead of `onInitialization`.

The `onInputProcessing` event handler is used to check incorrect inputs and verify the forwarding of attributes and the subsequent pages for further navigation. If no follow-on page has been specified, the page's `onInitialization` event handler is used to continue navigation within the BSP. On the other hand, if a follow-on page has been defined, the user will navigate automatically to this new BSP page. The follow-on page may be determined from the navigation structure or specified in the program code.[12] The requested page is then created according to the known processing flow and is output in the user's browser. A user action can now be made and the processing flow is restarted. With each navigation, the underlying page object is destroyed again. A range of specifications needs to be observed during development to ensure that the `onInputProcessing` event handler is triggered. These specifications are discussed in detail in Section 5.5.

**Processing flow in the stateful model**  Because the processing flow is similar to the stateless model, we will focus only on the differences here. The most important feature is that the page object is retained[13] for the entire duration of a session. When a BSP is first called, the `onCreate` event handler is called exactly once. If a navigation action is carried out within the BSP, the page object remains and `onCreate` will not be called again. The `onDestroy` event handler is called only if the system changes to stateless mode in the meantime. Otherwise, processing takes place in the stateless situation.

**Exit**  A stateful BSP application can be exited in two ways. The first option is to append special system parameters to the URL. The parameter `sap-sessioncmd=close` exits the application. These special URL system parameters are described in Section 3.3.2. The second option is to end the session with a time-out mechanism. If a BSP application is idle—that is, if no more actions are being carried out that result in another request/response cycle—a timeout intervenes after a time specified in the instance profile.

---

12  Within this event handler, you can also determine a follow-on page dynamically by reviewing the usage details. You can find more information on this later in Chapter 5.

13  The life cycle of a page object can be specified on the page level, request level, or for the entire session.

The timeout also occurs if the Web browser is closed without the BSP application's being explicitly closed first. Because the SAP Web AS does not recognize when the Web browser is closed, you need to consider this behavior when implementing a BSP application.

A local ABAP class is generated from a BSP page during the runtime. The page layout and the various event handlers are methods of this class. The server-side scripting contained in a page is translated into code of the generated layout method. The page attributes are also translated into method parameters of the generated class.

### 3.3.4  Model-View-Controller Design Pattern (MVC)

In software development, a *design pattern* is—in the broadest sense—a written document describing a general solution to a problem that occurs repeatedly in a multitude of projects. Patterns provide a formal description of the problem, the solution, and other factors. In object-oriented development, a pattern of this type may contain descriptions of objects and classes, including their individual components and dependencies. A collection of these patterns is a *pattern framework*.

**Design pattern**

The MVC pattern describes the methodology for efficient linking of the user interface to the underlying data model. It is widely distributed in programming in languages such as Java, Smalltalk, C, and C++.[14]

The MVC pattern contains a clear separation between the process flow, application logic (data model), and presentation logic. The formal division of these three areas is achieved using the three objects Model, View, and Controller, indicating that complex BSP applications can be divided into logical units. This division of BSP applications into units has several advantages. For example, changes to the user interface have no effect on the application logic. Conversely, data can be presented multiple times in different display formats simultaneously. Clever update mechanisms change the data for an update in all displays.

**Separation of process flow, application, and interface**

#### Interaction of the MVC components

The components have already been introduced in brief in Section 3.3.1, but are explained here once more for the purpose of clarification.

---

14  It is this that entitles the MVC model to call itself a design pattern. A basic requirement here is the level of distribution.

▶ **Model**

The *Model* represents the logical structure of the data underlying the application. For example, it provides methods such as backend services for data collection and processing. This component is responsible almost exclusively for implementing the application logic (business logic) and therefore does not contain any kind of user interface information.

A Model may have several Views that are realized using the relevant view pages.

▶ **View**

*Views* in typical applications consist of classes for the representation of the graphical elements of the user interface, such as buttons, menus, and dialog boxes. Views enable the visualization of user interface elements.

In the SAP Web AS, Views are implemented as concrete characteristics of BSP pages. They contain HTML code and ABAP for rendering the user interface.

To visualize the status, either a view sends queries to the Model or the Model informs the view of possible status changes. The view displayed to the client forwards user actions, such as clicking on a Submit button, to an assigned Controller.

Views have neither event handlers nor auto page attributes. Page attributes are filled by the Controller.

▶ **Controller**

Controllers are the classes that establish the link between the Model and the View. They implement the decision-making process for responding to user inputs, and they control the process flow. Input data from the user accepted by the View is forwarded to the Model and triggers changes to the application data using the relevant method calls. The controller then causes Views to be executed, or changes the Views' status.

When using controllers, you should consider the following points:

▷ Controllers are derived from either the base class CL_BSP_ CONTROLLER2 (see Appendix A) or other Controllers. This is easiest to achieve, as Figure 3.20 shows, via the forward navigation when creating a View.

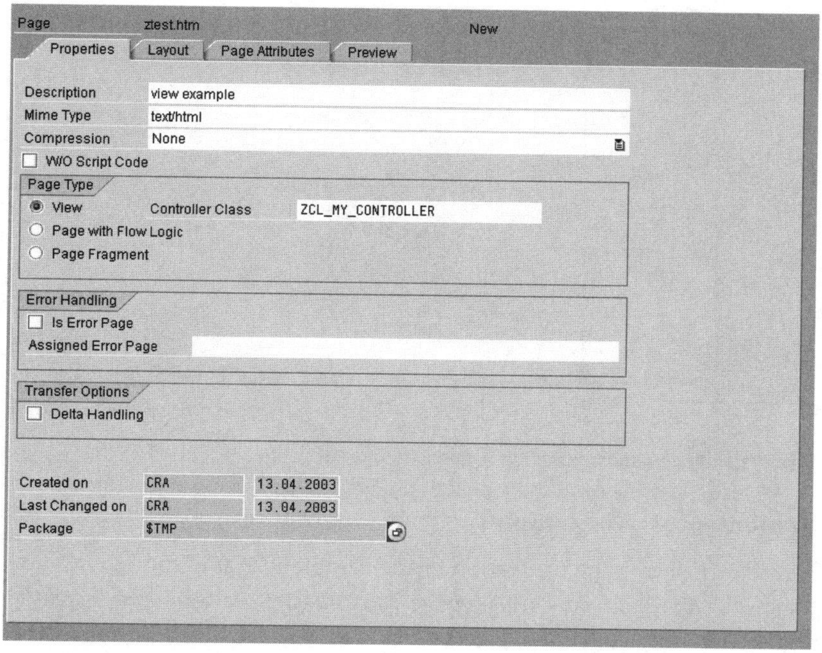

**Figure 3.20** Creating a controller via forward navigation

▶ Controllers can control Views only from their own BSP application; however, the controls can be transferred to Controllers from other applications.

▶ A controller's life cycle is restricted to one call by default. By using the ID, the life cycle is taken from the settings of the controller properties.

▶ Redirects are also possible using Controllers.

▶ Controllers can be reached from outside via a URL. They typically have the extension *.do*. A typical call might look like this:
*http://www.my-webas.de/sap/bc/bsp/sap/zcode/start.do?sap-client=100*

Figure 3.21 shows a schematic view of the connections between the components Model, View, and Controller.

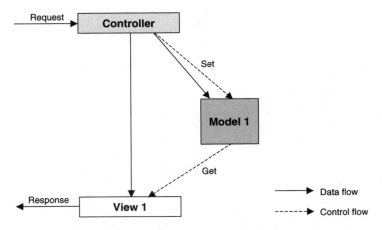

**Figure 3.21** Schematic interaction of the MVC components

## Implementation examples

**Simple implementation**

Figure 3.14 shows the navigation in an example BSP application with flow logic. In a BSP application using the MVC Design Pattern, the display in Figure 3.22 would apply in the same way. Each of the BSP pages has implemented all three components. The Views are each called directly by their assigned Controller. It is possible to navigate between the BSP pages via a redirect. It is also possible to assign to each Controller several Models or Views, and a "mixed mode" with typical BSP pages.

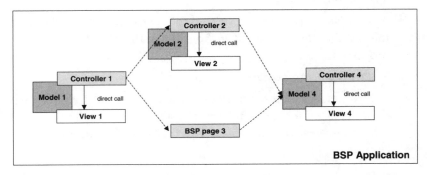

**Figure 3.22** Simple BSP application with MVC

**Multiple Views**

A Controller can control multiple Views in succession. With the corresponding flow control, it can also call these Views selectively, which is illustrated in Figure 3.23.

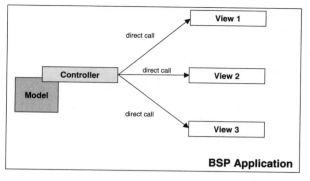

**Figure 3.23** Multiple views per controller

The flexibility is reflected, in particular, when combining the two previous options (i.e., multiple Views and simple implementation of MVC). In this example, a main Controller controls the central distribution (this main Controller does not require a separate View). This form of implementation is shown in Figure 3.24.

**Flexibility using central distribution**

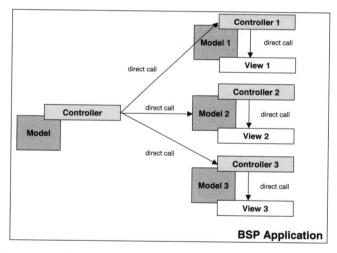

**Figure 3.24** A main controller controls the central distribution

It is also possible to generate a BSP page dynamically from multiple Views. However, this form of making components is not easy to manage. Figure 3.25 illustrates this way of using Controllers.

**Making components**

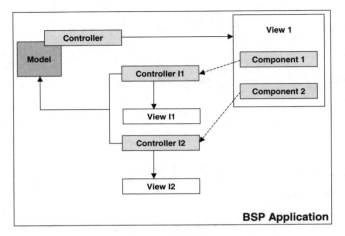

**Figure 3.25** Making components of BSP pages with MVC

Controllers from other applications can also be called. These examples show that there is a variety of combination options that allow virtually every conceivable implementation form. In addition, with all these combinations, BSP pages can be linked to the flow logic.

### Combination of MVC with previous BSPs

The techniques for the BSP application programming model, when understood with the following rules, contribute to form the newly integrated MVC Design Pattern:

▶ Views can be called only by Controllers. Exception: A call as an error page permits direct use of a View.

▶ Controllers can call a Controller using the `call` tag or the `goto` tag. However, they cannot call any pages using these tags.

▶ Transfers of pages to Controllers and back may take place using redirect via the navigation methods.

In a BSP application, both pages with flow logic and Controllers and Views may be present.

### Advantages of the MVC Design Pattern

The use of the MVC design pattern requires a certain level of implementation work. This work is rewarded with the corresponding advantages:

▶ **Maintainability**
Thanks to the clean division of the presentation logic, flow control, and application logic, the structure is simplified. This simplification of struc-

ture makes maintenance much easier. Designers can focus on the design, and application designers can focus on the application.

▶ **Performance**
The targeted use of the `goto` navigation reduces the number of required redirects and continues to use the same work process, which frequently saves resources.

You should consider the increased amount of required work very carefully. The more complex a project or the more complex the requirements placed on a BSP application become, the more beneficial it is to use the MVC Design Pattern.

**Estimating the work required and the advantages**

## 3.4    Including Mobile Clients

As you have already learned, the client PC on which a Web browser is running is the central presentation layer in the foreground. At the same time, the use of mobile terminals for business applications is becoming increasingly important. These mobile devices form the presentation layer for what is known as *mobile business*, which covers the non-location-specific procurement, processing, and provision of information of all kinds. Mobile business permits the processing of business and communication processes using mobile devices, suitable services, and network infrastructures. Its uses seem to be unlimited. Significant potential markets and varied applications can be identified in particular in the fields of procurement, sales, service, production, and logistics.

**Mobile business**

The mobile terminals used include WAP[15] compatible mobile telephones, laptops, and handhelds (PDAs). Enhancements to data transfer technology will allow high-volume applications to be created, even on these varied types of devices. This includes the UMTS standard permitting transfer rates of up to 2 MBit/s, for example.

**Variety of terminals**

An important problem in development for mobile business is the variety of possible terminals. Often there is no standardization, or if there is, preparing Web applications for specific devices is complicated because the display varies from device to device. The problematic categories of mobile terminals are:

---

15  WAP stands for *Wireless Application Protocol*. It is one of the most important standard for implementing Internet communication and interactive services for mobile phones and other mobile terminals. The markup language Wireless Markup Language (WML) and the corresponding programming language WMLScript realize data communication via WAP.

► **Display properties**

Displays are exceptionally varied. Some device displays are black-and-white, while other device displays support greyscale or permit color display at different levels of quality. Display size and resolution also vary by model.

► **Input methods**

Depending on the device, normal keyboards, telephone keypads, or on-screen input via keyboard or handwriting recognition can be used.

► **Markup languages**

For displaying the contents, different markup languages are supported depending on the device. This could be HTML or a limited variant, for example. In addition, various Wireless Markup Language (WML) versions are used.

► **Browser variants**

The different mobile terminals support different Wireless Application Protocol (WAP) browser versions. Despite the WAP standard, different devices are not guaranteed to display the same document in the same way because markup tags in particular are interpreted differently or are not evaluated. Different WAP browsers need different WML pages.

► **Graphical formats**

If graphics need to be displayed, you need to consider the supported graphics formats. In the worst-case scenario, multiple formats should be provided with different color depths and sizes.

These properties must be considered when developing Web applications for mobile terminals. This is the only way to ensure error-free and convenient operations with these devices. To resolve these problems, it is critical that a mobile-compatible server identifies and analyzes the client in terms of its technical characteristics. The server can use the information acquired in this way to prepare the response according to the capabilities of the client.

As illustrated in Figure 3.26, SAP Web AS supports the device-related development of Web applications for mobile terminals. These mobile extensions have been available since Release 6.10 in the form of a device detection process and a special interface `IF_CLIENT_INFO` that is part of the ICF.

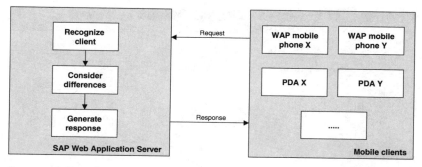

**Figure 3.26** Considering different mobile clients

The device detection function uses the content of a client HTTP request to determine the device type, and in the process allocates the values assigned to this device type to an instance of the implementation of interface IF_CLIENT_INFO. The detection process is used to specify the HTTP request header fields "Accept" and "User Agent" provided in the HTTP request by the requesting device.

**Device detection**

To identify the terminal, the content of the header field "User_Agent" is compared to an entry from the table MOB_DEVCFG (see Figure 3.27). This table is available on SAP Web AS and already contains various known terminals. Other devices can be added if required. If the device is found in the table, the stored values are used to fill the instance.

In the table, the "priority" column is also used to consider the precision in the assignment process. Here, the value "1" requires an exact match between the requesting client and the table entry. If no match is found during the comparison process, the device-detection process attempts to assign the terminal to a superior device type of priority levels 2 and 3.

If in the "User_Agent" column, the HTTP request header contains a character string starting with "SIE-", the terminal is detected as a device type from the manufacturer Siemens and the values for the general device type siemensGeneric are used to fill the instance. Here, it is assumed that all devices from a single manufacturer will use the same browser for the display.

If the device-detection process fails because no matching entry can be found, the HTTP request header field Accept is evaluated. This field contains the supported content type of the requesting mobile terminal. The device can now be assigned either the type wmlGeneric for WAP-compatible terminals, or the type htmlGeneric for HTML-compatible mobile terminals.

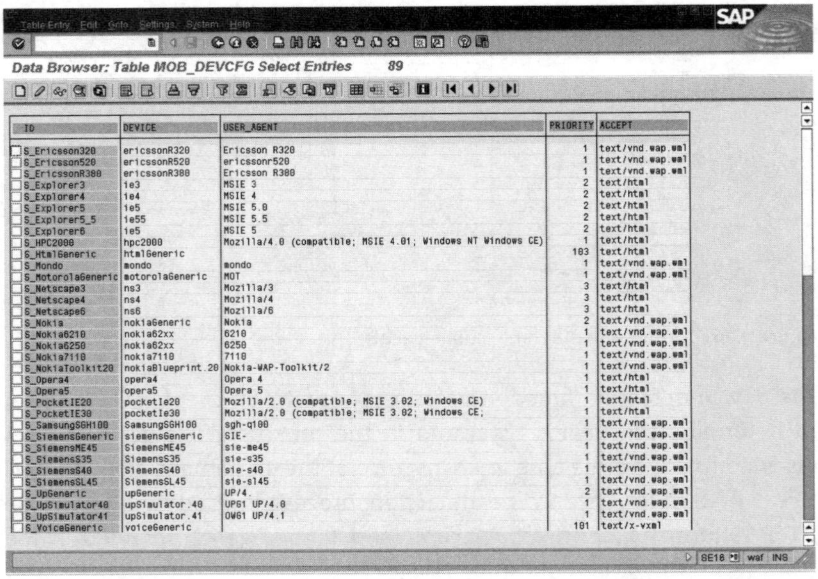


| ID | DEVICE | USER_AGENT | PRIORITY | ACCEPT |
|---|---|---|---|---|
| S_Ericsson320 | ericssonR320 | Ericsson R320 | 1 | text/vnd.wap.wml |
| S_Ericsson520 | ericssonR520 | ericssonr520 | 1 | text/vnd.wap.wml |
| S_EricssonR380 | ericssonR380 | Ericsson R380 | 1 | text/vnd.wap.wml |
| S_Explorer3 | ie3 | MSIE 3 | 2 | text/html |
| S_Explorer4 | ie4 | MSIE 4 | 2 | text/html |
| S_Explorer5 | ie5 | MSIE 5.0 | 2 | text/html |
| S_Explorer5_5 | ie55 | MSIE 5.5 | 2 | text/html |
| S_Explorer6 | ie5 | MSIE 5 | 2 | text/html |
| S_HPC2000 | hpc2000 | Mozilla/4.0 (compatible; MSIE 4.01; Windows NT Windows CE) | 1 | text/html |
| S_HtmlGeneric | htmlGeneric | | 103 | text/html |
| S_Mondo | mondo | mondo | 1 | text/vnd.wap.wml |
| S_MotorolaGeneric | motorolaGeneric | MOT | 1 | text/vnd.wap.wml |
| S_Netscape3 | ns3 | Mozilla/3 | 3 | text/html |
| S_Netscape4 | ns4 | Mozilla/4 | 3 | text/html |
| S_Netscape6 | ns6 | Mozilla/6 | 3 | text/html |
| S_Nokia | nokiaGeneric | Nokia | 2 | text/vnd.wap.wml |
| S_Nokia6210 | nokia62xx | 6210 | 1 | text/vnd.wap.wml |
| S_Nokia6250 | nokia62xx | 6250 | 1 | text/vnd.wap.wml |
| S_Nokia7110 | nokia7110 | 7110 | 1 | text/vnd.wap.wml |
| S_NokiaToolkit20 | nokiaBlueprint.20 | Nokia-WAP-Toolkit/2 | 1 | text/vnd.wap.wml |
| S_Opera4 | opera4 | Opera 4 | 1 | text/html |
| S_Opera5 | opera5 | Opera 5 | 1 | text/html |
| S_PocketIE20 | pocketIe20 | Mozilla/2.0 (compatible; MSIE 3.02; Windows CE) | 1 | text/html |
| S_PocketIE30 | pocketIe30 | Mozilla/2.0 (compatible; MSIE 3.02; Windows CE; | 1 | text/html |
| S_SamsungSGH100 | SamsungSGH100 | sgh-q100 | 1 | text/vnd.wap.wml |
| S_SiemensGeneric | siemensGeneric | SIE- | 1 | text/vnd.wap.wml |
| S_SiemensME45 | SiemensME45 | sie-me45 | 1 | text/vnd.wap.wml |
| S_SiemensS35 | SiemensS35 | sie-s35 | 1 | text/vnd.wap.wml |
| S_SiemensS40 | SiemensS40 | sie-s40 | 1 | text/vnd.wap.wml |
| S_SiemensSL45 | SiemensSL45 | sie-sl45 | 1 | text/vnd.wap.wml |
| S_UpGeneric | upGeneric | UP/4. | 2 | text/vnd.wap.wml |
| S_UpSimulator40 | upSimulator.40 | UP61 UP/4.0 | 1 | text/vnd.wap.wml |
| S_UpSimulator41 | upSimulator.41 | OW61 UP/4.1 | 1 | text/vnd.wap.wml |
| S_VoiceGeneric | voiceGeneric | | 101 | text/x-vxml |

**Figure 3.27** Identification of mobile terminals using the table MOB_DEVCFG

The instance created then describes properties and methods for the mobile terminal and provides information on the device's browser characteristics—that is, all the necessary information for developing device-specific Web applications (e.g., BSPs).

**The interface IF_CLIENT_INFO**

As you have already learned, this instance is an implementation of the interface `IF_CLIENT_INFO`. It contains several methods for evaluating the different display options of Web applications on different browsers and terminals.

The interface's properties and methods are accessed via the `runtime` object within the BSP application. This principle is explained in the following example, which can be implemented in the event handler `onInitialization`:

```
DATA: client_info TYPE REF TO IF_CLIENT_INFO.
client_info = runtime->client_info.
```

The methods and properties can then be accessed. An overview of the various methods of the interface `IF_CLIENT_INFO` is provided in Appendix A.2. The following example determines the width of the screen in pixels, for example:

```
DATA: l_pixel_width TYPE float.
l_pixel_width = client_info->get_pixel_width( ).
```

Whether the client accepts WML as a markup language can also be determined manually from the request via the runtime object:

```
DATA: is_wml TYPE flag. " does client support WML?
IF request->get_header_field( name = 'accept' ) CS
'wml'.
   is_wml = 'X'.
ENDIF.
```

# 4    Development: Tools

*This chapter introduces you to the necessary tools for developing BSP applications. By integrating the new BSP tools into the standard development environment, as experienced developers, you should soon feel at home and be able to take advantage of the new options that guarantee both straightforward and rapid development of Web applications.*

The SAP R/3 System's development environment, the *ABAP Workbench*, is a powerful tool. Since Release 6.10 of the SAP Basis system, the development environment's central starting point is called the *Object Navigator*. The Object Navigator functions replace the functions of the Repository Browser, which has moved one level lower in the hierarchy. This functionality was changed because the development environment has been extended by a number of features and proves to be very advantageous in daily use. **ABAP Workbench**

For a brief introduction to additional general development tools, the *Repository Info System* and *Transport Organizer*, see Section 4.1; for a more thorough introduction, we suggest that you refer to the online Help. The *MIME Repository* and the *Tag Browser* are necessary to BSP development and are located in the Web Application Builder (WAB) area. We will describe them in greater detail in Section 4.2.

The *Web Application Builder (WAB)*, as a part of the newly integrated Repository Browser, is also discussed extensively in Section 4.2. In this section, you will find all the tools that are relevant to the development of BSP applications. The following sections focus on the tools for the *BAPI Browser*, *Online Text Repository* (OTR), *XSLT Editor*, and *Version Administration*. Also covered are the *WebDAV Interface* and the *Service Maintenance*, which are equally important to the development of BSPs. **Web Application Builder**

## 4.1    Object Navigator

### 4.1.1    Introduction

As a higher-level administration tool, the Object Navigator is called using the Transaction SE80.

You can move through the navigation and tool areas separately. To change from one area to the next, simply double-click in the area in which you are currently in.

The initial screen of the Object Navigator is shown in Figure 4.1.

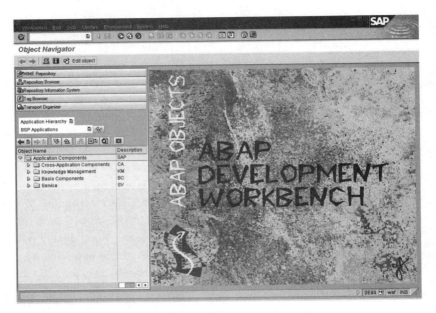

**Figure 4.1** Initial screen of the Object Navigator

Navigation areas The screen is divided into several independent areas in which to navigate. Figure 4.2 highlights these areas.

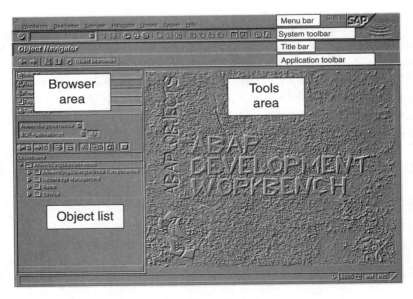

**Figure 4.2** Schematic diagram of the Object Navigator

These areas of the Object Navigator are:

▶ **Toolbars**

The menu bar and toolbars can also be divided into separate areas:

▷ **Menu bar**

The menus displayed here depend on which application is currently in use. Only the available menu items are visible.

▷ **System toolbar**

The system toolbar's icons are available on every R/3 screen. Icons that are not available are dimmed or shaded in gray. If you hold the cursor over an icon, a *Tooltip* opens, which shows the icon's function and the function key setting.

The input field in the left-hand area is represented as a *command field*. You can enter and execute transaction codes directly by pressing Enter. All available commands are listed when you position the cursor inside the field and press F1.

▷ **Title bar**

The title bar designates the tool and the function available in the tools area.

▷ **Application toolbar**

The application toolbar shows which icons are available in the currently displayed application.

All functions on the toolbars always refer to the tool that is currently available in the tools area.

▶ **Browser area**

Various browsers are available to choose from here. Because these browsers are described in greater detail in later sections, we have provided only a brief introduction here.

The available browsers are the:

▷ **MIME Repository**

Displays all existing MIME object directories on the system.

▷ **Repository Browser**

Displays the Repository objects (development objects) as object lists. A double-click (forward navigation) starts the editor of the tool assigned in the tools area.

▷ This browser is automatically activated when calling Transaction SE80.

▷ **Repository Info System**

Displays all objects of the Info System.

► **Tag Library**
Lists all available tags for Web applications. The list also includes BSP directives and BSP extensions.

► **Transport Organizer**
Enables quick access to the transport requests available on the system.

► **Object list**
Offers a hierarchically arranged overview of all development objects of a selected category of the respective browser tool. The hierarchical display has a separately assigned application toolbar (see Section 4.1.3), which permits rapid navigation within the hierarchy structure. The relationships between the objects are also reflected here. The object list is the most important navigation utility in the development environment.

Operations can also be simultaneously executed on several objects in the object list. To do so, hold down the Shift or Ctrl button while clicking on all objects that are to be included. Then, select the appropriate operation from the context menu. The context menus here are analogous to the context menus in the Microsoft Windows user interface.

► **Tools area**
Displays the tool used to edit the current development object. By double-clicking on an object in the object list, the work list, or the navigation stack, or when navigating using the application toolbar, the appropriate tool is automatically displayed.

► **Status bar**
Displays information on the system's current status, such as warnings and errors. In the right-hand area, system information is displayed. Here you can select relevant options from a drop-down list.

If the system response to your input is different from what you expected, look at the information in this area. For additional information, try double-clicking in this area.

**Additional components** ► **Important general function keys**

► **F1 key**
Press the Help button (F1) to see notes on fields, menus, functions, and messages.

► **F4 key**
Press the matchcode button (F4) to see information on possible input values. Alternatively, click the button to the right of a selected field for Field Help.

▶ **Navigation stack**

Use the *Navigation stack* to get an overview of the navigation steps in the Object Navigator. To display this useful tool, press Ctrl + Shift + F4 simultaneously inside the lower part of the tools area (see Figure 4.3). Double-clicking on an object in the stack displays the object in the tools area. Therefore, you can navigate among the objects already "visited."

The Navigation stack is not always available.

| Page | default_us.htm | | | Active | | |
|------|------|------|------|------|------|------|
| Properties | Layout | Event Handler | Page Attributes | Type Definitions | Preview | |

```
<%@page language="abap" %>
<html>
  <head>
    <link rel="stylesheet" href="z_flight.css">
    <title> FlyAnotherDay: Start </title>
  </head>
  <body>
    <center>
      <a href="information_us.htm?uname=<%= name %>">
        <img src="intro.jpg" alt="Welcome Picture" border="0">
      </a>
      <h2> Hello <%= name %>, </h2>
      <br>
      <h2> Welcome to FlyAnotherDay! </h2>
      <br>
      <a href="information_us.htm?uname=<%= name %>">
```

| | Li 14, Co 10 | | Ln 1 - Ln 16 of 21 lines |
|---|---|---|---|

Navigation stack

| Object type | Object name | Subobject name |
|------|------|------|
| Class | Z_CL_FLIGHT | |
| BSP Application | ZCRA | |
| BSP Page | Z_FLIGHT | DEFAULT_US.HTM |
| | Object Navigator Initial Screen | |

**Figure 4.3** The Navigation stack in the tools area

▶ **Worklist**

The *Worklist* is another practical utility. You can use it to help you specifically compile objects from different areas. And because the Worklist can be individually saved for each user, it's always available.

You can open the Worklist by selecting the **Utilities · Worklist · Display** menu option (see Figure 4.4). To record objects in the Worklist, select **Insert current object**.

Using this utility, you can maintain bookmarks for a particular row in the source text. The Editor does not have this feature. An object that has been recorded in the Worklist, however, does have this feature.

| Page | default_us.htm | | | | Active | |
|---|---|---|---|---|---|---|
| Properties | Layout | Event Handler | Page Attributes | Type Definitions | Preview | |

```
<%@page language="abap" %>
<html>
  <head>
    <link rel="stylesheet" href="z_flight.css">
    <title> FlyAnotherDay: Start </title>
  </head>
  <body>
    <center>
      <a href="information_us.htm?uname=<%= name %>">
        <img src="intro.jpg" alt="Welcome Picture" border="0">
      </a>
      <h2> Hello <%= name %>, </h2>
      <br>
      <h2> Welcome to FlyAnotherDay! </h2>
      <br>
      <a href="information us.htm?uname=<% name %>">
```

| | Li 13, Co 11 | | Ln 1 - Ln 16 of 21 lines |
|---|---|---|---|

Display Worklist

| Object type | Object name | Subobject name |
|---|---|---|
| BSP Page | Z_FLIGHT | DEFAULT_US.HTM |
| BSP Application | SBSPEXT_BSP | |
| BSP Controller | ZCRA | START.DO |

**Figure 4.4** The Worklist Display

The different functions in the Object Navigator can often be reached in several ways. Available options include: toolbars, menu bars, the context menu (displayed by right-clicking the mouse), the forward navigation (by double-clicking), as well as other transactions[1]. Understandably, this book does not show every method of navigation, because users each have certain preferences and, in time, will develop their own system of navigation.

### 4.1.2 Configuration

Within any professional development environment, you should be able to customize your environment to meet your personal requirements. The SAP Web Application Server (SAP Web AS) is certainly no exception. You can find the Configuration menu for user-specific settings by selecting **Utilities Settings**.

---

1 As a matter of fact, the Object Navigator only nests some of the transactions within the tools area. For instance, you can access the Class Builder also via Transaction SE24.

When developing BSP applications, it's worth mentioning the following settings on the various tabs (see Figure 4.5):

▶ **Workbench (General)**

  ▷ **Display background picture**
  The initial screen in the Object Navigator displays the background picture when activating settings.

  ▷ **Browser Selection**
  Here, components of the browser area can be hidden to make the screen clearer.

If you accidentally close the browser, don't worry; it can be displayed again.

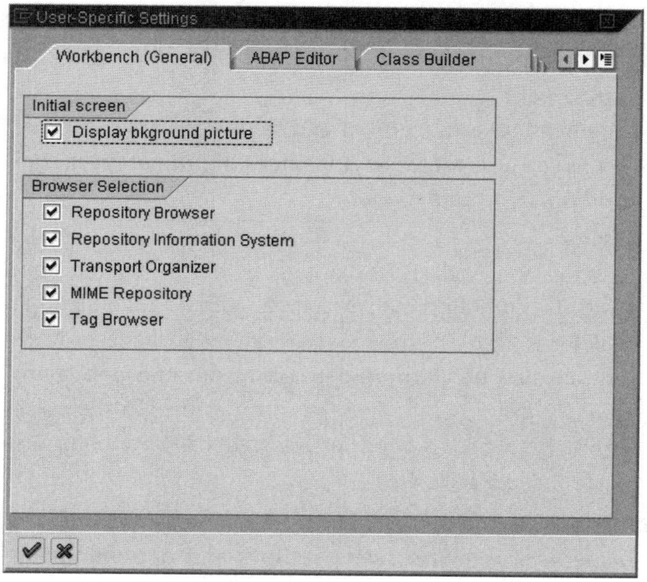

Figure 4.5  User-specific settings—Workbench (general)

▶ **ABAP Editor**

  ▷ **Front-end Editor**                                                                  Editor
  In this editor mode, the source code of an ABAP program is loaded into the frontend and can be edited there.

  ▷ **Back-end Editor**
  The traditional, backend line editor is not used with BSP application development.

**Upper-/lowercase conversion in disp mode**
By setting the flag, the source text in the display mode will be presented according to the Pretty Printer settings under **Convert upper-/lowercase**. If this option is not activated, the source text will be reproduced in the same format in which it is stored in the database.

Pretty Printer

**Indent**
Inserts an indentation into the ABAP source text, for example, all command lines for a particular event are shifted two spaces to the right.

**Convert upper-/lowercase**
The display of the source text can be standardized. Using this option, you can format the entire source text in lowercase, uppercase, uppercase keywords, or lowercase keywords. However, literals and comments are not affected by this option.

Split screen

**Window Arrangement**
You can set the window arrangement and several program comparison options. You can also set the arrangement of programs for comparison in addition to other parameters.

HTTP Debugging

**HTTP Debugging**
By using the activation flag, HTTP Debugging can be turned completely on or off. This function makes it possible to debug BSP applications in real time, that is, upon execution by a client browser. Another user can also be permitted to carry out the debugging, which is useful, for example, if a general Internet user in the corresponding service is to be assigned access rights. IP Matching can also be requested (see Figure 4.6).

**Class Builder**
The *Class Builder* is where you select settings and options for displaying the components of global classes or interfaces. These settings and options are particularly of value when using object-oriented programming with the Class Builder. Using the Display filter, you can either extend or restrict the default display. To restrict the display of class components by instance or static components (see Figure 4.7), use the Scope filter.

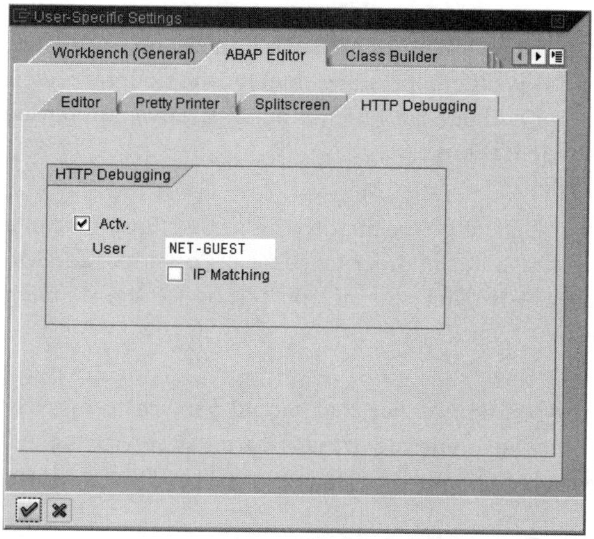

**Figure 4.6** User-specific settings—ABAP editor

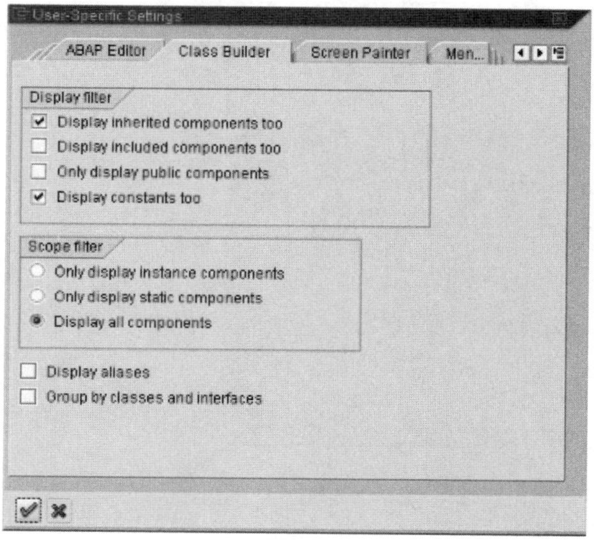

**Figure 4.7** User-specific settings—Class Builder

▶ **Business Server Pages**

▷ **Log**

Enter the protocol, which is used to call BSP applications directly. Possible values are "HTTP" and "HTTPS".

- **Application Server**

  Enter the name of the mySAP Business Suite Application Server. The name must be fully qualified, including domain and country codes. Alternatively, the IP address can be entered. This server should be used to test BSP applications.

- **Port Number**

  Enter the port number for connecting to the mySAP Business Suite Application Server. Use this number for test calls from BSP applications. If this field is left blank, the default setting for the standard BSP service is used.

- **Name of service**

  Enter the name of the BSP service that should be used to test BSP applications. If no name is entered, the standard BSP service is automatically used.

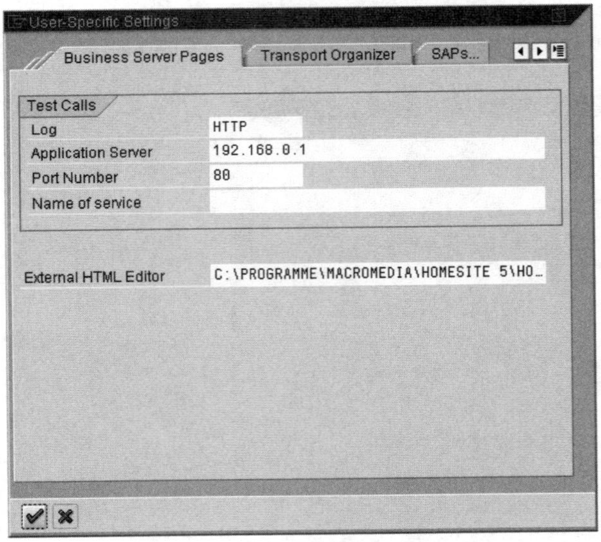

**Figure 4.8** User-specific settings for BSPs

**External HTML Editor**

- **External HTML Editor**

  Enter any program installed on the client that is intended to be used as an editor for the layout part of BSP pages. To start the program, from the Editor, select the menu option **Edit Start Local HTML Editor** or press Ctrl + F4 (see Figure 4.8).

### 4.1.3 Repository Browser

The *Repository Browser* is the standard tool of the ABAP development environment. Available objects can be selected from ordered object lists. In this way, for example, all objects in a BSP application can be displayed in a clear and hierarchical arrangement (see Figure 4.9).

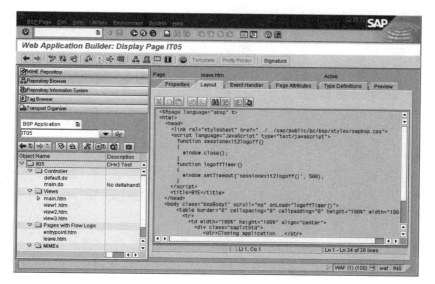

**Figure 4.9** Repository Browser—straightforward list of the objects

The object lists are displayed in the form of hierarchical structures. For example, below the browser area, the category (e.g., BSP Application) and a subset of that category (to reduce the number of results) are displayed.

Objects can be selected according to the following categories (see Figure 4.10):

▶ **Application Hierarchy**
In the SAP application hierarchy, the structure of all development objects in the R/3 system is displayed in a list, which is arranged hierarchically by application component(s), component identifier, and the packages contained within.

▶ **Package**
List of all objects of a package.

The package replaces the development classes used in earlier releases of R/3.

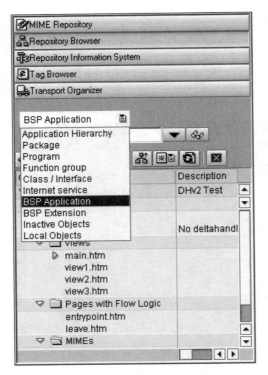

**Figure 4.10** The categories of the Repository Browser

▶ **Program**
List of all part objects of an ABAP program.

▶ **Function group**
List of all function modules and their part objects, which are defined within a function group.

▶ **Class/Interface**
List of all components of a global class. In addition, super classes and all inherited and redefined methods of the current class are displayed.

▶ **Internet service**
List of all part objects of an Internet service: description of service, themes, language resources, HTML templates, and MIME objects. Because the objects displayed in this list belong to the Internet Transaction Server (ITS), these objects are not relevant here.

▶ **BSP Application**
List of all the part objects of a BSP application. When selecting a BSP application, the corresponding environment of the Web Application Builder is called up.

► **Inactive Objects**

List of all of the user's inactive objects. Both local (no transport request assigned) and transportable objects are displayed.

► **Local Objects**

List of objects that belong to the *$TMP* package and are not transported beyond this point. You can assign local objects to another package for transport purposes.

**Figure 4.11** The Object List Application toolbar

The following functions can be applied to the corresponding object list using the application toolbar (see Figure 4.11):

► **Previous object list**

Backward navigation in the object list display with history.

► **Next object list**

Forward navigation in the object list display with history.

► **Expand all nodes**

Expands completely all nodes of the object list.

► **Collapse all nodes**

Closes completely all nodes of the object list.

► **Display superordinated object list**

Displays the next higher level in the hierarchy. After displaying the part objects of a program or application, the object list of assigned packages is displayed.

► **Favorites**

Allows favorites to be entered. The currently displayed object list can be directly recorded in the favorites list. You can also edit the entries of the existing favorites list.

The Favorites function is also highly suitable for quickly navigating between user-related objects that are frequently required.

► **Refresh object list**

Refreshes the display of the current object list. You can update changes that have been made in another mode, whereas changes made in the same mode are automatically updated. In the latter case, a refresh is not necessary.

▶ **Close Browser**

Closes the navigation area.

By double-clicking, objects from the list are displayed in the tools area with the appropriate editor. As in other browsers, various operations can be executed on the objects using the context menu (see Figure 4.12). In Section 4.2, we'll introduce important functionalities for BSP application development.

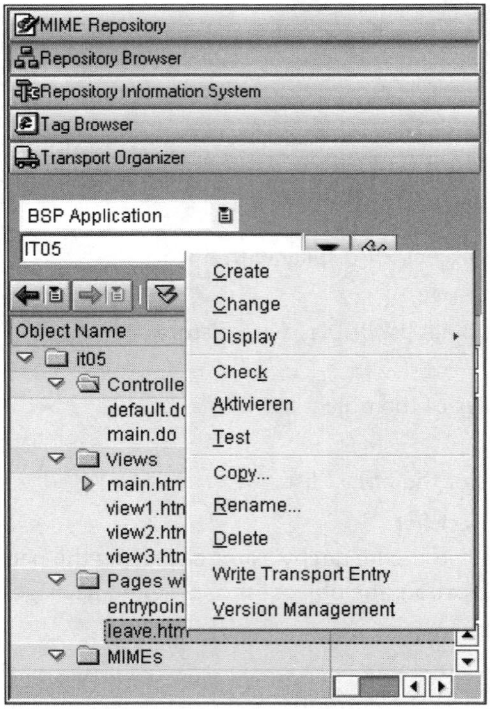

**Figure 4.12** Context menu for "BSP Page"-type objects

### 4.1.4 Repository Info System

Repository Info System vs. application hierarchy

Similar to the application hierarchy of the Repository Browser, the ABAP Workbench Info system is a tool that you can use to navigate and find objects quickly. Unlike the application hierarchy, using the *Repository Info System* enables you to search for objects of a particular object type using selection parameters (see Figure 4.13). Wildcard searches are also possible.

In the list of results, objects can be displayed directly in the corresponding editor using forward navigation.

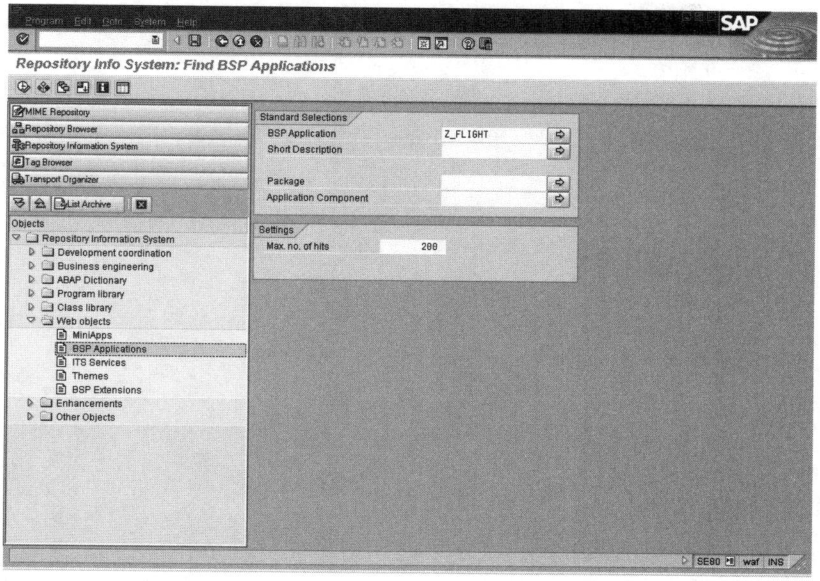

**Figure 4.13** The Repository Info System

### 4.1.5 Transport Organizer

The *Transport Organizer* shows requests that are currently on the system (see Figure 4.14). You can limit or restrict the number of jobs that are displayed by modifying a setting underneath the browser area. A range of frequently used functions for transport management can be accessed via the context menu. These functions include:

► Create, Change, Display, and Delete

► Check

► Add User... (i.e., assigning developers)

► Release (i.e., releasing transport jobs)

## 4.2 Web Application Builder

The *SAP Web Application Builder (WAB)* is the tool that creates and edits BSP applications in the SAP Web AS environment. To be more precise, the WAB is not a tool; rather, it is a collection of tools that are managed by a single interface. Once again, we see the relevance of the concept of the ABAP Development Workbench—a collection of tools managed together in one interface.

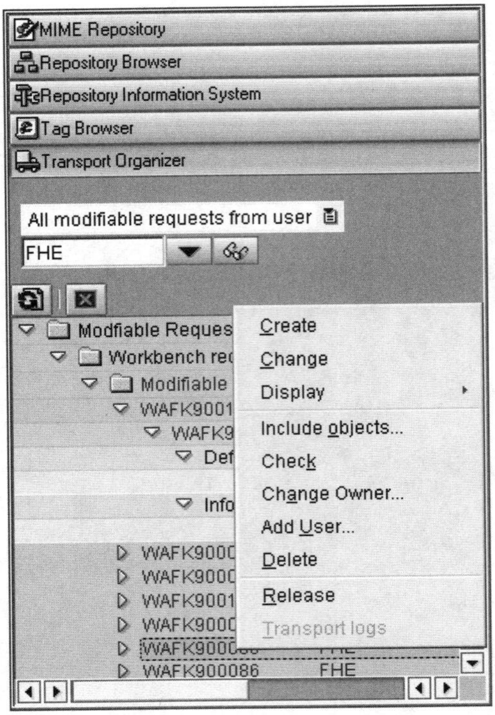

**Figure 4.14** Transport Organizer—the context menu of a job

In the following sections, you'll learn about the *Editor*, *Version Management*, the *MIME Repository*, the *Tag Browser*, and the *Theme Editor*.

### 4.2.1 Editor

The *Editor* (see Figure 4.15) is certainly the most frequently used tool. In principle, it is very similar to the other editors of the SAP R/3 system. Many functionalities and the basic working method are the same for all editors, independent of whether the editor is a class editor, the ABAP Editor, or a BSP editor.

In this context, the following three areas are significant (see Figure 4.2 in Section 4.1):

1. The menu bar

2. The application toolbar

3. The appropriate tools area including tabs, the editor toolbar, and the corresponding context menu

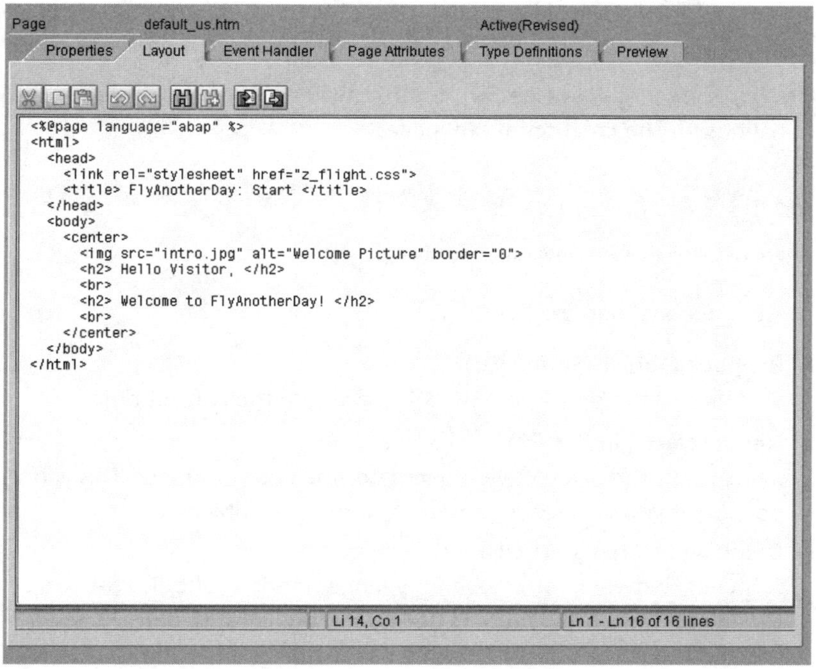

| Properties | Layout | Event Handler | Page Attributes | Type Definitions | Preview |
|---|---|---|---|---|---|

```
<%@page language="abap" %>
<html>
  <head>
    <link rel="stylesheet" href="z_flight.css">
    <title> FlyAnotherDay: Start </title>
  </head>
  <body>
    <center>
      <img src="intro.jpg" alt="Welcome Picture" border="0">
      <h2> Hello Visitor, </h2>
      <br>
      <h2> Welcome to FlyAnotherDay! </h2>
      <br>
    </center>
  </body>
</html>
```

Li 14, Co 1                          Ln 1 - Ln 16 of 16 lines

**Figure 4.15** The Editor tool with tabs and the Editor toolbar

The *Menu bar* is the most extensive navigation utility. From here, you can execute most functions and call all other relevant tools. Note the following options:

**Menu bar**

▶ **Edit—Start Local HTML Editor**
Starts the external editor, which was specified as the editor in the settings (see Section 4.1.2). Faster access is possible using the key combination Ctrl + F4.

▶ **Goto**
Enables you to launch the BAPI Browser, the Online Text Repository (OTR), the Theme Editor, and the translation tool.

▶ **Utilities**
Allows you to reset the server cache, incl. all cached MIMEs, for example, or locate the Breakpoint Administration or the Version Management.

During the development phase, MIME objects may be frequently exchanged or updated. In certain circumstances, when the server caching is not switched off,[2] these modifications are not immediately replaced in

---

2   In certain development environments, not switching off the server caching is advisable.

the cache when a page is reloaded. Using the Refresh Server Cache function, you can empty the cache and therefore resolve this problem.

Application toolbar

The *Application toolbar* (see Figure 4.16) makes available a range of functionalities for the creation of BSP pages.

**Figure 4.16** The Editor—Application toolbar

These functionalities are:

▶ **Previous Object (Shift + F6)**
Switches to the previous active object before the current object.

▶ **Next Object (Shift + F2)**
Switches to the next active object after the current object. This is only possible if you've already jumped to a previous object.

▶ **Display <-> Change (Ctrl + F1)**
Switches between display and change modes. Should the object already be locked by another developer, this information is shown in the status bar.

In this case, the system name of the user who has locked the object is also included. This enables you to request access rights[3] for the development object.

▶ **Active <-> Inactive (Shift + F8)**
Switches between the active and the inactive versions of the current object. This function can provide you with a quick overview of the changes, for example.

▶ **Other Object (Shift + F5)**
You can select another object with this icon and use it to search for other objects. This function enables you to change objects quickly.

▶ **Check (Ctrl + F2)**
The current object is checked (statistical check of the source text according to syntax rules to ensure formal correctness). Depending on the condition of the object, this can be the active or inactive version. There is no automatic save.

---

3 Access rights do not refer to transport requests, but rather to exiting the object or making changes to the display.

▶ **Activate (Ctrl + F3)**
The current object is activated, that is, the inactive version is changed to an active version[4] that is visible and available to all. The object is saved.

▶ **Where-used list (Ctrl + Shift + F3)**
The **Where-used list** can be executed on objects when you want to know wherever the objects have been employed.

Unfortunately, the **Where-used list** cannot be used for all objects within the BSP application development, that is, there are limitations to its use.

▶ **Test/Execute (F8)**
The page is loaded into the browser. It is advisable to activate the object before loading.

▶ **Display object list (Ctrl + Shift + F5)**
Shows the object list in the object list area for the object currently displayed in the tools area (see Section 4.1).

▶ **Display navigation window (Ctrl + Shift + F4)**
The navigation window (see Section 4.1) is displayed below the tools area.

▶ **Full screen on/off (Shift + F12)**
Shows/hides the Object Browser and object list. The tools area is expanded as needed.

▶ **Application help (Ctrl + F8)**
Opens the online Help.

▶ **Set/Delete Breakpoint (Ctrl+ Shift + F12)**
Sets a breakpoint in the row where the cursor is currently located. If a breakpoint cannot be set in this row because the row contains no command keyword, the breakpoint is set in the first preceding row that meets this condition.

▶ **Template (Ctrl + F6)**
This button enables you to have pattern calls (e.g., from function modules or methods) pregenerated.

This functionality is not available for the layout section of BSP pages.

4 For a more in-depth introduction to the activation concept in the SAP R/3 system, please refer to the online Help.

► **Pretty Printer (Shift + F1)**

The *Syntax Beautifier* formats the code listings. This functionality is particularly useful for BSP extensions and ABAP coding. For HTML coding, there is no Pretty Printer functionality.

► **Signature (Ctrl + Shift + F10)**

The signature stands for the combination of the formal parameters and their properties, which "describe" the object interface. Regarding the Event Handler, all available runtime objects are displayed (see Figure 4.17). Double-clicking on an object reference leads to the corresponding interface with the description of all the methods.

| Page | default_us.htm | | Active | |
|---|---|---|---|---|
| Properties | Layout | Event Handler | Page Attributes | Type Definitions | Preview |

OnInitialization

| Typ | Parameter | Type Assgn. |
|---|---|---|
| | RUNTIME | TYPE REF TO IF_BSP_RUNTIME |
| | APPLICATION | TYPE REF TO Z_CL_FLIGHT |
| | PAGE_CONTEXT | TYPE REF TO IF_BSP_PAGE_CONTEXT |
| | PAGE | TYPE REF TO IF_BSP_PAGE |
| | REQUEST | TYPE REF TO IF_HTTP_REQUEST |
| | RESPONSE | TYPE REF TO IF_HTTP_RESPONSE |

```
* event handler for data retrieval
* local data objects
DATA: lv_persnumber TYPE ad_persnum,
      lv_name_first TYPE ad_namefir,
      lv_name_last  TYPE ad_namelas.

* get personal number
SELECT SINGLE persnumber
       FROM  usr21
       INTO  lv_persnumber
       WHERE bname = sy-uname.

IF sy-subrc = 0.
* get complete user name - firstname and lastname
  SELECT SINGLE name_first name_last
         FROM  adrp
         INTO  (lv_name_first, lv_name_last)
         WHERE persnumber = lv_persnumber.

  IF sy-subrc = 0.
```

| Li 1, Co 1 | Ln 1 - Ln 21 of 29 lines |

**Figure 4.17** The signature of an event handler

**Editor toolbar**  Unlike the Application toolbar, the *Editor toolbar* (see Figure 4.18) makes functions available that are directly associated with the Editor.

The keyboard shortcuts are identical to those used in Microsoft programs.

**Figure 4.18** The Editor toolbar

▶ **Cut (Ctrl + X)**

The selected source code is copied to the clipboard and removed from the coding.

▶ **Copy (Ctrl + C)**

The selected source code is copied to the clipboard.

▶ **Paste (Ctrl + V)**

The contents of the clipboard are inserted into the place where the cursor is located in the source code.

▶ **Undo (Ctrl + Z)**

The last change is undone.

▶ **Redo (Ctrl + Y)**

The last change that was undone is done again.

▶ **Find/Replace (Ctrl + F)**

Enables you to search for particular strings, especially in large source texts.

The standard operating-system functionality is used.

▶ **Find Next (Ctrl + G)**

The string entered in a Find/Replace search is searched again.

▶ **Load from a local file**

The contents of a local file are inserted into the source code of the page.

The contents that are loaded completely replace the previous contents. As long as these contents are not saved, you can restore the original status by exiting the Editor. Therefore, we recommend that you check the local file beforehand.

▶ **Save as local file**

The contents of the current window are saved locally on the client as an ASCII file.

Only the contents of the current window are saved, which means, for example, that this method is not suitable for saving a complete BSP page.

All functionalities of the Editor toolbar are also available in the context menu.

**Context menu**

## 4.2.2 Version Management

Advantages *Version Management* is an important utility and is available to all objects of the ABAP Workbench. There are various reasons for using Version Management. From the developer's point of view, the following advantages are particularly noteworthy:

▶ **Control**

The developer can get an overview of which "change cycles" his or her developments have undergone.

▶ **Restore**

Where necessary, old versions can be restored. This restoration of old versions is useful, for example, when further developments of the coding prove to be impractical or erroneous.

Version Management can be easily reached from the Web Application Builder (WAB) using the menu bar. The **Utilities Versions** menu option offers the following submenus:

▶ **Version Management**

This submenu enables you to open the Version Overview. There are two databases (see Figure 4.19), in which the versions are stored:

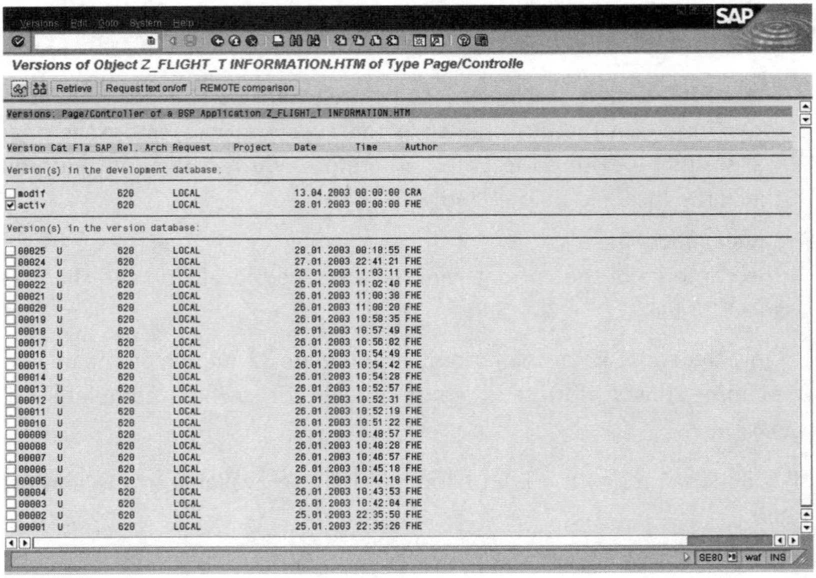

**Figure 4.19** Version Overview within Version Management

► **Development Database**

In this database, both the current active versions and the inactive versions are stored.

► **Version Database**

In this database, which is displayed under the Development Database, the historical versions are stored. Different kinds of information are displayed here, such as the time and release status of the version's creation. Additionally, the corresponding transport request (either for the imported version or the request where the object is currently being edited) is displayed if it exists. Another important column is *Type*. Here you will find how the version was created. "U" means *user requested*; "I" means *imported*.

The following functions can be accessed via the Application toolbar (see Figure 4.20):

► **Display (F7)**

The selected version is shown in the editor in display mode.

► **Compare (F8)**

A comparison can be displayed if two versions are selected. Different representations can be selected for a better overview.

► **Retrieve (Ctrl + F5)**

The selected version is restored.

The current version in the editor is permanently deleted.

► **Request text on/off (F6)**

More information can be shown.

► **REMOTE comparison (Shift + F8)**

Executes the same functionality as Compare. However, a remote target system can be selected here.

The print function is also available in the menu bar.

| &ℓ₀ 🔠 | Retrieve | Request text on/off | REMOTE comparison |

**Figure 4.20** The Application toolbar within Version Management

► **Generate version**

A "snapshot" of the current development status is taken and stored in the Version Database.

The active, not the inactive, version is saved. Therefore, it is recommended that you check beforehand to determine whether the current version is activated.

► **Return to active version**

The active version is loaded from the Development Database. Intermediate changes to the coding can be lost here.

 If an object is successfully transported, temporary versions from the Version Database are deleted.

### 4.2.3 MIME Repository

In the *MIME Repository*, one of the Web tools and an area of the database, all MIMEs are stored as objects, which are also integrated into the development environment. In this way, MIMEs can be grouped in transport requests and transported together with the application.

There are many objects that the SAP Web AS accepts as MIME objects. The object name extension is of importance for organizing. You can find a complete list in Appendix A.4.

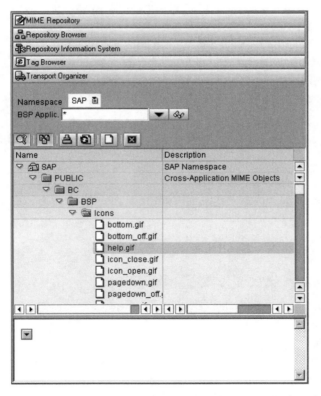

**Figure 4.21** Navigation in the MIME Repository with a display of a selected MIME Object

Navigation is achieved by using a browser that displays MIME objects in a hierarchical structure. These MIME objects are arranged according to the scheme.

**Navigation using the Hierarchy Structure Display**

```
Namespace — BSP application name — Subfolder.
```

Below the browser area, two fields are available to help you narrow down the selection—here, a namespace and a BSP application can be set as defaults. The public folder with MIMEs available for all applications is always shown as the uppermost entry. An object can be selected by double-clicking.

In contrast with other tools, selected objects are not shown in the tools area, but rather below the browser area in the object list (see Figure 4.21).

All relevant functions can be executed using the context menu (see Figure 4.22). These functions include:

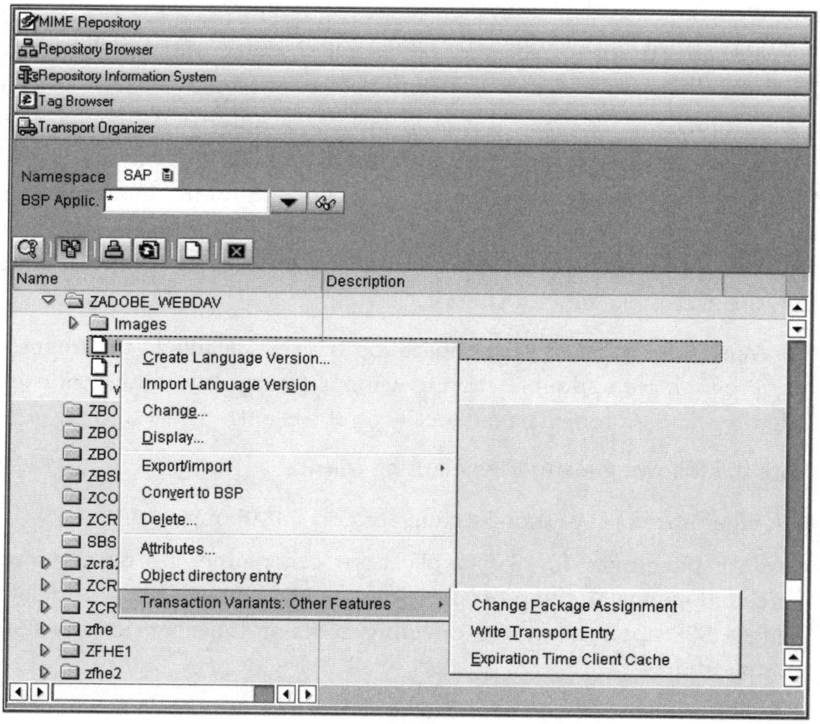

**Context menu**

**Figure 4.22** The context menu of MIME objects

- ► Creating subdirectories and objects
- ► Importing objects[5]
- ► Assigning transport entries
- ► Creating language versions[6]
- ► Editing and exporting objects locally
- ► Converting to BSP pages with flow logic

**Mass import**  A mass import of MIME objects through the WebDAV interface is possible. Instructions for this mass import are provided in Section 4.4. In this way, layout pages (e.g., in HTML, XHTML, or XML format) can be imported into the system. You will find the menu option **Convert to BSP** in the context menu to convert a MIME object to a BSP page.

MIME objects can be placed directly in the layout pages of BSP applications by dragging and dropping. In this case, the relevant path and the object name are inserted into the source text.

This importing of MIME objects also works for all BSP applications. For example, MIMEs from other BSP applications can be used in the own application.

 The authorization check is also valid for MIME objects! If an object of another application is used, the authorization check of the other application goes into effect for this object (see Section 4.3 for more information on service data settings). We recommend that you store objects applicable to more than one application in the *public* directory to ensure that they are accessible without checks.

**MIME list in the Repository browser**  The MIME object list of each application is also available in the Repository Browser. Here, double-clicking will not display, but rather will execute the standard tool assigned locally on the client.

**Special features**  Note the following features when using MIMEs:

- ► A where-used list cannot be generated on MIME objects.
- ► MIME directories for BSP applications can neither be created nor deleted manually. The procedure is automatic when creating or deleting a BSP application. The directory contains the name of the BSP application.
- ► MIME objects can also be moved or copied within the MIME Repository by dragging and dropping.

---

5  Several objects can also be selected simultaneously in a client folder.
6  Appropriately assigned MIME objects are used depending on the logon language.

## 4.2.4 Tag Browser

The *Tag Browser* displays all available tags for Web applications, which includes the tags of various versions of the page layout languages HTML, XHTML, WML, and XSLT, as well as the BSP extensions and *BSP directives*. You can place all tags in the layout window of BSP pages by dragging and dropping. In addition to the tags, the attributes are also displayed, when available.

With one exception, there are no context menus available. The exception applies where you can call documentation for BSP extensions.

You can restrict the number of tags displayed by selecting **Tags in BSP Pages** in the field below the browser area (see Figure 4.23).

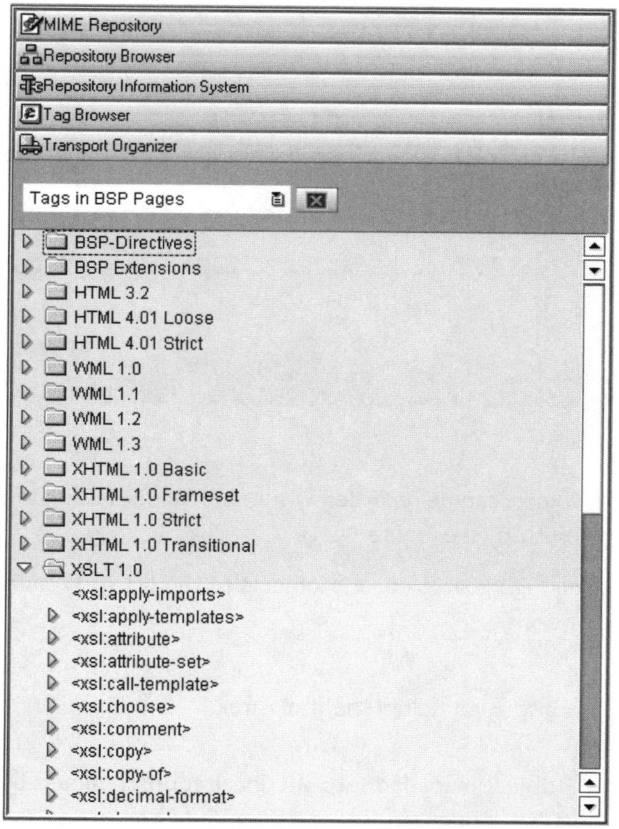

Figure 4.23 The Tag Browser

### 4.2.5 Theme Editor

In Section 3.3.1 we discussed the purpose of themes. In order for a MIME to be replaced at runtime, several conditions must be met: a theme has to be created; replacement definitions of objects must be assigned; and finally, the theme of a BSP application must also be signed.

**Creating a theme**
You can access the Theme Editor using the **Other Object ...** function in the application toolbar. Here, a new object can be created, or an existing theme can be selected and edited.

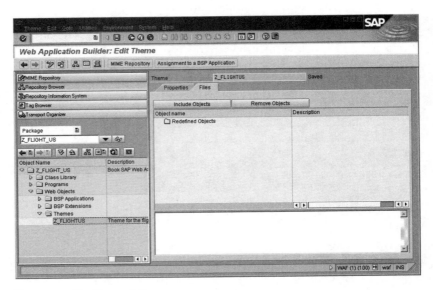

**Figure 4.24** The Theme Editor

In the Theme Editor, objects can be recorded within the tab files using the **Include Objects** pushbutton (see Figure 4.24).

The context menu (see Figure 4.25) of the objects in the list of themes offers the following options:

▶ Display
The MIME object is displayed below the tools area.

▶ Change
The selected MIME object is loaded into the local editor assigned by the client (this must be configured in the appropriate context of the operating system). Changes are applied after exiting the editor using a security prompt.

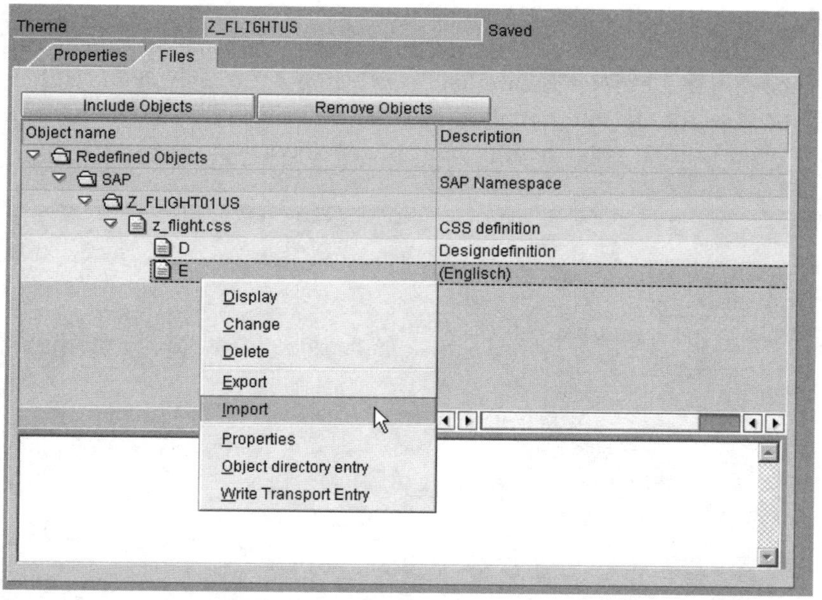

| Theme | Z_FLIGHTUS | Saved |
|---|---|---|

Properties | Files

| Include Objects | Remove Objects |
|---|---|

| Object name | Description |
|---|---|
| ▽ 🗁 Redefined Objects | |
| ▽ 🗁 SAP | SAP Namespace |
| ▽ 🗁 Z_FLIGHT01US | |
| ▽ 🗋 z_flight.css | CSS definition |
| 🗋 D | Designdefinition |
| 🗋 E | (Englisch) |

- Display
- Change
- Delete
- Export
- Import
- Properties
- Object directory entry
- Write Transport Entry

**Figure 4.25** Theme Editor—the context menu

▶ **Delete**
The selected object is deleted from the context of the theme.

▶ **Export**
The selected object is exported to the local client.

▶ **Import**
The object for redefinition is transferred from the local client to the server and stored as a *physical object* (*PHIO*).

By double-clicking on the object afterwards, you can ensure that the original object has indeed been redefined.

▶ **Properties**
A variety of information on the object can be displayed.

▶ **Object directory entry**
Assignment to a package and administrator can be changed.

▶ **Write transport entry**
The object can be assigned a transport request.[7]

All changes only occur on the pages of the BSP application when the theme of the particular BSP application is explicitly assigned. There are the following two options:

---

7  MIME objects are not automatically transported.

▶ **Properties tab of the BSP application**

On the Properties tab of the BSP application, the name of a theme can be entered into the **Theme** field (see Figure 4.26). This theme is then used as the default theme during runtime, unless it is redefined by a client-specific assignment (see list item below).

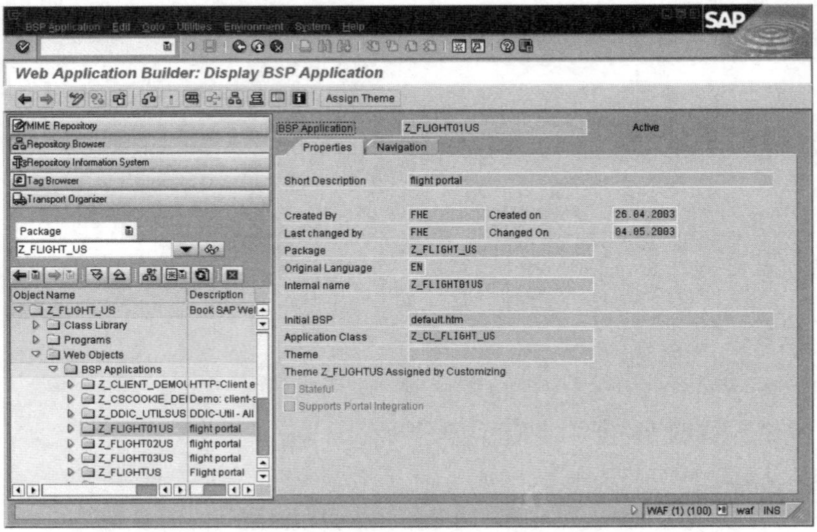

**Figure 4.26** Assignment of a theme on the Properties tab of a BSP application

▶ **Assignment using "Assign theme"**

From the menu option **Goto Assign Theme**, the BSP application can be assigned a theme. This assignment takes place without changing the BSP application itself and is client-specific. During runtime, it controls a theme entered in the Properties tab of the BSP application.

By clicking the **Assignment to a BSP Application** pushbutton (see Figure 4.24) located in the application toolbar, you can automatically assign the theme to several BSP applications.

If language versions have been set to a MIME object, each one of these language versions can be assigned its own object for a more refined definition. Figure 4.27 shows an example. Here, the MIME *flag_small.jpg*, which is available in two language versions, is "layered" according to the separate languages designated in the refined definition. Therefore, themes can be multilingual and correspondingly flexible.

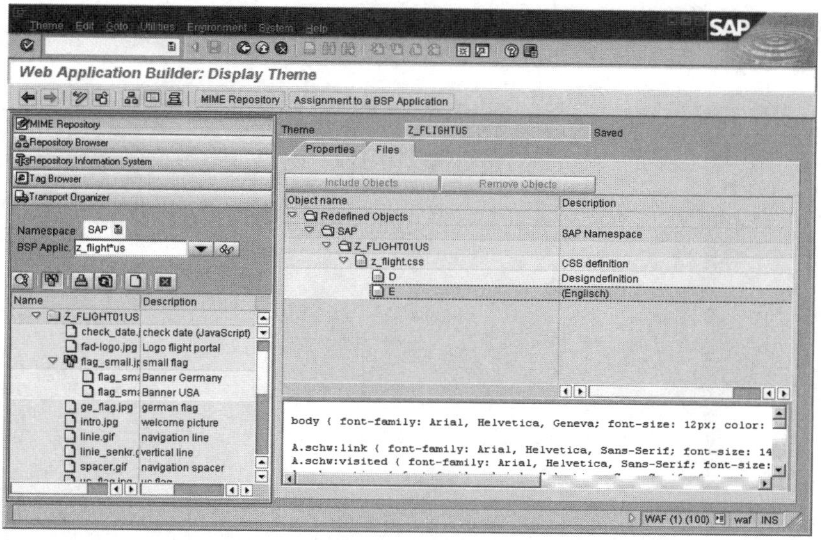

![Web Application Builder: Display Theme screenshot showing MIME Repository, theme Z_FLIGHTUS, properties and files including redefined objects and CSS definition](screenshot)

**Figure 4.27** Theme—refined definition in language versions of a MIME object

## 4.3 Service maintenance

A BSP application can be remotely accessed only by maintaining a service order and its activation. On the one hand, services store the necessary security requirements and logon data for the particular application. The goal is to allow only authorized Web access to the system. On the other hand, the connection between the URL and the HTTP request handler is established. Along with the service maintenance, useful tools for monitoring and troubleshooting will also be introduced.

**Purpose**

### 4.3.1 Services

The maintenance of services takes place through Transaction SICF. The services are maintained in the form of a hierarchy structure starting from the default host. In Figure 4.28, a few existing services are listed. They can be found under the `sap` services (SAP namespace).

Customers and partners who have their own namespaces available should have a node on the highest level of the HTTP service hierarchy. This node should be labeled with the customer's name. Now, all of their own services can be placed in this node.

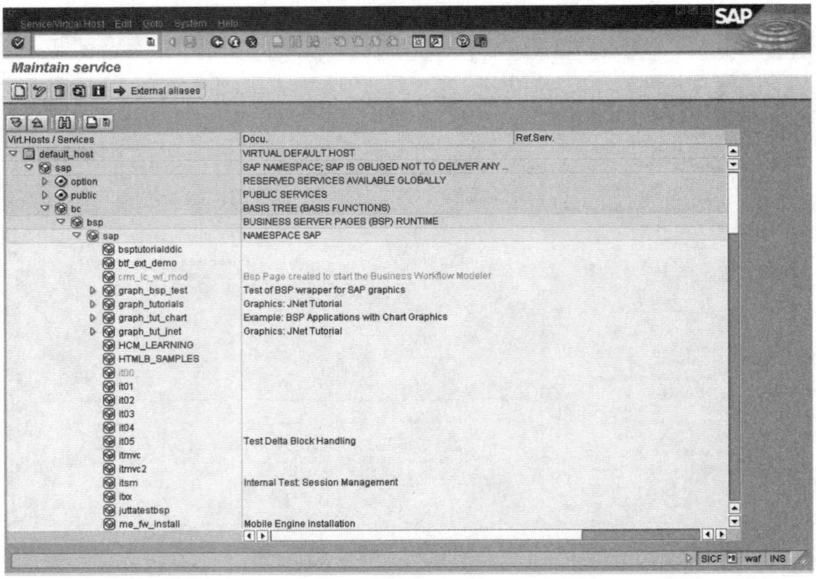

Figure 4.28 Maintaining services

**Creating services**

Since Release 6.20 of the SAP Web AS, node entries are automatically created and activated in the ICF service hierarchy for newly created BSP applications. (The name of the corresponding service node relates to the name of the BSP application.) In Release 6.10, this was not the case—services still had to be created manually. If you want to use these older applications with Release 6.20, you must select the particular BSP application. Double-clicking on the BSP application opens it. A message will be displayed, which should be confirmed. Finally, a transport request is assigned. In the background, the corresponding service is created. The activation state of this service is inherited from the superior level service.

A service name can contain a maximum of 15 characters. Prior to Release 6.20, BSP applications could be created whereby the name length was greater than 15 characters. In this case, it is advisable to copy these BSP applications to an application with a shorter name so that these services can be automatically created.

Of course, a service can also be created manually. This is necessary, for instance, when the corresponding service for a BSP application is missing. In the Web browser, you would see the following error message: BSP exception: »Cannot start application xxx. Use Transaction SICF to create an application node.«

To create a service manually, select the appropriate place in the service hierarchy and create a service using the **New Sub-element** context menu. In the pop-up window that opens, enter both the name of the service and the service element (in this case a standalone service) selected (see Figure 4.29).

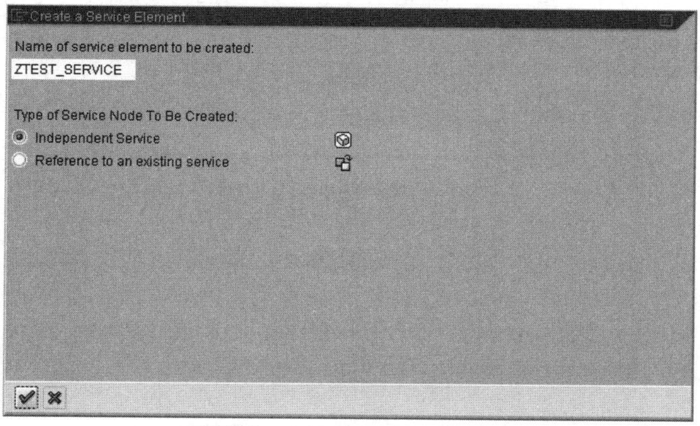

**Figure 4.29** Manual creation of a service

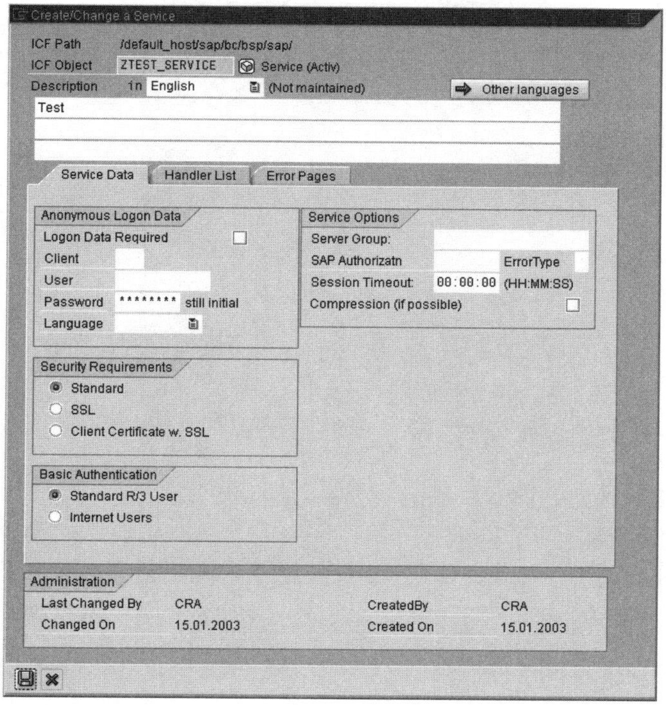

**Figure 4.30** Defining properties of a service

When the entry has been confirmed, another window opens, in which you can enter the detailed settings for the service (see Figure 4.30).

The window for the service to be created contains some interesting information and allows the properties to be updated. First, the ICF path and the ICF object are shown. For each service, a language-dependent description can be stored. Below that there are three updateable areas, which you can access via the tabs: **Service Data**, **Handler List**, and **Error Pages**. The **Service Data** tab sets the logon data and necessary security requirements required for this service. We have already extensively introduced the **Service Data** tab (see Section 2.5.1). In the **Error Pages** tab, which we have also previously introduced, you can create separate error pages for logon or application errors, as well as store redirects to other pages. However, the **Handler List** tab has yet to be described. One or several HTTP request handlers can be stored here (see Section 2.3), which are called up consecutively to edit the service. You can control these request handlers by using the return code during programming (see Figure 4.31).

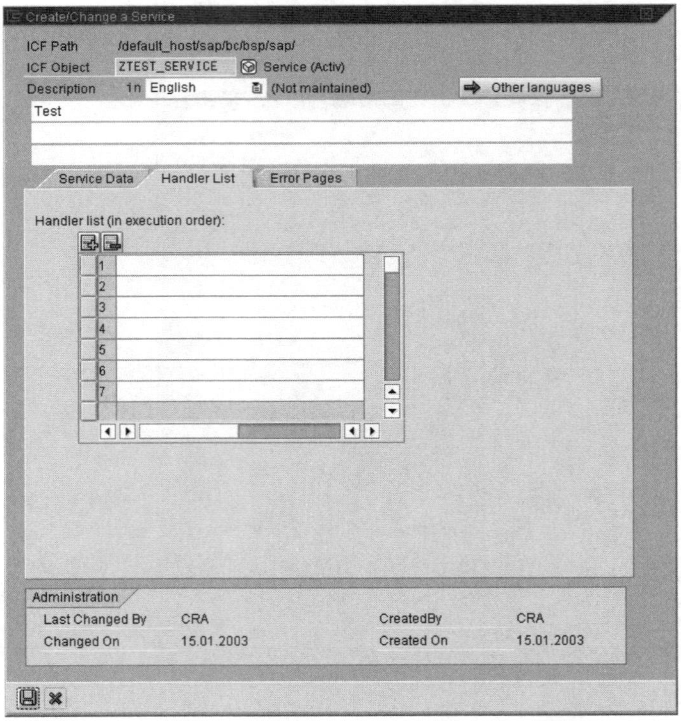

**Figure 4.31** The Handler List of a service

In this case, there is no handler entered that can answer a corresponding request. Therefore, a corresponding handler in the superior node is searched. In this example, a service was created below the service for processing `sap/bc/bsp` BSP applications. Behind this service, the HTTP request handler `CL_HTTP_EXT_BSP`, supplied by SAP, is defined for processing BSP applications. This handler is then used when the URL is called. When automatically generating a service for a BSP application, the system also creates the corresponding entry just below this service.

When installing the SAP Web AS, various kinds of Web applications are included by default. The corresponding services are automatically stored in the service hierarchy (also known as the *HTTP Service hierarchy*). However, these corresponding services are initially deactivated by default. Also supplied is the aforementioned service for executing BSP applications under `sap/bc/bsp`. In order to use the applications that you want, they must be manually activated (as explained below).

A service supplied in the standard installation is the ping service. This service can test whether the SAP Web AS is accessible. The ping service can be found under `sap/public/ping`. All services on the public node[8] are different from the typical services offered in that a system user must log on. The results of the public ping service are displayed in Figure 4.32.

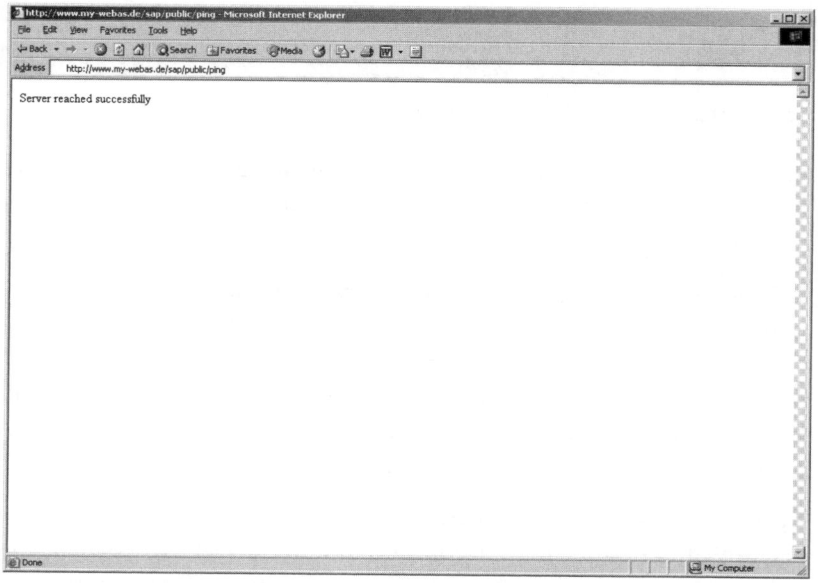

**Figure 4.32** Calling the ping service

---

8  No separate services can be set directly below the public node.

Services, if they are created as a component of a package, are linked to the Change and Transport System. If anonymous logon data is stored in the service, it will be deleted during transport.

**Activation and deactivation of services**

Only activated services can be executed remotely through a Web browser. Should you access a deactivated service, an error message is displayed in the browser (see Figure 4.33).

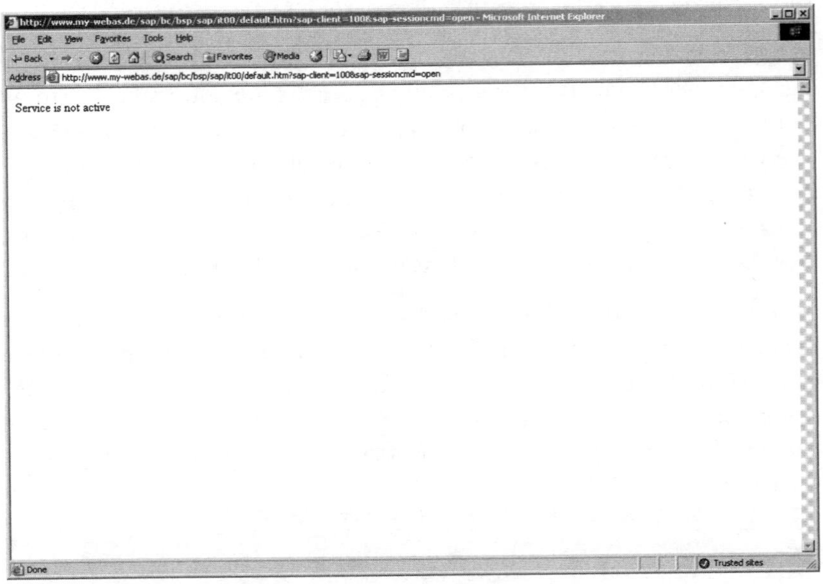


**Figure 4.33** Accessing a BSP application with a deactivated service entry

All active services are displayed in a black font; all deactivated services are displayed in a gray font; and all subservices of deactivated services are displayed in a blue font (see Figure 4.34).

In Figure 4.34, the `sap/bc/bsp/sap` service, including all of its subservices, is deactivated. For this reason, this service is colored gray and the services under it are blue (e.g., `sap/bc/bsp/sap/it05`). The `sap/bc/bsp/sap/it00` service remains gray, that is, deactivated, since this service had already been deactivated earlier. In the example in Figure 4.34, the `sap/public` service remains an active service.

If you want to activate or deactivate a service, follow these instructions: Ensure that the required service is located in the HTTP Service hierarchy and then select this service. You can now set up the service using the context menu. A pop-up window opens, in which you must designate the extent of the activation or deactivation (see Figure 4.35 for an example of an activation).

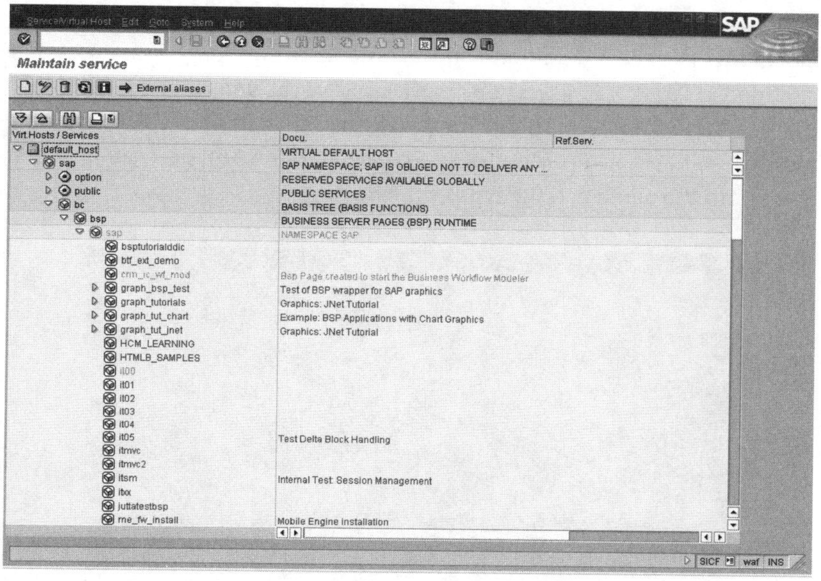

**Figure 4.34** Activated and deactivated services in the HTTP service hierarchy

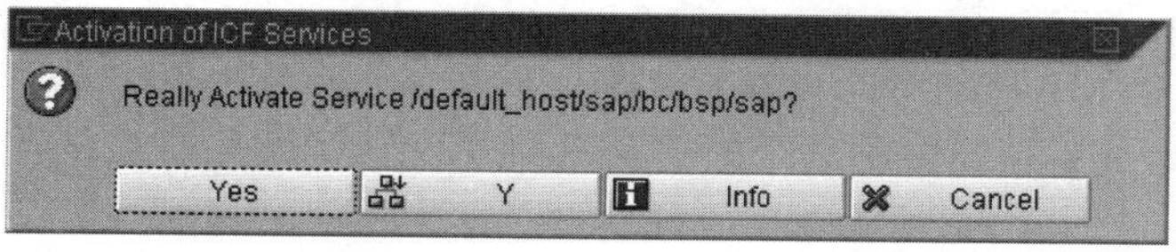

**Figure 4.35** Activation of a service

If you select **Yes**, only the selected service itself will be activated or deactivated. If you select **Yes** with the hierarchy structure icon, all services under this service (subservices) will be activated or deactivated.

Do not delete a service in order to block external access to a BSP application. Deactivating the corresponding service will suffice. In particular, services supplied by SAP should not be deleted; instead, they should be deactivated if they are not required.

Because activated services represent a security risk if they can be remotely accessed via HTTP, you should ensure that only those services that are actually required are activated, and that only users with the corresponding rights have access to these services.

**Virtual Hosts**   The SAP Web AS supports the concept of virtual hosts and virtual servers. In this context, a server can be addressed with different host/port combinations. The standard host is represented in the HTTP service hierarchy by the default host, which corresponds to the virtual host with the number 0. In the SAP Web AS, each virtual host corresponds to a separate ICF service hierarchy. To create additional hosts, the corresponding system profile parameter (is/HTTP/virt_host_<n>, in this case) must be set up. When this parameter has been set up, a new virtual host can be created using the toolbar. Then, a pop-up window opens (see Figure 4.36), prompting you to enter both the name and the type of the host.

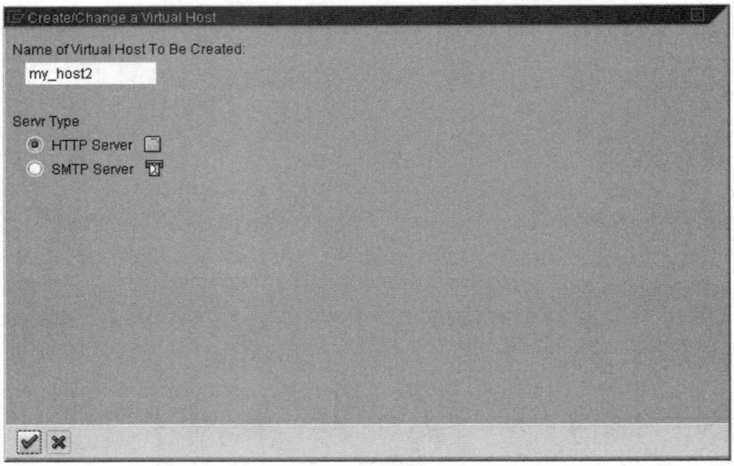

**Figure 4.36**  Creating a virtual host

When you have created a virtual host, you can update different attributes of the host (see Figure 4.37). In addition to the description of the virtual host, you can capture host data, including the number of the host from the profile parameters, service data, error pages, and also a default service.

In addition to the virtual host, internal and external aliases play an important role as additional service elements. In principle, an alias corresponds to a reference to a service entry within the ICF hierarchy. The advantage of an alias is that it enables you to access the corresponding BSP application with an abbreviated URL.

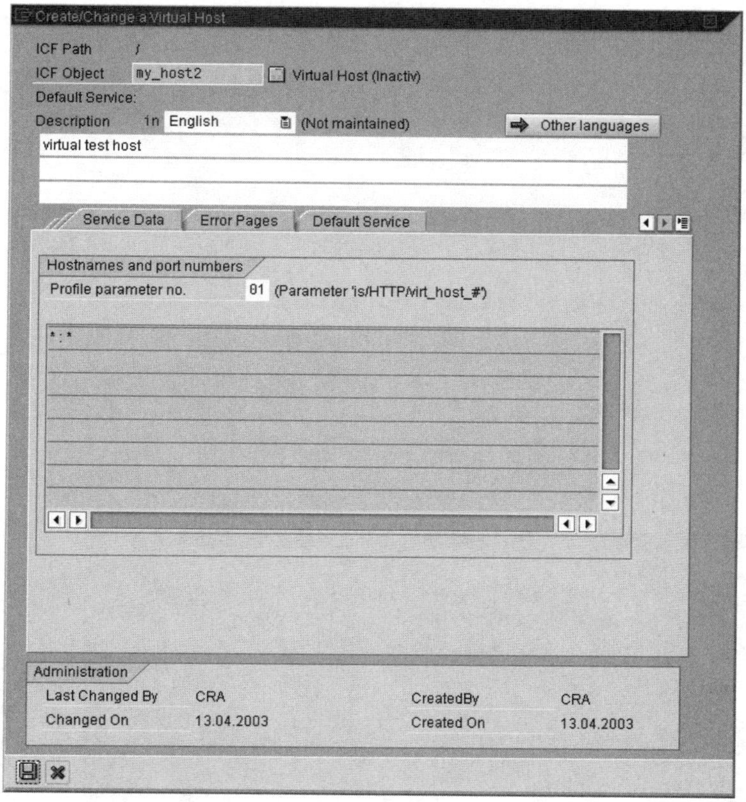

**Figure 4.37** Setting the properties of a virtual host

Internal alias

Creating an internal alias is similar to creating a typical ICF service. First, the position in the HTTP Service hierarchy should be marked. In this case, by using **New Sub-element** in the context menu, an alias is created in an existing service (see Figure 4.38).

After selecting the **Alias** option and entering the name, the properties of the alias can be updated in the next window (see Figure 4.39).

Next to the familiar tabs for maintaining service data and error pages you'll find a reference to a service in the ICF hierarchy in the **Alias Trgt** tab. In this example, the ping service is selected. Next, the alias must be activated. Now, using the alias, the ping service can also be addressed with the following URL:

*http://www.my-webas.de/sap/my_alias*

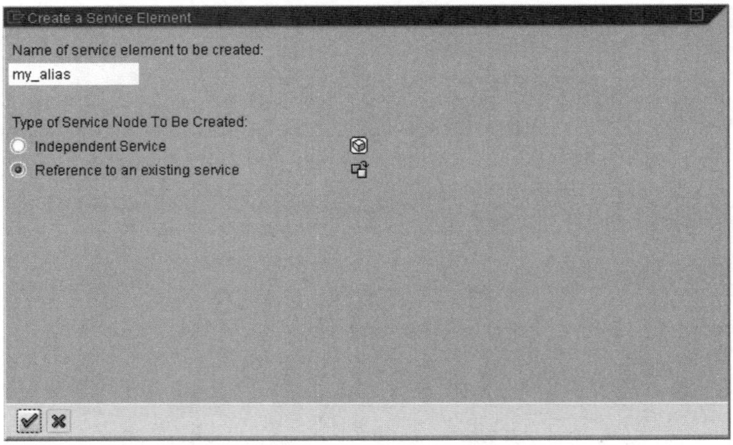

**Figure 4.38** Creating an internal alias

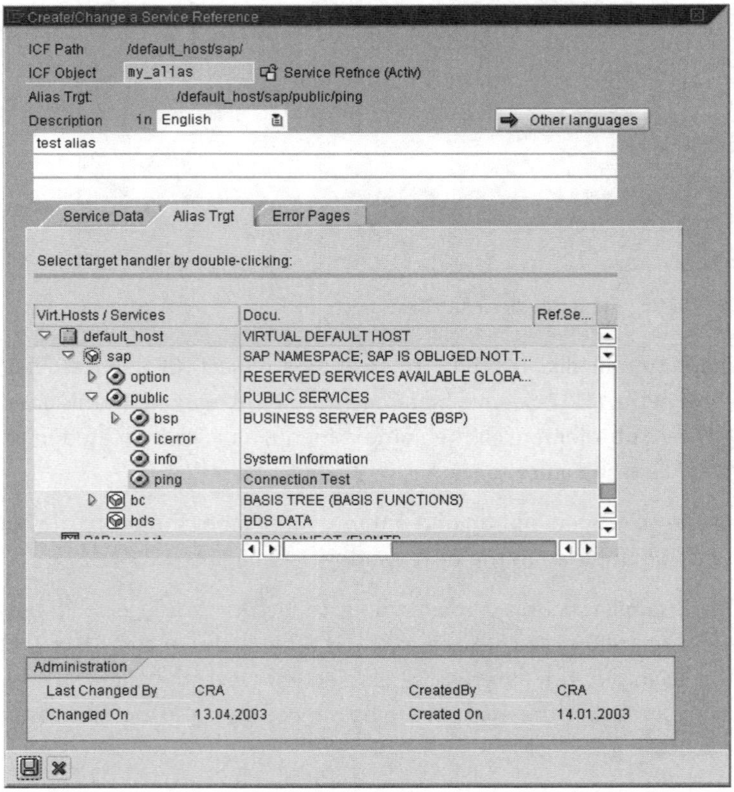

**Figure 4.39** Setting the alias target for an internal alias

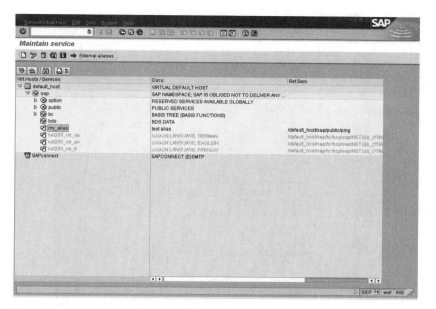

**Figure 4.40** An internal alias in the ICF hierarchy

When the URL is resolved, this request is then redirected to the ping service using the alias defined. The alias created is shown in Figure 4.40.

In addition to an internal alias, you can also create an external alias. An external alias can also refer to a service within the ICF service hierarchy. However, when assigning a name, you must adhere to the following schema:

**External alias**

```
/name1/name2/name3/...
```

One particular advantage to an external alias is the freedom allowed in assigning a name to the alias. In doing so, path names are more user-friendly, that is, the naming convention is not linked to the ICF path entries.

To create an external alias, the corresponding maintenance interface should be changed. This can be done by clicking the **External aliases** button. Now the cursor is positioned on the default host and the context menu is called. Select the menu option **Create new External Alias**. In the window that opens, the properties of the external alias can be set in the **Service data**, **Trg Element,** and **Error Pages** tabs (see Figure 4.41). In the **Trg Element** tab, open the service to be edited by double-clicking. In this case, the ping service is again selected as an example.

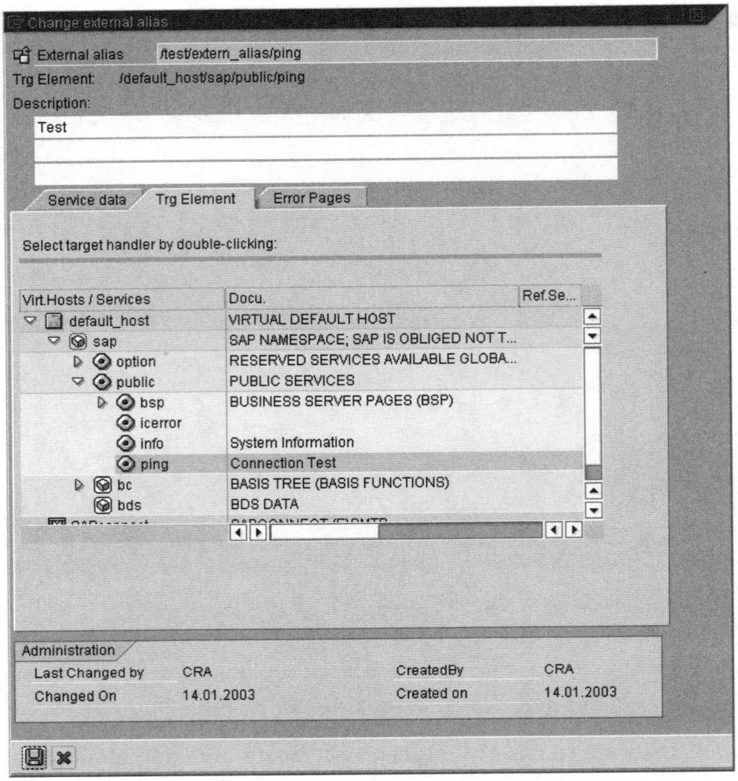

**Figure 4.41** Updating the properties of an external alias

By clicking the **Save** button, the external alias is created (see Figure 4.42).
Calling the ping service using the external alias can be done as follows:

*http://www.my-webas.de/test/extern_alias/ping*

Otherwise, an external alias is treated like an internal alias. The string of
the external alias in the URL of the incoming request is evaluated and
assigned an alias. Next, the service assigned to this alias is called, that is,
the HTTP request handler is defined in this service.

An external alias can be transported by selecting the menu option **External alias · Manual Transport Connection** or by clicking the pushbutton
with the transport icon.

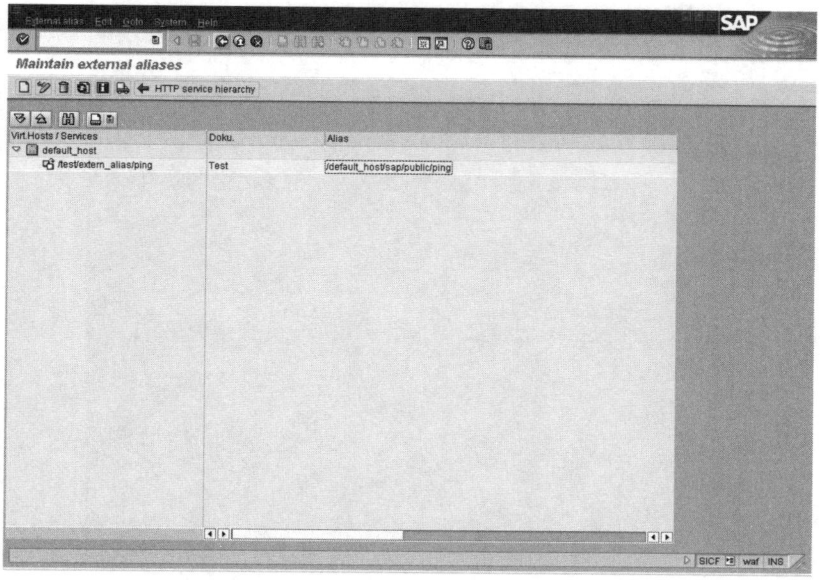

Maintain external aliases

HTTP service hierarchy

| Virt.Hosts / Services | Doku. | Alias |
|---|---|---|
| default_host | | |
| /test/extern_alias/ping | Test | /default_host/sap/public/ping |

SICF  waf  INS

**Figure 4.42**  An external alias

You cannot create further subservices or sub-aliases in the ICF service hierarchy beneath the alias created. Essentially, an alias does not differentiate between uppercase and lowercase letters.

The service data of an alias controls the service data of the corresponding service. Therefore, the need to control logon data could be a reason for creating an alias. An existing service can then be accessed with other logon data or another logon procedure.

When you select the **Edit Parse URL** menu option, you'll discover an interesting utility. For a particular URL, this utility allows you to see how it will be parsed in the HTTP service hierarchy when searching for services, aliases, and so forth. The example in Figure 4.43 shows how a URL is parsed.

**URL parsing**

Transaction SICF also provides a variety of tools, which support monitoring and troubleshooting in Web applications. These tools includes HTTP debugging, trace, and the runtime analysis, which are described in the following sections.

**Tools for monitoring and troubleshooting**

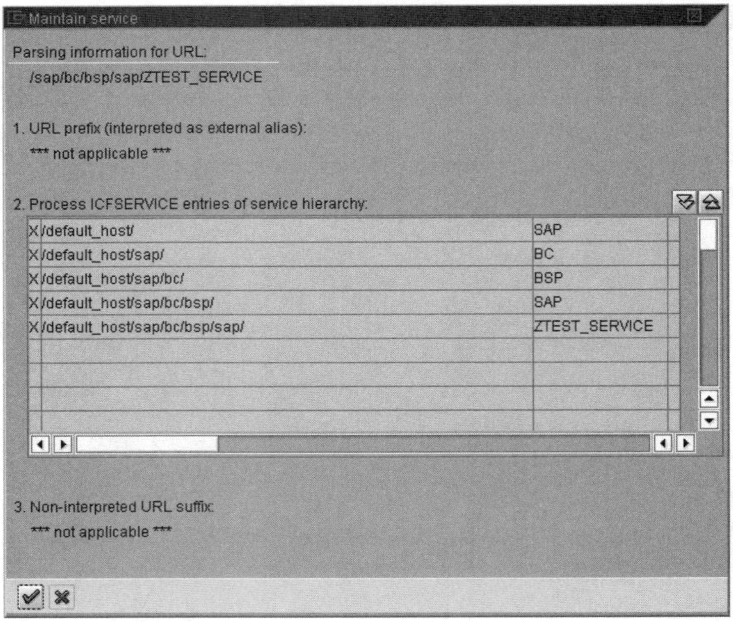

**Figure 4.43** Parsing a URL in the ICF service hierarchy

## 4.3.2 HTTP Debugging

HTTP debugging for a particular user can be activated by selecting the **Edit Debugging** menu option. After debugging is activated, a new debugging mode is opened when you enter the appropriate URL. In this mode, the handler can be debugged. The window with the debugging settings allows you to enter the user, the duration of validity, and the optional setting of additional breakpoints (see Figure 4.44). If the check box **Only calls from SAP GUI-IP** is checked, the debugging will start only if the HTTP client's IP address and the SAP GUI are identical. The second check box activates the system debugging.

You can specify additional HTTP breakpoints on two occasions. In the first instance, both the virtual host and the URL path can be specified, and you can set a breakpoint in the first rows of the HTTP request handlers of the corresponding service. In the second instance, the handler class itself can be specified. In this case, you set an HTTP breakpoint in the first rows of this handler class.

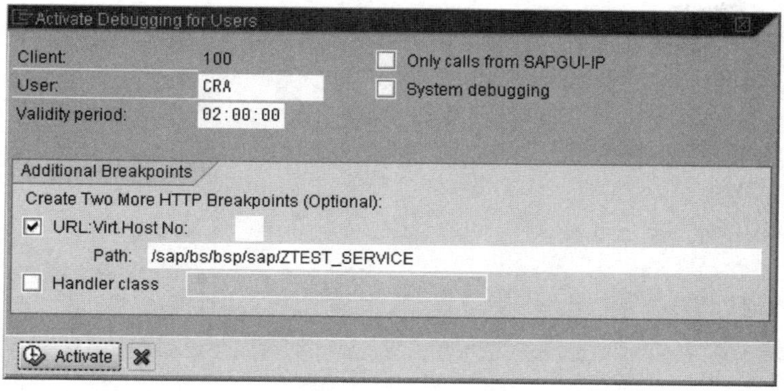

**Figure 4.44** Activating HTTP debugging for users

If debugging fails to launch in spite of the aforementioned settings, check the following:

▶ Whether the current client matches the user's client, which should be activated for debugging

▶ Whether the user specified in the service is also the user specified for debugging in the local settings

### 4.3.3 Trace

The function of a *trace* is to record different kinds of technical information that have been collected during the execution of an application. This information can then be used in error analysis and troubleshooting. To turn the trace on, select the **Edit Trace** menu option. In the Activate Trace for URL window, you can enter the protocol (HTTP or SMTP), the URL path in the ICF, the duration of validity, and the trace level (see Figure 4.45). If the **Only calls from SAP GUI-IP** check box is activated (checked), the trace will start only if the HTTP client's IP address and the SAP GUI are identical. By clicking on the **Activate** button to confirm that the IP address and the SAP GUI are identical, the trace is switched on.

To display the trace, select the **Edit Trace Display trace** menu option. Figure 4.46 shows an example of a user trace file.

Figure 4.45 Activating the trace for a URL

Figure 4.46 The trace file

### 4.3.4 Runtime Analysis

By using the runtime analysis, you can get an overview of a request's processing time. To activate the runtime analysis, select the **Edit Runtime Analysis** menu option. In the **Activate Runtime Analysis for URL** window that opens (see Figure 4.47), you can define the protocol (HTTP or SMTP), the URL path in the ICF, and the duration of validity for the activation. After clicking on the **Activate** button to confirm, the runtime analysis is started. If the corresponding BSP application is started at this point, the runtime data is saved to a measurement data file.

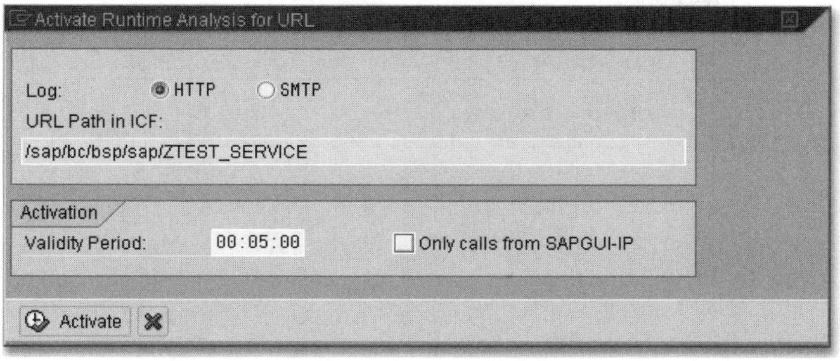

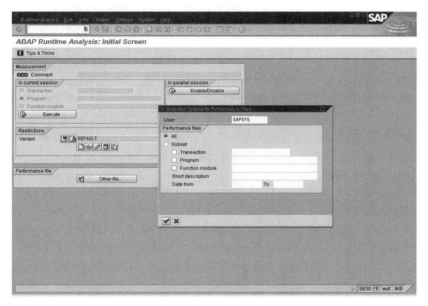

**Figure 4.47** Activating the runtime analysis for a URL

You can view the analysis using Transaction SE30. Click on the **Other file** button and enter *SAPSYS* in the User field (see Figure 4.48). A list of the recorded requests will be displayed in another window (see Figure 4.49).

**Figure 4.48** The results of a runtime analysis using Transaction SE30

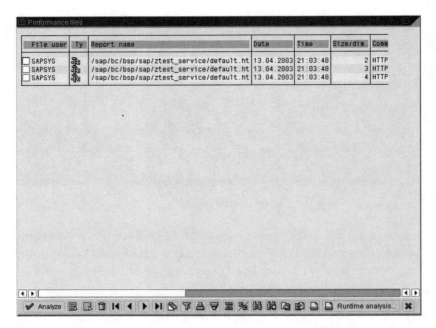

**Figure 4.49** The Measurement Data File with the available list of recorded requests

You can select an entry from this list and display it on a separate screen. The runtime analysis produced can consequently serve as a starting point for further optimizing the program coding (see Figure 4.50).

To get an overview of which functionalities discussed here are active on the system, a server monitor is available. To access this monitor, select the **Edit Server Monitor** menu option. Note that the overview (i.e., those functionalities listed as active) can be restricted to the local system or to the entire system. In this case, Figure 4.51 shows that no debugging, no trace, and one runtime session have been concurrently activated on the local system.

Because the monitoring and troubleshooting tools that we just introduced slow the system's performance and take up necessary system resources, you should activate the Runtime Analysis for only as long as is necessary.

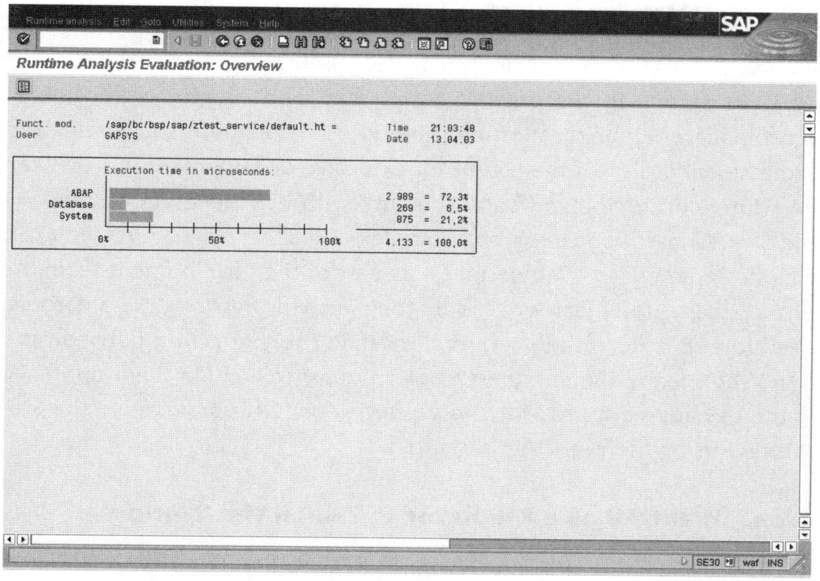

**Figure 4.50** The evaluation of a Runtime Analysis

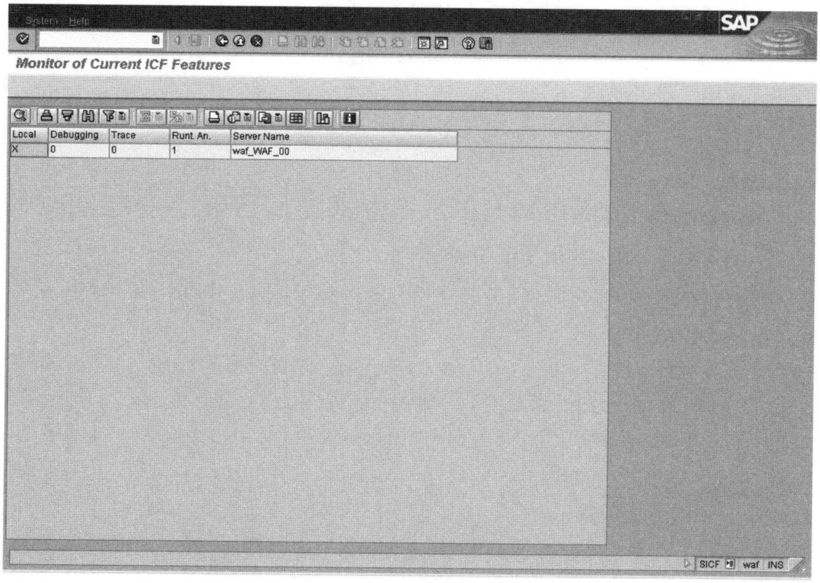

**Figure 4.51** The Server Monitor in ICF (local view)

## 4.4 WebDAV Interface

Professional layout design

A Web application is not limited to technical and functional points of view. In particular, the graphic design can ease or hinder the overall acceptance of an application by the end user. Yet the management and professional design of the layout for extensive development projects can be a time-consuming and confusing task with the tools that accompany the SAP Web AS. For designing complex and attractive layouts, you can include experienced Web designers as part of the development team. As a rule, these designers work with their own professional layout tools. Therefore, it is necessary to carefully define the interaction between the SAP Web AS and the designers' tools in order to include them optimally in the development process. The support required is provided in the SAP Web AS using the WebDAV interface.

### 4.4.1 WebDAV as a Mediator Between the Worlds

WebDAV

The standard *Web-based Distributed Authoring and Versioning* (*WebDAV*) was brought to life by companies such as Microsoft, Netscape, Novell, IBM, and Xerox, and since then has been developed and monitored by the independent IETF WebDAV Working Group.

WebDAV supports Web-based, collaborative work based on standard Internet technologies, by which the WWW protocol, HTTP, was extended by the appropriate services. These services are:

Services

▶ **Propfind**
Collects data (*Properties*) such as creation, date, and author names.

▶ **Overwrite protection/locking**
Prevents several users from working on a document concurrently.

▶ **Access control**
Manages the restrictions of access rights. The definition of the Web-DAV standard assumes that all WebDAV-capable applications support *HTTP Digest Authentication* (an authentication mechanism based on cryptographic hashes).

▶ **Version management**
Allows document versions to be managed. In doing so, important version statuses can be saved, either manually or automatically, for later access. Version management also enables several people to work on an object at the same time.

▶ **Namespace management/collections**

Ensures that all central components of a Web site, such as external images, are collected.

▶ **Advanced collections**

Provides a mechanism that can be used to display network resources in a hierarchical structure. *Ordered collections*, which are not restricted to HTTP resources, can, for example, be sorted and displayed automatically as specified by the client.

*Advanced collections* offer the additional option to reference. This referencing can be compared to a symbolic link in modern file systems. A file exists only once; however, it can appear to "physically" exist in different directories.

Through these executable services, WebDAV provides an infrastructure that enables developers without special knowledge to produce Web content using WebDAV-capable tools to collaborate on and to manage the content, without needing to use a specific client.

In order for this process to work, the SAP Web AS assumes the role of a WebDAV server and the corresponding design tool assumes the role of a WebDAV client. For this purpose, a WebDAV service runs on the application server, which requires a special HTTP request handler that implements the Web-DAV protocol via a remote connection. The WebDAV client/server scenario is displayed in Figure 4.52.

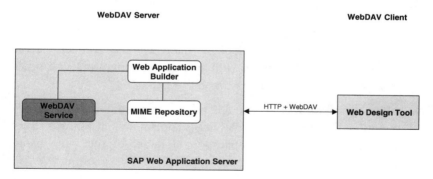

**Figure 4.52** WebDAV client and WebDAV server

The *Web Application Builder (WAB)* is the development environment on the SAP Web AS. Here, for example, the basic structure of a page can be implemented (the layout structure in particular, along with the business and flow logic) before it is processed with the design tool. Further editing of the pages with the external tool is accomplished with a Check-out/

Check-in mechanism via WebDAV. Finally, all MIME objects (e.g., graphics or new Web pages created with the external editor) are stored in the corresponding MIME directory of the BSP application in the MIME repository (see Section 4.2.3).

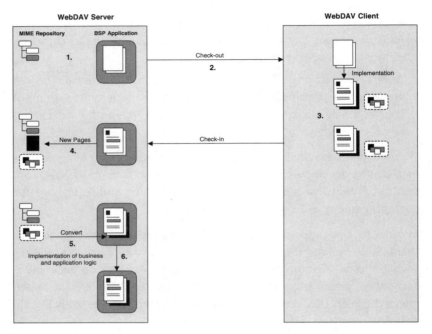

**Figure 4.53** The process of creating pages with external tools in WebDAV

The principal process, which is introduced in the following steps, shows the interaction between the WebDAV client and the WebDAV server when implementing Web pages with an external design tool. The separate stages of this process are illustrated in Figure 4.53.

**Principal process**

1. A BSP application with several BSP pages is created in the Web Application Builder (WAB). These BSP pages contain an initial layout structure. Similar to the BSP application, a folder of the same name (denoted by the dark-gray color of the BSP application and MIME directory) is created in the MIME repository.

2. These BSP pages should now be edited by an external tool. Therefore, the pages are now checked out—that is, they are locked for other users.

3. On the WebDAV client-side, editing can now take place—that is, the checked-out objects can be edited. In addition, new MIME objects, including static HTML pages, can be inserted. You can also use all the external editor's tools.

Finally, new Web pages (represented by the checkered or patterned Web page) can be created and saved.

4. The final Web pages and newly added MIME objects can be checked in again. In the process, the newly saved Web pages can be imported into the MIME repository as static pages. These Web pages will also be assigned to the BSP application package.

5. The static Web pages can now be converted to BSP pages, if necessary.

6. The layout of the BSP pages is now complete. The BSP pages can be finalized with the necessary business and application logic in the editor of the WAB.

The WebDAV service is implemented using the global ABAP class CL_HTTP_WEBDAV_SKWF. The corresponding service is maintained in Transaction SICF (see Section 4.3). The corresponding service path is sap/bc/bsp/bsp_dev (see Figure 4.54).

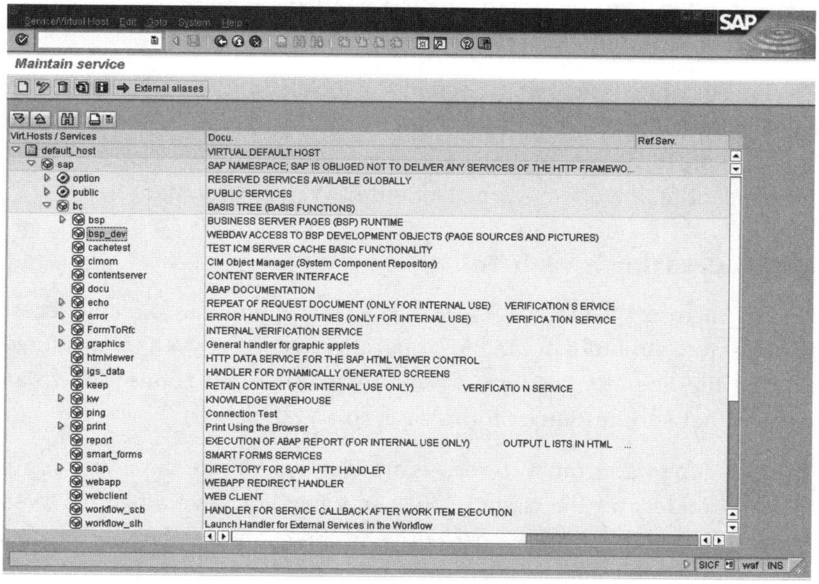

**Figure 4.54** The WebDAV service in Transaction SICF

In the standard installation, the handler is already correctly installed and as a rule should not be changed (apart from its activation). However, for security purposes it is advisable to provide access via the WebDAV with a password-protected logon.

**Locking files** Files that are currently being edited can be locked so that they are not changed by another member of the development team at the same time. The WebDAV client can set explicit locks on objects. If another user accesses a locked object, that user will receive a message alerting him or her that the object is locked. The object can then be opened only in *read-only* mode. Therefore, this check-in/check-out file system both increases productivity and fosters cooperation among the team members. When the page modifications are complete, the corresponding lock is lifted. The unlocked page is once again available to the development team for further editing.

With WebDAV's help, SAP Web AS provides the seamless integration of standard tools that also support WebDAV, such as Macromedia DreamWeaver, Adobe GoLive, and Microsoft Office. Many operating systems, such as Microsoft Windows 95/98/NT/2000/XP and Apple Mac OS X, as well as various Web servers, such as Apache and Microsoft IIS, support WebDAV. Therefore, a wide range of systems, infrastructures, and applications can be connected with WebDAV and represented as a single, virtual, and distributed file system.

**Adobe GoLive 6.0** For the example described in Section 4.4.3, Adobe GoLive Release 6.0 is used as the external design tool. With its native support for the WebDAV standard protocol, GoLive Release 6.0 provides all the functions required for efficient teamwork in a group-oriented Web environment.

### 4.4.2 Creating a Web Folder

**Web folders** Under Microsoft Windows 95/98/NT/2000/XP, you can directly access the directory structure of the BSP application using the Web folders function on the operating system. A Web folder creates a connection to an external network resource (in this case, to a Web server).[9]

The files and folders on Web servers are displayed in the same way as are files and folders on the client. However, when you save a file in a Web folder, it is saved not on the hard drive of the computer, but on the corresponding Web server.

---

9 Web folders are available only on Web servers that support WEC (Web Extender Client), FrontPage Extensions, or DAV (Distributed Authoring and Versioning) protocols.

In the following example, a Web folder will be created for access on the SAP Web AS (Web server). Web folders can be created under Microsoft Windows 95/98/NT/2000/XP in the *Network Neighborhood* folder using the Add Network Place Wizard (see Figure 4.55).[10]

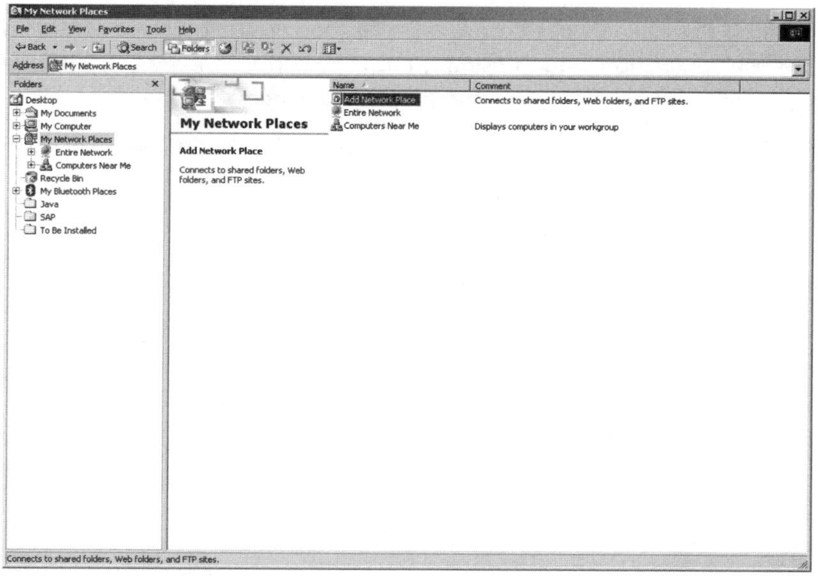

**Figure 4.55** Creating a Web folder using the Add Network Place Wizard

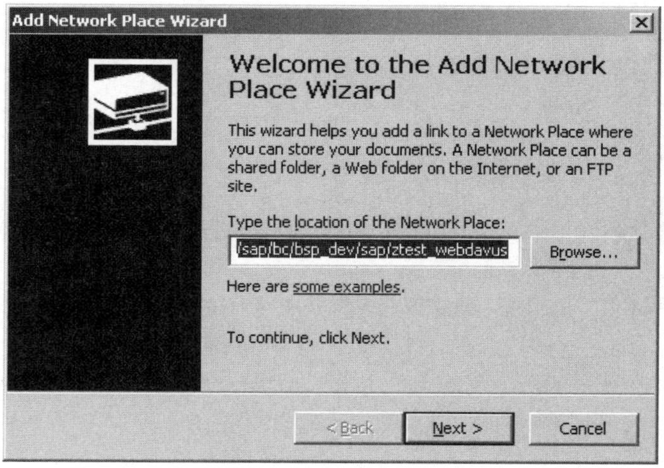

**Figure 4.56** Entering the path of the Web server

---

10 You can also create a web folder directly in Internet Explorer. However, this might cause some problems (see also Microsoft Knowledge Base, Article No. 290227)

When the Add Network Place wizard is started, a window opens, which prompts you for the location of the Web folder (see Figure 4.56).[11]

Now, enter the address of the BSP application in the following format:

*http://hostname/sap/bc/bsp_dev/sap/BSP-Applikation*

Because this URL usually corresponds to the URL that is used to access the BSP application, you can simply copy the corresponding URL into the input field above. Then make the following changes:

1. Replace the *bsp* service node with the *bsp_dev* WebDAV service.
2. Remove the URL mangling code in brackets.
3. Remove the BSP page name and any connected URL query string parameters (with the following exception; in some cases the client is necessary).

For example, the following URL

*http://www.my-webas.de/sap(jktxyBZ==)/bc/bsp/sap/ztest_webdav/ default.htm?sap-client=100&name=value*

should be changed to

*http://www.my-webas.de/sap/bc/bsp_dev/sap/ztest_webdav/*

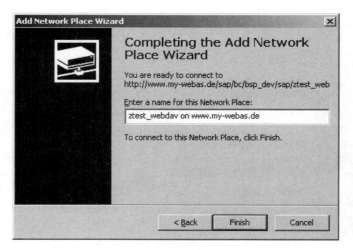

**Figure 4.57** Naming the Web folder

---

11  This example was done on a Windows 2000 system. The image may vary depending on the operating system used.

After confirming the location by clicking on the **Next** button, additional authentication may be required from the SAP Web AS, depending on how the service has been set up. Once this authentication has been confirmed, you can enter a name for the Web folder in the next window (see Figure 4.57).

By clicking on the **Finish** button, the Web folder is created in Network Neighborhood/My Network Places. In this folder, you will now find the MIME objects, BSP pages, page fragments, and views of the associated BSP application. In Figure 4.58, the objects in the development environment and the corresponding objects of the Web folder are listed. You can now edit these objects using the Web folder and the appropriate tools.

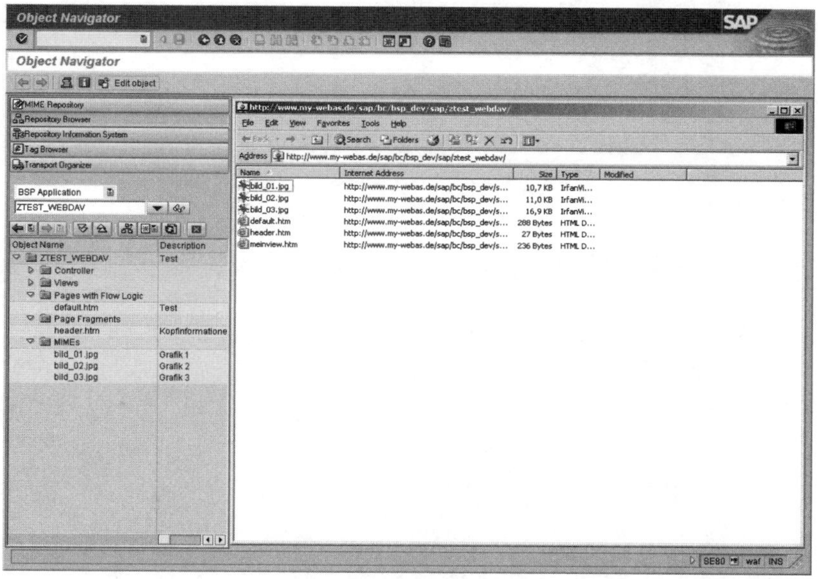

**Figure 4.58** An open Web folder

If new objects are copied to the Web folder, such as a new image or a new Web page, these objects are stored in the MIME application directory (see Figure 4.59 for an example of a new Web page).

**Inserting MIMEs**

This static Web page can now be converted to a BSP page (a page with flow logic). In order to do so, the page must be selected and the context menu opened. Start conversion by selecting the **Convert to BSP** menu option on the context menu (see Figure 4.60).

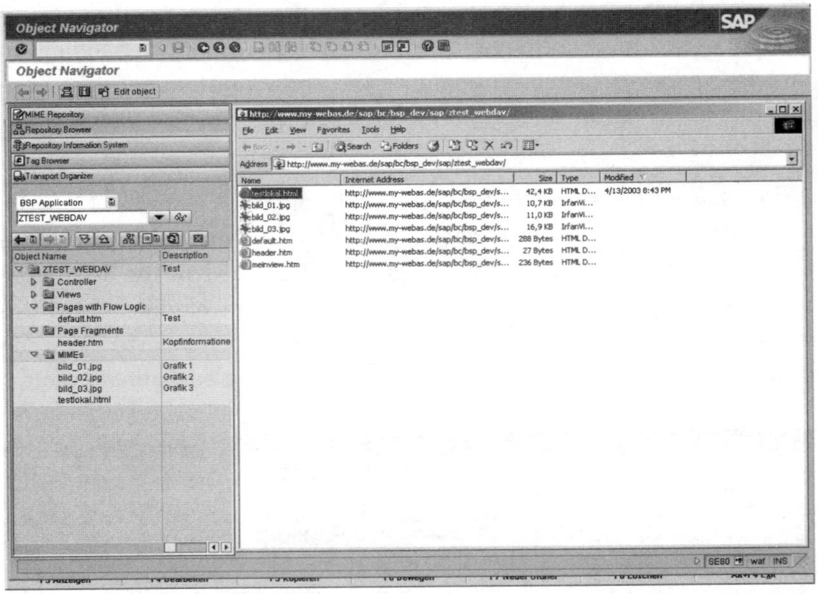

**Figure 4.59** Inserting a new Web page

**Figure 4.60** Converting a static Web page

The import function of the MIME repository browser makes it easy to import MIMEs from a folder; however, when importing entire directory structures, this method of importing MIMEs is not practical. A far better solution is to initialize a mass import using the WebDAV interface and the Web folders principle. The MIMEs can simply be transferred from the file directory on the hard drive to the specified directory in the MIME repository. Then, all imported MIMEs become components of the MIME repository and are assigned to the package of the corresponding BSP application by default.

**Mass import of MIMEs**

You can also copy entire directories, including their subdirectories. In this case, the corresponding directory structures are adopted in the MIME Repository.

### 4.4.3 Creation and Management of a BSP Application Layout Using Adobe GoLive 6.0

In order to follow this section properly, we recommend that you install Adobe GoLive 6.0. After it has been successfully installed, you can start the Adobe GoLive program.

When creating a BSP application layout, you must first create a structure for several sample pages using a template. Select **New Site** from the **File** menu; a site wizard starts automatically. In the GoLive Site Wizard's welcome screen, select the **Single User** option and confirm the settings by clicking on the **Next** button (see Figure 4.61).

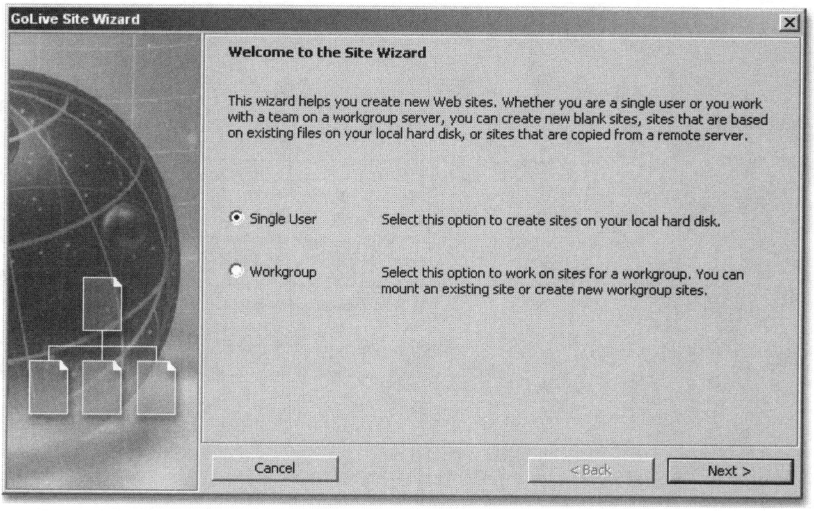

**Figure 4.61** Starting the GoLive Site Wizard

Another screen is displayed. In the Options for Local Sites window, select the **Copy from Template** option and confirm this setting by clicking on the **Next** button (see Figure 4.62).

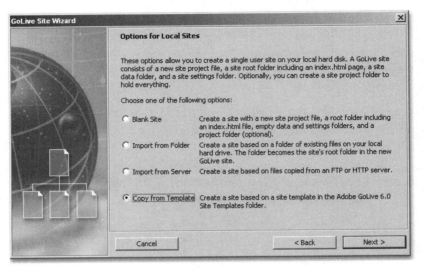

**Figure 4.62** Options for the Web site to be created

Figure 4.63 shows the following window, which prompts you to search for and choose a Web site template. You must also enter a name for the new Web site. Click **Next** to confirm your selection.

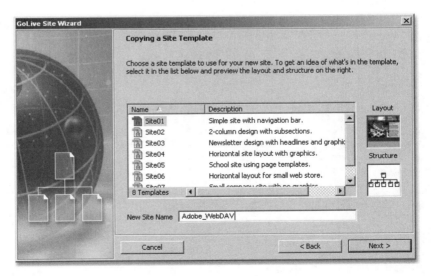

**Figure 4.63** Creating a new Web site using a template

In the next window, you are prompted to enter a local location where the generated pages should be saved. Confirm your new site location by clicking the **Finish** button (see Figure 4.64).

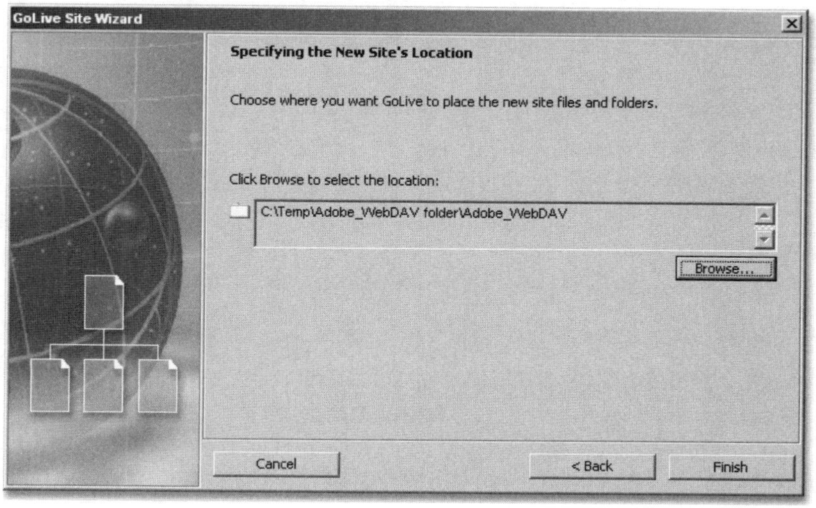

**Figure 4.64** Local directory structure for Web sites

Next, a framework (or view) for the selection of templates is generated. This view is displayed in a split screen (Site view). At this point, you can further develop or customize the Web site using the extensive tools that are available in Adobe GoLive (see Figure 4.65).

Now, you must enter the specifications of the WebDAV server (in this case, of the SAP Web AS). To do this, select the **Site Settings ...** menu option. To make the necessary settings, select **FTP & WebDAV Server**. Because no server has been entered, you must enter a new server. Open the combo box in the **WebDAV** area and select **Edit Server** from the drop-down list (see Figure 4.66).

In the next window, you can enter all the necessary specifications of the WebDAV server. First, assign a nickname to the server. Then enter the server data (server), the associated service URL (directory) of the BSP application, and, where applicable, the logon data (username and password). Confirm your specifications by clicking **OK** (see Figure 4.67).

Now all required settings to access the WebDAV have been entered.

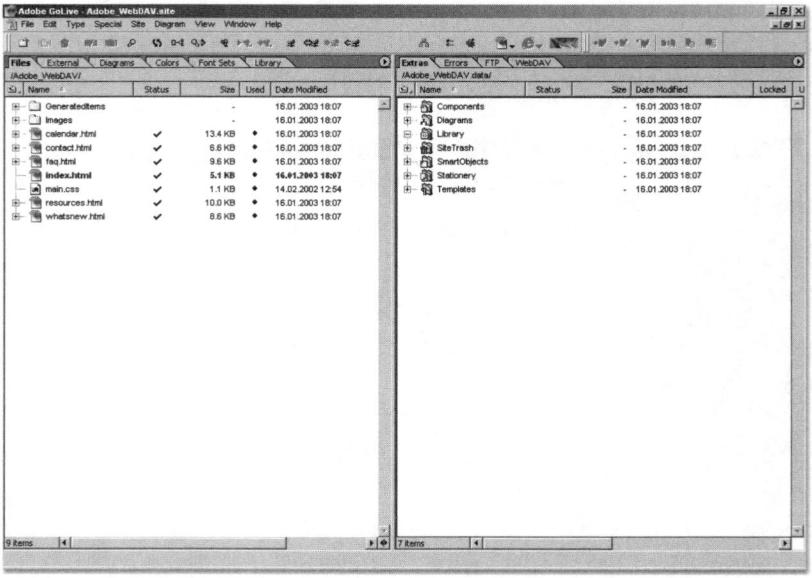

**Figure 4.65** The Site view of the generated Web site

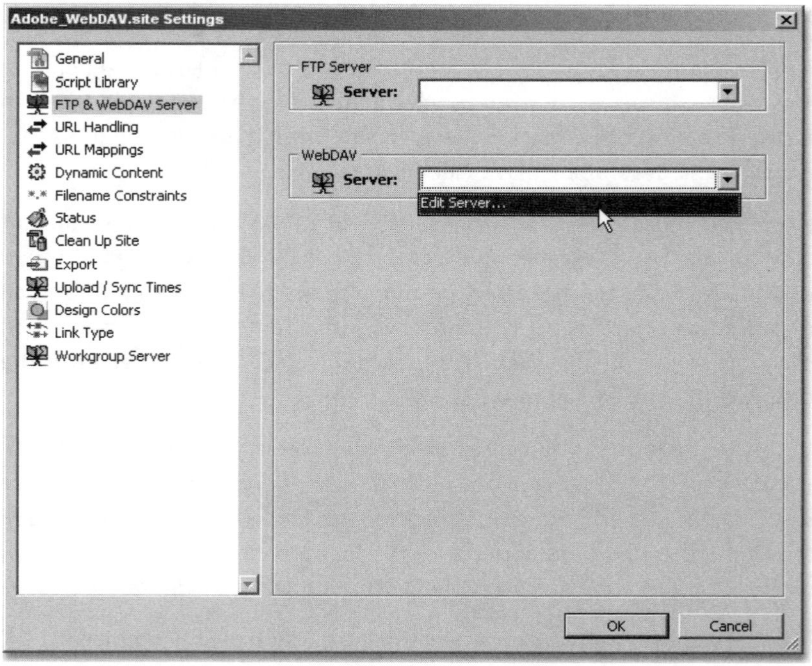

**Figure 4.66** Entering the WebDAV settings

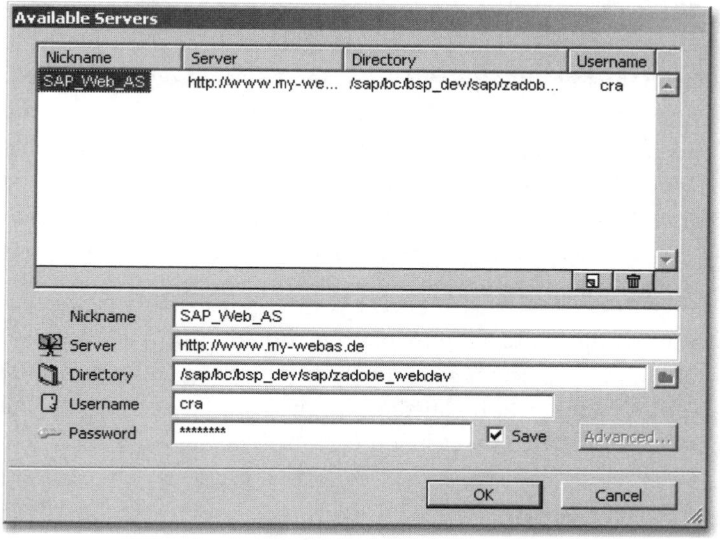

**Figure 4.67** Settings for access to the WebDAV server

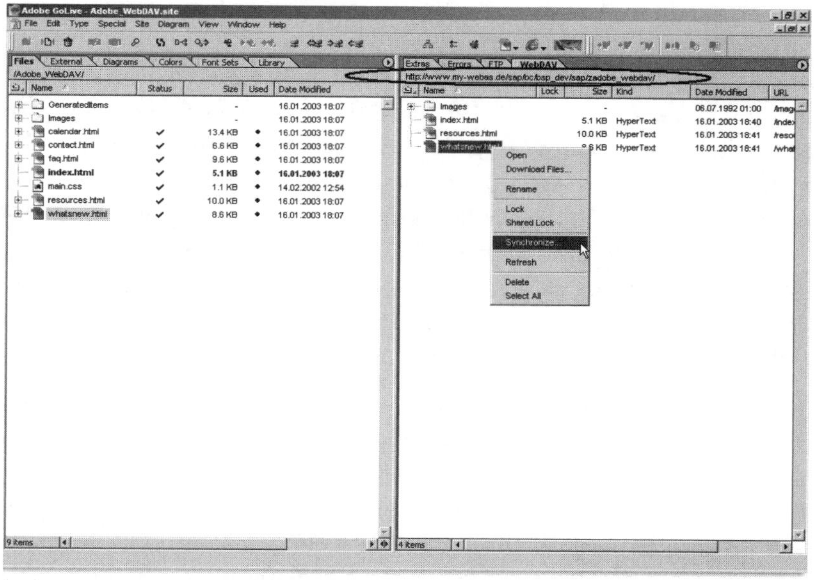

**Figure 4.68** An active WebDAV connection

Select the **Site WebDAV Server Connect** menu option to establish a connection to the WebDAV server. If this connection is successful, select the **WebDAV** tab in the right-hand window of the Site view (see Figure 4.68). The URL of the active connection to the WebDAV server is displayed in the status bar (see circled area). The right-hand window contains the contents of the application directory on the WebDAV server. You can move the objects created in Adobe from the left-hand window of the Site view to the right-hand window by dragging and dropping. In so doing, the objects are automatically copied to the application directory on the server.

Figure 4.68 shows the context menu for objects on the application server. From this menu, you can access such functions as locking and synchronizing. The WebDAV connection can then be deactivated again using the **Site WebDAV Server Disconnect** menu option.

## 4.5 BAPI Browser

RFMs
Reusable modular program components are encapsulated in the SAP environment in the form of ABAP function modules. By using *Remote Function Calls* (*RFCs*), these function modules can be executed on another system via a defined application programming interface (API). In order for this to work, the function modules must be marked "Remote-enabled module" and must adhere to certain design rules. Then these function modules can be labeled as *RFC-enabled Function Modules* (*RFMs*). The problem, however, is that RFCs can also access functions that are themselves executed within the system. Consequently, because these functions' interfaces are not concerned primarily with the external calling program, we cannot always ensure the stability of these interfaces, for example, when a new release is installed. Each change to the interface makes the functionality useless and introduces changes to the programming.

BAPIs
However, with the increased growth of the Internet, the necessity for a controlled, standardized, and business-oriented interface for the comprehensive use of the internal SAP functionality through external applications has become imperative. The *Business Application Programming Interfaces* (*BAPIs*) were unveiled as a central component of SAP's Business Frameworks. The BAPIs represent a subset of RFMs as an open and standardized interface; technically, the BAPIs can operate as RFC-capable function modules. A BAPI encapsulates the complex application functionalities using these stable interfaces and allows access to standardized business transactions in the form of Business Object Methods. These business objects are defined and managed in the *Business Object Reposi-*

*tory*. In addition, SAP guarantees that the interfaces will remain constant after new releases. In the meantime, over 1000 BAPIs exist for diverse fields of business.

Typically, the SAP Web AS, as an upstream system, accesses the RFMs and BAPIs from downstream backend systems. The problem, however, is that the SAP Web AS does not recognize the RFMs or BAPIs, and therefore does not make all necessary structures and dictionary definitions available for determining the type of interface for the function modules. However, this metadata is required in order to implement a correct function call. To avoid manually recording the definitions, a special tool, the *BAPI Browser*, has been made available. This browser drastically reduces the workload and therefore enables smooth implementation of the function calls.

You can start the BAPI Browser from the Page editor of the Web Application Builder (WAB). To do so, select the **Goto BAPI Browser** menu option. The BAPI Browser opens in a separate window (see Figure 4.69).

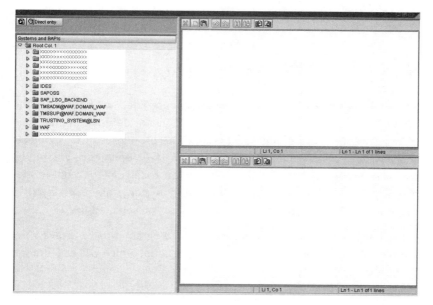

**Figure 4.69** The BAPI Browser

In the left-hand window of the BAPI Browser, all stored RFC destinations for this system are listed. RFC destinations for other required backend systems can be created using Transaction SM59. To select a BAPI, you first need to choose the target system that you want from the hierarchy structure (**Open folder**). From the list that is displayed, you can select the required BAPI with a double click (see Figure 4.70).

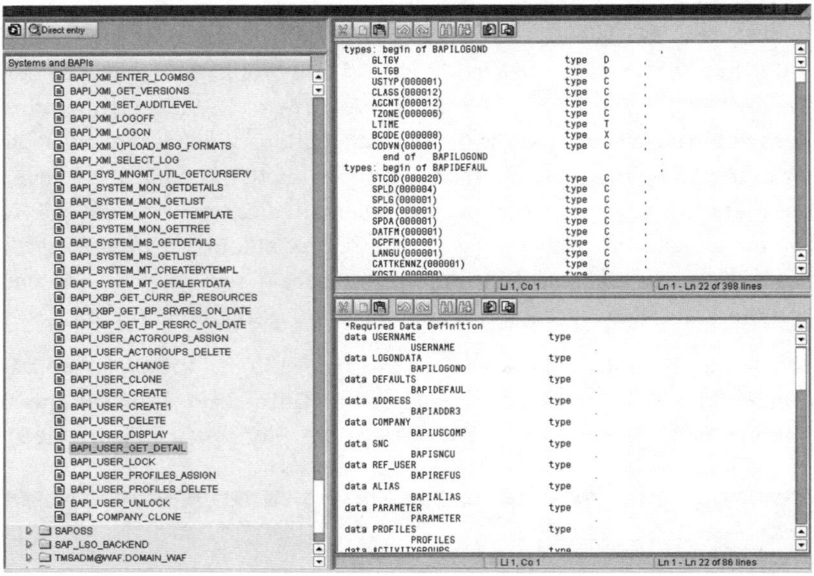

**Figure 4.70** A selected BAPI in the BAPI Browser

Now both windows on the right-hand side are filled with content. The top window contains necessary type definitions for determining the type of interface. The type definitions describe the properties of data objects and serve as a template for creating them. The type definitions created by the BAPI Browser shown in this window are based on the built-in elementary ABAP data types. The lower window contains necessary data definitions and a pregenerated sample call for the selected BAPI.

The typing or the structures necessary for programming, and even the sample call, can now be copied to the application, which will execute the BAPI call.

During the procedure introduced here, only the BAPIs of the corresponding system are displayed. However, if you want to access RFMs, click on the **Direct entry** button in the upper left area of the BAPI Browser. The Select Target System and BAPI window opens (see Figure 4.71).

![Select Target System and BAPI dialog box showing BAPI Name and Target System fields]

**Figure 4.71** Direct entry of RFMs and BAPIs

In the **BAPI Name** field, you can enter either BAPIs or RFMs. In the **Target System** field, you can then enter the RFC destination of the target system on which the function modules are to be executed. The corresponding type definitions, data definitions, and the example call are generated as described above.

Despite this useful tool, that is, the BAPI Browser, you may want to enter the necessary information (i.e., dictionary definitions, etc.) manually by typing it into the Data Dictionary. This is particularly useful when the typing is needed in a number of places and in different program elements.

## 4.6 Online Text Repository

The multilingual capability of Web applications is an important pre-requisite for their success. A multitude of different users located in different regions around the world can participate in collaborative applications. The fact that these users can use a particular Web application in their preferred language is critical to the acceptance of a solution. Therefore, the specified language of a Web application must be considered from the beginning of development and supported with suitable tools.

**Global Web applications**

The *Online Text Repository* (*OTR*) supports the registration and translation of texts in BSP applications. The OTR is a central storage area for these texts and makes services available for editing them.

**OTR**

By using OTR texts in BSP applications, texts are displayed depending on the logon language. If the texts to be displayed are not available in the logon language, they are shown in the system language (see Figure 4.72).

Language-specific texts are stored independently of the associated BSP page, which is merely referenced to OTR texts. Changes to a BSP page have no effect on the texts, and vice versa. Therefore, the texts can be translated independently of the BSP page. The OTR supports two types of text: short texts and long texts.

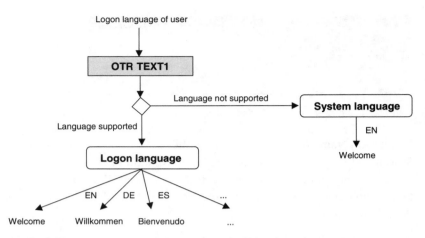

Figure 4.72 OTR—Language-specific texts in Web applications

 Objects in the OTR are always assigned to a package.

**OTR short texts** Short texts can be up to 255 characters long. If the text appears often in the BSP application, it is preferable to use short texts. Then the *alias text* is created and addressed via an alias name in the OTR. This text can then be addressed and employed through the package using this alias, making it more reusable and requiring only a single translation of the text. Alias texts are addressed within the layout of a BSP page using the following OTR directive:

```
<%= OTR(package name/alias name) %>
```

The OTR short texts can also be addressed from the ABAP. You can access the texts using either the GET_OTR_TEXT method of the runtime object RUNTIME or the GET_TEXT method of the CL_BSP_GET_TEXT_BY_ALIAS class.[12]

OTR short texts can be created in three ways: through the forward navigation from a BSP application, using the OTR Browser, or through the SOTR_EDIT transaction.

**Forward navigation** If the OTR directive described above is entered in the layout section, the OTR text can be input by double-clicking on this entry (see Figure 4.73).

---

12 You will find more information on classes and interfaces in Appendix A.

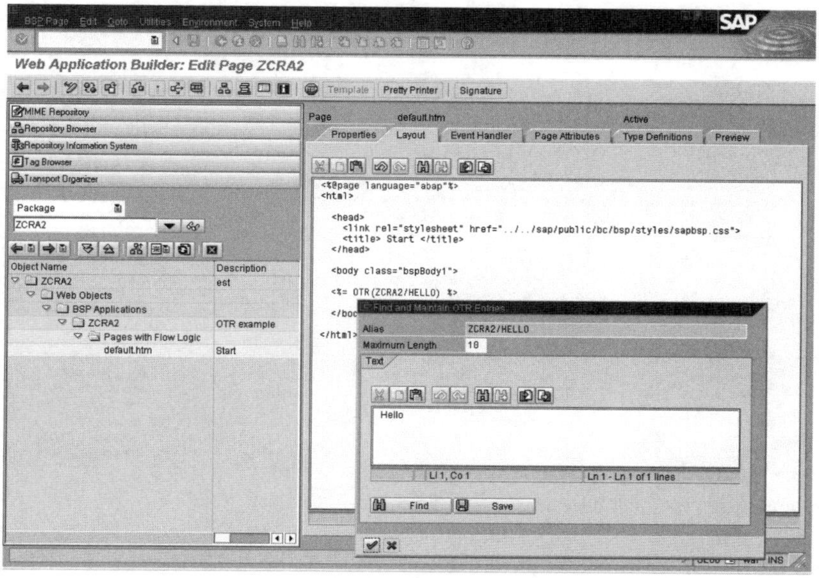

**Figure 4.73** Creating OTR entries in BSP applications through Forward Navigation

If you don't assign the alias a package name, the system will do it automatically. You can enter a maximum length for the translation of the text. This maximum length describes the space available for the translation into the various languages. If you don't know what your system needs, choose a longer length. If, however, you don't enter a length, the length of the input text is proposed. You should maintain the text in the logon language; then, the entry can be saved.

The second possibility to maintain OTR texts is to link directly to the OTR Browser from the Web Application Builder (WAB) using the **Goto Online Text Repository Browser** menu option. As a result, the browser is opened in a pop-up window in which two packages are offered: the currently edited package and a standard package called SOTR_VOCABULARY_ BASIC. The standard package contains general texts in the language installed on the particular system that can be used across packets. These texts can be used in any application and will therefore drastically reduce your workload.

**OTR Browser**

To create a new OTR text, choose the corresponding package and click on the **Create** icon from the toolbar (see Figure 4.74; the Create icon is circled).

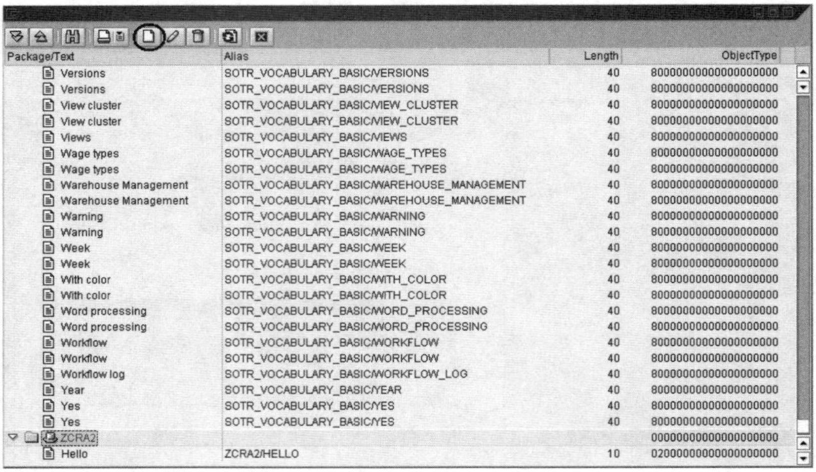
Package/Text
Alias
Length
ObjectType
Versions | SOTR_VOCABULARY_BASIC/VERSIONS | 40 | 80000000000000000000
Versions | SOTR_VOCABULARY_BASIC/VERSIONS | 40 | 80000000000000000000
View cluster | SOTR_VOCABULARY_BASIC/VIEW_CLUSTER | 40 | 80000000000000000000
View cluster | SOTR_VOCABULARY_BASIC/VIEW_CLUSTER | 40 | 80000000000000000000
Views | SOTR_VOCABULARY_BASIC/VIEWS | 40 | 80000000000000000000
Wage types | SOTR_VOCABULARY_BASIC/WAGE_TYPES | 40 | 80000000000000000000
Wage types | SOTR_VOCABULARY_BASIC/WAGE_TYPES | 40 | 80000000000000000000
Warehouse Management | SOTR_VOCABULARY_BASIC/WAREHOUSE_MANAGEMENT | 40 | 80000000000000000000
Warehouse Management | SOTR_VOCABULARY_BASIC/WAREHOUSE_MANAGEMENT | 40 | 80000000000000000000
Warning | SOTR_VOCABULARY_BASIC/WARNING | 40 | 80000000000000000000
Warning | SOTR_VOCABULARY_BASIC/WARNING | 40 | 80000000000000000000
Week | SOTR_VOCABULARY_BASIC/WEEK | 40 | 80000000000000000000
Week | SOTR_VOCABULARY_BASIC/WEEK | 40 | 80000000000000000000
With color | SOTR_VOCABULARY_BASIC/WITH_COLOR | 40 | 80000000000000000000
With color | SOTR_VOCABULARY_BASIC/WITH_COLOR | 40 | 80000000000000000000
Word processing | SOTR_VOCABULARY_BASIC/WORD_PROCESSING | 40 | 80000000000000000000
Word processing | SOTR_VOCABULARY_BASIC/WORD_PROCESSING | 40 | 80000000000000000000
Workflow | SOTR_VOCABULARY_BASIC/WORKFLOW | 40 | 80000000000000000000
Workflow | SOTR_VOCABULARY_BASIC/WORKFLOW | 40 | 80000000000000000000
Workflow log | SOTR_VOCABULARY_BASIC/WORKFLOW_LOG | 40 | 80000000000000000000
Year | SOTR_VOCABULARY_BASIC/YEAR | 40 | 80000000000000000000
Yes | SOTR_VOCABULARY_BASIC/YES | 40 | 80000000000000000000
Yes | SOTR_VOCABULARY_BASIC/YES | 40 | 80000000000000000000
ZCRA2 | | | 00000000000000000000
Hello | ZCRA2/HELLO | 10 | 02000000000000000000

**Figure 4.74** The OTR Browser

The pop-up window for entering and maintaining OTR texts opens. After you enter the new OTR text, save it.

**SOTR_EDIT** A third possibility is that the SOTR_EDIT transaction can be used to create OTR texts. After starting the transaction, the specified original language, the alias, and the text can be maintained here (see Figure 4.75).

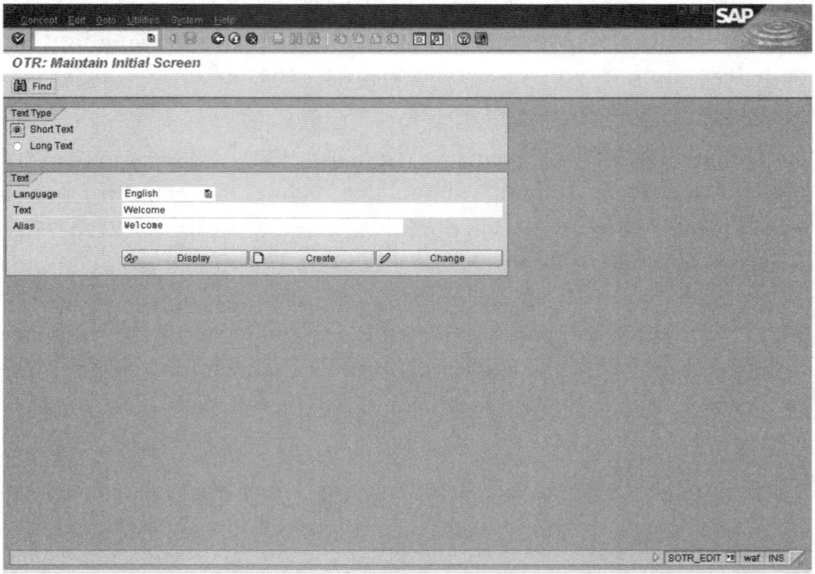
SAP
OTR: Maintain Initial Screen
Find
Text Type
Short Text
Long Text
Text
Language
English
Text
Welcome
Alias
Welcome
Display
Create
Change
SOTR_EDIT
waf
INS

**Figure 4.75** The SOTR_EDIT transaction

After confirming the text that you entered, you should enter the package and object type (WAPP for BSP pages) on the next screen. In some cases, the required maximum length of the text must be corrected. When you save your specifications, a pop-up window opens (see Figure 4.76). Check the attributes and confirm your entry (i.e., confirm the creation of an OTR concept).

For every OTR object, a context in the form of an OTR concept is man- **OTR concept** aged. Here, in the OTR concept, the most diverse information is stored. This data includes administration information such as author, date, package, original language, original system, and translation level. In addition, the OTR concept enables an overview of the translations in other languages, supported abbreviations for this text, and access to the **Where-used list** of the text. Categorization of the text's various uses can be stored in the form of a comment.

By saving the OTR concept, the OTR text element is created in the system.

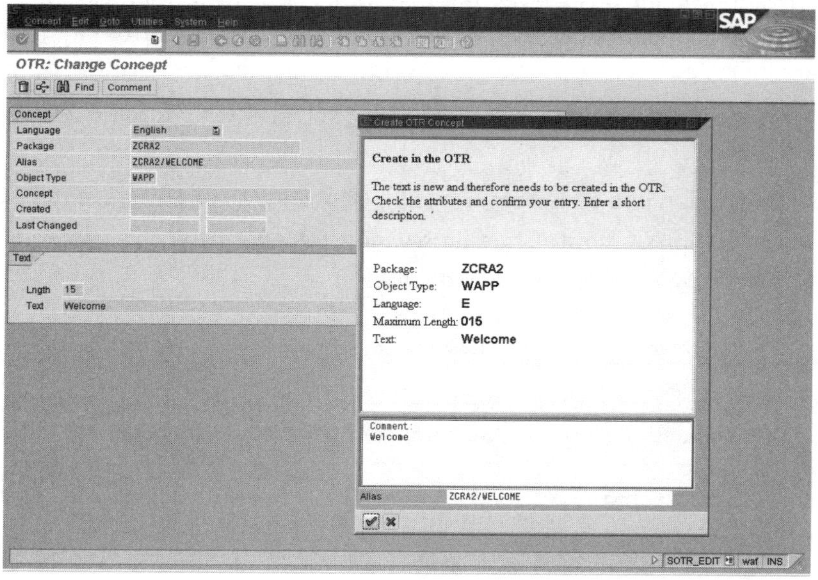

**Figure 4.76** Creating an OTR concept

Long texts can contain more than 255 characters and often appear only **OTR Long Texts** once and are therefore rarely reused. Long texts are placed in the layout of a BSP page using special tags:

```
<OTR> preferred text </OTR>
```

When generating a BSP page, these OTR text fragments are automatically redirected to the OTR.

The *SAP translation tool* (Transaction SE63) can be used to translate OTR short texts and OTR long texts. OTR long texts can also be translated from the WAB using the **Goto Translation** menu option.

**OTR Transport** The OTR is linked to the Change and Transport System. The OTR texts are transported together with the corresponding object. When an OTR text is first created, it is transferred to a transportable change request, if it is not already assigned to a local or private package.

## 4.7 The XSLT Editor

**Transformation of XML Documents** The *eXtensible Stylesheet Language* (*XSL*) includes both a transformation language (XSLT) and a formatting language (XSL-FO). The formatting language provides elements that set how the XML should be displayed (e.g., font, size, color, etc.); it therefore has a similar role to that of CSS for HTML documents. However, the transformation language provides elements that define how an XML document should be transformed into another XML document or another output format (e.g., HTML, RTF, etc.).

There are three different categories for converting XML documents (see Figure 4.77):

▶ Conversion into a display form (e.g., HTML, WML, XHTML, etc.)
▶ Conversion of the structure (into various XML formats)
▶ Conversion into ABAP data structures

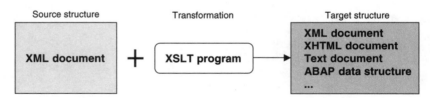

**Figure 4.77** XSL transformations

XML is therefore a good standard to use for exchanging data between systems with XSL/XSLT. If necessary, new dialects of the output structures are produced. In this way, an XML-based system coupling and system connection can be established.

**XSL/XSLT support in SAP Web AS** The *SAP XSLT processor* has been available since Release 6.10 as a component of the core SAP Web Application Server (SAP Web AS). SAP XSLT is an SAP implementation that conforms to the W3C specification for version XSLT 1.0.

The *XSLT Editor*, available in the SAP Web AS, enables transformations and their execution to be defined on the application server. The editor is completely integrated into the Workbench as a development tool and is linked to the correction and transport group. XSLT programs are stand-alone repository objects. The extent of the functions of the XSLT editor includes the following possibilities:

▶ Creating or editing XSLT programs using the Tag Browser

▶ Checking, activating, testing, and debugging transformations

To create an XSLT transformation, do the following:

Select a package. Then, select the **Create More XSL Transformation** menu option on the context menu (see Figure 4.78).

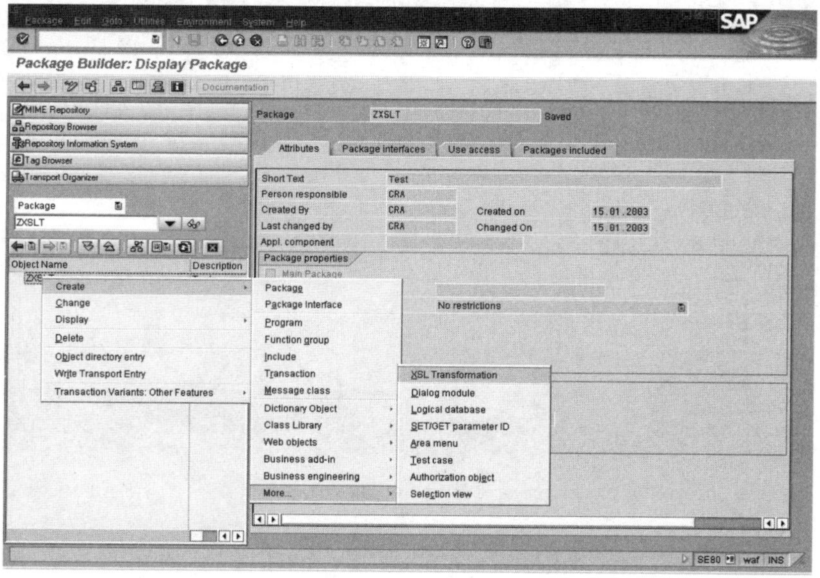

**Figure 4.78** Creating an XSL transformation

The Create XSLT Program window opens. In the **XSLT Program** field, enter the name of the XSLT program. In the **Description** field, enter a description for the repository object (see Figure 4.79).

After you have confirmed the name of the program and the description of the object, the XSLT program is created. A source text structure has already been generated for this program (see Figure 4.80). The source text prototype produced contains a few important default settings, namely, the XSL version used, the XSL namespace, and the SAP namespace.

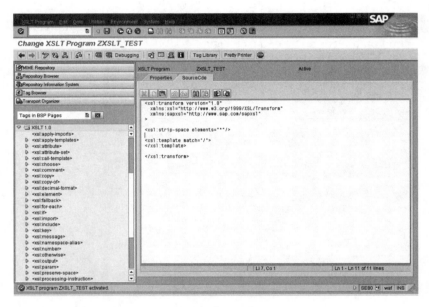

**Figure 4.79** Updating the name and description of an XSLT program

Using the Tag Browser, you can access all of the supported XSLT commands. Now you can begin the actual programming of the transformation.

**Figure 4.80** Editing the source text using the Tag Browser

To call a transformation, you can use the new ABAP language element CALL TRANSFORMATION. This language element supports the following transformations:

▶ XML to XML
▶ XML to ABAP
▶ ABAP to XML
▶ ABAP to ABAP

You can find the exact syntax in *ABAP Objects—The Official Reference* by Horst Keller and Joachim Jacobitz, which is also published by SAP PRESS.

# 5    Practical Exercise: Creating BSP Applications

*In Goethe's Faust, Mephistopheles says, "Grey is, young friend, all theory: And green of life the golden tree." As you will see, developing Web applications using the basic principles and tools introduced so far is relatively easy.*

In this chapter, we use a scenario and numerous additional examples to breathe life into the rather theoretical remarks made in previous chapters. The Web application, or more accurately, the BSP application, that you will develop contains all the basic functions necessary for a flight booking portal. This Web-based portal provides end users with the following functions:

- ▶ Display of available flights
- ▶ Search for flights
- ▶ Booking flights
- ▶ Display of the user's reservations
- ▶ Additional functions

**Functions**

We will introduce various technologies and concepts step-by-step based on the flight booking portal. Figure 5.1 gives an overview about the application's main process and the functions that are to be implemented. The main process consists of searching for and booking the requested flight. For the actual booking, users will be switched from a public area of the application to a protected area that requires logging on to the system.

Several options for implementing functions often exist. In this chapter, we share our experience from various projects, which we believe can help to guide and support you in the development of your Web application. Here, we track the development of the portal from beginning to end. We will deviate from this approach only rarely to introduce important details or alternatives regarding the implementation of functions.

New processes and functions are presented in detail when they are first introduced. When these concepts are referred to again later in the course of development, we assume that readers will already be familiar with them.

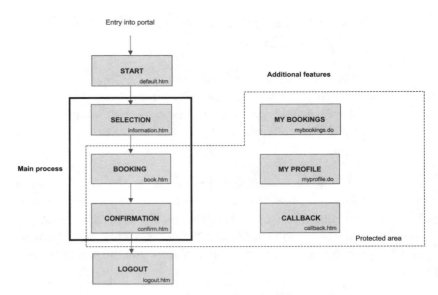

Figure 5.1 The Flight Booking Portal under development

## 5.1 The First BSP Application

Our first BSP application contains the welcome page for the flight booking portal. To produce the welcome page, we must first create a BSP application as a "container" for the components of our Web application. In an additional step, we will add the first Web page and link a graphic to it. To conclude, we will look at the results in our Web browser.

### 5.1.1 Creating a BSP Application

Before you can create a BSP application, you must first log on to the SAP Web Application Server from the SAP GUI. Next, you use SAP Easy Access Menu **(Overview Object Navigator)** or Transaction SE80 to enter the development environment. The object list that is displayed contains a drop-down box from which you can select various types of objects. In this case, select **BSP application** (see Figure 5.2)

After selecting this object type, you can enter the name of the BSP application in the entry field that appears below. In typical cases, we recommend that you create a BSP application within the customer namespace: it must begin with a "Y*" or a "Z*" and contain a maximum of 15 characters. In this example, the name of the BSP application is Z_FLIGHTUS. After you enter the application name, confirm it by clicking on the **Display** button (glasses icon). A dialog box opens, informing you that the application does not exist, and prompts you to create the object. To confirm the creation of the object, select **Yes** (see Figure 5.3).

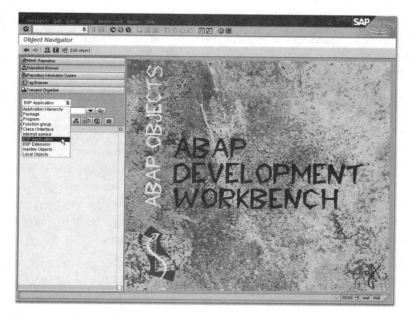

**Figure 5.2** Selecting the object type "BSP Application" in the Object Navigator

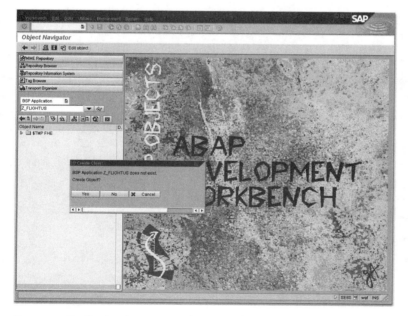

**Figure 5.3** Confirming the creation of a BSP application

After you confirm the creation of the object, an additional dialog box opens. Here, enter a short description of the BSP application being created (see Figure 5.4).

**Figure 5.4** Entering a short description for the BSP application

To confirm your entry, click the **Create** button (white sheet of paper icon). The next step assigns the BSP application to a package (see Figure 5.5). In this case, a package named Z_FLIGHT_US already exists; it was created with the Object Navigator. In general, packages are containers for all logically related development objects that are to be transported together into a subsequent system (such as a test system).

If the BSP application being created is a test or sample application that will not be transported into a production system, you can assign it as a local object to the *$TMP* package. Later, if you want, you can change the package assignment.

Confirm your entries by clicking the **Save** button (disk icon).

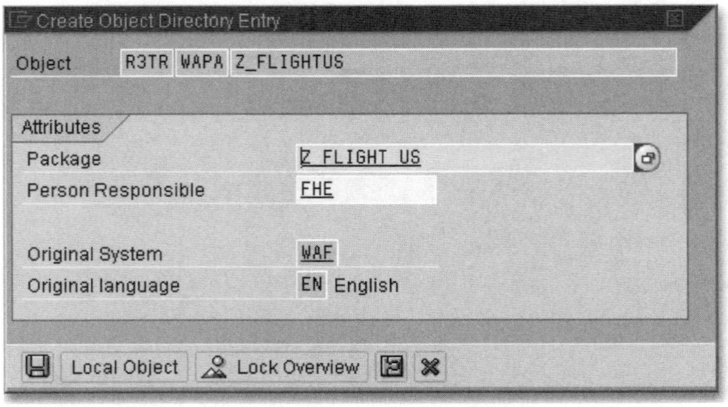

**Figure 5.5** Assigning a BSP application to a package

The development object is then entered in the transport requests that already exist. The first object is the BSP application; the second object is the ICF service entry that is automatically created along with the first object (see Figures 5.6 and 5.7). Confirm each assignment to a request by clicking on the green checkmark icon.

**Figure 5.6** Transport request for the BSP application

**Figure 5.7** Transport request for the corresponding ICF service

The system then updates the left window in the Object Navigator and displays the BSP application that has been created as a node. At first, the node is displayed in blue, which means that the BSP application has not yet been activated. You can double-click on the node to branch (connect) to the Web Application Builder (WAB). The BSP application is opened and the tools area shows the Properties and Navigation tabs of the BSP application. The Properties tab contains important information on the BSP application, such as who it was created by, last changed by, and the package assignment. You can also set the theme, application class, state model, and the start page (see Figure 5.8) in this tab. We will discuss these fields in greater detail later.

After following these steps, the BSP application is created in the system. As noted, the BSP application is still inactive, which you can see from the blue color in the left frame of the BSP application. You can also detect this when you look at the "inactive" entry (located to the right of the name of the BSP application, in the upper right part of the tools area).

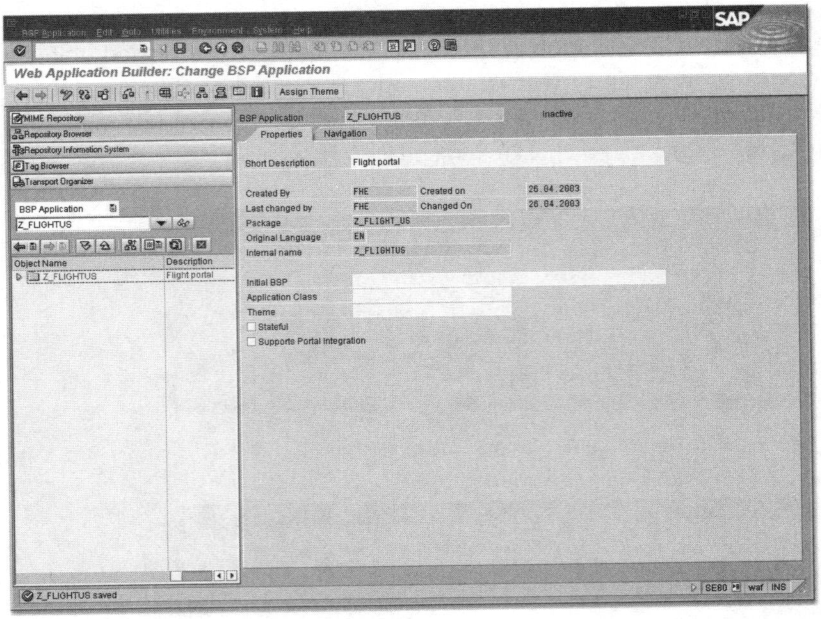

**Figure 5.8** Characteristics of the BSP application that has been created

You can activate the BSP application in several ways. By clicking the activate icon on the tool bar, with the keyboard (CTRL + F3), or via the context menu of the BSP application. If you're working with several inactive objects, a pop-up window opens and prompts you to select and activate the objects that are relevant to your work.

### 5.1.2 Creating a BSP Page

After you've created the BSP application, you can now create the first BSP page as the entry point to the flight booking portal. Name this BSP page *default.htm*.

To create the page, select the empty BSP application in the object list. From the context menu, select **Create Page** (see Figure 5.9).

Then, a dialog window for creating a page opens (see Figure 5.10). Select the Page Type in addition the name of the page and enter an appropriate short description. In this case, select **Page with Flow Logic** as the Page Type.

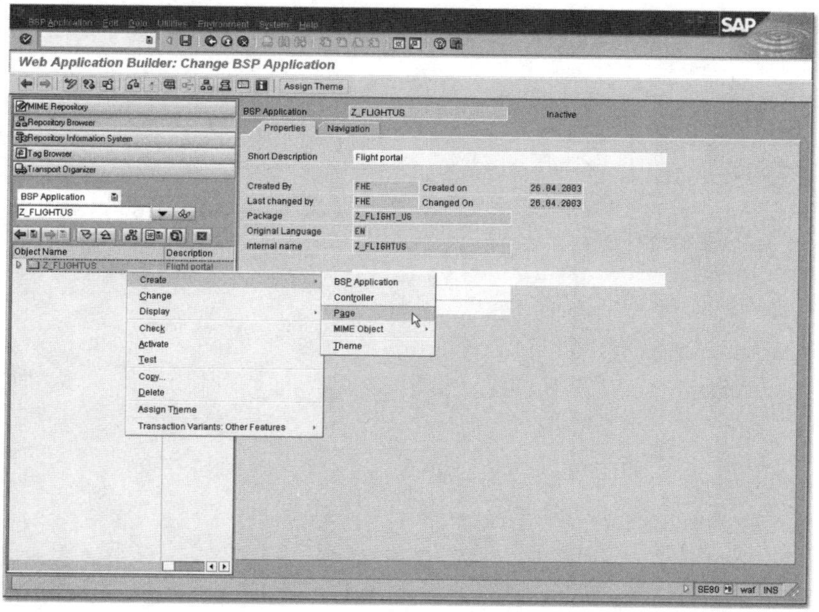

**Figure 5.9** Creating a BSP page

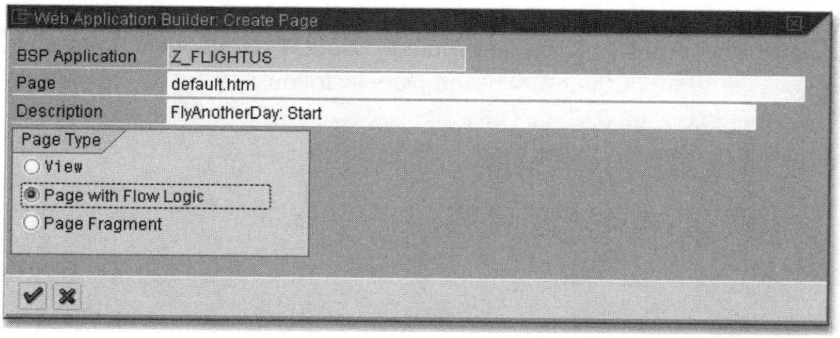

**Figure 5.10** Maintaining the description and page type for a BSP page

After you confirm your entries, a basic template for this BSP page appears in the editing window of the **Layout** tab (see Figure 5.11). The first line shows a special, blue statement that is required for server-side scripting.

An automatically generated basic HTML template is then created. The header tag is supplied with a proprietary SAP style sheet and a title with the short description of the page entered previously. The body tag does not contain any additional components; therefore, the Web browser first displays an empty HTML page, which has a status of "new," that is, it has not yet been saved.

**Basic HTML template**

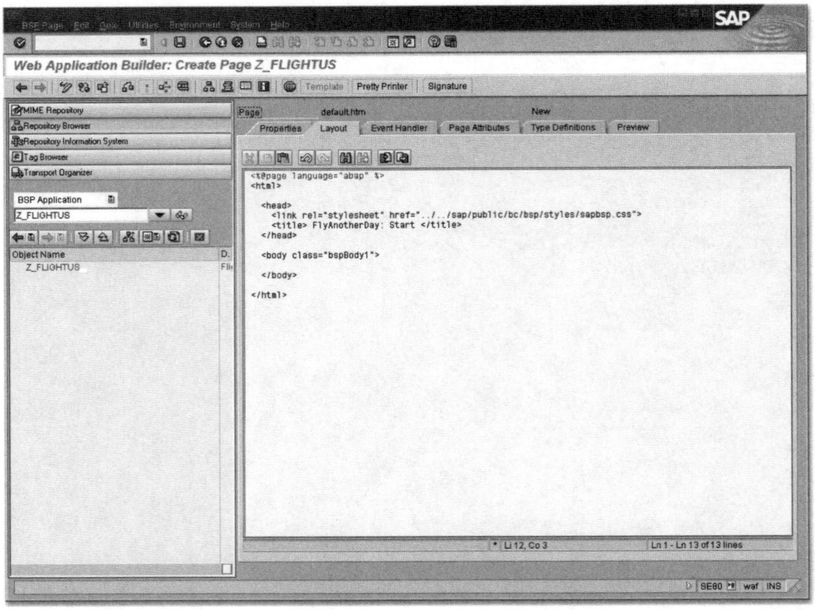

**Figure 5.11** The Layout template of the first BSP page

To give the page some life, additional HTML code is now added to the page. In this example, the page should output a simple welcoming text, which is entered in the body of the page as follows:

**Listing 5.1** A simple welcoming text

```
<CENTER>
    <H2> Hello Guest, </H2>
    <BR>
    <H2> Welcome to FlyAnotherDay! </H2>
</CENTER>
```

You can save the BSP page by using the system toolbar. The status of the page then changes to "inactive." Then, you can activate the page by using the application toolbar. In the following sections, the object list of the BSP application is enhanced with additional entries. Here, a folder named *Pages with Flow Logic* was created, and the BSP page we created has been sorted into it. In addition, the BSP page now has an "active" status, which means that we can test it (see Figure 5.12).

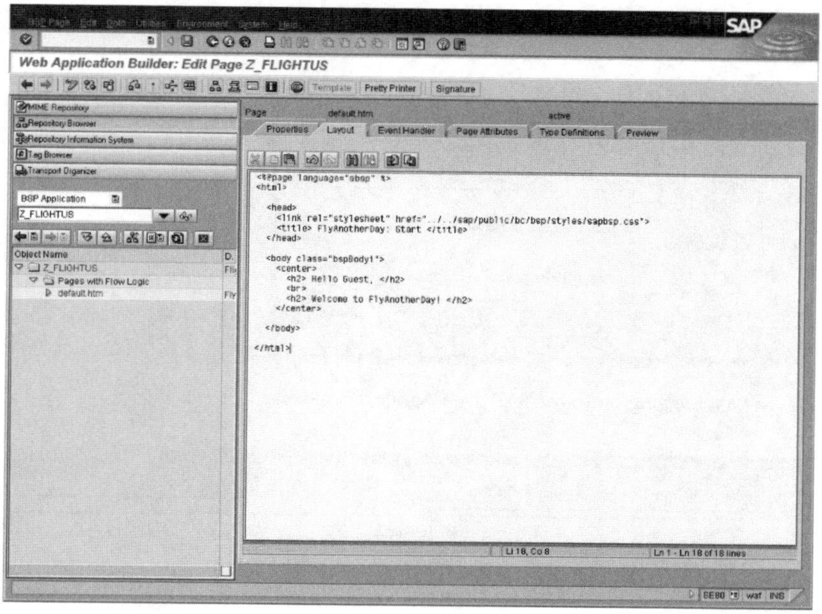

**Figure 5.12** Saved and activated BSP page

Now, let's look at the results of our page. We have two ways in which to review the results.

Testing

The first and recommended method is to test the page with the application toolbar. Doing so automatically starts Internet Explorer, which displays the BSP page of the BSP application. The advantage of this type of testing is that you can test the appearance and behavior of your Web application in a real-life environment. To perform the test, select the **Test/Execute** button from the application toolbar, or select F8. The first access to the SAP Web AS usually requires a logon, but this depends on the service settings for the BSP application. Basic authentication is typically set as the logon method in the service. To access SAP Web AS, enter your name and password in the window that opens (see Figure 5.13).

If authentication was successful, the browser displays the page (see Figure 5.14).

You must log on to the system again only if you have closed and then restarted the browser. Therefore, we recommend that you leave the browser open in the background, because doing so significantly accelerates testing any changes.

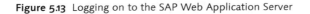

**Figure 5.13** Logging on to the SAP Web Application Server

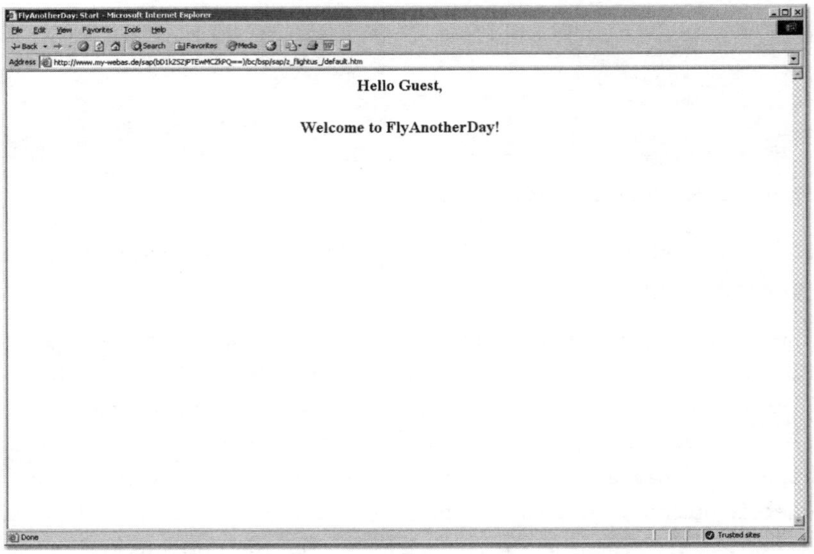

**Figure 5.14** The first BSP page in the Web browser

If you have logged on correctly, but the application does not display in the Web browser, look at the URL path in Internet Explorer to see if it contains a complete and qualified host name. If it doesn't, you can enter the host name from the development environment. Select **Tools Settings** from the menu and enter the name of the application server or the IP address in the **Business Server Pages** tab. The next time you test the BSP page, the system uses the correct URL and the page is displayed.

Internal Preview    The second method of testing the BSP page requires that you switch to the internal preview. Here, however, you can display only the static components of the layout: pure HTML and no server-side scripting. To use this approach when testing, select the **Preview** tab. Here, too, you must log on the first time you access the system. Figure 5.15 shows the results of the preview.

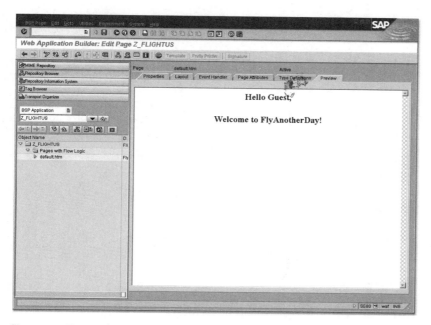

**Figure 5.15** Testing the page with the Preview function

You can use various tools to create the static HTML layout of a BSP page: the internal editor, the tag library, an external editor, and external design tools with the WebDAV interface. For the sample applications being developed in the following sections, we will use only the standard editor and the tag library.

**Notes**

You can set the start page of a BSP application in the application's Properties tab (see Figure 5.8). If you have done so, you don't need to enter the URL path (*default.htm* for example) in the Web browser to display the start page. The start page that you set will display automatically.

The **Properties** tab of the BSP page contains important information, such as the last change, the creator, the package assignment, and the URL. It also contains various setting options that ensure the integration and performance of the page for the most varied requirements (see Figure 5.16).

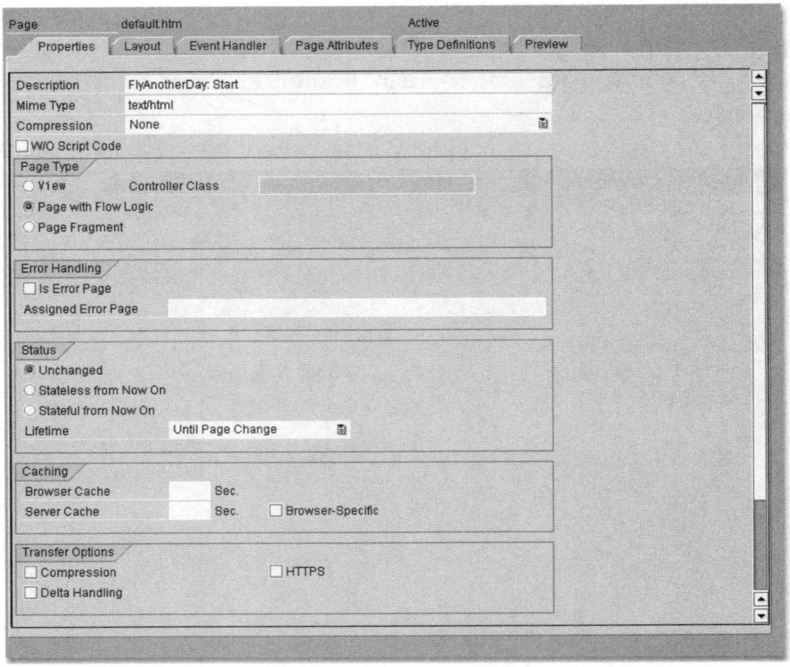

| Page | default.htm | | | | Active | |
| --- | --- | --- | --- | --- | --- | --- |

| Properties | Layout | Event Handler | Page Attributes | Type Definitions | Preview |
| --- | --- | --- | --- | --- | --- |

Description    FlyAnotherDay: Start
Mime Type      text/html
Compression    None
☐ W/O Script Code

Page Type
○ View          Controller Class
◉ Page with Flow Logic
○ Page Fragment

Error Handling
☐ Is Error Page
Assigned Error Page

Status
◉ Unchanged
○ Stateless from Now On
○ Stateful from Now On
Lifetime        Until Page Change

Caching
Browser Cache        Sec.
Server Cache         Sec.        ☐ Browser-Specific

Transfer Options
☐ Compression                     ☐ HTTPS
☐ Delta Handling

**Figure 5.16**  Properties of a BSP page (Excerpt)

### 5.1.3  Graphic Objects

The result of the first page is not yet very exiting. As a welcome page, it's still rather simple. That's why in the next step, we introduce more sophisticated graphic elements to the start page. To meet our goal, we'll have to link and display a local graphic, which means that we must import the graphic as a MIME object into the corresponding MIME directory of the application.

**Importing MIME objects**

Use the object browser to switch to the MIME repository. Once there, you can search the MIME directory that belongs to the BSP application of the same name. In our example, the MIME directory is named *Z_FLIGHTUS*. Use the context menu to call up the entry for importing MIME objects. Now you can search for the MIME object that you want in the local file system and then confirm your selection. You can also maintain a description of the graphic in the following dialog window.

**Linking a MIME object**

Once you have imported the MIME objects you can switch back to the Repository browser. An additional folder, *Mimes*, has been created in the object list. The folder contains all MIMEs specific to the application. You can now drag and drop the graphic into the location in the layout that you have chosen. The name of the graphic and the relative path to the object are automatically transferred into the layout. The only task that remains is to embed an appropriate `img` tag (see Figure 5.17).

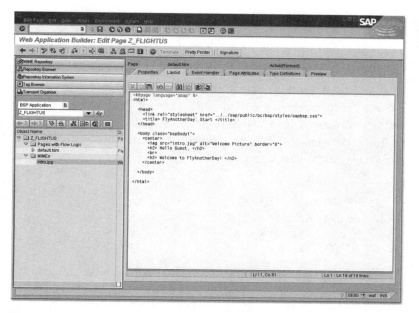

**Figure 5.17** Inserting a graphic from the MIME directory

**Figure 5.18** The Welcome page with the linked image

You can now save the page again and display it. Figure 5.18 shows the resulting page in the Web browser.

## 5.2 Server-Side Scripting

You can use server-side scripting to add dynamic elements to a Web page. Implement this scripting code in the **Layout** tab of a BSP page.

**Inline Code** Special tags (BSP directives) are available to embed server-side scripting and make it recognizable for BSP runtime. The tags <% and %> are used for scripting instructions. The resulting program code is also called *inline code*. The code appears in blue to differentiate it from the customary layout language, such as HTML:

```
<HTML>
   ... HTML-Tags (black)
   <% Scripting-Code (blue) %>
   ... HTML-Tags (black)
</HTML>
```

The SAP Web AS uses the proprietary SAP language, ABAP, as the scripting language. Accordingly, when using server-side scripting, you must first set the language being used in a BSP page. To do so, use *BSP directives*. If you recall the automatic generation of our first BSP page, you'll note that the first blue line was a BSP directive. There are various kinds of BSP directives, which we will introduce later in this discussion. Set ABAP as the scripting language in a BSP page with the following BSP page directive:

```
<%@page language="abap" %>
```

The formal layout of a BSP page that uses server-side scripting appears as follows:

```
<%@page language="abap" %>
<HTML>
   ... HTML-Tags (black)
   <% Scripting-Code (blue) %>
   ... HTML-Tags (black)
</HTML>
```

To clarify the use of ABAP as the scripting language, we will create a new BSP application that contains a BSP page. The page outputs a text five times on the page; each time, the text appears in a larger font. Figure 5.19 shows the coding.

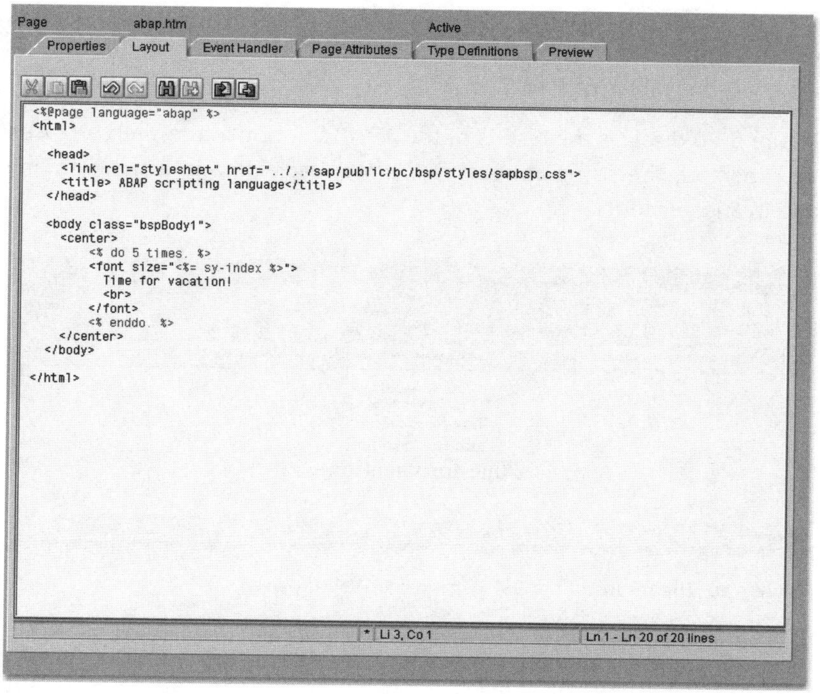

**Figure 5.19** Source code with ABAP as the server-side scripting language

As you can see in Figure 5.19, you can program quite easily in ABAP within the `Script` tag, which suggests that the program code that was entered adheres to the syntax rules of ABAP-OO. You can also trigger a syntax check from the application toolbar.

**Example**

The syntax check applies only to the server-side scripting. The HTML code itself is not checked.

The previous example programs a simple loop. Typical HTML coding appears within the loop, which processes the HTML coding five times. The HTML body contains a simple font definition, a text to be displayed, and a line break. The `size` attribute of the `Font` tag changes the font size; ABAP scripting does the rest.

Another BSP directive, the *print directive,* is used here to define to output the content of an ABAP variable. It has the following structure:

**Print Directive**

```
<%= variable name %>
```

This example outputs the contents of the ABAP variable `sy-index`, which contains the current loop counter. At runtime, the attribute is assigned the values of 1 to 5.

Figure 5.20 displays the results of the ABAP solution in the Web browser. As expected, the string appears five times, each time in a separate line and in a larger font.

**Figure 5.20** The results of the BSP page in the Web Browser

```
<html>

  <head>
    <link rel="stylesheet" href="../../sap/public/bc/bsp/styles/sapbsp.css">
    <title> ABAP scripting language</title>
  </head>

  <body class="bspBody1">
    <center>

        <font size="1 ">
          Time for vacation!
          <br>
        </font>

        <font size="2 ">
          Time for vacation!
          <br>
        </font>

        <font size="3 ">
          Time for vacation!
          <br>
        </font>

        <font size="4 ">
          Time for vacation!
          <br>
        </font>

        <font size="5 ">
          Time for vacation!
          <br>
        </font>

    </center>
  </body>

</html>
```

**Figure 5.21** The source text of the BSP page in Internet Explorer

In Internet Explorer, you can use the **View Source** menu to display the source code of the Web page. As you would expect, the BSP runtime environment generates pure HTML, which it then sends to the Web browser for display (see Figure 5.21).

Of course, you can also declare variables within the layout and use them in the scripting part. However, the layout is the wrong place to implement complex business logic. In a later section, you'll learn more about this.

## 5.3 Page Fragments

Page fragments are used to store frequently repeated components of a layout in their own pages (fragments). This functionality means that you can create modules for BSP pages. A typical example is a header fragment that contains the logo and descriptive information of a company. To conform to corporate identity policies, the header fragment should appear on all pages. The use of page fragments increases the efficiency of development, guarantees the application a uniform appearance, reduces the need for maintenance, and above all, is a proven concept for complex BSP pages. It guarantees a high level of flexibility and significantly increases the manageability of implementing difficult layouts. Therefore, we can unreservedly recommend the extensive use of page fragments.

The enhancement of the flight portal requires a new BSP page, which will be created with page fragments. This page offers flights that can later be chosen for booking. To accomplish this task, we will create a new BSP page named *information.htm*. This page will consist of five page fragments.

To create a page fragment, select a BSP page or the corresponding folder and then select **Create** from the context menu. The familiar dialog window for the creation of a BSP page opens. Enter the appropriate name and a description. Now, select **Page Fragment** as the page type and confirm your entries. Figure 5.22 shows the creation of the header fragment. **Creating**

Save and activate the page fragment. In addition to this fragment, you will also create additional fragments for the navigation, information, selection, and footer areas of the new BSP page by using the same procedure. The page fragments are collected in an individual folder named *Page Fragments*. When you open a page fragment, the BSP page directive that sets the script language being used is automatically added to the page (see Figure 5.23).

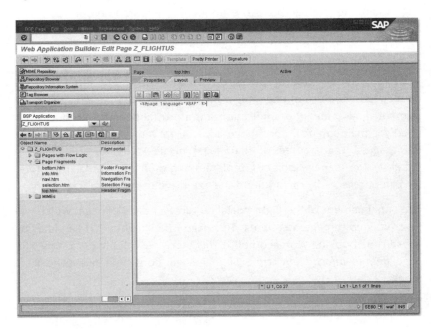

**Figure 5.22** Creating a page fragment

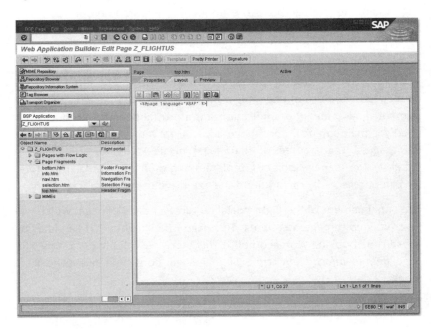

**Figure 5.23** Overview of the created page fragments

Unlike a BSP page, a page fragment contains only three tabs: **Properties**, **Layout**, and **Preview**. Figure 5.24 summarizes the properties of such a page.

You cannot call a page fragment independently: it must always be used in the context of a BSP page.

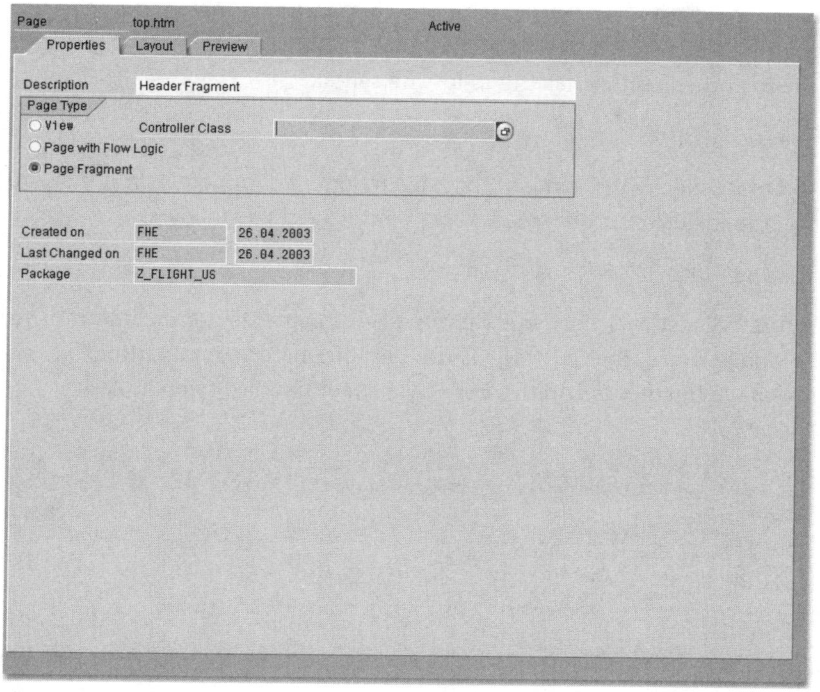

**Figure 5.24** The properties of a page fragment

Once you have successfully created the page fragments, you fill them with the appropriate content. As is the case with BSP pages, here you can use static HTML and dynamic server-side scripting. In this example, the header and the navigation fragment contain additional graphics and HTML instructions. To this end, the graphics were already imported into the appropriate MIME directory (see Figure 5.23).

**Filling**

Now, you should think about the uniform appearance of the entire BSP application. You can develop and link a Cascading Style Sheet (CSS) for the uniform definition and use of fonts, font sizes, buttons, and so on. You work with a CSS just like you would a typical MIME object. To link the CSS to the BSP page, remove the reference to the old style sheet and enter the new one:

**CSS**

```
<LINK rel="stylesheet" href="z_flight.css">
```

To use the various style elements of the CSS, they must be placed into the corresponding HTML tags.

**Including**    After you create the page fragments, they must be included in the BSP page that uses them. An additional BSP directive exists for this purpose. The include directive has the following syntax:

```
<%@include file="page fragment" %>
```

You must specify the name of the page fragment completely. In our example, the inclusion of the header fragment appears as follows:

```
<%@include file="top.htm" %>
```

Figure 5.25 shows how the various page fragments are included in the BSP page. Here, the BSP page is used as a frame or container for the various page fragments and the new style sheet has also been added.

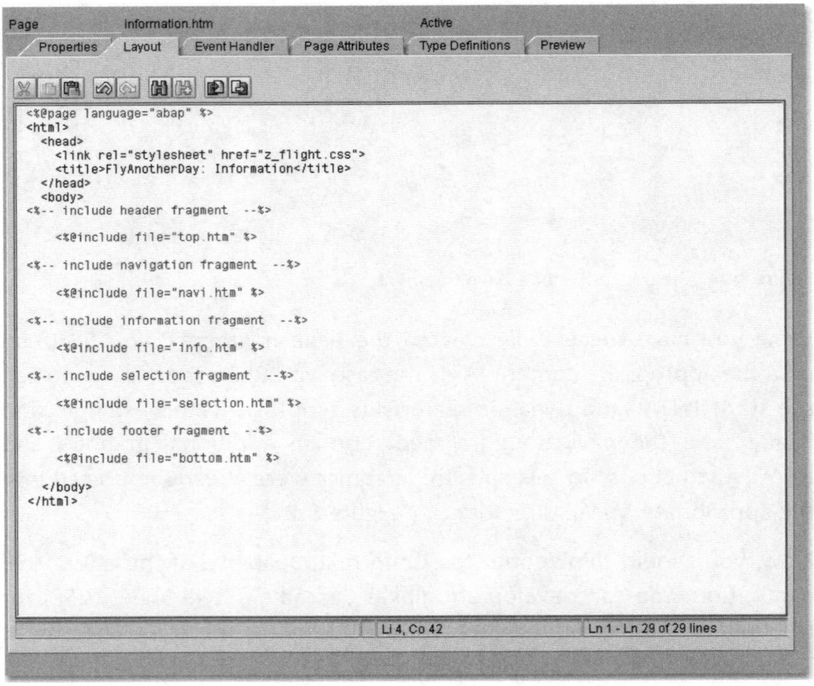

**Figure 5.25** A BSP page with page fragments Included

**Comments**    When you examine the source code, you might have noticed a new BSP directive. It permits you to comment on the program coding. The comment directive has the following syntax:

```
<%-- Comment --%>
```

Meaningful comments significantly help the reader to comprehend a listing; therefore, you should use them frequently.

The following list highlights some pointers on the design and use of page fragments:

► The level at which you decide to work with modules depends on the complexity of the application and the planned reuse of individual fragments. A high level of modules (fragmentation to the smallest level) increases flexibility and reusability, but at some point, this level of fragmentation has a negative affect on manageability.

► When a BSP page includes page fragments, all the pages can use only one, uniform, server-side scripting language.

► Note that during the composition of all page fragments and the corresponding BSP page, a valid HTML document is always produced. Otherwise, the client browser can produce an unwanted interpretation (for example, it might completely ignore the coding).

► As with BSP pages, you can develop static and dynamic parts within a page fragment. You can also submit page fragments for a syntax check. A page fragment can generally be included in several BSP pages. When you perform a syntax check, a dialog window opens, in which you can select the corresponding BSP page. In this context, you can also use variables of the parent BSP page in the scripting portion of the page fragment; however, ensure that you submit these page fragments to syntax checks as well.

Figure 5.26 shows the results of the new page. At this point, only two (header and navigation fragments) of the five page fragments have been populated with contents. The empty page fragments are therefore not yet shown.

Now we must create the connection between our start page and the new information page. Click on the image on the start page and the navigation to the information page is triggerd. The following coding is inserted into *default.htm*:

```
<A href="information.htm">
    <img src="intro.jpg" alt="Welcome Picture"
    border="0">
</A>
```

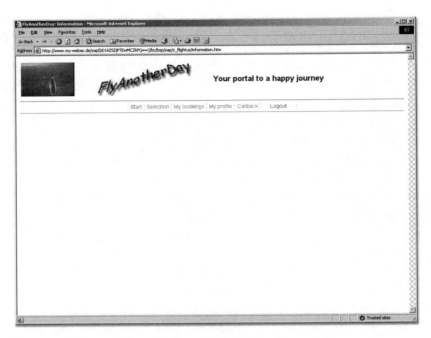

**Figure 5.26** The new information page in the flight booking portal

To make the site easy for visitors to navigate, we add a text link that also guarantees navigation to the information page:

```
<A href="information.htm"> Click image to proceed... </A>
```

## 5.4    Data Retrieval

So far, we have primarily concentrated on the technical aspects of the layout of the Web application. Now, however, we will redirect our focus. The following section examines retrieving data from the SAP tables available in the SAP Web AS, declaring variables, and displaying the retrieved data. All these tasks point to an additional central aspect of developing BSP applications: the implementation of flow and business logic. As previously noted, ideally, these areas are separated from the design of the layout. Our goal is to take the first step by greeting each visitor personally on the Welcome page. Instead of the impersonal greeting, "Hello Guest," all visitors will be greeted with their full name, based upon their logon data. In terms of technical development, this means selecting the name from the appropriate database table, storing the results temporarily in an appropriate data structure, and then outputting the name to the layout.

The second step is to retrieve available flights from the database system and display them in a table on the information page. Here, too, data must be read according to a selection criterion, saved in an internal structure, and ultimately displayed. In essence, the logic here is the same as that used for personalization.

An understanding of the data definition and the visibility of a BSP page are prerequisites for all the partial steps in the various scenarios.

You can define data objects and data types at various locations within a BSP page. This ability to define data has a direct influence on the visibility of the defined objects, that is, on their usability in the various components of a BSP page. A declaration can occur at the following points:

**Data Definitions**

▶ **Layout**

You can use this variant (see Figure 5.27) to create the required data objects and data type definitions in the layout of a BSP page. Visibility is then limited to the layout of the BSP page and all the page fragments included in this page. You can create these local declarations as inline code.

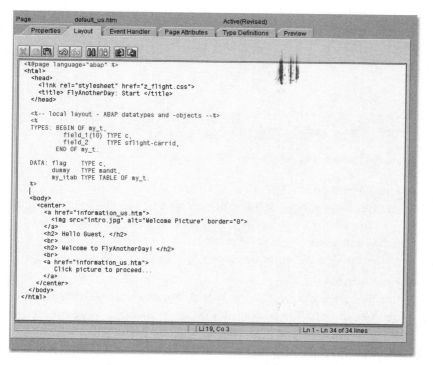

**Figure 5.27** Sample data definitions in layout

Declarations in the layout should be limited to a minimum and serve only to support dynamic elements.

▶ **Event Handler**
You can create data definitions in the event handler. If you do so, the visibility of the data definitions is local and limited to each event handler. Figure 5.28 shows a simple declaration of data object and data type definitions.

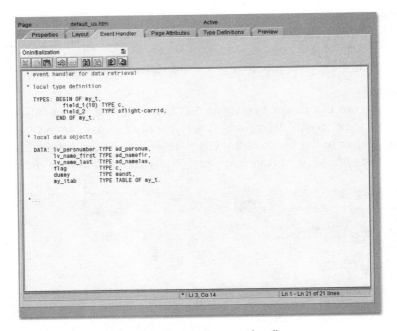

**Figure 5.28** Sample data definitions in the event handler

▶ **Type Definitions**
You can use the **Type Definitions** tab in a BSP page to create BSP-global type definitions. These type definitions can be used within the entire BSP page: in all event handlers and in the layout. Figure 5.29 shows the declaration of two global types in the type definitions.

▶ **Page Attributes**
In a BSP page, you can use the **Page Attributes** tab to declare BSP-global data objects. The page attributes are available at various times: in all event handlers and in the layout of a BSP page. Note that you cannot declare type definitions in the **Page Attributes** tab. See Figure 5.30 for some sample definitions of data objects, including some definitions that use the type definitions you have created.

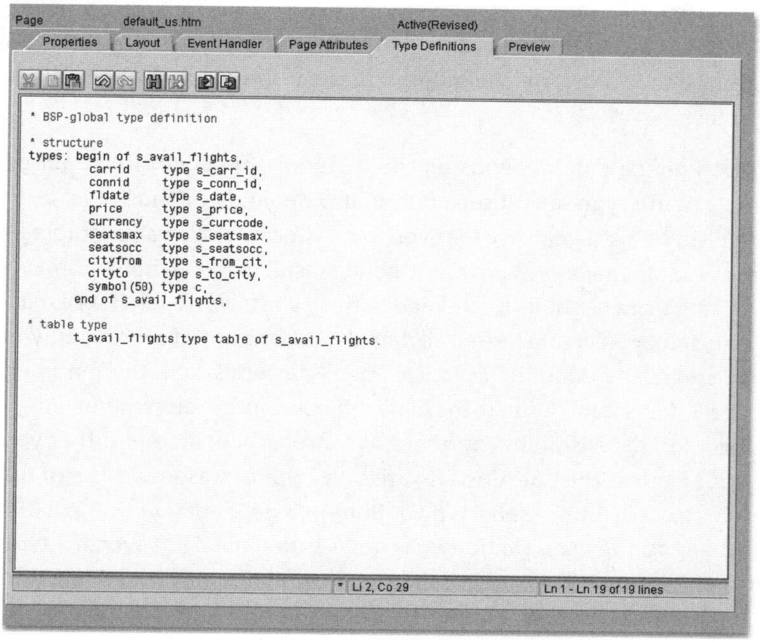

**Figure 5.29** Sample BSP-global type definitions

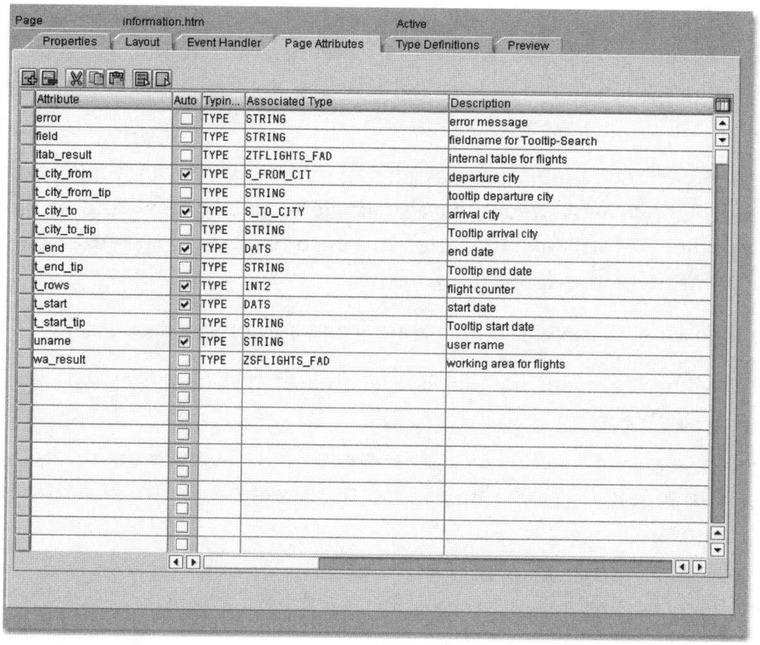

**Figure 5.30** Sample definition of BSP-global data objects (Page attributes)

**Data Dictionary**  Of course, you can also classify the data objects you use directly in the Data Dictionary with the help of the ABAP dictionary types. This method corresponds to global type definitions that can be used in all development objects.

Where you define data depends on the required visibility of the required data objects and type definitions. But, it also depends on individual taste and the level of manageability that you want. Consider a small example. A auxiliary variable that stores an intermediate result in the layout and that is required there can certainly be defined in the layout. However, if, as a matter of principle, you want to keep all data definitions out of the layout, you can also create the data object in the Page Attributes tab. Keep in mind that page effects can occur if the data object is used elsewhere—in an event handler, for example. Therefore, we strongly recommend that you avoid this practice. The question also arises regarding reasonable use of the BSP-global type definitions. If a type definition is needed only within a BSP page, adding to the Data Dictionary is not worthwhile. However, if a type is used more frequently—and in other development objects—adding it to the Data Dictionary makes a great deal of sense.

**Event Handler**  Every BSP page owns specific points in time and follows a very particular processing flow. Event handlers map the various points in time. Both flow control and access to the business logic of the BSP application in the ABAP-OO context are established within the handlers. See Section 3.3.3 for a detailed description of the processing flow and the individual event handlers.

In general, we recommend storing the business logic in an application class. For simpler cases, you can also implement business logic in the event handler. We will take the latter approach in the following examples until we introduce the application class.

In the following, the event handlers are listed and briefly described:

▶ The onCreate event handler is executed first. It initializes data and generates objects.

▶ The onRequest event handler is executed at every request (every access to a BSP page). It can be used to recreate data structures from the request.

▶ The onInitialization event handler is used to retrieve data, in particular, reading data from a database.

▶ The onManipulation event handler can be used to manipulate the flow of HTTP data stream after the layout has been processed.

▶ The `onInputProcessing` event handler is used to process user entries, to navigate to subsequent pages, and to transfer parameters to subsequent pages.

For our purposes, we will first use the `onInitialization` event handler.

### 5.4.1 Scenario 1: Customization of the Start Page

Now that you have been introduced to the basics, we can turn to the implementation of the first sample scenario. Here, we want to use the logon data to determine the full user name and display it in the layout. Because this process deals with data retrieval, the name will be determined in the `onInitialization` event handler. To determine the personnel number of the current user from the logon name (in the runtime structure `sy-uname`), we employ User Table USR21. The personnel number will then be used to select the first and last name from the address table ADRP.

For implementation, open the BSP page *default.htm*. Select the **Event Handler** tab and then select the `onInitialization` event handler in the drop-down box. Then switch to change mode so that the event handler can accept entries (white background: see Figure 5.31).

Implementing the Event Handler

Within the editor, enter the following code to determine the personnel number:

```
SELECT  SINGLE  persnumber
                FROM   usr21
                INTO   lv_persnumber
                WHERE  bname = sy-uname
```

The result of the selection is a personnel number stored in the variable `lv_persnumber`. The following code determines the first and last name of the user based upon this number:

```
SELECT  SINGLE  name_first name_last
                FROM   adrp
                INTO   (lv_name_first, lv_name_last)
                WHERE  persnumber = lv_persnumber.
```

The results of this selection are stored in two variables: one variable provides intermediate storage of the first name (`lv_name_first`) and the other variable provides intermediate storage of the last name (`lv_name_last`).

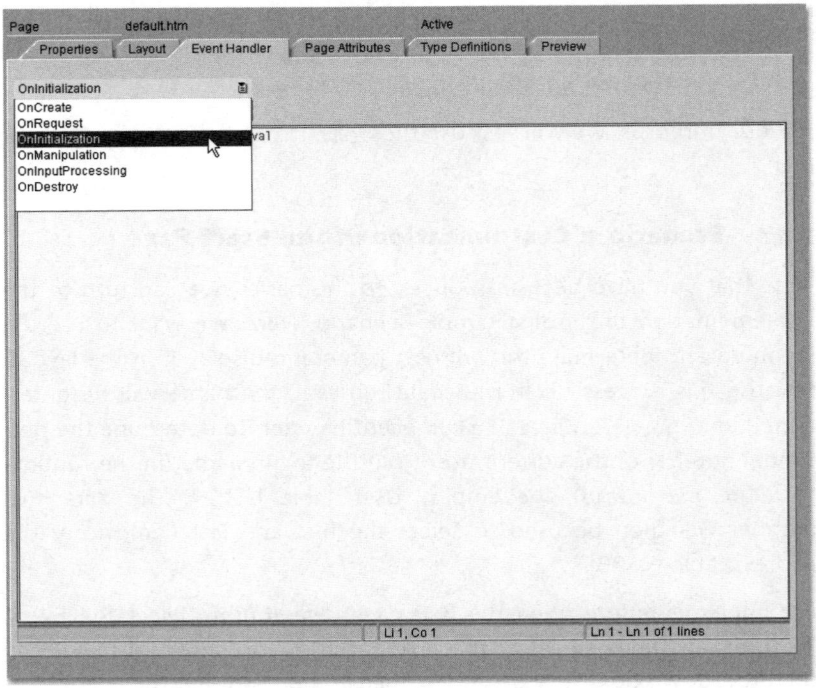

**Figure 5.31** Opening the onInitialization Event Handler

The results are summarized in the `name` variable, which contains the complete name and will be used in the layout to output the information. The following code shows how the complete name is generated from the two components:

```
CONCATENATE lv_name_first lv_name_last
    INTO name SEPARATED BY space.
```

Now we need to perform the required data declaration. The event handler needs the variables `lv_persnumber`, `lv_name_first`, and `lv_name_last` only locally. Create the variables there and type them as follows:

```
DATA: lv_persnumber TYPE ad_persnum,
      lv_name_first TYPE ad_namefir,
      lv_name_last  TYPE ad_namelas.
```

Note that the data definition should be located at the start of the coding for the event handler. Doing so is good programming style and increases manageability.

The declaration of the variable name behaves differently: it is needed in both the event handler and in the page layout. Accordingly, this global variable is created as a page attribute. Open the **Page Attributes** tab and create the page attribute with the type `string` (see Figure 5.32).

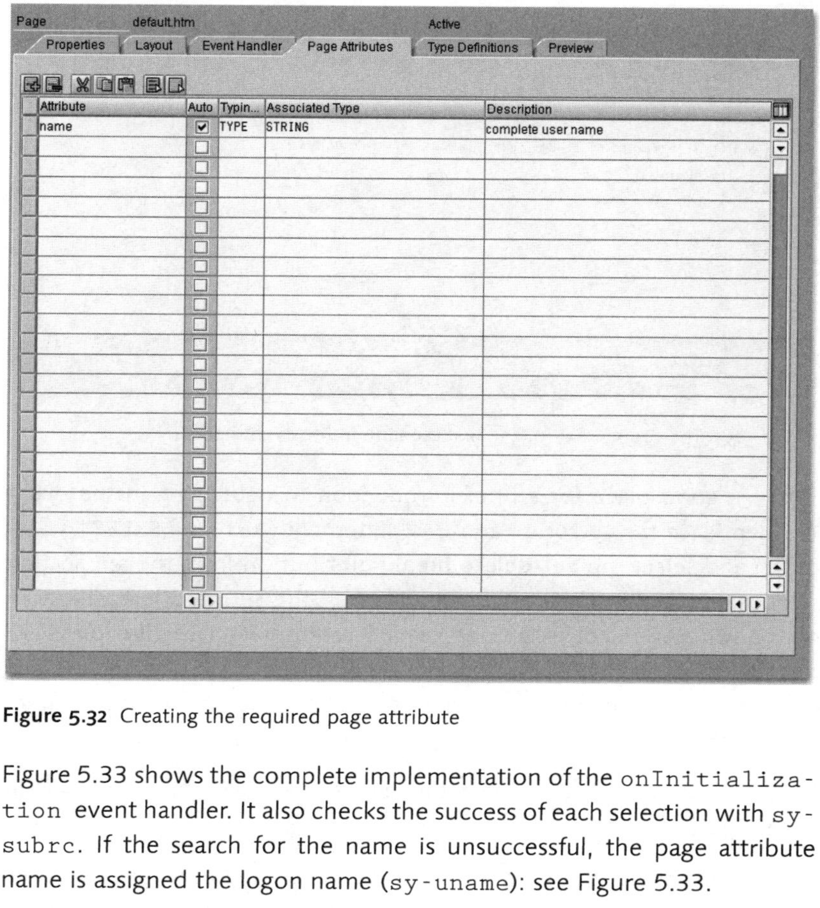

**Creating a Page attribute**

**Figure 5.32** Creating the required page attribute

Figure 5.33 shows the complete implementation of the `onInitialization` event handler. It also checks the success of each selection with `sy-subrc`. If the search for the name is unsuccessful, the page attribute name is assigned the logon name (`sy-uname`): see Figure 5.33.

Do not forget to comment on the source code regularly. Save your entries, check the syntax, and then activate the BSP page.

Properties | Layout | Event Handler | Page Attributes | Type Definitions | Preview

OnInitialization

```
* event handler for data retrieval
* local data objects
DATA: lv_persnumber TYPE ad_persnum,
      lv_name_first TYPE ad_namefir,
      lv_name_last  TYPE ad_namelas.

* get personal id number
SELECT SINGLE persnumber
       FROM   usr21
       INTO   lv_persnumber
       WHERE  bname = sy-uname.

IF sy-subrc = 0.
* get complete user name - firstname and lastname
  SELECT SINGLE name_first name_last
         FROM   adrp
         INTO   (lv_name_first, lv_name_last)
         WHERE  persnumber = lv_persnumber.

  IF sy-subrc = 0.
* build complete name
    CONCATENATE lv_name_first lv_name_last INTO name SEPARATED BY space.
  ELSE.
    name = sy-uname.
  ENDIF.

ELSE.
  name = sy-uname.
ENDIF.
```

                                          Li 29, Co 7                    Ln 1 - Ln 29 of 29 lines

**Figure 5.33** The source text for the first scenario in the event handler

**Debugging**  This is a good place for a brief introduction to debugging in the event handler. Place the cursor on an ABAP statement (such as a SELECT statement) and select the **Set/delete breakpoint** button from the application toolbar (stop icon). These actions will color the selected line yellow. A dialog window might also open, which prompts you to turn on HTTP debugging. Now, when you execute a BSP page, an additional mode is opened in which the debugger has been started. The most common functions of the debugger are available in this mode (see Figure 5.34).

You can also set a breakpoint in the layout of the BSP page, but only in scripting statements.

To conclude the customization of the start page, the only task that now remains is to adjust the output in the layout. Switch to the layout view and replace the greeting with the following code:

```
<H2> Hello <%= name %>, </H2>
```

This code displays the name of the logged-on user. Figure 5.35 shows the new appearance of the BSP page.

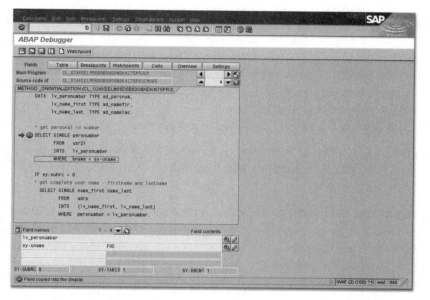

**Figure 5.34** Debugging an event handler

**Figure 5.35** The results of the first scenario in the Web Browser

### 5.4.2 Scenario 2: Displaying Flights

This scenario enhances the information page of the flight booking portal so that the page includes a table listing the available flights. Users can employ the displayed flights as a starting point for booking or for further searches. Implementation occurs in the page fragment *info.htm* that has already been created. In the first step, we will select the flight data, store it in an internal table, and then display it properly in the layout.

 When you call the flight data generator, ensure that the flight data model is populated with appropriate data records. You can use report SAPBC_ DATA_GENERATOR.

Selection of the flight data also occurs in the onInitialization event handler. You can use a database view available in the system to select the data. The view is called SFLIGHTS2 and is a component of the flight data model. Of course, you can also program the selection manually. However, the view helps to keep the sample data manageable. When the page is first called, it should display a maximum of six flights for the next ten days as the default. Next to the information on individual flights, an additional column will contain an icon that indicates the availability of seats. To populate that column, we will use various MIME graphics from the *Public* folder of the MIME repository. To implement the selection from the database, switch to the onInitialization event handler for BSP page *information.htm*.

**Declarations and constants**

**Listing 5.2** Data retrieval in the event handler

```
CONSTANTS:
  co_day_spread TYPE i VALUE 10,
" Time horizon (10 days)
  co_level3 TYPE p decimals 2 VALUE '100.00',
" Completely booked (100%)
  co_level2 TYPE p decimals 2 VALUE '70.00',
" Booking level 2 (70%)
  co_level3_mime TYPE string VALUE
'../PUBLIC/BC/ICONS/S_S_TL_R.GIF', "MIME-Path
  co_level2_mime TYPE string VALUE
'../PUBLIC/BC/ICONS/S_S_TL_Y.GIF', "MIME-Path
  co_level1_mime TYPE string VALUE
'../PUBLIC/BC/ICONS/S_S_TL_G.GIF'. "MIME-Path
DATA:
  lv_day_start TYPE sy-datum,
  lv_day_end TYPE sy-datum,
```

```
   lv_seatsmax TYPE s_seatsmax,
   lv_seatsocc TYPE s_seatsocc,
   lv_calc TYPE p DECIMALS 2.
```

```
* Set time horizon
lv_day_start = sy-datum.
lv_day_end = lv_day_start + co_day_spread.
```
Time horizon

```
* Selection of flight data
SELECT  carrid connid fldate price currency seatsmax
        seatsocc cityfrom cityto
   FROM sflights2 UP TO 6 ROWS
   INTO TABLE itab_result
   WHERE fldate BETWEEN lv_day_start AND lv_day_end.
```
Select flights

The first step creates the declarations needed for the constants and data objects used.

Flight selection is to be limited to a period covering the next ten days, which requires filling the corresponding variables. For example, lv_day_start contains the current date, and lv_day_end contains the last day of the period. The co_day_spread constant maps the overall period.

The next step selects flights from the view discussed above. The selection limits the number of results to six flights and considers the time period defined in the WHERE clause.

The selection contains table fields that are important for output or additional processing within the application. Here, we will select the abbreviation of the airline (carrid), the flight connection (connid), the date of the flight (fldate), the price of the flight (price), the currency of the flight price (currency), the number of available seats (seatsmax), the number of occupied seats (seatsocc), the departure city (cityfrom), and the destination city (cityto). The results of the selection are placed into an internal table. This is a special type of table that was created with global type definitions. Figure 5.36 shows the definition of the corresponding structure and the table definition that belongs to it.

The generated type, s_avail_flights, represents a flat structure type that contains all the fields to be selected. It also includes the symbol and symbol_desc fields. The first field records the path to the MIME object that will be displayed; the second field records a description (tool tip) of the graphic. The table type t_avail_flights was created based upon this structure type.

```
* BSP-global type definitions

* Structure
types: begin of s_avail_flights,
         carrid           type s_carr_id,
         connid           type s_conn_id,
         fldate           type s_date,
         price            type s_price,
         currency         type s_currcode,
         seatsmax         type s_seatsmax,
         seatsocc         type s_seatsocc,
         cityfrom         type s_from_cit,
         cityto           type s_to_city,
         symbol(50)       type c,
         symbol_desc(40)  type c,
       end of s_avail_flights,

* Table type
         t_avail_flights type table of s_avail_flights.
```

**Figure 5.36** The required type definition

These type declarations are used to define an internal table and a working area for the table. You should now make the following data declaration in the page attributes

```
DATA itab_result TYPE t_avail_flights.
DATA wa_result TYPE s_avail_flights.
```

Now we complete the missing paths for symbols in the internal table by using the following model:

▶ Full or overbooked flights receive a red traffic light, meaning that no seats are available.

▶ If a flight is more than 70% booked, a yellow traffic light is displayed, meaning that only limited seats are available.

▶ All loads under 70% receive a green traffic light, signaling that a relatively large number of seats are available.

Constants define the paths to the icons in the MIME directory (*Public* directory); see the previous example. The load is calculated from the fields seatsmax and seatsocc, which are available for every data record. Finally, the local variable `lv_calc` contains the results of the load calculation. The internal table is then supplemented with the appropriate entries for the MIME paths in the `symbol` field and the corresponding description in the `symbol_desc` field:

**Listing 5.3** Adding the MIME graphics

```
* Adding the MIME graphics
LOOP AT itab_result INTO wa_result.
  lv_seatsmax = wa_result-seatsmax.
  lv_seatsocc = wa_result-seatsocc.
  lv_calc = lv_seatsocc * 100 / lv_seatsmax.
  IF lv_calc >= co_level3.
* Completely booked/overbooked -> red traffic light
    wa_result-symbol = co_level3_mime.
    wa_result-symbol_desc = 'No more seats available!'.
  ELSEIF lv_calc > co_level2."
* Level of utilization > 70% -> yellow traffic light
    wa_result-symbol = co_level2_mime.
    wa_result-symbol_desc = 'Only limited seats
                            available!'
  ELSE.
    wa_result-symbol = co_level1_mime."
* Level of utilization <= 70% -> green traffic light
    wa_result-symbol = co_level1_mine.
    wa_result-symbol_desc = 'A lot of seats available!'
  ENDIF.
  MODIFY itab_result
    FROM wa_result TRANSPORTING symbol_desc.
  CLEAR wa_result.
ENDLOOP.
```

Now the table must be output to the layout. Switch to the page fragment *info.htm* and implement an HTML table. You can use the Tag Browser's drag and drop to get table components. Fine-tune the layout even further by using the linked style sheet. Output occurs with a simple loop statement.

**Listing 5.4** The output in the source code

```
<TABLE border="1">
  <TR>
    <TD class="graum">
     Carrier
    </TD>
    <TD class="graum">
      Connection
    </TD>
    <TD class="graum">
      Flight date
    </TD>
    <TD class="graum">
      Price
    </TD>
    <TD class="graum">
      Currency
    </TD>
    <TD class="graum">
      Departure
    </TD>
    <TD class="graum">
      Arrival
    </TD>
    <TD class="graum">
      Availability
    </TD>
  </TR>
  <% LOOP AT itab_result INTO wa_result. %>
  <TR>
    <TD class="hgrau" align="center">
      <%= wa_result-carrid %>
    </TD>
    <TD class="hgrau" align="center">
      <%= wa_result-connid %>
    </TD>
    <TD class="hgrau" align="center">
      <%= wa_result-fldate %>
    </TD>
```

```
<TD class="hgrau">
  <%= wa_result-price %>
</TD>
<TD class="hgrau" align="center">
  <%= wa_result-currency %>
</TD>
<TD class="hgrau">
  <%= wa_result-cityfrom %>
</TD>
<TD class="hgrau">
  <%= wa_result-cityto %>
</TD>
<TD class="hgrau" align="center">
  <IMG src="<%= wa_result-symbol %>"
       alt="<%= wa_result-symbol_desc %>">
</TD>
</TR>
<% ENDLOOP. %>
</TABLE>
```

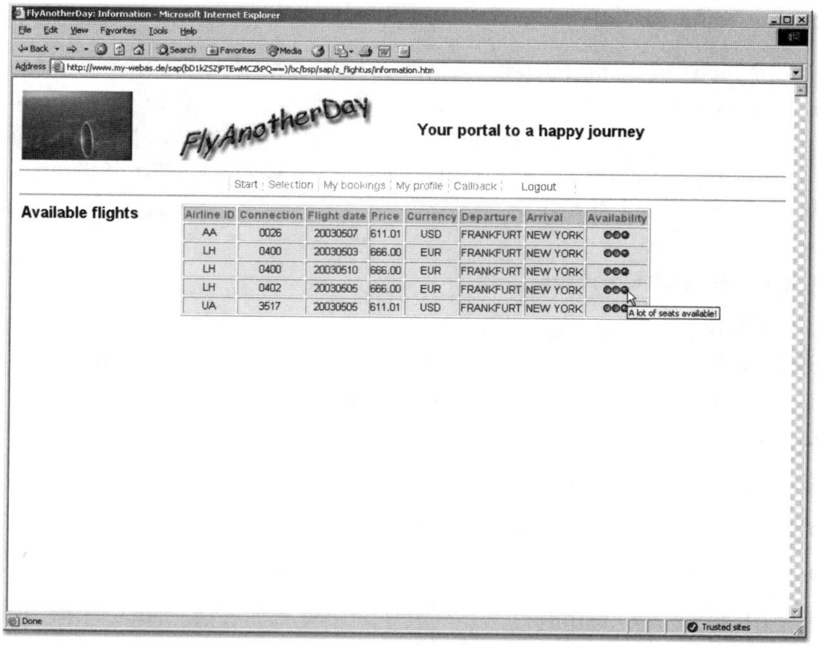

**Figure 5.37** The results of the flight selection in the Web browser

Once you have created the layout in the fragment, save and test the parent BSP page *information.htm*. Figure 5.37 shows how the results should appear.

As you probably noticed, the date of the flight is still displayed according to an internal format for display (format: yyyymmdd). We'll look at this problem later.

## 5.5    Processing User Entries and Navigation

This section focuses on the processing of user entries in HTML forms. The forms can be as complex as you want; they help capture data. Users trigger the transmission of forms by clicking on a **Submit** button. This action transfers the form data to the server where it can be processed further. After the additional processing, the user is directed toward another part of the application, or the system returns a message about the entries. For example, when users enter incorrect information, the system might return them to the form page so that they can correct the errors. However, if all the entries are correct, the data should be sent to the next page for further processing. In the context of BSP development, several options exist to ensure this behavior. The following section introduces the various options.

In our flight booking portal, we will supplement the information page with a form, which consists of five entry fields. Four fields limit the flight times and locations; one field limits the output list. Therefore, the entries made in the form are the selection criteria upon which the list of flights is redetermined and displayed.

### 5.5.1    Event Control

onInput_
Processing

In the BSP programming model, the onInputProcessing event handler is available for processing user entries and the subsequent navigation. The following conditions are required for the event handler to be triggered:

▶ A form must be defined within the BSP page.

▶ At least one **Submit** button must exist to transmit the form.

▶ The name of the button to be evaluated is "onInputProcessing."

The name of the button must be "onInputProcessing" because using the button and processing the event are linked to the name of the button. Unless at least one button conforms to this naming convention, the event handler is not called. The name of the event handler is not case- sensitive. Listing 5.5 shows an example of the correct definition of HTML form that complies with onInputProcessing:

**Listing 5.5** Defining an HTML Form

```
<FORM name="myform">
    <INPUT type="submit" name="onInputProcessing"
    value="Page 1">
</FORM>
```

Of course, you can design the form to include several **Submit** buttons to execute different server-side actions that must be evaluated. In this case, each button must have the name "onInputProcessing." However, the server page cannot determine which button was actually selected. To solve this problem, you can assign an additional ID to the hard definition of the name. This ID identifies the button and appears in parentheses next to the name. The ID is called the *event ID*.

The following example shows a form with three **Submit** buttons, each with a definition of its own event ID. Selecting each individual button enables the user to navigate to a different page. In the third example, the user is returned to the same page:

**Listing 5.6** An HTML form with three Submit buttons

```
<FORM name="myform">
<INPUT type="submit" name=
    "onInputProcessing(event_1)"
    value="to page 1">
<INPUT type="submit" name=
    "onInputProcessing(event_2)"
    value="to page 2">
<INPUT type="submit" name=
    "onInputProcessing(event_3)"
    value="to the same page">
</FORM>
```

In addition to information on that a button was pushed, the server also receives the button's ID. This information allows the event handler to distinguish between the buttons. To enable this feature, the `onInput-Processing` event handler has a global runtime object name `EVENT_ID` (the object type is `string`). When the button is pushed, this object is automatically populated with the event ID of the button. Listing 5.7 shows coding for differentiating cases in the event handler:

**Listing 5.7** Evaluating the EVENT_ID in the event handler

```
CASE event_id.
WHEN 'event_1':
* … check/process entries and then navigate to page 1
WHEN 'event_2':
* … check/process entries and then navigate to page 2
WHEN 'event_3':
* … check/process entries and then navigate to the
* same page
ENDCASE.
```

Unlike the name of the event handler, the name of the event ID is case-sensitive. Note this limitation during evaluations in the CASE statement.

## Dynamic Navigation to Subsequent Pages

To enable the design of dynamic navigation within a BSP application, an additional global runtime object, NAVIGATION, is available. This object is based upon the IF_BSP_NAVIGATION interface (see Appendix A.2) implemented by the CL_BSP_NAVIGATION class. The object enables various methods to trigger navigation. The two most important methods are the following:

▶ GOTO_PAGE
This method requires a parameter that provides the absolute or relative URL of the subsequent page.

Example: goto_page( 'page1.htm' ).

▶ NEXT_PAGE
Instead of listing a URL as the subsequent page, a navigation request determined in the Properties tab of a BSP application is provided.

Example: next_page( 'to_page_1' ).

Each of these methods produces an HTTP redirect: a new request is sent to the server with the HTTP method of GET.

With this information, we can now supplement the event handler with the appropriate navigation instructions. Our example uses the GOTO_PAGE method. Listing 5.8 shows the last example:

**Listing 5.8** Navigation to a subsequent page with the GOTO_PAGE method

```
CASE event_id.
  WHEN 'event_1':
  navigation->goto_page( 'page1.htm' ).
  WHEN 'event_2':
  navigation->goto_page( 'page2.htm' ).
  WHEN 'event_3':
* … nothing else needed: automatic navigation
ENDCASE.
```

If you want to navigate to the same page, you don't need to call a method: the page is automatically reloaded. This is always the result when the `onInputProcessing` event handler is processed and does not find any appropriate navigation.

Now, you can put this example into practice. Implement the HTML form given in Listing 5.8 in the body of a new BSP page. Then, create two different target pages (*page1.htm* and *page2.htm*) and implement the code of the flow control in the `onInputProcessing` event handler. Figure 5.38 shows the start page with the three buttons.

**Figure 5.38** The start page of the navigation sample via the event handler

When the second button is selected, the navigation goes to page 2 (see Figure 5.39).

At this point, testing the debugging is a good idea. Create a breakpoint in the `CASE` statement and look at the contents of the global object `EVENT_ID` at runtime so that you can complete the subsequent navigation.

Target page 2 - Microsoft Internet Explorer
File Edit View Favorites Tools Help
Back Search Favorites Media
Address http://www.my-webas.de/sap(bD1kZSZjPTEwMCZkPQ==)/bc/bsp/sap/z_nav_demous/page2.htm
Page 2
Done
Trusted sites

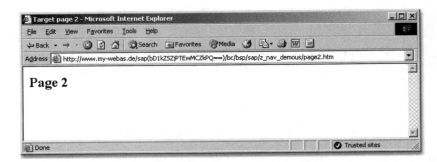

**Figure 5.39** The results of navigation

**Navigation requests**

As we just indicated, you can also navigate using navigation requests. You define navigation requests in the navigation structure of a BSP application; these requests represent the navigation edges of a navigation graph. Symbolic names (aliases) are assigned to the edges and used as references for navigation. This kind of navigation allows for targeted change of navigation paths in a BSP application, without, however, changing the source code. You can make the appropriate entries in the **Navigation** tab of your BSP application (see Figure 5.40).

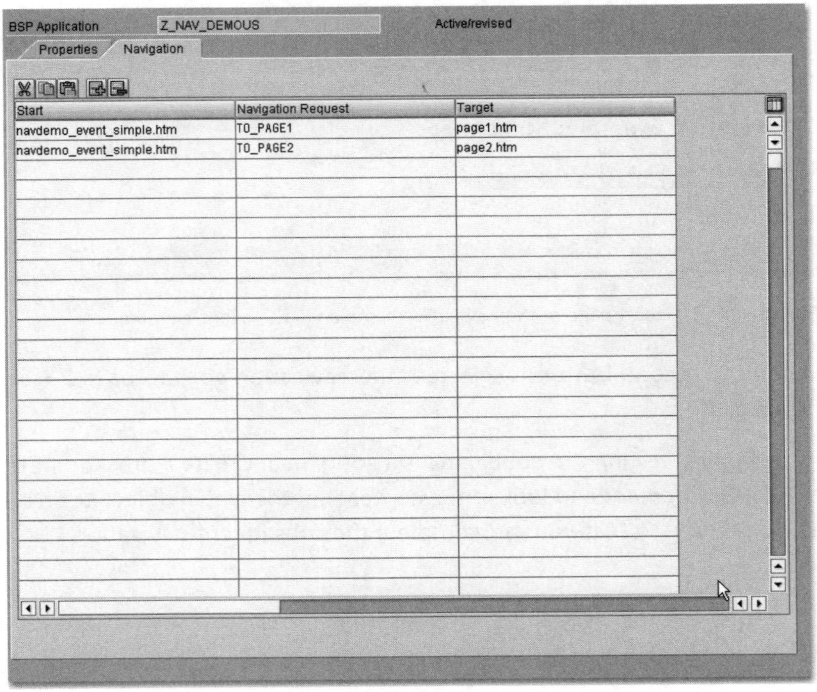

BSP Application
Z_NAV_DEMOUS
Active/revised
Properties
Navigation
Start
Navigation Request
Target
navdemo_event_simple.htm
TO_PAGE1
page1.htm
navdemo_event_simple.htm
TO_PAGE2
page2.htm

**Figure 5.40** Definition of a navigation request

When you use these navigation requests in the `onInputProcessing` event handler, you must use the NEXT_PAGE method. Listing 5.9 shows the modified coding for the last example:

**Listing 5.9** Navigation from the event handler with the NEXT_PAGE method

```
CASE event_id.
  WHEN 'event_1':
  navigation->next_page( 'to_page_1' ).
  WHEN 'event_2':
  navigation->next_page( 'to_page_2' ).
  WHEN 'event_3':
* ... nothing else required: automatic navigation
ENDCASE.
```

The actual navigation is executed only after you leave the event handler.

### Transferring Parameters Between BSP Pages

Along with the declaration of global data objects, page attributes function as (import) interfaces of a BSP page. Therefore, page attributes can be populated with external values by creating a page attribute with an auto flag. This kind of attribute is called an *automatic page attribute*.

**Automatic page attributes**

It's important to note that the automatic transfer of the field contents of a BSP page to the subsequent page is accomplished with the equivalency of names. An automatic page attribute with the same name must be defined on the target page for the name/value pairs of the form field to be transferred.

We'll use the previous example to better explain this idea. We'll record two text fields (`field_1` and `field_2`) in the form that already exists. The contents of these fields are to be transferred and output to the target page. Expand the layout of the start page to include the following entries:

```
Fieldname 1 <INPUT type="text" name="field_1"><BR>
Fieldname 2 <INPUT type="text" name="field_2"><BR><BR>
```

The SET_PARAMETER method of the runtime object NAVIGATION is used to transfer parameters to the subsequent page. You can execute this method in two ways. The abbreviated or short option appears as follows:

```
navigation->set_parameter( 'form_field_name' ).
```

Use of the short variant presupposes that the name of the form element in the layout and the automatic page attribute on the target page have the same name.

However, if the formula field name on the source page and the name of the automatic page attribute on the target page differ, you must use the following variant to guarantee that the names are equivalent:

```
navigation->set_parameter(name='form_field_name'
                          value=myform_field_value).
```

With this variant, you must also read the contents of the formula field into a variable (my_form_field_value) from the request manually. Here you can use an additional runtime object named REQUEST. This object is of the ICF_HTTP_REQUEST type and offers methods for working with the request. You can use the GET_FORM_FIELD to read a formula field.

Listing 5.10 shows the implementation of the onInputProcessing event handler with both of the variants introduced above:

**Listing 5.10** Transferring parameters with the SET_PARAMETER method

```
DATA: lv_help TYPE string.
CASE event_id.
  WHEN 'event_1'.
    navigation->set_parameter( 'field_1' ).
    navigation->set_parameter( 'field_2' ).
    navigation->goto_page( 'page1.htm' ).
  WHEN 'event_2'.
    lv_help = request->get_form_field( 'field_1' ).
    navigation->set_parameter( name = 'field_1' value
                               =lv_help ).
    lv_help = request->get_form_field( 'field_2' ).
    navigation->set_parameter( name = 'field_2' value
                               =lv_help ).
    navigation->goto_page( 'page2.htm' ).
  WHEN 'event_3'.
*  … nothing else required: automatic navigation
ENDCASE.
```

Now you must create the automatic page attributes on the target page. Open each page and enter the page attribute. Check the auto flag for each attribute (see Figure 5.41).

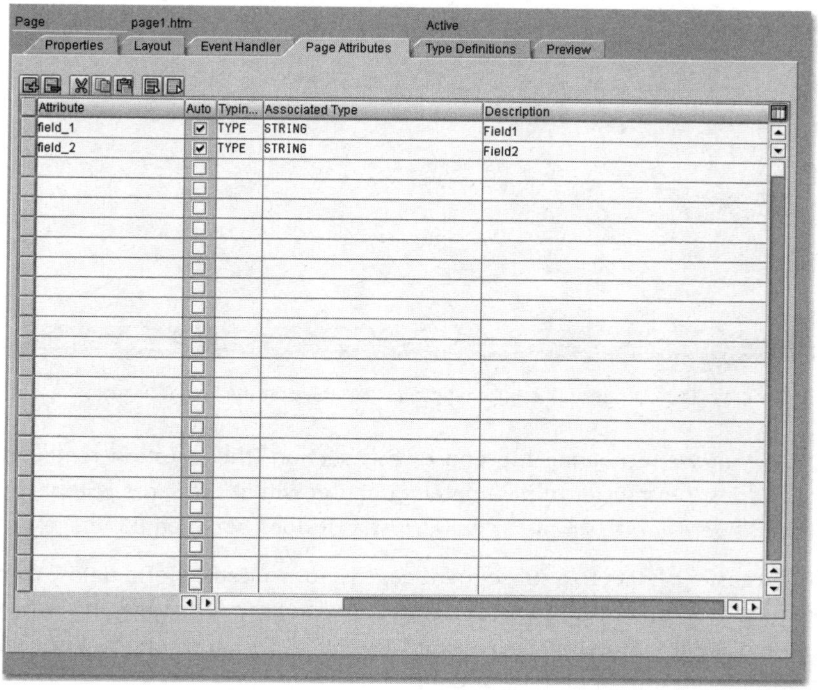

**Figure 5.41** Creating automatic page attributes

Figure 5.42 shows the start page for this example. You can enter character strings in the two text fields.

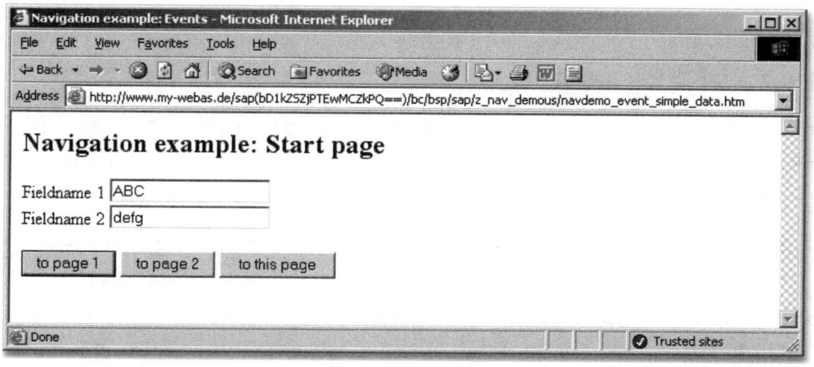

**Figure 5.42** The Start page

After navigating to the target page, the automatic page attributes are filled there. The contents of the variable are output to the layout (see Figure 5.43).

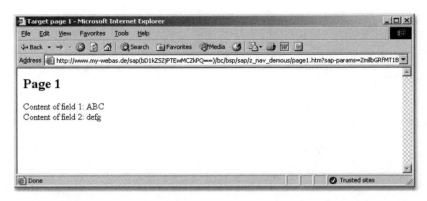

**Figure 5.43** The output of the automatic page variables on the Target page

Now that we're nearing the end of this section, the question remains: how does the transfer of parameters function within the same BSP page. The answer is quite simple: it works just as it does between BSP pages.

The transfer of data to a subsequent page is not limited to form fields. You can use this method to transfer any data to a subsequent page, including internal tables. However, because of the HTTP-GET restriction, you can transfer a maximum of 4 KB of data.

You can use the USE_AUTO_SUBMIT_FORM method of the NAVIGATION object to transfer a large amount of form data from the onInput-Processing event handler. This method performs the transfer of the data with HTTP-POST and is not subject to the size limitations previously noted.

### 5.5.2 URL Parameters

You can use additional options to transfer parameters between BSP pages. These options use traditional HTML methods instead of the onInputProcessing event handler.

**Name/Value Pair in the Link** With the first option, you transfer parameters from one page to the next in the URL. You simply add *name/value pairs* directly to the target reference, and then append a question mark (?). An ampersand (&) separates the individual pairs. The principle is the same as that discussed in Section 3.3.2 on calling a BSP application:

```
<Log>://<Host>:<Port>/<Naming_environment/<application_
name>/<Page>?<name1=value1>&<name2=value2>
```

An example:

```
<A href="http://www.my-webas.de/my-service.htm?
test=true"></A>
```

This case also requires an automatic page attribute with the same name on the target page if you want to transfer the value into the target variable automatically. In addition to the simplicity of its implementation, this variant offers another plus: you can use it to implement lists of links without any great effort. However, on the other page, you must remember that this technique does not use separate flow control. The following section builds a simple example. We will return to this topic later, in the context of selecting a flight in the flight booking portal.

### 5.5.3  HTML Form Control

The second option consists of assigning parameters to the <FORM> tag. Two attributes are available:

<form auto="..."
method"...">

1. `action`
   This attribute specifies a URI for processing form data. Clicking on the **Submit** button enables a user to navigate to the target address entered.

2. `method`
   This attribute determines how form data is transmitted: with the HTML methods POST or GET.

An example:

**Listing 5.11**  Transferring parameters in the <FORM> tag — Excerpt

```
<BODY>
  <FORM name="myform" action="http://www.my-webas.de/my-
  service.htm" method="GET">
    <INPUT type="text" name="test" value="true">
    <INPUT type="submit" value="Go!">
  </FORM>
</BODY>
```

Listing 5.11 affects exactly the same parameter transfer as the URL approach discussed in the previous section. With the latter variant, however, you can use the JavaScript event onSubmit() to influence the <FORM> tag attribute of the input tag parameter. Don't forget to create the corresponding automatic page attribute.

All three variants have advantages and disadvantages that you should evaluate:

▶ The simplicity of the principle speaks for the URL link. However, with this variant, you cannot control the target address with user entries. Flow control is not separated.

▶ Parameterization of the <FORM> tag does not share this disadvantage; however, it must be programmed with client-side JavaScript for complex behavior. Flow control is not separated.

▶ The variant with the event handler is the most flexible and largely separates flow control from presentation logic. However, this variant demands increased implementation efforts.

When you are unsure, we always recommend the third variant. The first variant is the preferred method only for simple tasks, such as simple output lists from which you navigate further. The second variant is especially not recommended when the target group does not use a uniformly defined browser, including the configuration settings. At least for professional Web development with JavaScript, the behavior of the application with deactivated JavaScript should be tested on the client page.

 Yet another variant exists: the *Model View Control* (MVC) *Design Pattern*. Because the MVC represents a completely different use of programming, we will discuss this topic later.

### 5.5.4  Enhancing the Flight Booking Portal

First, we will use the *default.htm* page to demonstrate data transfer with a name/value pair. The graphic link should not only proceed to the next page, but also transfer the user name.

Accordingly, we will enhance the source code from Section 5.3 with the reference:

```
<A href="information.htm?uname=<%= name %>">
   <IMG src="intro.jpg" alt="Welcome image"
   border="0">
</A>
```

The target page reference is followed by a question mark and then the name/value pair. The name of the pair is uname. We will use the ABAP variable name (previously populated in the event handler with the name) as the value portion. Now, when users click on the graphic, the variable uname is transferred with the value of name.

You can check this immediately. When you move the mouse pointer over the picture in the newly generated Web page, the status line shows the current name/value pair: see Figure 5.44.

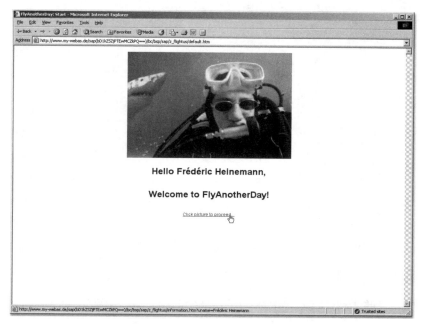

**Figure 5.44** The status line shows the populated name/value pair

The parameter can now be received on the target page. If an automatic page attribute with the same name exists, it is populated automatically. Create the automatic page attribute `uname` (of type `STRING`) in the BSP page *information.htm*. Don't forget to set the auto flag (see Figure 5.45).

We also want to use the new parameter right away, and this presents us with a good opportunity to populate the page fragment *bottom.htm*. The page fragment recognizes all page attributes automatically if it has been linked in a BSP page. We can therefore use the parameter without additional programming. Insert the following coding into the page fragment:

```
<HR>
<P>You are logged on as: <%= uname %>
```

You do not have to populate the `onInputProcessing` event handler in the BSP page *default.htm*. The "HTML automatism" (the process that happens in HTML code) handles the transfer of all parameters added to the URL.

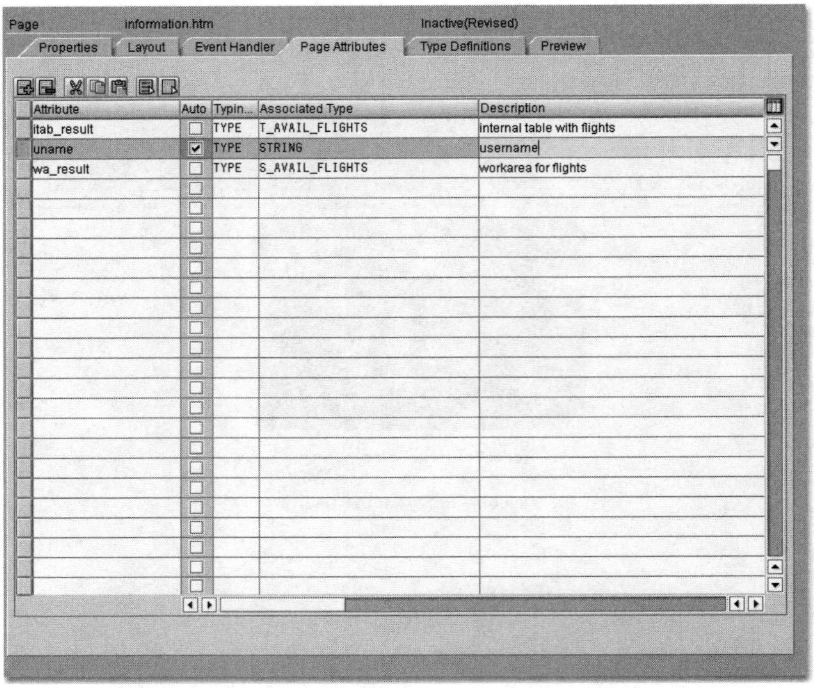

**Figure 5.45** **Figure 5.45** A new automatic page attribute for the name/value pair

Next, we teach the application how to record selection parameters for the flights to be displayed in the table. Populate the page fragment *selection.htm* and use the `onInputProcessing` event handler to transfer parameters.

Five entry fields are defined in a form so that the user can enter selection criteria. We also add a button that triggers the processing of the onInput-Processing event handler. For a design that is intended to be informative, the coding is placed into a table and enhanced with the CSS.

**Listing 5.12** The form in page fragment selection.htm—Excerpt

```
<FORM name="myform">
...
    <INPUT type="text" name="t_start" value="<%=
    t_start %>" size="10">
    <INPUT type="text" name="t_city_from" value="
    <%= t_city_from %>" size="20">
    <INPUT type="text" name="t_rows" value="<%=
    t_rows %>" size="3">
```

```
<INPUT type="text" name="t_end" value="<%=
t_end %>" size="10">
<INPUT type="text" name="t_city_to" value="<%=
t_city_to %>" size="20">
<INPUT type="hidden" name="uname" value="<%=
uname %>">
<INPUT type="submit" name=
"onInputProcessing(search)" value="search">
...
</FORM>
```

After you call the *information.htm* page with the search function or
update it with browser functions, the previous implementation will cause
the contents of the variable uname to be lost from page fragment *bot-
tom.htm*. To avoid this problem, we would typically insert the following
line into `onInputProcessing` for uniform implementation logic: `nav-
igation->set_parameter( 'uname' )`. However, we'll use this
opportunity to introduce the HTML command `<INPUT type="hid-
den">`. This command transfers the contents of the variable as a hidden
form field to the target page. The results are identical, regardless of the
approach taken.

In this case, the code for the event handler is very short, because when
you transmit the form, you don't need to do it with `SET_PARAMETER`:

**Listing 5.13** The event handler for processing user interaction

```
CASE event_id.
  WHEN 'search'.
  WHEN OTHERS.
ENDCASE.
```

Of course, the variables that contain the selections that have been
entered must be declared as an automatic page attribute:

**Listing 5.14** The required automatic Page attribute

```
DATA t_end TYPE char10.
DATA t_start TYPE char10.
DATA t_city_from TYPE s_from_cit.
DATA t_city_to TYPE s_to_city.
DATA t_rows TYPE int2.
```

To enable use of these parameters for database selection in the `onIni-tialization` event handler, the entries are processed and formatted as parameters. The selection is then adjusted accordingly. Simply replace the old code with the following:

**Listing 5.15** Setting the selection criteria

```
* set time horizon
IF t_start IS INITIAL.
   t_start = lv_day_start = sy-datum.
ELSE.
   lv_day_start = t_start.
ENDIF.
IF t_end IS INITIAL.
   t_end = lv_day_end = lv_day_start + co_day_spread.
ELSE.
   lv_day_end = t_end.
ENDIF.
* set the number of flights
IF t_rows IS INITIAL.
   t_rows = 6.
ENDIF.
* set the departure and arrival locations
IF t_city_from IS INITIAL.
   t_city_from = 'FRANKFURT'.
ENDIF.
IF t_city_to IS INITIAL.
   t_city_to = 'NEW YORK'.
ENDIF.
* selection of flight data
SELECT  carrid connid fldate price currency seatsmax
seatsocc cityfrom cityto
 FROM   sflights2 UP TO t_rows ROWS
 INTO   TABLE itab_result
 WHERE fldate BETWEEN lv_day_start AND lv_day_end
 AND cityfrom = t_city_from
 AND cityto = t_city_to.
```

If no parameters are entered, the variables are populated with the default values. Figure 5.46 shows the results of this action.

Figure 5.46  The selection of flights

At this point, the date is still output in the internal format. The same internal format must also be used in the entry fields for the selection. In addition, the departure and arrival locations must be entered in upper-case character. We'll discuss this in more detail later.

## 5.6    The Application Class

The application class encapsulates the business logic of a BSP application. This class, which you must create yourself, is a typical ABAP class. All event handlers and, if needed, the layout of every BSP page of the related BSP application can call the methods of the class. The runtime environment automatically creates a global runtime instance of the application class. The instance is addressed by the name APPLICATION and permits access to the methods of the class. There is no need to assign a special instance to the class. The application class is created in the Class Builder. We recommend that you create the application class (and other classes as well) in the customer namespace environment: begin the name with "Z_CL."

If you use your own constructor, ensure that it has no parameters.

For our flight booking portal, we will store the application logic, which contains the information garnered from a previous database selection, in its own application class. To perform this task, the application class must contain an attribute and two methods. The attribute records the results of the selection; the two methods select the data and enable access to it.

 Because further development of the flight booking portal increasingly demands changes in the program code, we will freeze the current state of the BSP application Z_FLIGHTUS and continue to work with a copy named Z_FLIGHT01US.

**Creating an application class**

First, we need to create an application class. In the Class Builder (access via Transaction SE24 or directly from the Object Navigator), create a public class named Z_CL_FLIGHT_US (see Figure 5.47).

 You can also enter the class to be created directly in the application class field on the **Properties** tab of the BSP application. Double click on this entry (forward navigation) to create the class. After a security query, you arrive at the **Create** dialog window, as shown in Figure 5.47.

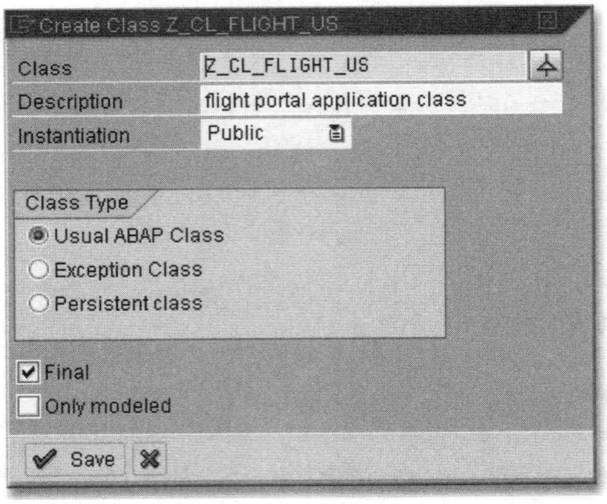

| Create Class Z_CL_FLIGHT_US | |
|---|---|
| Class | Z_CL_FLIGHT_US |
| Description | flight portal application class |
| Instantiation | Public |

Class Type
- ● Usual ABAP Class
- ○ Exception Class
- ○ Persistent class

☑ Final
☐ Only modeled

✔ Save ✖

**Figure 5.47** Creating an application class in the Class Builder

You must save the results of the selection. To do so, we use a typed attribute of the class. As you recall, we also typed the flight table within the BSP page *information.htm*. We can't use this type as a reference type because the class does not recognize it here. Accordingly, we have created a structure type, ZSFLIGHTS_FAD, and a table type, ZTFLIGHTS_FAD, in the Data Dictionary so that we can use them in the application class.

Now, it's reasonable to adjust the typing of the page attribute in the BSP page *information.htm*. The internal table ITAB_RESULT then is of type ZTFLIGHTS_FAD and the work area WA_RESULT is of type ZSFLIGHTS_ FAD.

Create the attribute M_SELFLIGHTS in the application class according to Figure 5.48.

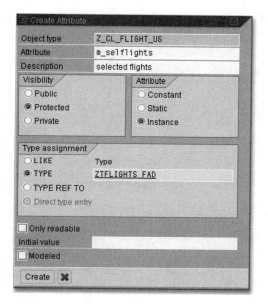

**Figure 5.48** Creating an attribute

Then create a public instance method named SELECT_FLIGHTS (see Figure 5.49). It will select the data and write the results to the attribute that you just created.

Now you can define the parameters of the method. We need the following import parameters in the interface of the method (see Figure 5.50).

Then implement the contents of the method. You can insert the existing source code from the event handler here. Now you just have to adjust the selection parameters. The method then appears as it does in Listing 5.16.

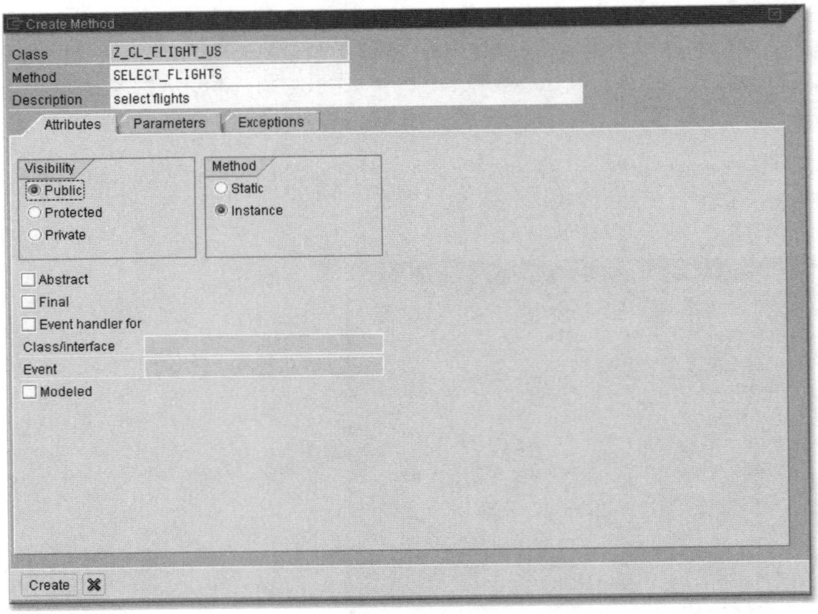

**Figure 5.49** The properties of the SELECT_FLIGHTS method

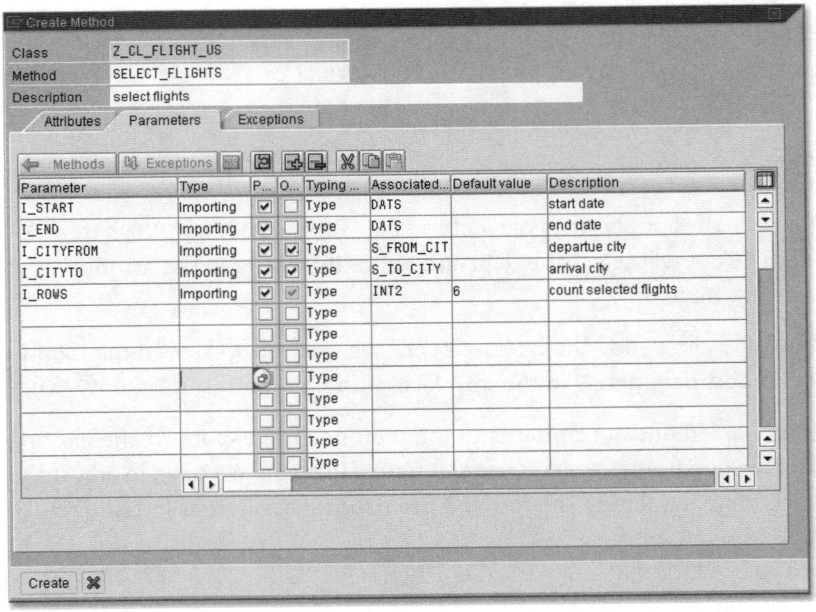

**Figure 5.50** The parameters of the SELECT_FLIGHTS method

**Listing 5.16** The source code of the SELECT_FLIGHTS method

```abap
METHOD select_flights .
  CONSTANTS:
    co_day_spread TYPE i VALUE 10,
" Time horizon (10 days)
    co_level3 TYPE p DECIMALS 2 VALUE '100.00',
" Completely booked (100%)
    co_level2 TYPE p DECIMALS 2 VALUE '70.00',
" Booking level 2 (70%)
      co_level3_mime TYPE string VALUE '../PUBLIC/BC/
ICONS/S_S_TL_R.GIF', " MIME-Path
      co_level2_mime TYPE string VALUE '../PUBLIC/BC/
ICONS/S_S_TL_Y.GIF', " MIME-Path
      co_level1_mime TYPE string VALUE '../PUBLIC/BC/
ICONS/S_S_TL_G.GIF'. " MIME-Path
  DATA:
    wa_selflights TYPE zsflights_fad,
    lv_seatsmax TYPE s_seatsmax,
    lv_seatsocc TYPE s_seatsocc,
    lv_calc TYPE p DECIMALS 2.
* Check mandatory parameters
  IF i_start IS INITIAL.
    i_start = sy-datum.
  ENDIF.
  IF i_end IS INITIAL.
    i_end = i_start + co_day_spread.
  ENDIF.
* Selecting the flight data
  SELECT  carrid connid fldate price currency seatsmax
          seatsocc cityfrom cityto
    FROM  sflights2 UP TO i_rows ROWS
    INTO  TABLE m_selflights
    WHERE fldate BETWEEN i_start AND i_end
    AND cityfrom = i_cityfrom
    AND cityto = i_cityto.
* Supplement the MIME graphics
  LOOP AT m_selflights INTO wa_selflights.
    lv_seatsmax = wa_selflights-seatsmax.
    lv_seatsocc = wa_selflights-seatsocc.
    lv_calc = lv_seatsocc * 100 / lv_seatsmax.
    IF lv_calc >= co_level3. " Completely booked/Over-
```

```
                                 booked -> red traffic light
           wa_selflights-symbol = co_level3_mime.
           wa_selflights-symbol_desc = 'No more seats
                                       available!'.
      ELSEIF lv_calc > co_level2. " Level of utilization >
            "70% -> yellow traffic light
           wa_selflights-symbol = co_level2_mime.
           wa_selflights-symbol_desc = 'Only limited
                                        seats available!'.
      ELSE.
           wa_selflights-symbol = co_level1_mime.
           " Level of utilization <= 70% -> green traffic
           " light
           wa_selflights-symbol_desc = 'A lot of seats
                                        available!'.
      ENDIF.
      MODIFY m_selflights FROM wa_selflights TRANSPORTING
      symbol symbol_desc.
      CLEAR wa_selflights.
    ENDLOOP.
  ENDMETHOD.
```

After the selection has been made and the flights stored in the attribute of the application class, you can access the flights externally with the GET_FLIGHTS method you will now create. You also create this method in the application class Z_CL_FLIGHT_US. As a formal interface parameter, this method suffices as a returning parameter R_SELFLIGHTS of type ZTFLIGHTS_FAD. Listing 5.17 shows the source code of the method.

**Listing 5.17** The source code of the GET_FLIGHTS method

```
METHOD get_flights.
  r_selflights = m_selflights.
ENDMETHOD.
```

The tasks within the application class for the purposes of this section are now completed. The results should appear as illustrated in Figure 5.51.

Save, test, and activate the class, then switch back to the BSP application.

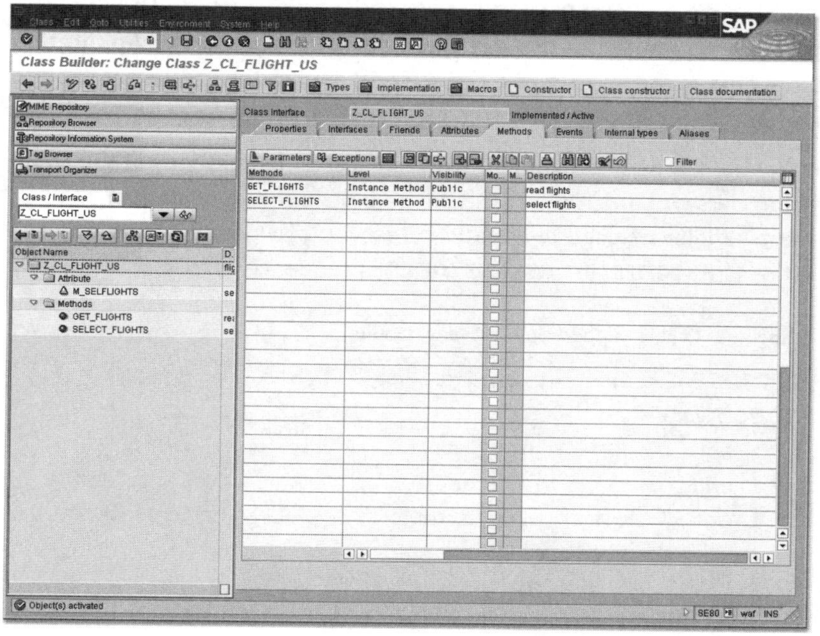

**Figure 5.51** The newly created application class

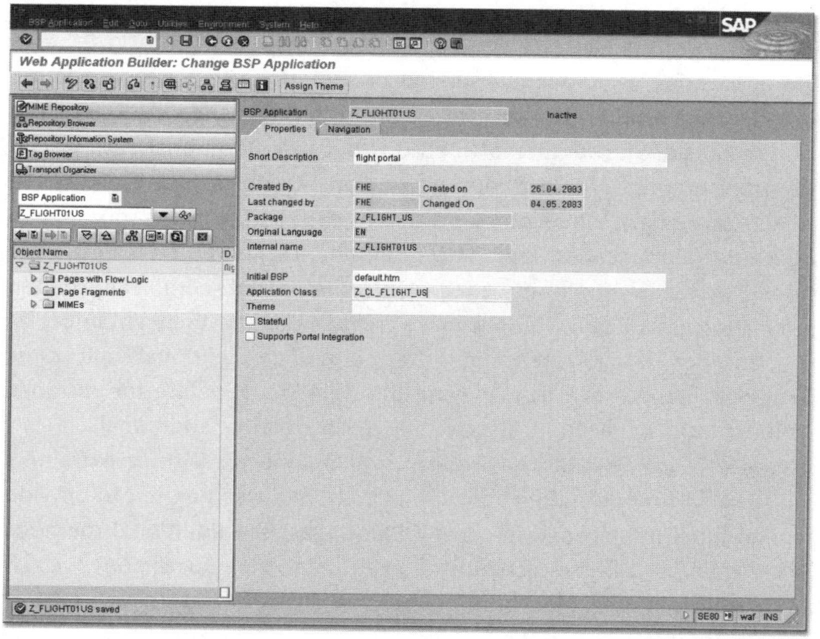

**Figure 5.52** Assigning the application class to a BSP application

<table>
<tr><td>

**Assigning the application class**

</td><td>

You assign a class to a BSP application with the properties of a BSP application. Here you enter the selected application class in the **Application Class** field of the Properties tab. Each BSP application can be assigned to exactly one application class (see Figure 5.52).

</td></tr>
<tr><td>

**Using the application class**

</td><td>

After you make the assignment, you can access the methods of the application class with the APPLICATION object. In the onInitialization event handler of page *information.htm*, you can now call the methods SELECT_FLIGHTS and GET_FLIGHTS in sequence as follows:

</td></tr>
</table>

**Listing 5.18** Calling methods in the Event Handler

```
CALL METHOD application->select_flights
  EXPORTING
    i_start    = lv_day_start
    i_end      = lv_day_end
    i_cityfrom = t_city_from
    i_cityto   = t_city_to
    i_rows     = t_rows.
itab_result = application->get_flights( ).
```

Use the template function to implement the method call. Doing so pre-generates the call with all the interface parameters for you. Optional parameters are commented out in the process.

The application logic is encapsulated in the application class. In larger projects, that would mean that the application class would have to record a disproportionate number of methods because additional calls would often be required within a method to transmit the results back to the caller. Accordingly, we recommend that as early as the design phase, you separate the application logic into additional classes by creating a class model. In our example, it's conceivable that as the complexity of the application grows, you would want to create a class for the flight information, another class for user administration, and an additional utility class for general tasks, such as retrieving the date. To populate the instance attribute, the application class would then call the additional classes, grouped according to tasks, with the usual OO mechanisms. In extremely complex class models, the application class could also be used to provide general functions needed in several BSP pages. The additional methods would then be called directly in the event handlers. Our experience has shown that only this method (i.e., creating different classes for different types of information or tasks) ensures that several developers can implement application logic simultaneously, without interfering with each other by locking the class. There is also an added advantage because maintenance of the coding is markedly better. Lastly, this approach increases the chances of reusing entire classes in additional projects.

## 5.7 Formatting the Output

One recurring problem is that the internal storage of an ABAP variable can differ significantly from how it should appear. You've probably already asked yourself why the date in our application looks so odd. This is due to the internal format of variables, which are output to the layout without undergoing a conversion. The same problem affects time and currency fields. These fields also require appropriate formatting. This section deals with the problem and presents a solution.

We use the PAGE object to format output. The PAGE object is another runtime object that's available in all event handlers and in the layout. It provides two methods that not only deliver the "correct" display of the date, but also can use the personal formatting settings in a given user's user profile.[1] The following section introduces the use of the two methods WRITE and TO_STRING.[2]

**PAGE Object**

The WRITE method can insert the contents of ABAP variables into HTML output as a string. The only condition is that the variable to be output is scalar. You call it as follows:

**The WRITE method**

```
<% page->write( parameter = value ). %>
```

The WRITE method recognizes the following parameters:

▶ `value` (type any)
The most important and only required parameter. The value transfers the name of the variable.

▶ `format` (type i)
The output format of the variables. This method recognizes the following constants:

▶ co_format_currency: output in currency format

▶ co_format_long: long output

▶ co_format_lower: output in lowercase characters

▶ co_format_none: standard formatting

---

1 Transaction SU01; for example, you can set the currency or date formats here.
2 In addition to formatting options, the PAGE object permits use of several additional methods to access information relevant to a page. See Appendix A.2 for a detailed description.

- co_format_short: short output
- co_format_upper: output in uppercase (capital) letters

▶ **outputlength** (type i)
Definition of the string's maximum output length.

▶ **num_decimals** (type i)
The number of places to display after the decimal point.

▶ **reference_value** (type c)
A reference value, such as the currency or unit of quantity.

**The TO_STRING method** You can also use the TO_STRING method as an alternative. It uses the same parameters as WRITE. Unlike WRITE, however, this method returns the formatted string as a returning parameter. The use of this method with the print directive in the layout appears as follows:

```
<%= page->to_string( parameter = value ) %>
```

Declare the ABAP variable correctly from the start: you must also assign a variable that stores a currency to a currency data type. Once you do so, you can simply transfer the NAME attribute; no other formatting specifications are required. At first, it might seem tempting to type all the data objects being used as strings. However, doing so can mean that maintenance will be more involved later on, when you parameterize methods and function modules. The following example is both simple and effective:

```
<P><% page->write( value = sy-datum ). %></P>
```

The date is no longer output in the internal format rather in a user-friendly format.

The formatting options permit formatting of the date, time, text, numbers, and currencies. Listing 5.19 shows some examples:

**Listing 5.19** Formatting options—Excerpt

```
<%= page->to_string( value = sy-datum format = if_bsp_
page~CO_FORMAT_SHORT ) %>
<%= page->to_string( value = sy-uzeit format = if_bsp_
page~CO_FORMAT_LONG ) %>
<%= page->to_string( value = 'abcABC' format = if_bsp_
page~CO_FORMAT_UPPER ) %>
<%= page->to_string( value = px format = if_bsp_page~CO_
FORMAT_CURRENCY reference_value = 'ITL' ) %>
```

The BSP application Z_PAGE_FORMAT contains a summary of the formatting options discussed here. Figure 5.53 shows the effects of the formatting at runtime.

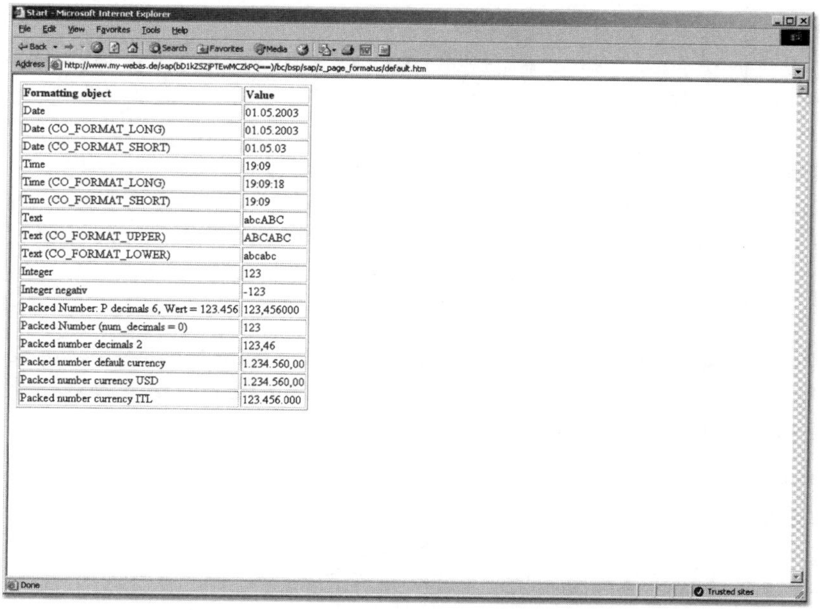

| Formatting object | Value |
|---|---|
| Date | 01.05.2003 |
| Date (CO_FORMAT_LONG) | 01.05.2003 |
| Date (CO_FORMAT_SHORT) | 01.05.03 |
| Time | 19:09 |
| Time (CO_FORMAT_LONG) | 19:09:18 |
| Time (CO_FORMAT_SHORT) | 19:09 |
| Text | abcABC |
| Text (CO_FORMAT_UPPER) | ABCABC |
| Text (CO_FORMAT_LOWER) | abcabc |
| Integer | 123 |
| Integer negativ | -123 |
| Packed Number: P decimals 6, Wert = 123.456 | 123,456000 |
| Packed Number (num_decimals = 0) | 123 |
| Packed number decimals 2 | 123,46 |
| Packed number default currency | 1.234.560,00 |
| Packed number currency USD | 1.234.560,00 |
| Packed number currency ITL | 123.456.000 |

**Figure 5.53** Formatted output of variables

**Outputting tables and input fields**

Next, we will adjust the output of our tables and input fields in the corresponding page fragments of the BSP page *information.htm*. All currency and date fields are to be displayed in a legible format.

To be able to use the type conversion of the TO_STRING method of the PAGE object, our first step changes the typing of the automatic page attribute for date fields, used in the page fragment *selection.htm*:

```
DATA t_start TYPE DATS.
DATA t_end TYPE DATS.
```

Next, the output of the date, departure city, and arrival city are adjusted in the page fragment *selection.htm*. The departure and arrival cities will be output automatically in capital letters. To adjust the output, change the <INPUT> tag's output in the form, as shown in Listing 5.20.

**Listing 5.20** Adjusting the output in the Entry Form—Excerpt

```
<INPUT type="text" name="t_start" value="<%= page->to_
string( value = t_start format = if_bsp_page~CO_FORMAT_
LONG ) %>" size="10">
<INPUT type="text" name="t_city_from" value="<%= page-
>to_string( value = t_city_from format = if_bsp_page~CO_
FORMAT_UPPER ) %>" size="20">
<INPUT type="text" name="t_end" value="<%= page->to_
string( value = t_end format = if_bsp_page~CO_FORMAT_
LONG ) %>" size="10">
<INPUT type="text" name="t_city_to" value="<%= page->to_
string( value = t_city_to format = if_bsp_page~CO_
FORMAT_UPPER ) %>" size="20">
```

The next step adjusts the output of the list of flights for the date and price fields. The prices will be formatted in the appropriate currency. Make the following changes in page fragment *info.htm*:

```
<%= page->to_string( value = wa_result-fldate format =
if_bsp_page~CO_FORMAT_LONG ) %>
<%= page->to_string( value = wa_result-price format =
if_bsp_page~CO_FORMAT_CURRENCY reference_value = wa_
result-currency ) %>
```

So that the database selection can also return results if the departure and arrival cities are entered in lowercase letters, a conversion to uppercase (capital) letters is performed in the `onInitialization` event handler. Here, you add the following code before the call of the methods of the application class:[3]

```
t_city_from = page->to_string( value = t_city_from for-
mat = if_bsp_page~co_format_upper ).
t_city_to = page->to_string( value = t_city_to format =
if_bsp_page~co_format_upper ).
```

Once you have executed the appropriate output formatting, you see the results shown in Figure 5.54. As the figure indicates, the formatting does more than display the date correctly. The change of the type in DATS also means that the date can be entered in the usual manner.

---

3  Alternatively, here you could also use the command TRANSLATE TO UPPER-
   CASE.

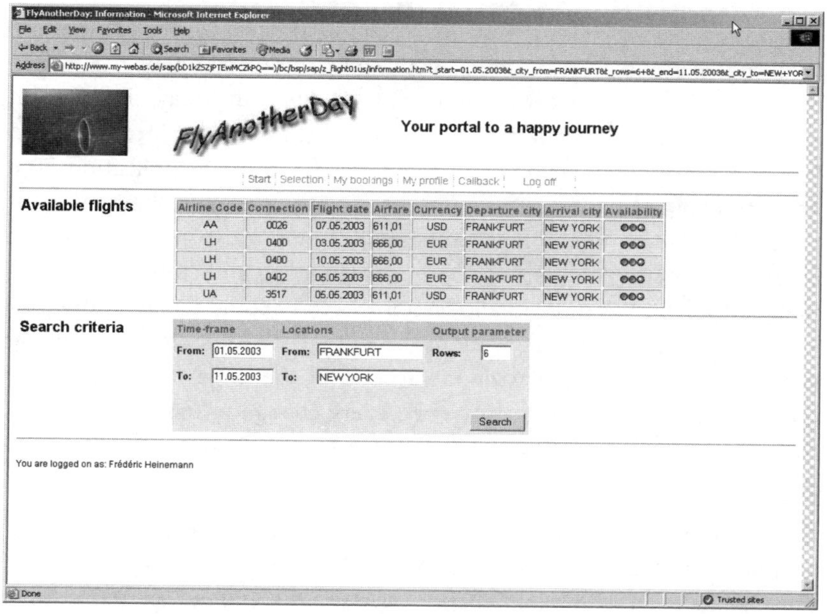

**Figure 5.54** Output formatting in the flight booking portal

You also can format variables with special, encoding print directives. The syntax is as follows:

**Special formatting options**

```
<%Encodingformat= Variable %>
```

The following four formatting options are available:

▶ **raw**

The variable is output according to its outgoing format, which corresponds to the standard BSP print directive.

▶ **html**

The variable is converted to output in a conforming HTML string: all special characters are replaced with special codes (entities). For example, the "<" character becomes "&lt;"

▶ **wml**

This setting corresponds to HTML coding. The only difference is that the output generated here conforms to WML.

▶ **url**

If a URL string is output in this manner, the result conforms to URL: all special characters are removed and replaced with permitted characters. For example, the "é" character is replaced with "%E9."

## 5.8    Multilingual Capabilities

Web applications are becoming increasingly more complex. Static text blocks controlled the Internet in its initial stages, but today, the Internet makes available full-valued applications. The applications' design and functions no longer need to hide behind a "normal" application. The growing comprehensive penetration of business processes beyond company boundaries means that Web applications must also increasingly respect international differences, such as language and culture. The multilingual capabilities of Web applications have become a mandatory prerequisite to ensure the applications' acceptance. At first, it might appear straightforward to create various versions of the pages and then store them in various subfolders. However, every change in the layout or of a text element then quickly degenerates into comprehensive and error-prone work.

BSP applications use the support of the SAP development environment. Multilingual capabilities are completely integrated into that environment; they can be used with minimal effort. We use the Online Text Repository.

**OTR**    With the *Online Text Repository* (*OTR*), your Web applications can offer texts in multiple languages. We'll now use this design to afford not only English-speaking users, but also German-speaking users, a chance to use the flight booking portal comfortably. In our example, we'll offer the welcome page and the information page in both languages. We'll start the process by displaying two national flags on the start page. When users select a flag, the display changes to the appropriate language. The text literals used on all BSP pages are marked as OTR texts (see Section 4.6) and can be translated as such. You can use OTR long texts to create both long texts and texts used only once. You can use OTR short texts for recurring texts in your application. The following BSP directive outputs OTR short texts:

```
<%= OTR(package_name/alias) %>
```

A short text always belongs to a package and is addressed via a symbolic ID, or alias. The alias can contain up to 50 characters. Open the page *default.htm* and change to the layout view. Replace the first line of the welcoming text with the second line (below):

```
<H2> Hello <%= name %>, </H2>
```

```
<H2> <%= OTR(Z_FLIGHT_US/HELLO) %> <%= name %>, </H2>
```

Create the text with forward navigation (see Figure 5.55).

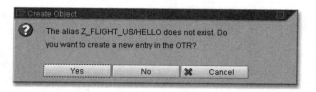

**Figure 5.55** Creating a text with forward navigation

When the dialog window opens (see Figure 5.56), enter the text to be used by this alias. You also have to set a maximum length for the translation that is to follow.

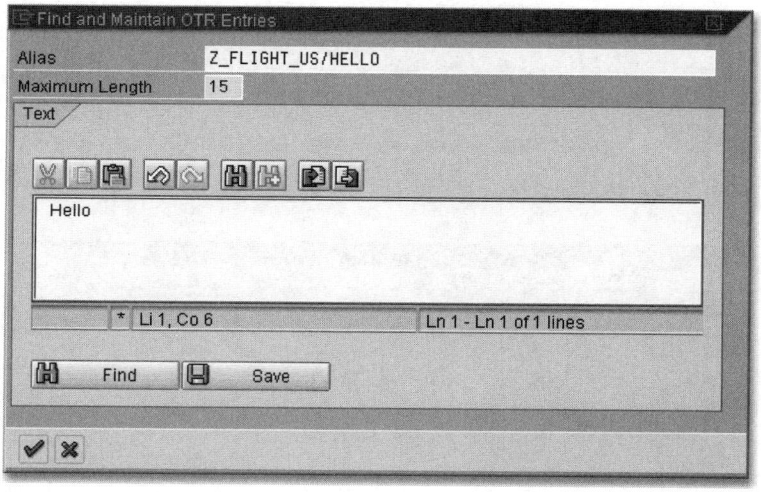

**Figure 5.56** Entering an OTR short text

Then save your entries and assign the OTR text to change request. Translation occurs in Transaction SE63. In the transaction, use the menu to select **Translation · Online Text Repository (OTR) · Short Texts**. In the dialog window that opens (see Figure 5.57), enter the package, the source language, the target language, and the text from the OTR. You can use the list of suggested values for the OTR. To process the actual translation, click on the **Edit** button.

You can now translate the text in the screen that is displayed. After you save your entry, the status line shows a confirmation and the status of the translation changes from red to green (see Figure 5.58).

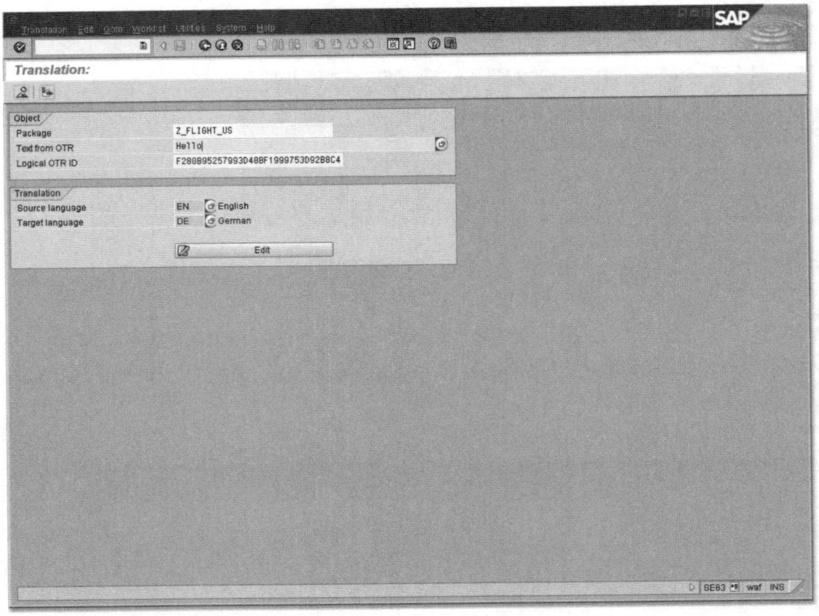

**Figure 5.57** Translating OTR short texts

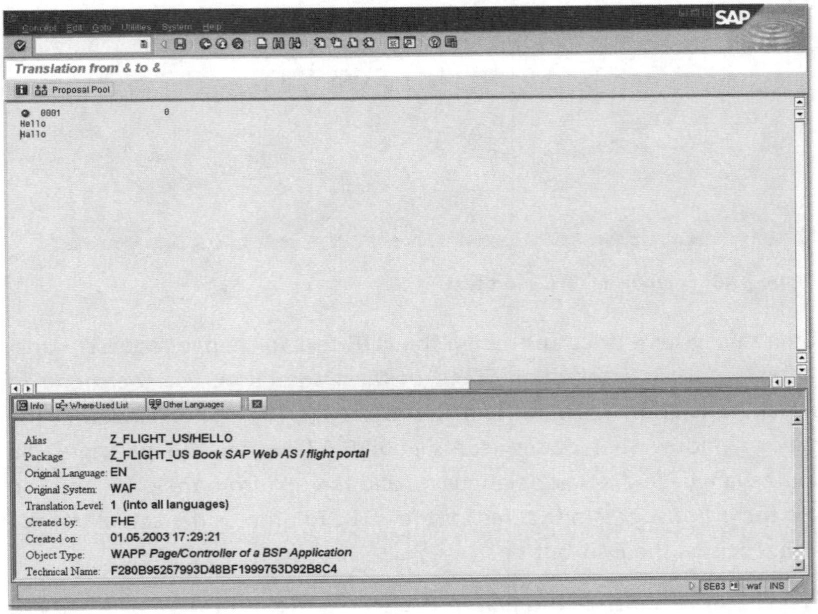

**Figure 5.58** A successful translation

These actions end the translation of the OTR text. To include multilingual elements in the entire page, you must replace all text literals on the welcome page with the appropriate OTR short texts.

A package named SOTR_VOCABULARY_BASIC already exists. It contains a number of translated OTR short texts that you can use in your BSP application. If you try to create a text that is already a component of the package, the system will notify you that it already exists. You can use the texts that already exist or create your own OTR short texts.

Now we need to explain how to change the language of our BSP application at runtime. Here we use the URL parameter sap-language. This parameter is also assigned the ISO language ID of the selected language and is then appended to the existing URL link. Listing 5.21 shows the syntax for the linked images.

**Changing the system language**

**Listing 5.21** Changing the language version

```
<A href="default.htm?sap-language=en">
    <img src="us_flag.jpg" alt="<%= OTR(Z_FLIGHTUS/
    CLANG) %>" border="0">
</A>
<A href="default.htm?sap-language=de">
    <img src="ge_flag.jpg" alt="<%= OTR(Z_FLIGHTUS/
    CLANG) %>" border="0">
</A>
```

Since the page is reloaded when the language is changed, there's no point in determining the user name again in the onInitialization event handler. Accordingly, the page attribute name is marked as an automatic page attribute, and the event handler simply checks to see if the attribute has already been populated.

The change from English to German allows the welcome page of our application to appear as shown in Figure 5.59.

You can also store an internal alias that uses a preset language in service maintenance (see Section 4.3). The alias then refers to the actual BSP application. You must create an alias for each language. Then you will only have to set the link of each national flag to refer to the appropriate alias.

Multilingual Capabilities    **329**

**Figure 5.59** The Welcome page in German

We will now adjust the page fragments *top.htm*, *navi.htm*, *info.htm*, *selection.htm*, and *bottom.htm*. Open the pages and replace all text literals with the appropriate OTR short texts.

Our application class also uses language-dependent texts to describe icons. To include the translation of these texts, you can create them as text elements. Replace the coding for the original text assignment in the first line below with the coding in the second line:

```
wa_selflights-symbol_desc = 'No more seats available!'.
```

```
wa_selflights-symbol_desc = TEXT-010.
```

Double-click on the text element TEXT-010 to go to the maintenance tool for text elements; once there, store a number and corresponding text for each of your texts. Here, too, you must enter the number of characters available for later translation in the last column (see Figure 5.60).

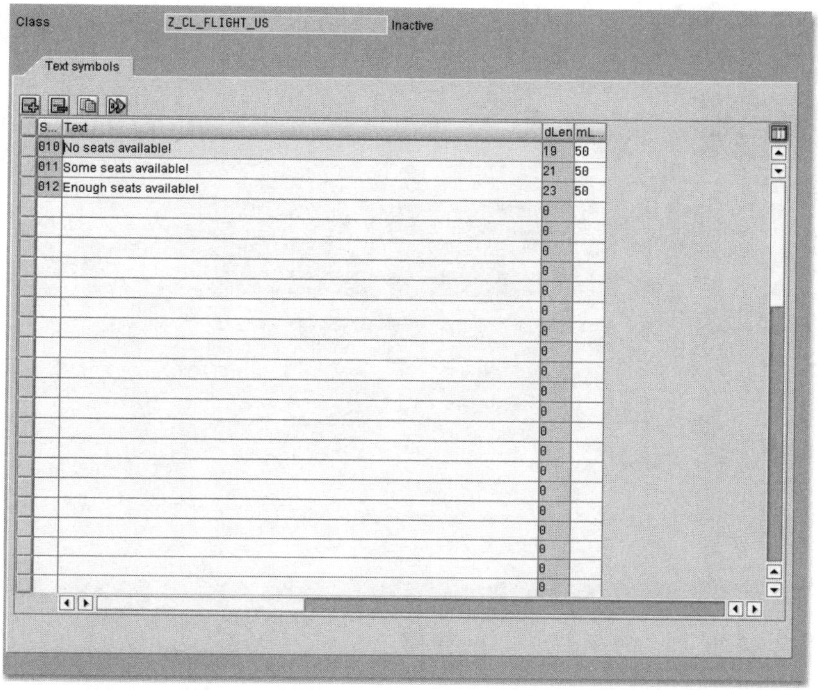

| S... | Text | dLen | mL... |
|---|---|---|---|
| 010 | No seats available! | 19 | 50 |
| 011 | Some seats available! | 21 | 50 |
| 012 | Enough seats available! | 23 | 50 |
| | | 0 | |
| | | 0 | |
| | | 0 | |
| | | 0 | |
| | | 0 | |
| | | 0 | |
| | | 0 | |
| | | 0 | |
| | | 0 | |
| | | 0 | |
| | | 0 | |
| | | 0 | |
| | | 0 | |
| | | 0 | |
| | | 0 | |
| | | 0 | |
| | | 0 | |

**Figure 5.60** Creating text elements

Take the translation of the text elements from the Class Builder via the menu **Go To Translation**.

The CL_BSP_GET_TEXT_BY_ALIAS class enables access to OTR short texts. To accomplish this task, a static method called GET_TEXT is available. The OTR alias and the language are to be transferred as parameters of the method. To use this method, the OTR short texts are created as usual. Now you can use these texts in your application class and in the event handlers. For the previous example, you would use the texts in the application class as follows:

```
wa_selflights-symbol_desc =          cl_bsp_get_text_by_
alias=>get_text( alias = 'Z_FLIGHTUS/NOSEATS' language =
sy-langu ).
```

The result of the German BSP page appears in the browser as shown in Figure 5.61.

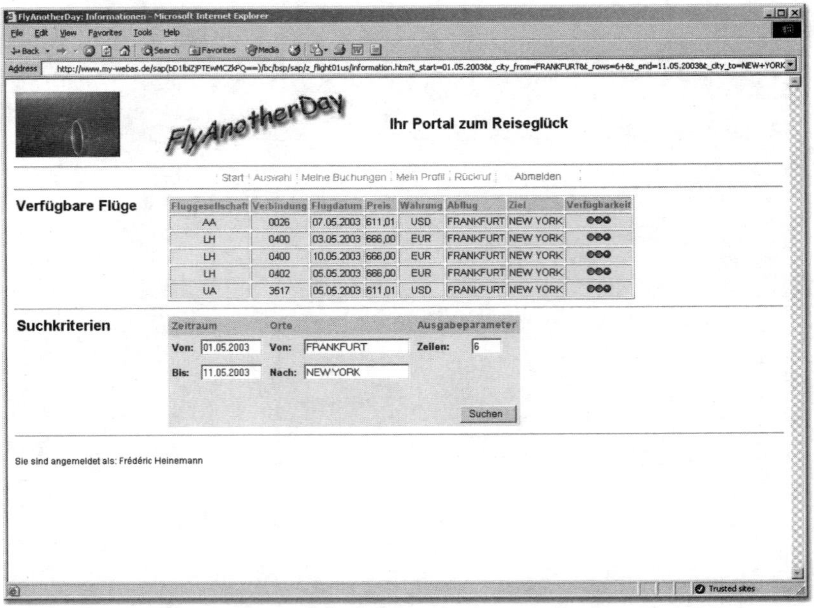

**Figure 5.61** The translated information page

## 5.9 Dictionary Services for BSP Applications

The technical properties of the declared data objects partly control the display of page attributes and locally defined variables in the context of formatting the layout of a BSP page. If typing occurs with the types in the Data Dictionary, you also have available additional properties, such as language dependency, various lengths of field identifiers, value areas, and so on.

However, to avoid limiting the display options from the very start, not all the available type properties are used automatically at runtime. Consider the date in our application as an example: the date is output without formatting if you do not explicitly customize the display (see Section 5.7). Here, we use the methods page->write() and page->to_string.

DDIC-Services  You have numerous additional options in which to use metadata from the repository that are relatively easy to implement. With the service object DDIC util, you can provide the Web application with definitions and information about the ABAP parameters that are used.

The runtime object runtime recognizes the object reference (of type IF_BSP_ServiceS) of the attribute ddic_util. In order for the method to recognize the object to which results should be returned, a reference to the corresponding dictionary object is transferred as an importing parameter. The language (LANGU) can be transferred as an optional parameter in all methods. If it isn't transferred, the method automatically uses the system language.

The following is a list of most of the available methods (see also Appendix A.2):

▶ GET_FIELD_LABEL

**Field description**

This method returns the longest field ID for an elementary data object as a field label. You can use it to describe a field displayed on a Web page in more detail.

An example that returns the field label of a data object in English appears as follows:

```
user_label = runtime->ddic_utils->get_field_label(
                 data_object_ref = dataref
                 langu            = 'E' ).
```

In Figure 5.62, this code would be the contents of the field ID "heading."

▶ GET_QUICKINFO

**Tool tip**

Calling this method provides the short description of the base elementary data object with a reference to the Data Dictionary. It is well-suited for the creation of tool tips with concise, application-specific text, such as field labels.

Example:

```
user_info  = runtime->ddic_utils->get_quickinfo(
                 data_object_ref = dataref ).
```

In Figure 5.62, this would be the contents of the field "short description."

▶ GET_DAY_COLLECTION/GET_MONTH_COLLECTION

**Calendar data**

This method returns the names of the days of the week or month stored in the Dictionary as a table of type DAYCOLLTAB or MONCOLL-TAB. The table has three columns: INDEX, ID, and TEXT. ID is the standard DIN, language-dependent abbreviation taken from the factory calendar.

Example:

```
CALL METHOD runtime->ddic_utils->get_day_collection
     EXPORTING      langu    = sy-langu
     CHANGING       day_tab  = tage.
```

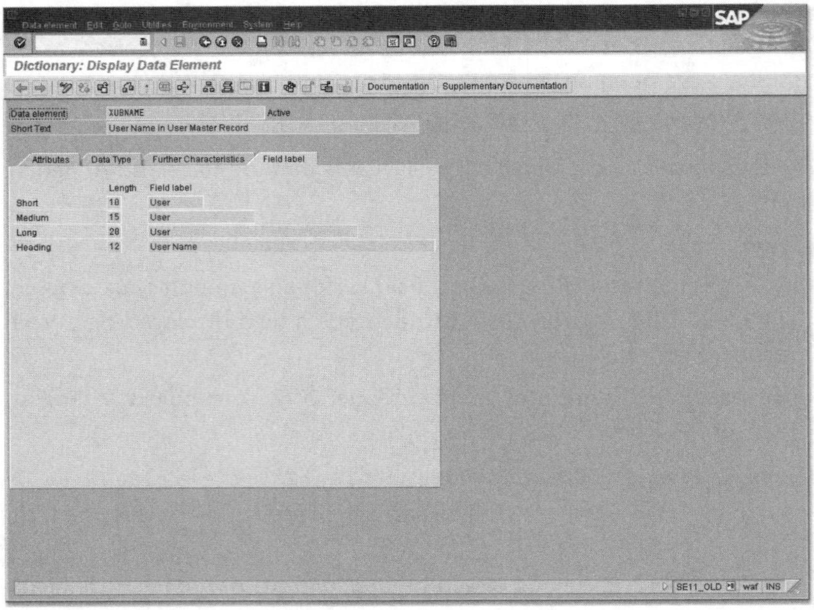

Figure 5.62 Displaying a dictionary element

**VCARD NAME** ▶ GET_HISTORY_ID/GET_LOCAL_HISTORY_ID

These fields can be assigned to a field history to support user entries in input fields (currently only for Internet Explorer 5.0 and above). The data is encrypted and stored on the client side. Unlike the local history ID, the global history ID is application-independent. The history ID is also assigned to an HTML input field by setting the VCARD_NAME attribute. If no VCARD_NAME attribute is entered, the NAME attribute is used to capture or detect the history.

Example:

```
carrid_his  = runtime->ddic_utils->get_history_id(
                        data_object_ref = datarefl ).
```

The HTML call then appears as follows:

```
<INPUT type="text"
       name="carrid_val"
       vcard_name="<%= carrid_his %>" />
```

The HTML attribute VCARD_NAME can also be assigned to any string, as long as the string is unique and identical during every HTML call of the field.

► GET_SIMPLE_HELPVALUES

This method delivers a list of values from a simple menu of suggested values. It's similar to using F4 Help in typical screen programming. The Help values best suited for simple suggested values are those returned as a two-column list of values (fixed values, for example). The second column should be a text column or another adequate means of visualizing the values in the first column.

This function will be expanded consecutively in later releases of the SAP Web AS.

Example:

```
CALL METHOD      runtime->ddic_utils->get_simple_
                 helpvalues
     EXPORTING   data_object_ref = dataref1
     CHANGING    helpvalue_tab   = helpvaluelist.
```

In typical cases, helpvaluelist should have the type of an appropriate two-column table. Listing 5.22, Listing 5.23, and Figure 5.63 combine to form a complete example.

In the following section, we'll introduce an example with the most important methods so that you can reconstruct it. This example is available for download from the SAP PRESS Internet site. The BSP application is named Z_DDIC_UTILS.

First, we'll show the coding for the onInitialization event handler in which the DDIC service methods are executed.

**Listing 5.22** Use of DDIC UTIL methods—onInitialization event handler

```
DATA: dataref1 TYPE REF TO data,
      dataref2 TYPE REF TO data,
      user     TYPE usr01,
      flight   TYPE sflight.
TRY.
* get data reference from variable
    GET REFERENCE OF user-bname    INTO dataref1.
    GET REFERENCE OF flight-carrid INTO dataref2.
* GET_FIELDLABEL
    user_label   = runtime->ddic_utils->get_field_label(
                            data_object_ref = dataref1
                            langu           = 'E' ).
* GET_QUICKINFO
    user_info    = runtime->ddic_utils->get_quickinfo(
```

```
                        data_object_ref = dataref1 ).
        carrid_title = runtime->ddic_utils->get_quickinfo(
                        data_object_ref = dataref2 ).
*  GET_HISTORY_ID
    carrid_his   = runtime->ddic_utils->get_history_id(
                        data_object_ref = dataref2 ).
*  GET_SIMPLE_HELPVALUES
      CALL METHOD       runtime->ddic_utils->get_simple_hel-
                        pvalues
          EXPORTING  data_object_ref = dataref2
          CHANGING   helpvalue_tab   = airlinelist.
*  Error handling
    CATCH cx_bsp_services.
       " ...
ENDTRY.
```

In the first step, a reference to the relevant data object is generated with the GET REFERENCE method. The corresponding references are then transferred to the method as interface parameters.

**Help values**  The most interesting aspect here is the retrieval of the Help values with the GET_SIMPLE_HELPVALUES method. The referenced data object, flight-carrid, has the domain type S_CARR_ID, which is assigned as a value table to SCARR. This table contains all the airlines (carriers) in the data model of SAPBCTRAVEL.

We generally recommend integrating error-handling when using these method calls. Doing so ensures the stability of the programs. Nothing is worse for users visiting an Internet site than an internal server error.

The layout coding follows next:

**Listing 5.23** Use of DDIC UTIL methods—layout <BODY> portion

```
<H2>Example page for the use of DDIC-Utils</H2>
<FORM method="post">
  <TABLE>
<%-- Example for GET_FIELD_LABEL/GET_FIELD_INFO  --%>
    <TR>
      <TD class="gw">GET_FIELD_LABEL/<br>GET_FIELD_
      INFO</TD>
      <TD><SPAN title="<%= user_info %>"><%= user_label
      %>:<%= sy-uname %></SPAN></TD>
    </TR>
```

```
<%-- Example for GET_SIMPLE_HELPVALUES                    --%>
   <TR>
     <TD class="gw">GET_SIMPLE_HELPVALUES</TD>
     <TD>
       <% data wa like line of airlinelist. %>
       <SELECT name="carrid">
         <% loop at airlinelist into wa. %>
         <OPTION value="<%= wa-key %>"><%= wa-value
         %></OPTION>
         <% endloop. %>
       </SELECT></TD>
   </TR>
<%-- Example for GET_HISTROY_ID                        --%>
   <TR>
     <TD class="gw">GET_HISTROY_ID</TD>
     <TD><INPUT type="text" name="carrid_val" vcard_
     name="<%= carrid_his %>" title=
     "<%= carrid_title %>"/>
       <INPUT type="submit" name="callme"
       value="Page is reloaded"/></TD>
   </TR>
  </TABLE>
 </FORM>
```

The most interesting part here is the formatting of the drop-down list. The internal table, `airlinelist`, is searched to populate a `<SELECT>` tag correctly. The values from the value column are displayed and the key value of the selected element from the drop-down list is transferred to the subsequent page. If "American Airlines" is selected, the parameter CARRID is populated with the value "AA" and transmitted by clicking on the **Submit** button.

Figure 5.64 shows the use of the Web application.

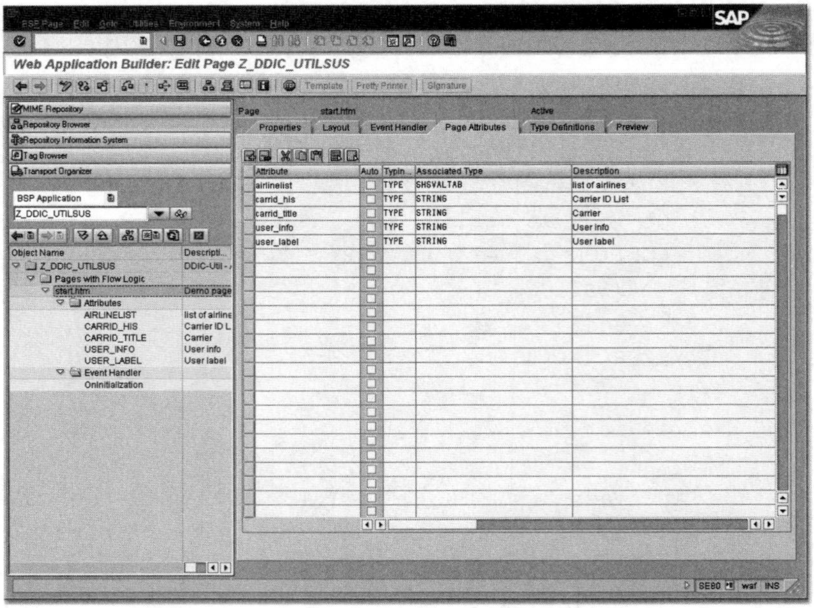

**Figure 5.63** Use of DDIC UTIL methods—Page attributes

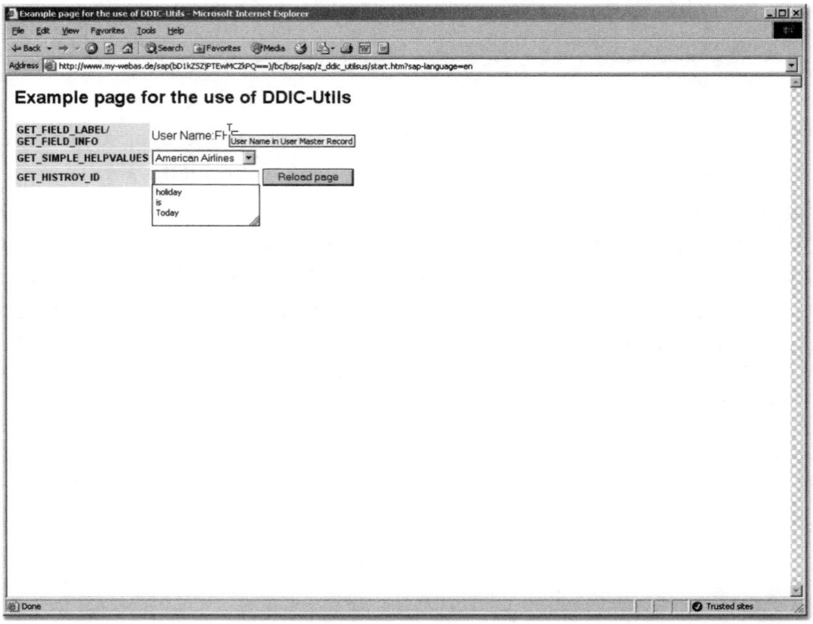

**Figure 5.64** Example DDIC page for Listing 5.23

Now we can use our knowledge in the flight portal. All input fields of the selection are to receive a tool tip as a "quick info." Because we have to create the data before we can display it on the page, we'll call the corresponding method in the `onInitialization` event handler. In order to have the tool tip variables also available on the layout page, we first need the page attribute for the corresponding tool tip (see Figure 5.65).

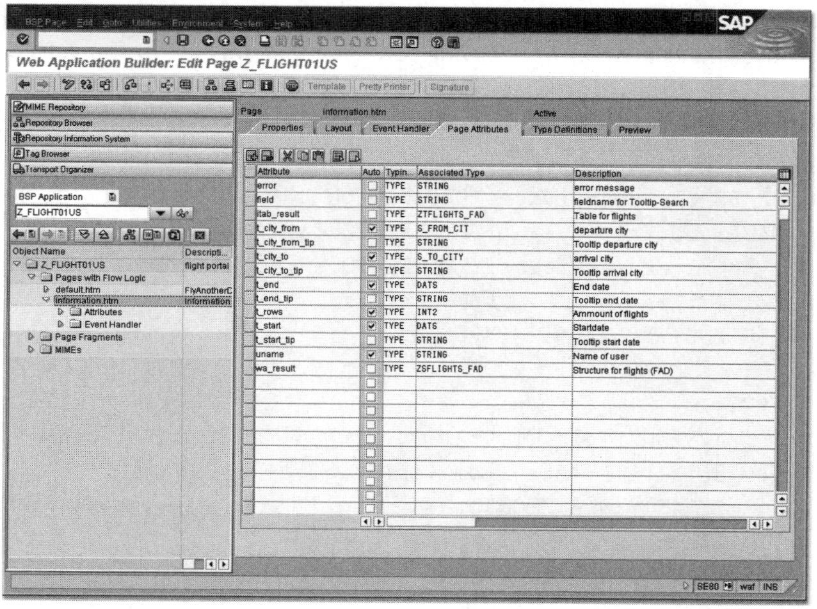

**Figure 5.65** Enhancing the Page attribute with tool tips

The next step adjusts the output in the layout. The following listing excerpt is an example of this step. The `<INPUT>` tag for the starting date is expanded with the attribute title. The other affected fields should be treated similarly.

```
<TD class="hgrau">
  <INPUT type="text" name="t_start" title="<%= t_start_
                                              tip%>"
       value="<%= page->to_string( value = t_start
       format = if_bsp_page~CO_FORMAT_LONG ) %>"
       size="10">
</TD>
```

The only thing missing now is data retrieval. Here, we have two options: we can retrieve the data directly in the event handler or we can use the application class. The advantages of the second option are obvious:

▶ A clean separation of the application logic

▶ Reusability of the method for any fields, without having to perform an individual data declaration each time for data retrieval

▶ Separation and reusability reduce the complexity and probability of error that can occur from having several programming efforts involved

**Listing 5.24** The method for enhancing the Selection fields

```
METHOD get_tooltip.
  CLASS cl_bsp_services DEFINITION LOAD.
  DATA: dataref        TYPE REF TO data,
        l_ex_services TYPE REF TO cx_bsp_services,
        typename       TYPE string.
  FIELD-SYMBOLS: <f> TYPE ANY.

  TRY.
      ASSIGN field TO <f>.
* get data reference from variable
      IF <f> IS ASSIGNED.
        typename = <f>.
        CREATE DATA dataref TYPE (typename).
      ENDIF.
      UNASSIGN <f>.

* GET_QUICKINFO
      tooltip = cl_bsp_services=>get_quickinfo(
                              data_object_ref =
                              dataref ).

* Error handling
    CATCH cx_bsp_services INTO l_ex_services.
*     catch exception into message
      error_msg = l_ex_services->get_text( ).
  ENDTRY.

ENDMETHOD.                             "get_tooltip
```

Figure 5.66 shows the required interface parameters.

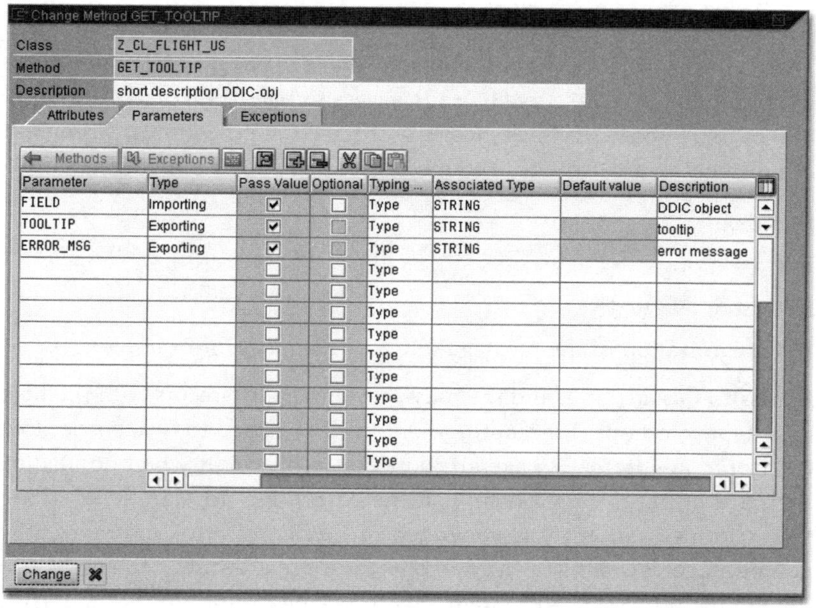

**Figure 5.66** Interface parameters of the GET_TOOLTIP method

## 5.10 Checking and Handling Entries

The checking and handling of user entries in HTML forms is a task that is constantly repeated. Checking data is indispensable when transmitting information that is valid only in the context of the application to subsequent pages. Users must be notified if the check of the entries fails. In the ideal case, users are returned to a new form that highlights the incorrect entries and explains the situation.

Our flight booking portal uses a form in which users can enter their selection criteria to search for flights. Until now, the solution has allowed users to enter text freely. So far, we've also assumed that users know what entries the Web application needs in order to generate the corresponding list of flights. If erroneous entries occurred, the application would return an empty list of flights. Now we want to check all entries of incorrect entries. We'll introduce two different designs to reaching our goal. The first design uses an additional global object for checking and handling entries. The second design uses client-side JavaScript.

### 5.10.1 The message Object

The `message` object realizes a class to manage messages and notifications of any kind. In this case, we'll use this class to handle incorrect entries in BSP pages. In order to track incorrect entries, the object must store a list of messages in an attribute. The messages consist of the following:

▶ Index

▶ Condition

▶ Descriptive text

▶ Categorization of the message (error or warning, for example)

Checking automatic page attributes Access to this attribute and the messages it contains occurs with the help of suitable methods. The `message` object can be used to type entries that are stored in automatic page attributes. If errors occur when populating the page attribute—for example, if the entries are not converted in the target format—an entry is generated in the list of error messages. The condition corresponds to the name of the page attribute and serves as a unique ID in the list. A constant sets the categorization of the message. Of course, you can also add your own error messages to the object so that you can administer completely self-contained checks.

The object is available in all event handlers and in the layout. You reference the object with the PAGE object as follows:

```
page->messages->method_name( ).
```

When using the `message` object, the primary processing flow works as follows. First, user entries from the form are accepted; this data is processed in the `onInputProcessing` event handler. Next, the entries are verified according to the stored application logic. Checking the type also occurs for automatic page attributes. If no errors occur, the system navigates to the next page (i.e., you are brought to the next page). If required, parameters are also transferred to the next page. If errors occur, they are collected in the `message` object. Afterwards, the same page is reloaded. The page outputs the error messages in the correct locations on the page, so that users can respond (see Figure 5.67).

The corresponding flow control occurs automatically; it must be realized in the event handler with `navigation->goto_page()`. It is unnecessary in this case, because every time the **Search** button is activated, processing occurs on the same page.

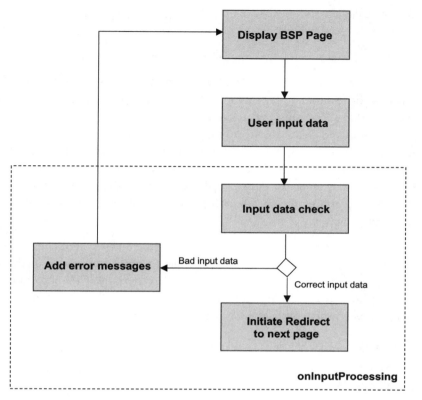

**Figure 5.67** Processing user entries with the message Object

The following list is a brief introduction to the most important methods of the message object that are relevant to our example. See Appendix A.2 for a more detailed description.

▶ NUM_MESSAGES
This method returns the number of errors stored in the message object. You can also use this method to determine if errors have occurred.

▶ ADD_MESSAGE
Use this method to add messages to the message object. This method enables you to freely select the condition and the text.

▶ ASSERT_MESSAGE
Calling this method returns the error text for a message. Access to the message occurs via the condition.

You can calculate the number of errors during assignment to an automatic page attribute as follows:

```
count_errors = page->messages->num_messages( ).
```

However, this check is usually insufficient. In our example, the start date must not be less than today's date, and the end date must be greater than the start date. To ensure that these values are correct, we need to store some checks and create some messages in the event of errors. The coding is provided in Listing 5.25 and is to be entered in the onInputProcessing event handler. From the coding, you can see that a check of the date is triggered only when it can be populated correctly according to its type. In addition, entries for the departure and arrival cities are absolutely required.

In this connection, however, the plausibility of the entries is not checked. The entries, at this point, can also be checked more thoroughly in the coding. For example, you can use table SPFLI to verify if the locations entered exist, and, in a later step, if there is actually a flight (or connection) between the two locations.

**Listing 5.25** Checking entries with the message object

```
CLASS cl_bsp_get_text_by_alias DEFINITION LOAD.
DATA message TYPE string.
* Is the automatic page attribute populated correctly?
IF page->messages->num_messages( ) EQ 0.
* Check to see if the start date is valid
  IF t_start < sy-datum.
    message = cl_bsp_get_text_by_alias=>get_text( alias
    = 'Z_FLIGHTUS/ERRSTART' language = sy-langu ).
    page->messages->add_message(
      condition = 't_start'
      message = message
      severity = page->messages->co_severity_error ).
  ENDIF.
* Check to see if end date is greater than start date
  IF t_end < t_start.
    message = cl_bsp_get_text_by_alias=>get_text( alias
    = 'Z_FLIGHTUS/ERREND' language = sy-langu ).
    page->messages->add_message(
      condition = 't_end'
      message = message
```

```
      severity = page->messages->co_severity_error ).
   ENDIF.
 * Check to see if the departure city is populated
   IF t_city_from IS INITIAL.
      message = cl_bsp_get_text_by_alias=>get_text( alias
      = 'Z_FLIGHTUS/ERRCITYF' language = sy-langu ).
      page->messages->add_message(
         condition = 't_city_from'
         message = message
         severity = page->messages->co_severity_error ).
   ENDIF.
 * Check to see if the arrival city is populated
   IF t_city_to IS INITIAL.
      message = cl_bsp_get_text_by_alias=>get_text( alias
      = 'Z_FLIGHTUS/ERRCITYT' language = sy-langu ).
      page->messages->add_message(
         condition = 't_city_to'
         message = message
         severity = page->messages->co_severity_error ).
   ENDIF.
ENDIF.
```

The constant `co_severity_error` helps to categorize the message and is an example of a typical error. Keep in mind that the message texts must be created as language-dependent in the OTR and linked as shown.

Once the entry check has occurred, the page is reloaded. Selecting the flights based on the entries provided does make sense, but only if the entries were valid. To ensure that the entries were indeed valid, we use the `onInitialization` event handler to check if errors have occurred.

```
IF page->messages->num_messages( ) EQ 0.
   * Normal processing...
ELSE.
   * Output of the error message...
ENDIF.
```

Any errors that occur are output to the layout in the line beneath the affected input field. To access the message, we use the ASSERT_MES-SAGE method and the condition. Listing 5.26 shows how this method is employed. The error messages are output beneath the input fields.

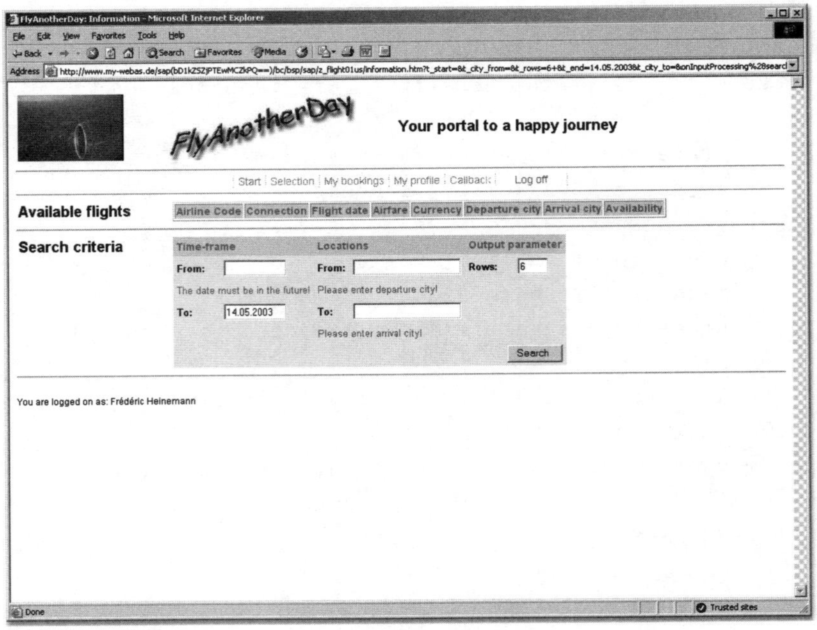

**Figure 5.68** Error-handling with the `message` object

**Listing 5.26** The form with error output—Excerpt

```
<TR>
<TD class="hgrau">
  <INPUT type="text" name="t_rows" value="<%= t_rows %>"
  size="3"><BR>
  <FONT color="red">
    <%= page->messages->assert_message( 't_rows' ) %>
  </FONT>
</TD>
<TD colspan="2" class="hgrau">
  <FONT color="red"><%= page->messages->assert_message(
  't_start' ) %></FONT>
</TD>
<TD colspan="2" class="hgrau">
  <FONT color="red"><%= page->messages->assert_message(
  't_city_from' ) %></FONT>
</TD>
<TD colspan="2" class="hgrau">
  <FONT color="red"><%= page->messages->assert_message(
  't_end' ) %></FONT>
```

```
</TD>
<TD colspan="2" class="hgrau">
  <FONT color="red"><%= page->messages->assert_message(
  't_city_to' ) %></FONT>
</TD>
</TR>
```

Figure 5.68 shows the error messages generated based on the incorrect entry of the date and arrival city.

### 5.10.2 Client-Side JavaScript

As an alternative, or in addition to the previous methods, you can use JavaScript to check entries. JavaScript enables user-friendly access to all objects of an HTML form. You can check all the entries made in a form before you transmit it. For example, you can notify users of an error with a pop-up window. Of course, the use of this feature assumes that users have activated JavaScript for their Web browser. If you decide to use Java-Script, you must ensure that users have enabled it. A significant advantage of using JavaScript is that the checks occur on the client side, there-fore avoiding an additional roundtrip to the server, and ultimately, reducing the load on the network.

We'll now create an alternative page fragment named *selection_js.htm*, in which we will process all the required checks with client-side JavaScript. The following section explains the steps required to arrive at the client-side JavaScript solution.

The most elegant solution stores the various JavaScript functions in a spe-cific file so that you can still have a good overview of the layout. You store the file in the MIME Repository and link it to the HTML page with the fol-lowing instruction:

```
<SCRIPT src="JavaScript-File" type="text/javascript">
</SCRIPT>
```

This example checks the data. First, insert the following coding below the first line of *selection_js.htm*:

**Checking the date with JavaScript**

```
<SCRIPT src="check_date.js" type="text/javascript">
</SCRIPT>
```

Use any text editor to store the file named *check_date.js*, which contains the actual functions to check the date.

**Listing 5.27** JavaScript coding to check the date

```
function checkDate (mydate)
/* This function checks to see if the transferred date
   is valid.
   The following entry formats are checked: DD/D.MM/
   M.YYYY/YY/Y
   checkYear is used to check for a leap year.
   In the event of errors, pop-ups are generated that
   inform users
   about the type of error.
   Parameter:  mydate (value of the date field)
   Return value true - only for a completely valid date,
   otherwise false.
   Reuse only with the permission of the authors
   Frederic Heinemann: frederic.heinemann@novasoft.de
   Christian Rau:      christian.rau@novasoft.de) */
{
```

Data declaration

```
   var year;
   var month;
   var day = new String();
   check = true;
   var helpstr = new String(mydate);
```

Checking for
Dot Notation

```
/* Separate the date into its individual components */
   if (helpstr.length > 4){
      pos = helpstr.indexOf('.');
      if (pos != -1){
         day = helpstr.slice(0,pos);
```

Checking the Day

```
/* Is the day a number? */
         if(isNaN(day) == true){
            check = false;
         }
         helpstr = helpstr.substr(pos + 1,help-
str.length);
         pos = helpstr.indexOf('.');
         if (pos != -1){
            month = helpstr.slice(0,pos);
```

Checking
the Month

```
/* Is the month a number? */
            if(isNaN(month) == true)
            check = false;
            }
```

```
               helpstr = helpstr.substr(pos + 1,help
               str.length);
               if (helpstr.length > 0){
                   year = helpstr;
/* Is the year a number? */
                   for (var i=0;i < year.length;i++){
                     if(isNaN(year) == true)
                   check = false;
                     }
                   }
                   else{
                     check = false;
                   }
             }
             else{
               check = false;
             }
         }
         else{
           check = false;
           alert("Please use dots to format the date.");
           return false;
         }
     }
     else{
       check = false;
     }
   if (check == true){
     dummy = "0";
     if (day.length == 1) day = dummy.concat(day);
     if (month.length == 1) month = dummy.concat(month);
/* Convert all strings to integers */
     var myday = day - 0;
     var mymonth = month - 0;
     var myyear = year - 0;
     if (myday < 01 || myday > 31){
       alert("Invalid day. Please correct.");
       return false;
     }
/* The year can be entered in one or two digits for the
   year */
```

```
           if (myyear < 1000){
             myyear+=2000;
           }
           if (myyear < 1990 || myyear > 3200){
             alert("Invalid year entered. Please correct.");
             return false;
           }
```
**Checking for the correct month**
```
           if (mymonth < 01 || mymonth > 12){
             alert("Invalid month. Please correct.");
             return false;
           }
```
**Checking for a leap year**
```
           if (mymonth == 02 && myday > 28){
             if (!checkYear(myyear)){
                 alert("This year is not a leap year. Please
                     correct.");
                 return false;
             }
           }

           return true;
         }
         else{
           errorStr = "You have not entered a valid date.
           Please correct.";
           alert(errorStr);
           return false;
         }
       }
```
**Method to check for a leap year**
```
       function checkYear(year)
       /* This function checks to see if the transferred date
          is a leap year.
          If it is, 1(true) is returned; if it is not, 0(false)
          is returned. */
       {
         return (((year % 4 == 0) && (year % 100 != 0)) ||
         (year % 400 == 0)) ? 1 : 0;
       }
```

After the initial data declaration, the date transferred to the method is first separated into its components (day, month, and year) and examined to verify if the dot notation was used. It is then checked to verify if the individual components consist of numerical characters only.

If the first part of the verification returns positive results, the strings are cast in integer types. Now we can calculate these values without the danger of generating an error message in the JavaScript interpreter. Next, the information is checked to verify if it actually represents a correct date. Note that the shortness of February and leap years are built into the checking of this information.

Next, we also want to check the number of rows with JavaScript. In this case, we insert code into the header area of the HTML document.

Typically, you can store the following code elsewhere for easier mainte-nance. In the context of this example, however, we'll use this opportunity to show you once again how to link this code directly in the layout.

Listing 5.28 shows the coding:

**Listing 5.28** JavaScript coding to check the number of rows

```
<SCRIPT type="text/javascript">
  function checkRows(rows) {
 <%--    Determines if a transferred value is an invalid
 number (NaN = Not a Number). --%>
 if(isNaN(rows) == true)
     {
       alert(rows + " Not a number!");
       return false;
     }
     else return true;
 }
</SCRIPT>
```

After the JavaScript functions have been implemented, the check func-tions are linked to the corresponding input fields. Here, we use the Java-Script event onBlur(), which is called when leaving an input field. Sup-plement the three input fields in the layout as shown in Listing 5.29:

**JavaScript event:**
**onBlur()**

**Listing 5.29** Linking Input fields in the JavaScript event

```
<INPUT type="text" name="t_start" title="<%= t_start_
tip%>"
value="<%= page->to_string( value = t_start format = if_
bsp_page~CO_FORMAT_LONG ) %>" size="10"
onBlur="checkDate(this.value)">
...
```

```
<INPUT type="text" name="t_rows" value="<%= t_rows %>"
size="3" onBlur="checkRows(this.value)">
...
<INPUT type="text" name="t_end" title="<%= t_end_tip%>"
value="<%= page->to_string( value = t_end format = if_
bsp_page~CO_FORMAT_LONG ) %>" size="10"
onBlur="checkDate(this.value)">
```

You can now test the BSP application with the newly inserted changes.
Figure 5.69 illustrates how an incorrect entry triggers JavaScript to generate a pop-up window that requests a correction of the entry.

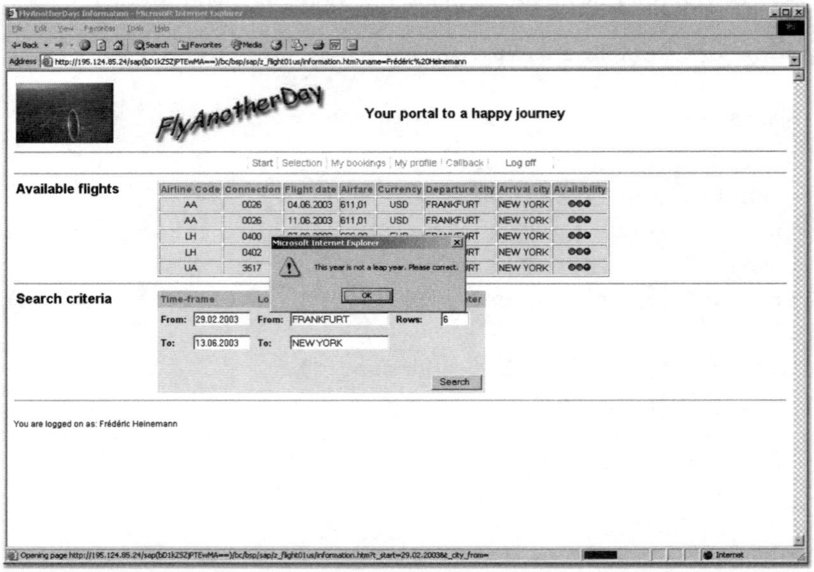

**Figure 5.69** The result of entering the date incorrectly

The best way to avoid producing incorrect entries is not to enable them at
all. Specifically, that means preselecting all entries (by using Help values)
and limiting free-text entries to a minimum. Therefore, we recommend
combining client-side JavaScript and the `message` object. In this case,
however, ensure that you test how the application behaves if JavaScript is
deactivated.

## 5.11 State Models

You can execute BSP applications in two state models: *stateful* means that the application content is retained after a response; *stateless* means that the application context is lost after a response. See Section 3.3.3 for more information on the state model. The primary advantage of stateful programming is that the instance of the application class is retained. All data stored in attributes can be reused after a request. This feature facilitates comfortable programming. Our flight booking portal, however, was programmed in the stateless model, because as we proceed, we want to enable access to the BSP application for a very large group of users. In this case, programming in the stateless model is recommended to optimize the performance and the resource load for this target group.

This section examines the behavior of stateless and stateful applications in more detail. It then introduces various techniques to retain the data in a stateless application even after a request. The techniques that will be introduced include the following:

▶ Hidden form fields
▶ Client-side cookies
▶ Server-side cookies

We will then enhance the flight booking portal with server-side cookies.

Let's begin with a comparison of stateful and stateless applications. To illustrate the difference with a small example, we'll create a new BSP application named Z_STATE_DEMO_US.

Within the BSP application, create a new BSP page, *default.htm*, and store the following layout:

```
<%@page language="abap"%>
<HTML>
  <HEAD>
    <LINK rel="stylesheet" href="../../sap/public/bc/
    bsp/styles/sapbsp.css">
    <TITLE> Start </TITLE>
  </HEAD>
  <BODY class="bspBody1">
    <FORM method="GET">
      <H2>Contents of Counter:<%= application->
      m_counter %></H2>
```

```
        Stateful<INPUT type="checkbox" name="stateful"
            value="X"
        <% IF runtime->keep_context = 1. %> checked <%
        ENDIF. %>><br>
        <INPUT type="submit" name="onInputProces-
        sing(inc)" value="increase">
        <INPUT type="submit" name="onInputProces-
        sing(dec)" value="decrease">
        <INPUT type="submit" name="onInputProces-
        sing(res)" value="reset">
    </FORM>
  </BODY>
</HTML>
```

The layout of the BSP page displays the contents of a counter. A check box allows you to toggle between stateful and stateless. The three buttons enable you to increase, decrease, and reset the counter. You can set the state model at runtime with the KEEP_CONTEXT attribute of the runtime object runtime: the value 1 means stateful and the value 0 means stateless. The default setting is stateless. Setting the state model is established in the onInputProcessing event handler as follows:

```
DATA check TYPE char1.
check = request->get_form_field( 'stateful' ).
IF check EQ 'X'.
  runtime->keep_context = 1.
ELSE.
  IF runtime->keep_context = 1.
    application->reset( ).
  ENDIF.
  runtime->keep_context = 0.
ENDIF.
CASE event_id.
  WHEN 'dec'. application->dec_counter( ).
  WHEN 'inc'. application->inc_counter( ).
  WHEN 'res'. application->reset( ).
ENDCASE.
```

The actual functions of the counter are defined in a specific application class, Z_CL_STATE_DEMO_US. The application class has a public attribute, M_COUNTER, and three methods. The methods increase (INC_COUNTER), decrease (DEC_COUNTER), and initialize (RESET) the counter.

When the check box is activated, the event handler dynamically switches the application to stateful. After a request-response-cycle, the value of the attribute is retained so that the counter can continue to count upward (see Figure 5.70). Therefore, the application class retains the data over a roundtrip to the server. However, if the check box is not activated (stateless), the contents of the attribute are lost after each request, and counting upward is then impossible.

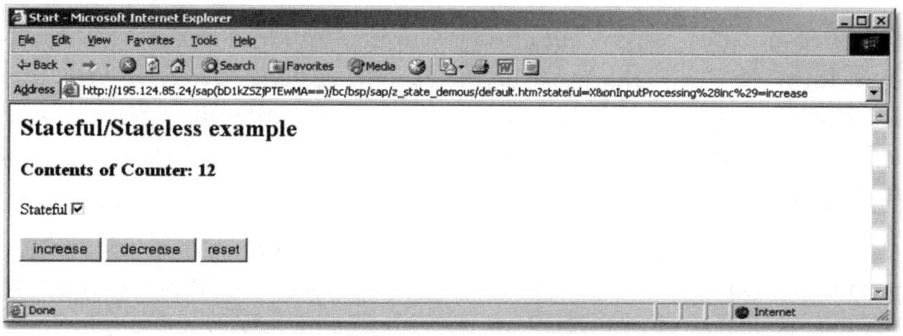

**Figure 5.70** The example in Stateful mode

We encourage you to experiment a little with the coding so that you can understand the behavior of the application, particularly the changes in state. You can set the state model statically using the properties of the BSP page.

To avoid repeated data retrieval in the stateless mode, you can use various techniques. We highly recommend using these techniques to ensure the performance of the application.

### 5.11.1   Hidden Form Fields

You can also store information in the *hidden form fields* of an HTML form and transmit them to the subsequent page by clicking on the **Submit** button. The HTML syntax to define these kinds of input fields is as follows:

```
<INPUT type="hidden" name="field_name" value="field_value">
```

The type of the input field is "hidden," which means that the contents of the input field are not displayed.

Naturally, you can see the information in the source text. Therefore, you should not use this technique to transmit confidential information.

The familiar processing in the onInputProcessing event handler with the NAVIGATION object is used to transfer the data to the subsequent page. It makes no difference if the type of the input field is "text" or "hidden." Use the following syntax to transfer the data:

```
navigation->set_parameter( 'field_name' ).
```

A corresponding automatic page attribute is then defined on the target page.

We have already used this function in our application. For example, a hidden form field (uname) exists in page fragments *selection.htm* and *selection_js.htm* to save the user name. The corresponding BSP page, *information.htm*, uses this form field in the onInputProcessing event handler to transfer parameters.

Hidden form fields are particularly well-suited to throughput information gathered from page to page. This is generally information relevant to additional flow and business logic (such as key fields). Because, in some circumstances, the information can involve a large number of fields, it's best to store this data in its own page fragment, because that guarantees a good overview and reduces the maintenance involved.

However, you cannot use this technique to transfer data from internal tables. Therefore, the following syntax does not work:

```
<INPUT type="hidden" name="field_name" value="<%= itab_
values">>
```

### 5.11.2 Client-Side Cookies

Client-side cookies are an additional option that you can use to save data after a request-response cycle. Section 3.2.5 introduced client-side cookies, and this section will explain how they are used. In general, you can store any information in a cookie. However, ensure that the data is transferred as a string and is stored on the client. If you use a complex cookie, such as one to save the contents of a shopping cart, in an internal table, you'll have to consider saving the data in a string (serialization). When reading the data string from the cookie, the information must be reconverted into the internal data structures.

In order for client-side cookies to function, the client side must, of course, accept them.

You can use the methods of the `IF_HTTP_ENTITY` interface to implement client-side cookies. Use the `SET_COOKIE` method to write a cookie. You can do this with the `RESPONSE` object. You can choose from two types of client-side cookies: persistent and temporary.

A *persistent cookie* is stored on the client computer until an expiration date is explicitly indicated. The computer retains the cookie when the user leaves the Web browser or turns off the computer.

**Persistent cookies**

*Temporary cookies*—also called *session cookies*—are stored in the memory of the Web browser rather than in the file system. They are deleted when a user closes the browser. Some browsers distinguish between the two types of cookies and inform the user about the type. Use the following syntax to generate a temporary cookie and a persistent cookie:

**Temporary cookies**

```
* Temporary cookie
response->set_cookie(
   EXPORTING name = cookie_name
             value = cookie_value
             expires = '' ).
* Persistent cookie
response->set_cookie(
   EXPORTING name = cookie_name
             value = cookie_value
             expires = 'Day, 27-Apr-04 18:30:00 GMT' ).
```

When generating a persistent cookie, ensure that the expiration date is entered according to HTTP specifications by using the format of DD-Mon-YYYY HH:MM:SS GMT. You can delete a persistent cookie by backdating the expiration date. The following example deletes a persistent cookie:

```
* Deleting a Cookie
response->set_cookie(
   EXPORTING name = cookie_name
             value = cookie_value
             expires = 'Day, 28-Oct-02 18:30:00 GMT' ).
```

Use the GET_COOKIE method with the REQUEST object to read a client-side cookie. The following syntax should be used:

**Reading**

```
request->get_cookie(
    EXPORTING name    = cookie_name
    IMPORTING value   = cookie_value
              expires = expires ).
```

In the following example, we'll change a simple visitor counter to a persistent client-side cookie. Create a new BSP application named Z_CSCOOKIE_DEMOUS and implement the layout of the BSP page *default.htm* as follows:

```
<%@page language="abap"%>
<HTML>
  <HEAD>
    <TITLE>Cookie</TITLE>
  </HEAD>
  <BODY>
    <FORM>
      <H2>Client-side permanent Cookie_DEMO</H2>
      <H3>This page was called <%= count_str %> times.
      </H3>
      <INPUT type="submit" value="reload" name="OnInput-
      Processing()">
    </FORM>
  </BODY>
</HTML>
```

The page attribute COUNT_STR is output in the layout. It contains the number of times the page was loaded, that is, information it calculated from the cookie. You can click the **reload** button to reload the page. The counter will increase incrementally (by one) and be updated in the display. Reading and setting the cookie occurs in the onInitialization event handler.

```
DATA: count   TYPE i.
CONSTANTS: cookie_name TYPE string VALUE 'Cookie-Demo'.
* Read the cookie
request->get_cookie(
      EXPORTING name    = cookie_name
      IMPORTING value   = count_str
                expires = date ).
date = 'Day, 27-Apr-04 12:00:00 GMT'.
* Increase counter
count = count_str.
count_str = count + 1.
* Update the cookie
response->set_cookie(
```

```
EXPORTING name    = cookie_name
          value   = count_str
          expires = date ).
```

Unique access to the client-side cookie occurs with the name of the cookie. Then, simple overwriting updates the cookie. Figure 5.71 illustrates the functions of this example.

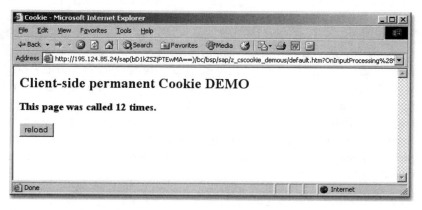

**Figure 5.71** A client-side cookie in action

You can verify if the cookie was stored permanently by closing and reopening the browser. When the application is called again, the old count will be displayed.

### 5.11.3 Server-Side Cookies

In addition to client-side cookies, you can also use server-side cookies to save data. These cookies offer you significant flexibility because they have no size restrictions and can save complex content. The contents of these pervasive cookies are stored in the database. A specific class, CL_BSP_SERVER_SIDE_COOKIES, is available to use with server-side cookies. You write a server-side cookie with the SET_SERVER_COOKIE method:

```
CALL METHOD cl_bsp_server_side_cookie=>set_server_
          cookie
  EXPORTING
    name                  = name
    application_name      = application_name
    application_namespace = application_namespace
    username              = username
    session_id            = session_id
```

```
        data_value              = data_value
        data_name               = data_name
*       expiry_time_abs         = expiry_time_abs
*       expiry_date_abs         = expiry_date_abs
*       expiry_time_rel         = expiry_time_rel
*       expiry_date_rel         = expiry_date_rel.
```

The name parameter gives the cookie a name you can choose at will. The next parameters point to the generated cookie and identify it uniquely. The available parameters include the name of the BSP application (`application_name`), the namespace of the BSP application (`application_namespace`), the user name (`username`), and the session ID (`session_id`). If you don't want to specify the parameters further (to generate a user and session-independent cookie, for example), you can set the value of the parameters with a dummy entry (such as "none"). However, if you want to use the data of the runtime environment to generate a session-dependent cookie, use the various attributes of the runtime object:

```
runtime->application_name
runtime->application_namespace
runtime->session_id
```

You can assign the user with `sy-uname`. However, to populate the username parameter correctly, you must execute a casting in a string.

Note that an implicit logon via an Internet user occurs for public areas of the Web. In this case, the specification of the cookie with the user name alone is insufficient. You must have an appropriate session ID.

The `data_value` and `data_name` parameters set the contents and name of the data object for the data to be saved. This approach is necessary because the cookie data is stored in a cluster table in the database. You can type the `data_value` parameter directly by creating a specific internal table for the data to be saved. We will also address this principle in the flight booking portal at an appropriate place. You must not forget that when reading the cookie, it once again writes to the corresponding target structure, because you would otherwise receive an error message.

Alternatively, you can write the data directly to a data cluster (of type `xstring`) with the ABAP command EXPORT. The following syntax shows you how to use the command:

```
DATA cookie_data TYPE xstring.
    EXPORT structure  FROM structure
           flat_field FROM flat_field
           table_data FROM table_data
           TO DATA BUFFER cookie_data.
```

You can then transfer the populated data object to the method. Finally, you can use the last parameter of the method to set the expiration date of the cookie. You can set an absolute or relative date or time. Relative settings are made in seconds or days, starting with the time of creation.

Use the GET_SERVER_COOKIE method to read a server-side cookie. The following syntax illustrates this method:

```
CALL METHOD cl_bsp_server_side_cookie=>get_server_cookie
   EXPORTING
     name                  = name
     application_name      = application_name
     application_namespace = application_namespace
     username              = username
     session_id            = session_id
     data_name             = data_name
   IMPORTING
     expiry_date           = expiry_date
     expiry_time           = expiry_time
   CHANGING
     data_value            = data_value.
```

The corresponding cookie is returned after calling this method. You can write and use the contents of the cookie (data_value) directly to the target structure (such as an internal table) that you have defined.

However, if you have transferred the data to the cookie with the EXPORT command, you can use the IMPORT command to write the data from the cluster back into the target structure. The following syntax shows this example:

```
IMPORT structure  FROM structure
       flat_field FROM flat_field
       table_data FROM table_data
       TO DATA BUFFER cookie_data.
```

The GET_LAST_ERROR and GET_LAST_ERROR_NAME methods allow you to perform a targeted query to determine if the cookie methods that have been called were executed properly. The first method returns an error code and the second method returns an explanatory description of the error. The following syntax shows how these methods work:

```
CALL METHOD cl_bsp_server_side_cookie=>get_last_error
  receiving
    rc    = rc.
CALL METHOD cl_bsp_server_side_cookie=>get_last_error_
          name
  receiving
    name  = rc_name.
```

Using server-side cookies in your application instead of application data significantly improves the performance of the applications, because they don't need to read from the database repeatedly.

### 5.11.4  Enhancing the Flight Booking Portal

The flight booking portal should store the entries for departure city, arrival city, and the number of lines to be displayed from *selection.htm* in a server-side cookie. When the application starts, it should check to see if a server-side cookie exists. If it does exist, the application reads the entries from the cookie and enters them in the automatic page attribute. The input fields are then pre-populated with the stored entries. The server-side cookie is updated each time the entries change.

Create a new BSP application named Z_FLIGHT02US. You can use the BSP application Z_FLIGHT01US as a template. Open the onInitialization event handler of the *information.htm* page and declare a data object to accept the cookie data:

```
DATA: l_cdata TYPE xstring.
```

In the first step, read the contents of the cookie named z_flight_data (case-sensitive) with the GET_SERVER_COOKIE method. The cookie should be stored as user-dependent: (l_uname contains sy-uname) and session-independent (z_flight). Implement the following method call at the beginning of the event handler:

```
CALL METHOD cl_bsp_server_side_cookie=>get_server_cookie
  EXPORTING
    name                  = 'z_flight_data'
    application_name      = runtime->application_name
    application_namespace = runtime->application_name-
                            space
    username              = l_uname
    session_id            = 'z_flight'
    data_name             = 'l_cdata'
  CHANGING
    data_value            = l_cdata.
```

Next, we check if the information was stored in the cookie. If it was, it is written from the data cluster back into our page attribute:

```
IF l_cdata IS NOT INITIAL.
  IMPORT t_city_from = t_city_from
         t_city_to   = t_city_to
         t_rows      = t_rows
         FROM DATA BUFFER l_cdata.
ENDIF.
```

Now, all the changes to the onInitialization event handler are completed. The rest of the code remains unchanged.

Setting the cookie occurs in the onInputProcessing event handler. As before, declare the cookie data object:

```
DATA: l_cdata TYPE xstring.
```

The entries from the entry form are now written to the data cluster with EXPORT:

```
EXPORT t_city_from FROM t_city_from
       t_city_to   FROM t_city_to
       t_rows      FROM t_rows
       TO DATA BUFFER l_cdata.
```

After the data object has been populated, the cookie is written to the database with the SET_SERVER_COOKIE method. If a cookie already exists, it is overwritten. The cookie is valid for 14 days.

```
CALL METHOD cl_bsp_server_side_cookie=>set_server_cookie
  EXPORTING
    name                  = 'z_flight_data'
```

```
application_name          = runtime->application_name
application_namespace = runtime->application_name-
                            space
username                  = l_uname
session_id                = 'z_flight'
data_value                = l_cdata
data_name                 = 'l_cdata'
expiry_date_rel           = 14.
```

## 5.12   BSP Extensions

The design of pages plays a central role in the development of BSP applications. The more complex the frontend is, the greater the effort required in creating pages. One task that occurs repeatedly is the generation of graphic and text elements to display menus, buttons, input fields, and so on. The use of *Cascading Style Sheets* (*CSS*: see Section 3.2.2) can significantly reduce some of the tasks involved in the overall effort. Nonetheless, changes can require the reworking of numerous elements. An additional limitation requires that some components, such as interaction with the user, must be programmed manually.

**BSP elements**   You can use BSP extensions to handle manual programming. In principle, a *BSP extension* is a container for BSP elements. Every element possesses attributes and is assigned to an ABAP class, which realizes the functions of the element. The attributes are the input parameters for the class. In typical cases, the class also handles the generating of the data stream for rendering on the Web site. This approach produces a higher level of flexibility. For example, the display of XML or WML can occur without any problems. BSP extensions are called within the layout of the BSP page in XML notation.

Here, unlike with the HTML layout, you can check the syntax of the BSP extensions during the syntax check in the development phase. Figure 5.72 illustrates the context.

SAP provides a series of predefined BSP extensions as part of the standard delivery of the SAP Web AS. We will examine the HTMLB extension and its use. Appendix A.3 provides an overview of the individual elements with sample graphics. The number of elements delivered is as comprehensive as the options available to parameterize the elements. A complete description of all the options is beyond the scope of this book, so we simply want to demonstrate what it's like to work with BSP extensions, in the context of our scenario. You can find additional information on individual elements and their attributes in the online documentation.

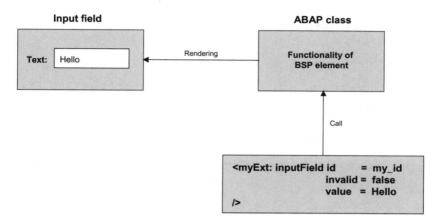

Figure 5.72 The BSP element

## 5.12.1 Using BSP Elements

First, we want to modify our information page so that it displays the internal table with the selected flight data in a BSP element. We can use the `tableView` element of the BSP extension HTMLB.

### Page Declarations

To use page declarations, we must first create the preconditions for the table based on the BSP extension.

As a matter of principle, the BSP extension must be declared in the source text before we can use a BSP element:

```
<%@extension name=extension_name prefix=prefix%>
```

**The BSP extension directive**

`extension_name` describes the name of the BSP extension, and the prefix functions as a namespace for all the BSP elements of the corresponding BSP extensions that will be used. The prefixes "sap" and "bsp" are reserved and cannot be used. A correct example that we can use in our application would read as follows:

```
<%@extension name="htmlb" prefix="htmlb"%>
```

Splitting the name and the extension can also quickly change the assignment of the requested BSP enhancement. You only need to change the entry in the BSP extension directive, and not the individual calls on the page.

**content element**     You will also need the `content` element. This BSP element makes available the context for the other elements in the BSP extension. It is called as follows:

```
<htmlb:content>
   ...
</htmlb:content>
```

**page and document elements**     Of course, you can also replace the HTML definitions `<HEAD>` and `<BODY>` with BSP elements. Although this approach has no disadvantages, it makes things more manageable. Here you can use the simple page element, or the more complex `document` element.

We'll examine the `document` element that allows us more freedom. It requires two subelements that must be specified:

▶ `documentHead`
This element also contains another subelement called `headInclude`. You can include your own CSS files, JS (JavaScript) files, and `<meta>` tags.

▶ `documentBody`
This element must contain all visual HTMLB elements.

**form element**     Before we can use the `tableView` element, we also require the `form` element. This element is equivalent to the HTML `<FORM>` tag:

```
<htmlb:form>
   . . .
</htmlb:form>
```

We will also insert the `form` element in the page with flow logic (*information.htm*). To save ourselves the unnecessary complexity inherent in coding and evaluating user input, we remove the previous HTML `<FORM>` tag from the page fragment *selection.htm*.

Now, all the required elements are specified. Let's examine the integration into the layout coding. The following syntax looks at the link to the layout coding. Listing 5.30 can replace almost all the coding of the *information.htm* page, except for the body content. Linking your own CSS files within the header block and linking the page fragment in the body block occurs as usual.

**Listing 5.30** The HTMLB context for BSP extensions

```
<%@page language="abap" %>
<%@extension name="htmlb" prefix="htmlb" %>
<htmlb:content design="DESIGN2002" >
  <htmlb:document>
    <htmlb:documentHead title="FlyAnotherDay: Informa-
    tion" >
      <htmlb:headInclude/>
      <link rel="stylesheet" href="z_flight.css">
    </htmlb:documentHead>
    <htmlb:documentBody>
      <htmlb:form id     = "myform"
                  method = "post" >
        <%-- Include header fragment          --%>
        <%@include file="top.htm" %>
        <%-- Include navigation fragment  --%>
        <%@include file="navi.htm" %>
        <%-- Include information fragment --%>
        <%@include file="info.htm" %>
        <%-- Include selection fragment   --%>
        <%@include file="selection.htm" %>
        <%-- Include footer fragment           --%>
        <%@include file="bottom.htm" %>
      </htmlb:form>
    </htmlb:documentBody>
  </htmlb:document>
</htmlb:content>
```

## button Element

Because we've removed the HTML `<FORM>` tag, we must first replace the **Search** button of the page fragment *selection.htm* with a BSP element for the purpose of consistency.

Here, we can use the button element. Because of its small number of attributes, it is easy to manage and therefore extremely well-suited for a first enhancement. Replace the call of `<INPUT type="submit"...>` in the coding with the following code:

**Button element**

```
<htmlb:button id      = "id_search"
              text    = "<%= otr(Z_FLIGHTUS/SEARCH) %>"
              onClick = "onInputProcessing()" />
```

Now let's look at the three attributes being used:

▶ id
The id attribute represents a unique, freely chosen name as a text literal. The id is used to identify an element uniquely in the context of input processing and flow control.

▶ text
The text attribute determines the text assigned to a button at runtime.

We also recommend using OTR functions with BSP elements whose contents are rendered at runtime at the presentation level.

▶ onClick
Use the onClick attribute to link to a server-side event.

Although this attribute is not mandatory, you should populate it, or the appropriate attribute, for a client-side call of event handling (onClientClick). Otherwise, no interaction and no event handler occurs.

### tableView Element

tableView element

The tableView element is next. This BSP element displays mass data in table-like layout. It requires a minimum of two parameters:

▶ id
This parameter is the unique identifier of the element and can be any string. It is used to identify the object during the entire runtime of the BSP page.

▶ table
This parameter (or attribute) is used for data binding. Typically, you would enter an internal table that is to be displayed, but first you have to populate the table appropriately. A message is issued if the table is empty.

First, we parameterize the element with this minimal configuration (additional attributes will be introduced later). We accept the previous HTML table definition from page fragment *info.htm* and replace it with the tableView element as shown in Listing 5.31.

**Listing 5.31** The call of the tableView element

```
<%@extension name="htmlb" prefix="htmlb" %>
  <htmlb:tableView id    = "flight_table"
                   table = "<%= itab_result %>" >
  </htmlb:tableView>
```

If you want to compare the HTML table with the BSP element table, simply expand the existing listing. Figure 5.73 illustrates the difference.

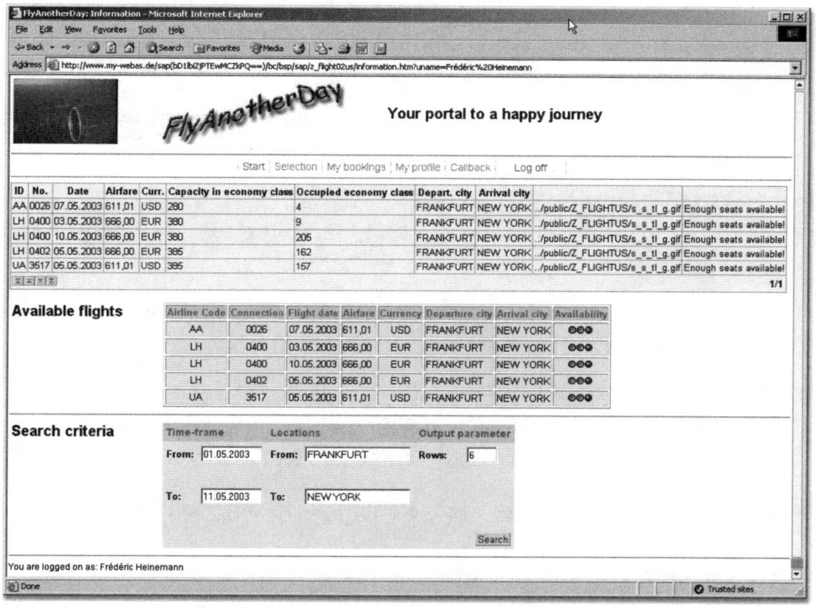

**Figure 5.73** Comparison of the HTML table and the BSP element table

The result is still not completely convincing, but at least we didn't have to deal with naming the columns and manually creating a loop to populate the HTML table. Note that the actual call was performed with three lines.

Next, we want to customize the visible columns. For selection and parameterization, you can use the `tableColumns` subelement, which also contains another subelement, `tableColumn`, to describe the individual columns.

**Columns in the tableView element**

The `tableColumn` element also "understands" various attributes. We'll briefly introduce some of these attributes based on the availability column:

**tableColumn element**

▶ `columnName`
This attribute is the only mandatory attribute. It contains the name of the field from the internal table.

▶ `type`
This attribute sets the type of the field. The default value is text, so that the column is formatted according to the type or the Dictionary information of the data source. In addition, the following values are available: `link` (hyperlinks), `image` (the column data is interpreted as URLs of images), `imagelink` (the image represents a link), `edit` (the cells of the column are displayed as input fields), and `button` (pushbutton).

▶ `title`
This attribute can override the column name derived from the table setting.

▶ `tooltipColumnKey`
When this attribute is set with a text literal, the text is displayed as a tool tip.

If the text literal for a table column refers to the same name, the contents of the current field of this column are displayed.

▶ `horizontalAlignment`
This attribute sets the horizontal alignment of the cell. Permissible values include: `left`, `center` (default), `right`, `justify`, and `char`.

Now we enhance the `tableView` element according to Listing 5.32.

**Listing 5.32** Parameterization of the columns of the tableView element

```
[ ... ]
  <htmlb:tableView id    = "flight_table"
                   table = "<%= itab_result %>" >
    <htmlb:tableViewColumns>
      <htmlb:tableViewColumn columnName="CARRID" >
      </htmlb:tableViewColumn>
      <htmlb:tableViewColumn columnName="CONNID" >
      </htmlb:tableViewColumn>
      <htmlb:tableViewColumn columnName="FLDATE" >
      </htmlb:tableViewColumn>
      <htmlb:tableViewColumn columnName="PRICE" >
      </htmlb:tableViewColumn>
      <htmlb:tableViewColumn columnName="CURRENCY" >
      </htmlb:tableViewColumn>
      <htmlb:tableViewColumn columnName="CITYFROM" >
```

```
    </htmlb:tableViewColumn>
    <htmlb:tableViewColumn columnName="CITYTO" >
    </htmlb:tableViewColumn>
    <htmlb:tableViewColumn columnName= "SYMBOL"
                   type= "IMAGE"
                   title= "Availability"
                   tooltipColumnKey    = "SYMBOL_DESC"
                   horizontalAlignment = "RIGHT" >
    </htmlb:tableViewColumn>
  </htmlb:tableViewColumns>
</htmlb:tableView>
```

You cannot specify individual columns for exclusion. If you want to choose the column display freely, you must define all the columns to be displayed individually or create a field list with a table from structure `TABLEVIEWCONTROL`.

The `tableView` element itself also "understands" a series of attributes that clarify how well it can perform. We'll introduce some of these attributes and insert them into our example:

▶ `headerText`

This attribute sets the contents of the table header. You can use any text that you want or an element from the Online Text Repository (OTR).

In theory, you can write a name for display control directly into the HTML tag, but this is not recommended. Doing so would undermine the basic principle of BSP extensions.

▶ `headerVisible`

Use this attribute to determine if the header line is visible or invisible. Permitted values include `false` (default) and `true`.

▶ `emptyTableText`

Use this attribute to define a text that is output if the table does not contain any rows.

▶ `fillUpEmptyRows`

Use this attribute to determine how to display empty rows. This condition is relevant only when the number of table rows is smaller than the number of visible rows that you have set. Permitted values include `false` (default) and `true`.

▶ `footerVisible`
Use this attribute to set the visibility of the footer. Permitted values include `true` (default) and `false`.

▶ `navigationMode`
Use this attribute to determine if the number of visible lines or the page number is output. Permitted values include `bypage` (default) and `byline`.

▶ `columnDefinitions`
Use this attribute to link a table of type `TABLEVIEWCONTROL` as a field list.

The `tableView` element can automatically use field identifiers—if they exist. In addition, this element automatically suppresses the display of any client fields that might exist.

You can enhance the `tableView` element with the attributes suggested in Listing 5.33. You can customize the behavior of the table by changing and expanding the attributes according to your own settings. No other minor steps are required to create multilingual capabilities. The maintenance of Data Dictionary types in multiple languages automatically supplies the table with language-dependent metadata. Here, too, a careful selection and definition of the data objects is useful.

**Listing 5.33** Enhancing the tableView element with additional attributes

```
<htmlb:tableView id              = "flight_table"
                 table           = "<%= itab_result %>"
                 emptyTableText  = "<%= otr(Z_FLIGHTUS/
                                    empty_table) %>"
                 headerText      = "<%= otr(Z_FLIGHTUS/
                                    INFOUE) %>"
                 headerVisible   = "TRUE"
                 fillUpEmptyRows = "FALSE"
                 visibleRowCount = "6"
                 navigationMode  = "BYPAGE"
                 footerVisible   = "TRUE" >
```

**Advancing the scenario: booking a flight**
In a later step, we will enhance the functions of our portal. So far, we could only display the flight. Now, we want to enable users to select a specific flight and navigate to the flight booking page.

First, we must adjust the presentation logic. The user selects a row and then sends the selected row for processing in the `onInputProcessing` event handler by clicking on the **Submit** button. Then, users should be able to navigate to the subsequent page, *book.htm*. Here, we will first expand our `tableView` element with an additional attribute:

```
selectionMode = "SINGLESELECT"
```

The attribute can accept the following values:

Selection variants

▶ `none`
This is the default value. No option for selection exists.

▶ `singleselect`
Exactly one row can be selected. At runtime, the result is in the `SELECTEDROWINDEX` attribute of the object of class `CL_BSP_EVENT_TABLEVIEW`.

▶ `multiselect`
Any number of rows can be selected.

▶ `lineedit`
The line can be edited when the user clicks on it. The editing mode for this line ends when the user selects another row.

▶ `multilineedit`
All selected lines can be edited. The editing mode ends when the user selects another line.

Next, we insert a booking button. Here we can copy and adjust the coding we already used for the **Search** button, as shown in Listing 5.34. Insert this coding beneath the table:

**Listing 5.34** Coding for the button element "Book"

```
<htmlb:button id      = "id_book"
              text    = "<%= otr(Z_FLIGHTUS/buttonBook) %>"
              tooltip = "<%= otr(Z_FLIGHTUS/book) %>"
              onClick = "onInputProcessing()" />
```

Granted, the appearance is not notable, but we'll deal with enhancements in the following section.

### gridLayout and gridCell Element

Table elements have always been used to position elements on a Web page in traditional HTML programming. The `gridLayout` element fulfills this task when using BSP elements. This element is comparable to the HTML `<TABLE>` tag. Each line of the `gridLayout` element can record an element. By default, the element itself does not have its own visible

Layout positioning with an HTML table

design. The internal element structure consists of `gridLayoutCell` elements, which correspond to the HTML `<TD>` element.

Because the subelements are positioned as coordinates, an element that corresponds to the HTML `<TR>` element isn't necessary. Just like HTML tables, `gridLayout` elements can be nested.

**gridLayout element**

The `gridLayout` element recognizes many attributes. The following attributes are relevant to us:

▶ `rowSize` (mandatory)
Sets the number of rows.

▶ `columnSize` (mandatory)
Sets the number of columns.

▶ `id`
Identifies the BSP element with a unique name. This attribute is used in event handling and data handling.

▶ `width`
Sets the width of the grid layout. The units valid for HTML are also valid here.

▶ `height`
Sets the height of the grid layout.

▶ `cellSpacing`
Sets the distance (spacing) between the cells in the grid.

▶ `cellPadding`
Sets the distance (padding) between a cell's frame and its contents.

▶ `style`
Sets the background color. Acceptable values are `alternating`, `transparent`, `standard` (default value), and `white`.

**gridLayoutCell element**

We can also introduce the `gridLayoutCell` element here:

▶ `id`
Identifies the BSP element with a unique name. This attribute is used in event handling and data handling.

▶ `rowIndex` (mandatory)
Sets the index for the row within the gridLayout element, in which the current element is to be positioned.

▶ `columnIndex` (mandatory)
Sets the index for the column within the gridLayout element, in which the current element is to be positioned.

▶ **horizontalAlignment**

Sets the horizontal alignment of a cell entry. Acceptable values are `left`, `center`, `right`, `justify`, and `char`.

▶ **verticalAlignment**

Sets the vertical alignment of a cell entry within a row. Acceptable values are `top`, `middle`, `bottom`, and `baseline`.

▶ **width**

Sets the width of a cell.

▶ **wrapping**

Sets whether text in a cell remains on one line, or is divided between lines.

▶ **colSpan**

Sets the number of columns that a cell can encompass.

▶ **backgroundColor**

Changes the background color of a cell in the `gridLayout` element.

▶ **style**

Sets the background color. Acceptable values are `alternating`, `transparent`, `standard` (default value), and `white`.

With this knowledge, we can center the output of the table and display the **Book** button at the lower right edge of the table. Listing 5.35 provides us with the required coding:

**Listing 5.35** Code to position the elements and the Book button

```
<htmlb:gridLayout id          = "outer"
                  columnSize = "1"
                  rowSize    = "1"
                  width      = "100%" >
  <htmlb:gridLayoutCell columnIndex          = "1"
                        rowIndex             = "1"
                        horizontalAlignment = "center" >
    <htmlb:gridLayout id          = "inner"
                      columnSize = "2"
                      rowSize    = "1"
                      cellSpacing = "5" >
      <htmlb:gridLayoutCell columnIndex = "1"
                            rowIndex    = "1" >
  [tableView...]
            </htmlb:tableViewColumn>
```

```
        </htmlb:tableViewColumns>
      </htmlb:tableView>
    </htmlb:gridLayoutCell>
    <htmlb:gridLayoutCell columnIndex       = "2"
                          rowIndex          = "1"
                          verticalAlignment = "BOT-
                                               TOM" >
      <htmlb:button id      = "id_book"
                    text    = "<%= otr(Z_FLIGHTUS/
                               buttonBook) %>"
                    tooltip = "<%= otr(Z_FLIGHTUS/
                               book) %>"
                    onClick = "onInputProcessing()" />
    </htmlb:gridLayoutCell>
  </htmlb:gridLayout>
</htmlb:gridLayoutCell>
</htmlb:gridLayout>
```

The result should look like the screen in Figure 5.74.

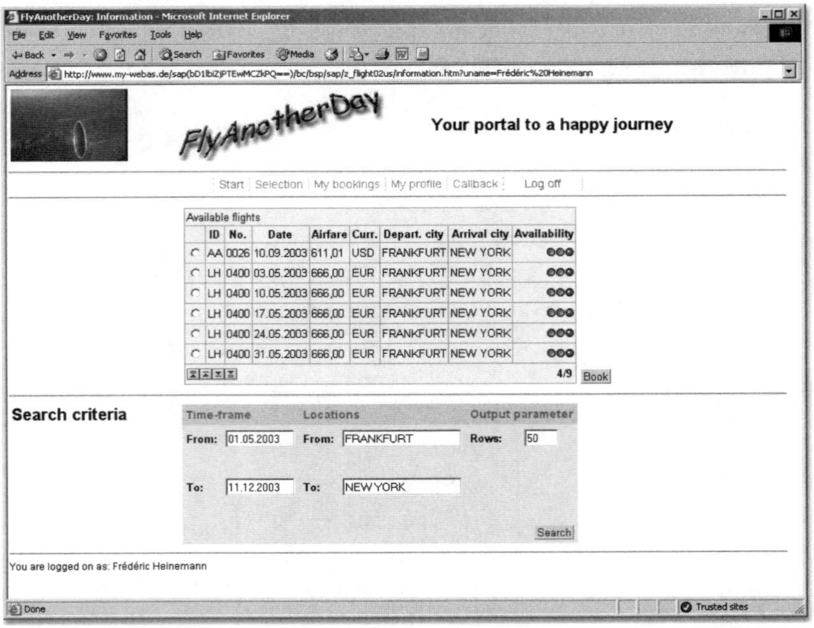

**Figure 5.74** A BSP element table with positioning aids and column parameterization

If you want to use a calendar as a data-entry aid for date fields, try the following coding. In page fragment *selection.htm*, replace the coding for the input field t_end (shown in the first coding block below) with the coding shown in the second block:

Data-entry aid: calendar

```
<input type="text" name="t_end" title="<%= t_end_tip%>"
    value="<%= page->to_string( value = t_end format
    =if_bsp_page~CO_FORMAT_LONG ) %>" size="10">
<br>
```

```
<htmlb:inputField id = "t_end" type = "date" required =
"true" firstDayOfWeek = "1" showHelp = "true" maxlength
= "10" value = "" description = "" />
```

Test how the new coding affects the information page of the Web application.

### Event Handling with BSP Elements

Now that our presentation logic has progressed to this point, we can examine the flow control next. We can identify the following events:[4]

Events on the page

▶ **Search**

When users click the **Search** button, the list of results should be updated (just as it was before). We'll address this event in the event handler so that we can demonstrate the difference between BSP elements as an example. However, we don't have to present any coding here. A redirect to the same page is sufficient.

▶ **Scroll**

Navigation elements are created automatically for the tableView element in the footer. However, these elements are only available for interaction when the number of result rows is greater than the setting for the maximum number of lines per page. The CL_BSP_ TABLEVIEW class, which is assigned to the BSP element, makes this function available automatically.

▶ **Book**

When users select a table row, by clicking the **Book** button, they can navigate to the booking page. This is the most interesting and comprehensive case; we will delve into this functionality in more detail below.

---

4 This section deals only with events that interact directly with the interface. We specifically do not address closing the browser, using the Back button, and so on.

When users click on one of the elements listed above, an event is generated that calls the `onInputProcessing` event handler. In the next step, this event must be identified correctly, the corresponding values queried, and errors caught.

We must first determine which event has been triggered. Accordingly, for security reasons, we check to see if the `EVENT_ID` of the event actually agrees with the BSP extension. Next, the required variables for event handling are declared. It's considered good programming to always place the declarations at the beginning, even if data declarations in ABAP are not required in that location. However, to provide a good overview of Listing 5.36, we won't adhere to this recommendation.

```
[...]
* Evaluating the triggered event
IF event_id = cl_htmlb_manager=>event_id.
   DATA: event          TYPE REF TO cl_htmlb_event,
         tv             TYPE REF TO cl_htmlb_tableview,
         button_event   TYPE REF TO cl_htmlb_event_button,
         tv_data        TYPE REF TO cl_htmlb_event_table-
                        view,
         wa_result      LIKE LINE OF itab_result.
```

The triggered event is then assigned to the declared object. We query the `get_event` method of `CL_HTMLB_MANAGER` class (see Appendix A.2).

```
event ?= cl_htmlb_manager=>get_event( runtime->server
   ->request ).
```

**The correct event?** We can now evaluate the populated `event` object. In this case, the `IF` portion is executed only if the type of element that generated the event is a button and the event itself is of type `click`. This evaluation ensures that the `tableView` event triggered by scrolling is ignored at this point. Another advantage of the design of the BSP extension is exhibited here: the scroll function is nonetheless executed automatically by the assigned class, `CL_HTMLB_TABLEVIEW`. No manual effort is required on the part of the developer.

The `name` attribute does not return the name of the individual button, as you might expect, but the name of the BSP element. To determine the runtime name of the object, you must query the `id` attribute.

```
* Button?
 IF event->name = 'button' AND event->event_type =
    'click'.
    button_event ?= event.
```

The button ID is evaluated next. In the first case, when the id_search but-    **Evaluating the ID**
ton triggered the event, no additional programming is required in this
scenario. The form automatically transfers any new selection parameters.
So far, the BSP element <htmlb:form> works just like its counterpart,
HTML <FORM>.

```
    CASE button_event->id.
        WHEN 'id_search'.   "Search
* No coding required: redirect occurs automatically
```

Now we'll look at the event of greatest interest to us. When the **Book**    **Data of the object**
button triggers the click event, the familiar class, CL_HTMLB_MANAGER, is
used to assign the request data of the object to the tv reference object. To
ensure the correct determination of the correct object, name and id are
transferred.

```
        WHEN 'id_book'.     "Book
            tv ?= cl_htmlb_manager=>get_data(
                        request = runtime->server->request
                        name    = 'tableView'
                        id      = 'flight_table' ).
```

If the tv (tableView) object is not empty, the event data is assigned to    **Setting the**
tv_data. You can then query the attribute selectedRowIndex that    **selected row**
returns the row marked in the tableView element when the event was
triggered.

```
        IF tv IS NOT INITIAL.
            tv_data = tv->data.
```

The selected row and the page attribute uname  are then set as transfer    **Transferring data**
values. A redirect to the page with flow logic, *book.htm*, then occurs:

**Listing 5.36** Event Handling of the BSP element

```
        IF tv_data->selectedrowindex IS NOT INITIAL.
            navigation->set_parameter(
                        name  = 'idx_data'
                        value = tv_data->selectedrow-
                                index ).
```

```
                navigation->set_parameter( 'uname' ).
                navigation->goto_page( 'book.htm' ).
            ENDIF.
        ENDIF.
    WHEN OTHERS.
    ENDCASE.
    ENDIF.
ENDIF.
```

**Securing the cor-
rect information** The question now arises of how the selected flight is moved to the page for booking flights; only the index of the selected row is transferred. You might think that the simplest solution is to execute the same SELECT statement in *book.htm*. This solution, however, has two disadvantages that make it inadvisable.

1. The selection data (t_city_from, t-city_to, t_start, and t_end) would also have to be transferred to the subsequent page.

2. There's no guarantee that the basic data of view SFLIGHTS2 has not changed. A change would create the possibility of transferring an incorrect flight connection.

Here again, we use the technique of server-side cookies. A server-side cookie is set in the onManipulation event. The cookie stores the entire itab_result table with the flight connection data as a persistent object (see Listing 5.37). The itab_result table can then be recreated and reused when generating the runtime object of the BSP page *book.htm*, without any changes in the database affecting the data.[5]

**Listing 5.37** Server-side cookie with the user's flight data table

```
data l_uname type string.
l_uname = sy-uname.
* Saving the cookie
call method cl_bsp_server_side_cookie=>set_server_cookie
    exporting
    name                     = 'z_flight_it'
    application_name         = runtime->application_name
    application_namespace    = runtime->application_name-
                               space
    username                 = l_uname
    session_id               = 'z_flight'
```

---

5  A productive environment would, of course, require implementation of a more complex solution to prevent the possibility of erroneous bookings.

```
data_value              = itab_result
data_name               = 'itab_result'
expiry_time_rel         = 3600.
```

Now you must consider simply reducing the `itab_result` table to exactly the one selected data record—before it becomes persistent. We've decided not to adopt that idea, so that a later enhancement can enable simultaneous selection of multiple flights with the attribute `selectionMode = "multiselect"`. As a general rule, you should always estimate the effort, costs, and benefits of each method that you employ.

### 5.12.2  Modifying BSP Elements

As delivered by SAP, the BSP extension HTMLB has an extensive range of functions. Nonetheless, using HTMLB without making any modifications in your own BSP applications makes sense in only a few cases. You must consider corporate design and changed functions. You have an opportunity to do so in the form of several options, which we'll introduce in the next section.

### Redefining the Design

A simple way of changing the underlying definition for the HTMLB extension is by setting the `themeRoot` attribute in the `content` element. Then, you only have to generate or modify those files for the CSS definitions and the graphics. The following section deals with the second option—modifications.

First, we create a new folder in the MIME Repository for the CSS files and graphic elements of the BSP elements that are to be modified. Open the context menu of the *PUBLIC* folder and select **Create Folder** (see Figure 5.75).

**Creating your own design**

Enter the name Z_FLIGHTUS in the dialog window that opens and assign it a meaningful description (see Figure 5.76).

In the same manner, create a subfolder, *HTMLB*, in the new folder. Now, copy the following folders and files—with the identical structure—from the MIME folder *PUBLIC/BC/HTLMB* into the folder that you just created:

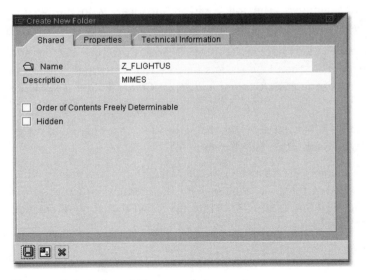

**Figure 5.75** Creating a new folder in the MIME Repository

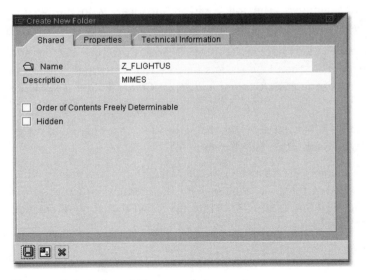

**Figure 5.76** Assigning a folder name during creation

► **Folder**

Because our scenario currently uses only the elements `tableView` and `button` (no graphic folder exists for the latter), copying the sub-folder *tableView* with its files will suffice. Instead of the predefined graphics, you can also import your own graphics into the subfolder. At runtime, the graphics determine the appearance of various graphic elements, such as the buttons for page navigation.

You can copy all the files simultaneously by using the mass selection, and then drag and drop them into the new folder.

► **Files**

These are all the files from the folder *HTMLB*. Depending on the type of browser that you have, the proper files are linked automatically at runtime.

If you can ensure that your productive application will be used only by a closed user group, all of whose members use a uniform browser, it will suffice to copy and modify only the required files:

*1x1.gif,    controls_default.css,    controls_default.js,    controls_ie4.css, controls_ie4.js,    controls_ie5.css,    controls_ie5.js,    controls_ie6.css, controls_nn4.css,   controls_nn4.js,   controls_nn4l.css,   controls_nn6.css, controls_nn6.js, htmlb_texts_en.js, mimesinfo.xml*

The new directory structure should resemble the directory in Figure 5.77.

Now we have fulfilled almost all the prerequisites necessary to generate your own design based upon the original files. The only thing missing is the new entry in the `themeRoot` attribute of the `content` element. If you have accepted our suggested name, the attribute is modified as follows:

```
<htmlb:content themeRoot = "../../public/Z_FLIGHTUS" >
```

Then, you can tailor the CSS files to fit your corporate design. However, you must ensure that you don't change the original name of the CSS elements. We'll demonstrate the issue with an example. Load the CSS file from the newly created folder (the folder loaded at runtime for the browser you currently use) into a CSS editor or any text editor with the context menu **Change**.

The CSS file is structured according to the pattern *controls_browsershort-description.css*: For the current version of Microsoft Internet Explorer, the file is *controls_ie6.css*.

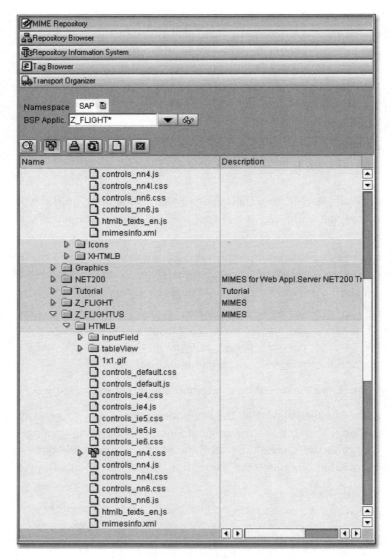

**Figure 5.77** The directory structure of your own design for the BSP extension HTMLB

Search for the `.sapTbvTitStd` element and replace it with the following lines:

**Listing 5.38** Replacing the Class element for the Table Header tableView element

```
.sapTbvTitStd {
 font-family: arial,sans-serif;
 font-size: larger;
```

```
color: #000000;
background-color: #EFF6FB;
font-weight: bold;
vertical-align: bottom;
padding: 2px;
}
```

Now save the file and close the editor so that the CSS file is written back to the MIME Repository. Execute the BSP application and look at the "new" information page.

If everything worked properly, the results should appear as illustrated in Figure 5.78.

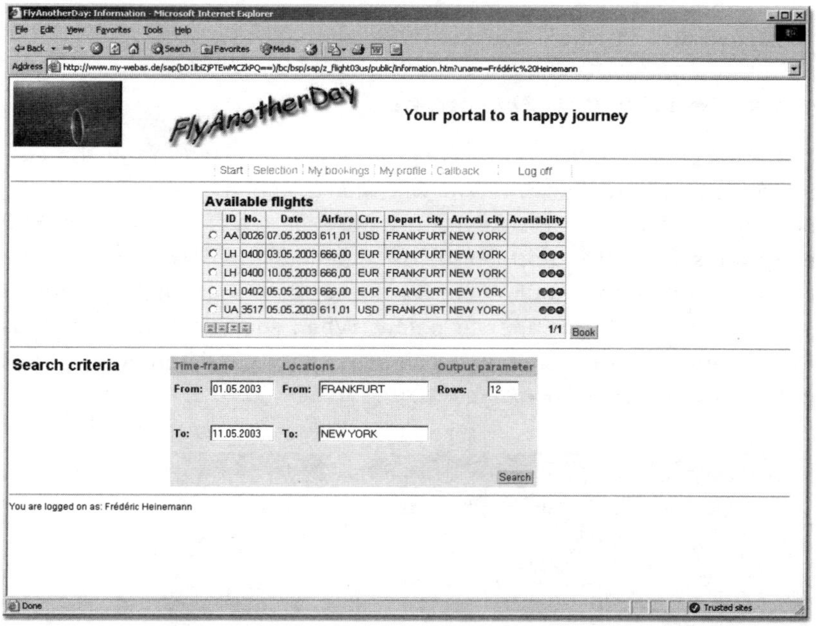

**Figure 5.78** The results of your own design

The effort needed to attain this result might seem great. However, just think—you are now completely free to redesign the HTMLB extension and you can still access the full range of functions. You only need to make a change once; however, this change will be made consistently across the entire Web application.

If you copy and modify the language selection of the initial page, you can also offer visitors various designs: just set a link in the initial page, using the following syntax as an example:

```
<A href="default.htm?uname=<%= name %>&pagedesign= ../
../public/Z_FLIGHTUS">
  <IMG src="myTheme.jpg" alt="<%= OTR(Z_FLIGHTUS/CTHEME)
  %>" border="0">
</A>
```

When you now query the value in the `onInitialization` event and assign it as a print directive to the `themeRoot` attribute, the Web user can decide how the page appears. The following is an example of the assignment:

```
<htmlb:content themeRoot = "<%= pagedesign %>" >
```

### 5.12.3  Creating BSP Extensions

In the following section, we'll create a new BSP extension in the customer-naming environment. We will then combine the modified and new elements in it. In the Repository Browser, select the category **BSP extensions** from the drop-down list. Enter "Z_FLIGHTUS" or another name that fulfills the requirements of the customer-naming environment into the input field that appears below. When you select the entry button, a dialog window opens, in which you can further describe the details of the new extension (see Figure 5.79).

| Create BSP Extension | |
|---|---|
| Enter details of the new BSP extension: | |
| Name | Z_FLIGHTUS |
| Default Prefix | zf |
| Short Text | BSP-elements |

**Figure 5.79**  Entering information for the new BSP extension

The default prefix is automatically displayed when using the assigned elements in the HTML layout. Once you confirm the entries with the following assignments for package and workbench order, the extension has been created successfully.

### 5.12.4 Generating BSP Elements

In this section, we address the generation of our own BSP element. The delimiter element element handles the individual navigation points in the page fragment *navi.htm*. Until now, the separation of the points has complicated matters. Accordingly, we'll describe the BSP element as a `delimiter` element. In the first step, we create the new element in our BSP extension Z_FLIGHTUS. In the Repository Browser, select the category **BSP extensions** and then the BSP extension Z_FLIGHTUS. Then use the context menu to select **Create BSP Element**. In the dialog window that opens, enter the information shown in Figure 5.80.

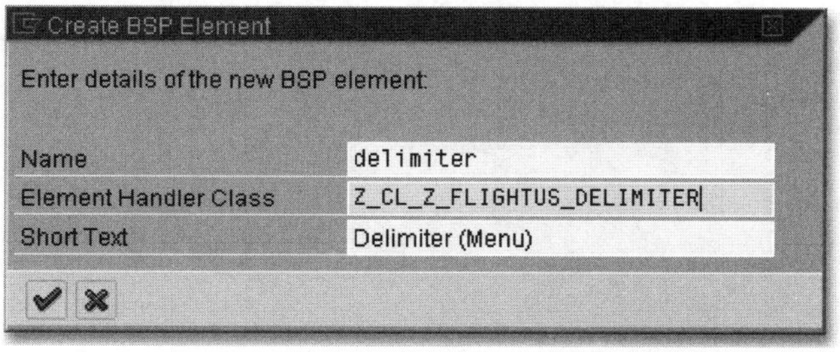

**Figure 5.80** Creating a delimiter element

The new BSP element is generated in the next step, including its element class, Z_CL_Z_FLIGHTUS_DELIMITER. The properties then appear as shown in Figure 5.81.

Next, we consider the attributes that we'll need. Therefore, we'll look more closely at the previous coding for the spacer bar in Listing 5.39. The following lines generate the bar and the space around it:

**Listing 5.39** Listing for the manual generation of a spacer bar

```
<%-- Spacer            --%>
<TD><IMG src="../../public/Z_FLIGHTUS/spacer.gif"
    width="1" height="1" border="0"></TD>
<TD><IMG src="../../public/Z_FLIGHTUS/linie_senkr.gif"
    border="0"></TD>
<TD><IMG src="../../public/Z_FLIGHTUS/spacer.gif"
    width="1" height="1" border="0"></TD>
```

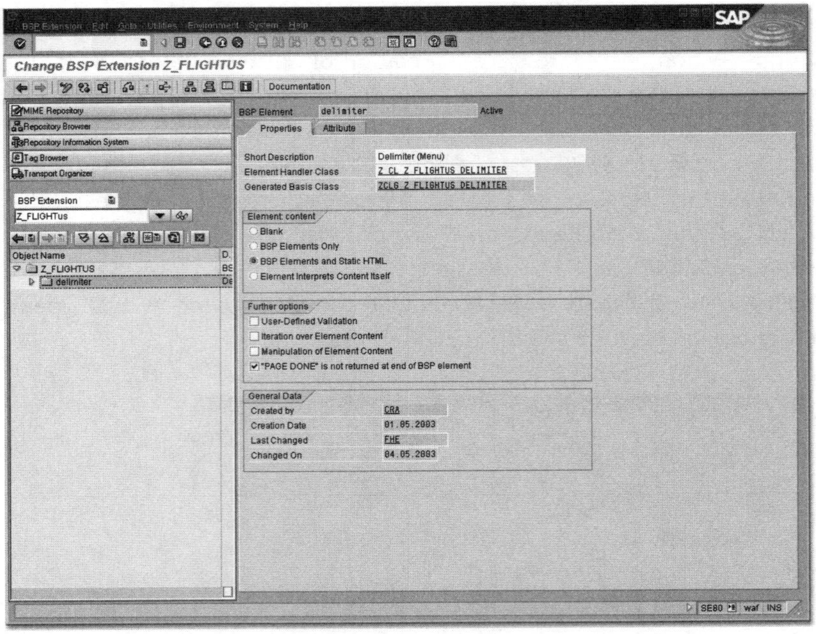

**Figure 5.81** The Properties tab of the delimiter element

We can identify the following attributes:

▶ `symbol`
The graphic for the division of the individual menu points should be variable. In one option, you can offer several hard-wired graphics. We've decided on a more flexible version in which developers provide the path to the graphic. Of course, we'll define this attribute as a mandatory attribute.

Permissible entries: String, default value: –

▶ `spacing`
You should be able to select the width of the spacing. For example, this attribute allows you to position the menu option for logout some distance away from the other choices. However, it's unnecessary for you to consider the height, because we'll set that at a fixed level.

Permissible entries: String, default value: 1

If you enable dynamic variable transfer for both attributes, you can also transfer ABAP variables at runtime with the print directive.

We create the attribute in the tab of the same name. See Figure 5.82 as a model for the entries.

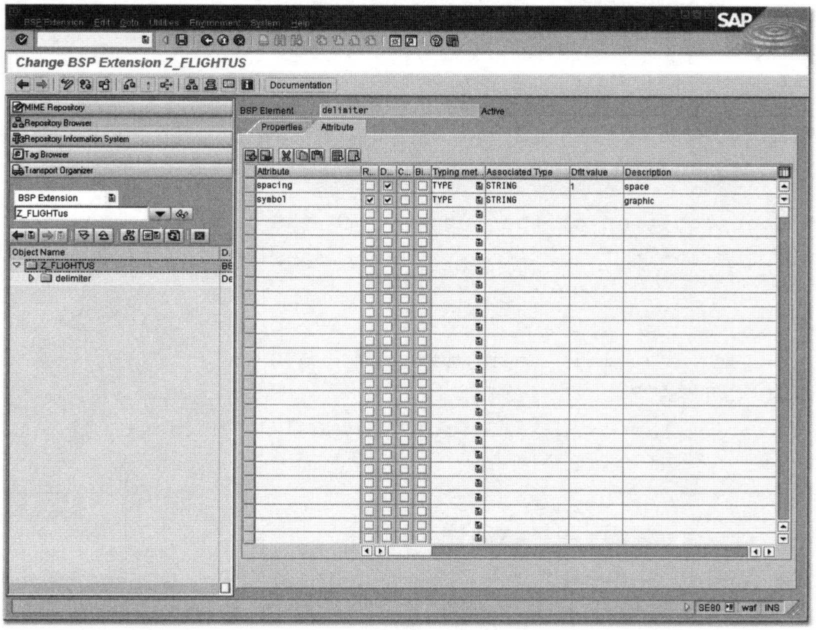

**Figure 5.82** The attributes for the delimiter element

Now we're only missing the implementation of the function, which we will do in the assigned class. Use forward navigation to go to class Z_CL_ Z_FLIGHTUS_DELIMITER. The basic class, ZCLG_Z_FLIGHTUS_ DELIMITER, and the attribute are already entered correctly, so we can start with the installation of the required coding. Here we need to redefine the IF_BSP_ELEMENT~DO_AT_BEGINNING interface method. The method is executed at the beginning of the call of the element. Let's look at the coding in Listing 5.40 in more detail:

**Listing 5.40** The DO_AT_BEGINNING method

```
* Data declaration
  DATA: out_string  TYPE string,
        help_string TYPE string.
  DATA: outstream   TYPE REF TO if_bsp_writer.
```

After the data declaration, the output stream of the outstream object reference is assigned with the get_out() method of the m_page_context interface attribute. You cannot write directly to the output stream.

```
* Assigning the output stream
  outstream = me->if_bsp_element~m_page_context->get_
              out( ).
```

Next, the HTML coding embedded in the output stream is concatenated successively in the helper variable out_string.

You can validate the parameters entered in method IF_BSP_ELE-MENT~COMPILE_TIME_IS_VALID or IF_BSP_ELEMENT~RUNTIME_IS_VALID when compiling or at runtime.

```
* Concatenation of the output with the flux compensator
  CONCATENATE '<TD><IMG src="../../public/Z_FLIGHTUS/
                spacer.gif" width="'
                spacing '" height="1" border="0"></TD>'
                INTO help_string.
  CONCATENATE help_string
                '<TD><IMG src="' symbol '" border="0">
                </TD>'
                help_string
                INTO out_string.
```

The output string that has been generated (out_string) is then inserted into the output stream (outstream):

```
* Rendering the HTML coding
  outstream->print_string( out_string ).
* Close
  rc = me->co_element_done.
```

To insert the new BSP element, we must now modify page fragment *navi.htm*. Our BSP element is available in the Tag Browser with Drag & Drop functionality. Drag the delimiter element from the BSP extension Z_FLIGHTUS into the browser. Here, the new BSP directive is simultaneously inserted into the code:

```
<%@extension name="Z_FLIGHTUS" prefix="zf" %>
```

Replace the old coding for the spacer with the new BSP element. Don't forget to set the spacing attribute for the last two spacers (see Figure 5.83).

Now, the coding is much clearer, and you can perform any required modifications centrally.

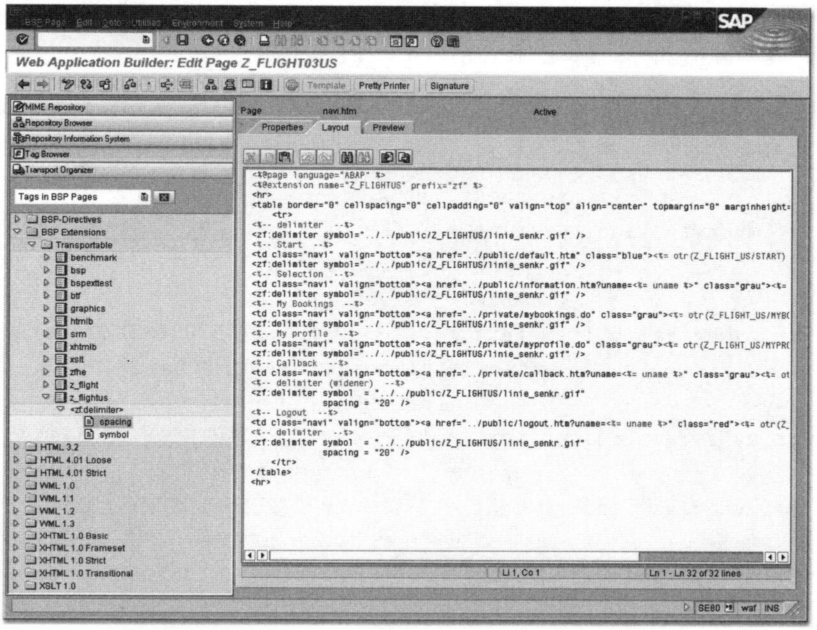

**Figure 5.83** The new listing for navi.htm

## 5.12.5 Composite Elements

You may want to call several BSP elements in the same configuration repeatedly. If you do, you'll soon learn that the effort required in combining and positioning these elements can increase each time significantly given the complexity of the BSP application. In addition, these iterative tasks can lead to errors that have negative effects on the layout in the client browser at runtime. *Composite elements* can help. They encase existing BSP elements in a common layout and enable you to iterate the elements by administering metadata (such as the number of subelements) centrally. You can also store additional information, such as style definitions or CSS class-element assignments in a central location. This feature allows you to generate code that is easily maintained and therefore enables you to use the components with versatility.

The navigation menu in our concrete scenario would seem predestined for encasement. Accordingly, with the right encasement into a composite element, the source would appear as follows:

**Grouping BSP elements**

**Listing 5.41** Page fragment navi.htm created with composite element myNavigation

```
<%@extension name="Z_FLIGHTUS" prefix="zf" %>
<HR>
<zf:myNavigation spacing = 1
                 delimiter = "../../public/Z_FLIGHTUS/
                 linie_senkr.gif">
<zf:myNavigationItem text = "><%= otr(Z_FLIGHTUS/START) %>"
                     ref = "default.htm"
                     color = "blue" />
<zf:myNavigationItem text = "<%= otr(Z_FLIGHTUS/SELEC) %>"
                     ref = "information.htm?uname=<%=
                     uname %>" />
<zf:myNavigationItem text = "<%= otr(Z_FLIGHTUS/MYBOOK) %>"
                     ref = "mybookings.do" />
<zf:myNavigationItem text = "<%= otr(Z_FLIGHTUS/MYPROF) %>"
                     ref = "myprofile.do" />
<zf:myNavigationItem text = "<%= otr(Z_FLIGHTUS/CALLB) %>"
                     ref = "callback.htm" />
<%-- Logout              --%>
<zf:myNavigationItem text = "<%= otr(Z_FLIGHTUS/LOGOFF) %>"
                     ref = "logout.htm"
                     color = "red" />
</zf:myNavigation>
```

In this example, we assume that the standard color of links is grey, and that using the color red automatically contributes to wider spacing. When you compare this coding with the original coding of the page fragment *navi.htm*, you can see how BSP extensions are truly powerful.

### 5.12.6 BSP Extension Expressions

**BEEs** You can use *BSP extension expressions* (*BEEs*) to overwrite the standard rendering of BSP elements—tabStrip or tableView elements, for example. That means that you can generate new BSP elements or HTML tags and write them to predefined locations in the page context (see Figure 5.84).

You define a BSP extension expression with the IF_BSP_BEE interface, which has two methods: RENDER and RENDER_TO_STRING. The first method writes the BEE into the current page context; the second method writes the BEE into a string. You can use various classes to implement the interface properly and enable the generation of a BEE in several ways:

CL_BSP_BEE_HTML, CL_BSP_BEE_IF_WRITER, CL_BSP_TABLE, and CL_BSP_BEE_XML. Using BEEs is particularly ideal for working in a tableView element. In this case, you can use the IF_HTMLB_ TABLEVIEW_ITERATOR interface and your own class to implement it properly. The class then gives you access to the rendering of tableView. You can also use BEEs within the iterator to modify the layout.

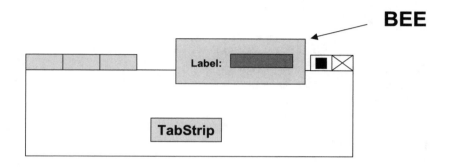

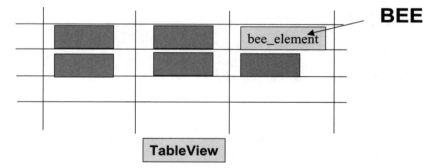

**Figure 5.84** Overwriting the standard rendering of BSP elements with BEEs

The BSP page *tableview.bsp* (see Figure 5.85) in the BSP application SBSPEXT_HTMLB provides an overview of the use of a tableView iterator and the use of BEEs).

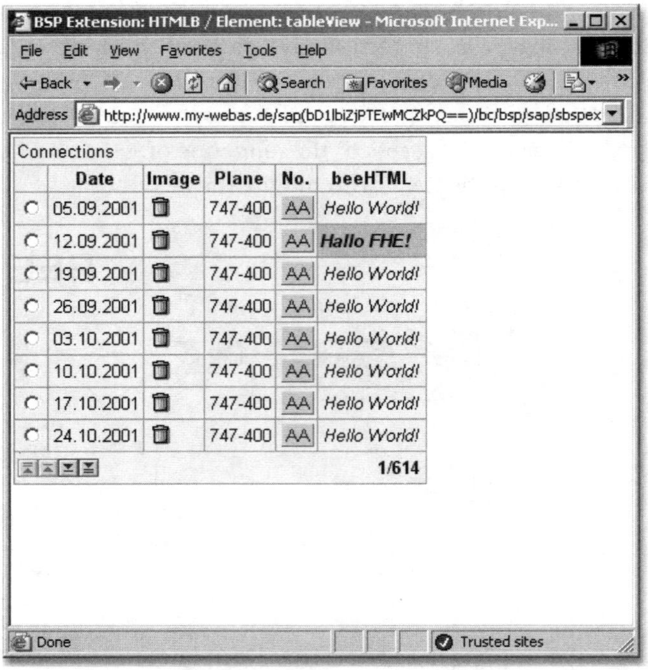

**Figure 5.85** The use of BEEs in a tableView

### 5.12.7 Scenario: Executing the Booking

As described, the page *book.htm* contains an index of the flight selected by the user. The onInitialization event handler uses the index to reselect the corresponding flight from the cookie. The page should redisplay the flight in a tableView element. Accordingly, the result is stored in an internal table, itab_fly. Listing 5.42 shows the event handler.

**Listing 5.42** The onInitialization event handler of Page book.htm

```
DATA l_uname TYPE string.
* Reading the customer number
userid = application->get_userid( ).
l_uname = sy-uname.
IF userid IS NOT INITIAL.
* Reading the cookies
  CALL METHOD cl_bsp_server_side_cookie=>get_server_
              cookie
    EXPORTING
      name                    = 'z_flight_it'
```

```
      application_name       = runtime->application_name
      application_namespace = runtime->application_name-
                               space
      username               = l_uname
      session_id             = 'z_flight'
      data_name              = 'itab_result'
    CHANGING
      data_value             = itab_result.
* Selecting the transferred row
   READ TABLE  itab_result
       INTO    wa_result
       INDEX   idx_data.
   APPEND wa_result TO itab_fly.
ENDIF.
```

As you can see from the listing, the GET_USERID method is used first to check if the user already has a customer number. The successful booking of a flight therefore requires some preparatory work.

The first step enhances the application class Z_CL_FLIGHT with additional methods. The BOOK_FLIGHT method books a flight and the CREATE_CUSTOMER method creates a new customer in flight table SCUSTOM. Each customer in table SCUSTOM has a customer number, which is a prerequisite for booking flights. Listing 5.43 provides the source text for the BOOK_FLIGHT method. The method calls two BAPIs to construct a flight booking. The booking data for a flight (booking_data) is required as an import parameter. The booking results in a booking number that is returned to the caller.

**New methods in the application class**

**Listing 5.43** The BOOK_FLIGHT method

```
METHOD book_flight.
  CALL FUNCTION 'BAPI_FLBOOKING_CREATEFROMDATA'
    EXPORTING
      booking_data   = booking_data
    IMPORTING
      bookingnumber = booking_number
    TABLES
      return         = return.
  CALL FUNCTION 'BAPI_TRANSACTION_COMMIT'
    EXPORTING
      wait = 'X'.
ENDMETHOD.
```

In Listing 5.44, you can see how a new customer for the flight booking portal is created. The import parameter customer_data provides the required customer data. The customer is then created in the system. The result is a customer number that identifies the customer uniquely. The number must be read manually from the return table.

**Listing 5.44** The CREATE_CUSTOMER method

```
METHOD create_customer.
  DATA: itab_return TYPE bapiret2_t,
        wa_return TYPE bapiret2,
        wa_flight_customer TYPE zflight_customer.
  CALL FUNCTION 'BAPI_FLCUST_CREATEFROMDATA'
    EXPORTING
      customer_data = customer_data
    TABLES
      return        = itab_return.
  CALL FUNCTION 'BAPI_TRANSACTION_COMMIT'
    EXPORTING
      wait = 'X'.
* Determine the customer number
  READ TABLE itab_return INTO wa_return WITH KEY type =
                                                  'S'.
  IF sy-subrc EQ 0.
    customer_number = wa_return-message_v2.
* Create/change the customer in the local
* table ZFLIGHT_CUSTOMER
    CALL METHOD me->set_userid
      EXPORTING
        i_username = sy-uname
        i_id       = customer_number.
ENDMETHOD.
```

In Listing 5.44, you can also see that the SAP customer name and the customer number that has been determined are written to a table that is specifically created in the Data Dictionary with the SET_USERID method (see Listing 5.45). Table ZFLIGHTUS_CUSTOMER enables us to quickly determine the customer number of a logged-on user. This involved a simple, client-dependent table with the client key and the user name.

**Listing 5.45** The SET_USERID method

```
METHOD set_userid.
  DATA:  wa TYPE zflight_customer.
  IF i_username IS INITIAL.
    wa-username = sy-uname.
  ELSE.
    wa-username = i_username.
  ENDIF.
  wa-id = i_id.
  MODIFY zflight_customer FROM wa.
ENDMETHOD.
```

The GET_USERID method reads the customer number (see Listing 5.46).

**Listing 5.46** The GET_USERID method

```
METHOD get_userid.
  SELECT SINGLE id
      FROM    zflight_customer
      INTO    r_userid
      WHERE   username EQ sy-uname.
ENDMETHOD.
```

In addition to booking flights, *book.htm* also regulates the creation of new users for booking flights. Creation is controlled by two page fragments. Page fragment *customer.htm* is used to create new customers; page fragment *gobook.htm* is used for the actual booking. Accordingly, a decision on one of the two page fragments depends on whether the user already has a customer number in table ZFLIGHT_CUSTOMER. As already noted, that determination occurs in the onInitialization event handler. The correct page fragment is displayed in the layout based upon userid.

```
<% if userid is initial. %>
  <%@include file="customer.htm" %>
<% else. %>
  <%@include file="gobook.htm" %>
<% endif. %>
```

If the customer number is found, page fragment *customer.htm* is loaded and the user is prompted to enter the personal data (see Figure 5.86).

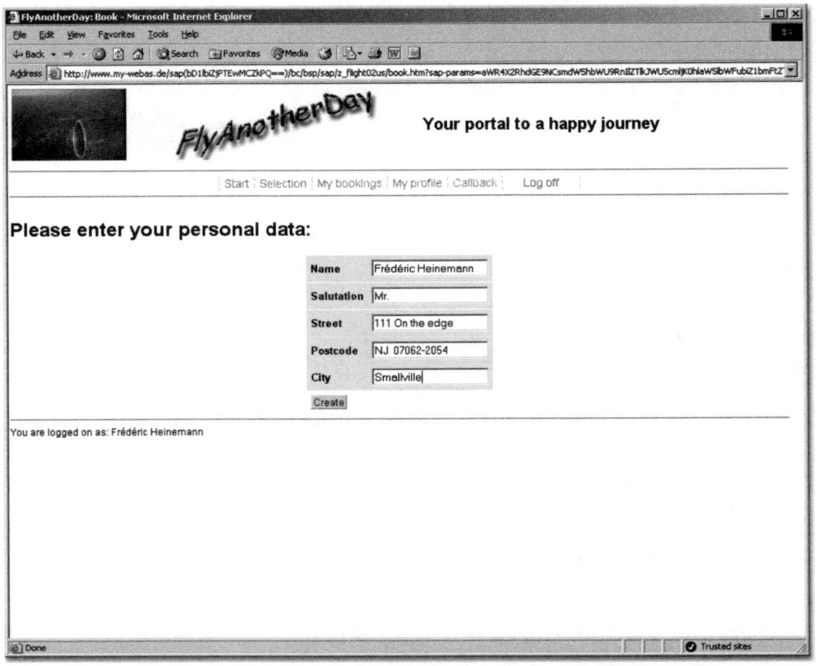

**Figure 5.86** Creating a customer

After saving the entries, the new user is created in the onInput-
Processing event handler of the BSP page *book.htm*. The source code
for creation of the customer appears as follows:

```
[...]
CASE button_event->id.
  WHEN 'id_customer'.
    customer_data-custname = request->get_form_field(
                             'custname' ).
    customer_data-form = request->get_form_field
                         ( 'form' ).
    customer_data-street = request->get_form_field(
                           'street' ).
    customer_data-postcode = request->get_form_field(
                             'postcode' ).
    customer_data-city = request->get_form_field
                         ( 'city' ).
    customer_data-custtype = 'P'. " Private customer
    CALL METHOD application->create_customer
```

```
EXPORTING
    customer_data   = customer_data
IMPORTING
    customer_number = userid.
navigation->set_parameter( name = 'idx_data'
                           value = idx_data ).
navigation->set_parameter( name = 'userid'
                           value = userid ).
navigation->set_parameter( name = 'uname'
                           value = uname ).
navigation->goto_page( 'book.htm' ).
```

As you can see in the code, all the customer data from the input field is transferred to the customer data structure, customer_data. After calling the application method to create a customer, a customer number is returned. We then reload *book.htm*: the assigned customer number is now displayed along with the selected flight (see Figure 5.87). If the user already has a customer number, this page is displayed immediately.

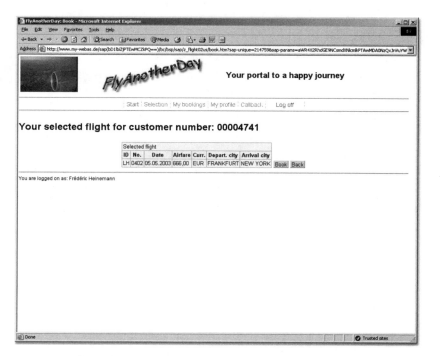

**Figure 5.87** The Booking page with a valid customer number

Clicking the **Book** button reloads the `onInputProcessing` event handler to execute the booking (see Figure 5.87). The following example shows the corresponding coding:

```
WHEN 'id_book'.
  booking_data-airlineid = request->get_form_field(
                             'carrid' ).
  booking_data-connectid = request->get_form_field(
                             'connid' ).
  booking_data-flightdate = request->get_form_field(
                              'fldate' ).
  booking_data-customerid = request->get_form_field(
                              'userid' ).
  booking_data-class = 'Y'.             " Economy
  booking_data-agencynum = '00000093'. " Default-
                                       " Travel agency
  CALL METHOD application->book_flight
    EXPORTING
      booking_data   = booking_data
    IMPORTING
      booking_number = booking_number.
  navigation->set_parameter(
    name = 'booking_number'
    value = booking_number ).
  navigation->set_parameter( 'uname' ).
  navigation->goto_page( 'confirm.htm' ).
```

The required booking data is entered into the `booking_data` structure. Once the booking has occurred, a booking number is returned, which we then transfer to the subsequent page, *confirm.htm*. This page is displayed to show the results of the booking (see Figure 5.88).

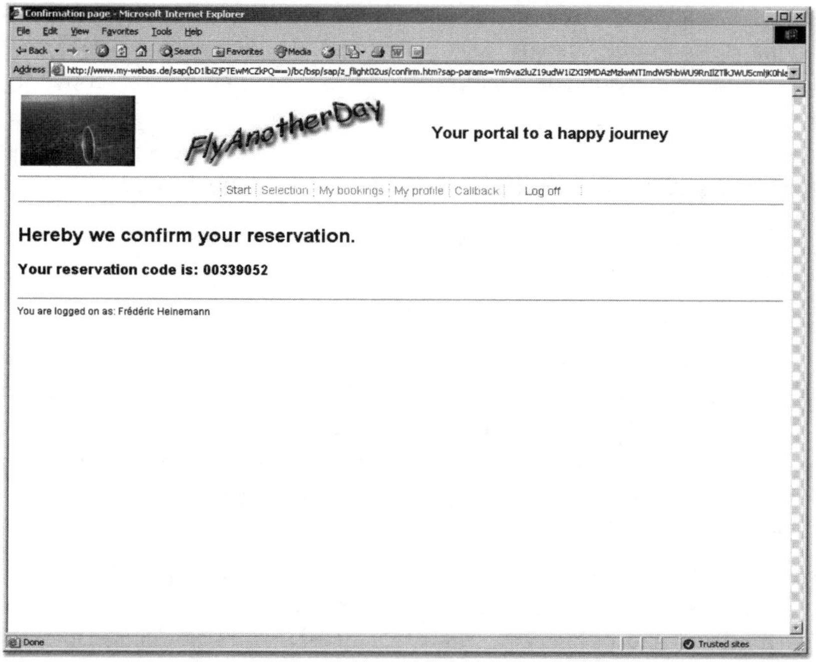

**Figure 5.88** A successful booking

## 5.13 Public and Protected Access Areas

You have identified a group of users that can and should work with your Web application. You can also divide your application into public areas, accessible to all users, and into protected areas, accessible only to special groups of users. Many Internet applications offer free access to general information. If users request special information, generally available only to members, they must first register. After they register, users receive a user name and password that permits them to access the protected areas.

In our scenario, the flight booking portal is completely protected right now. Users can access the portal only with their SAP user names and passwords. So, let's change that now to make access to the flight booking portal (*default.htm*), searching for flights (*information.htm*), and closing the application (*logout.htm*) freely accessible (see Section 5.1). Users will no longer need any authentication for these particular pages. However, if users want to book a flight or view their personal data, they must authenticate themselves. They will be authenticated as standard SAP users, as they were previously. The protected areas will include BSP pages *book.htm* and *confirm.htm*.

The conversion of our application into public and protected areas involves numerous changes to the source code. Accordingly, we'll now work with a copy of Z_FLIGHT02US, and name the copy Z_FLIGHT03US.

### 5.13.1 Applications with Public and Protected Areas

To develop a Web application with public and protected areas, you have the following options to create the division:

▶ **Divided applications**
You can separate your application into two distinct applications: one to cover the public areas and one to cover the protected areas. You can store logon information in the service maintenance of each application. You would store a default (anonymous) user for the public area and require a logon (for a SAP user, for example) for the protected area.

▶ **Partitioned application**
In this option, the complete application functions as one application, which is partitioned into two subtrees (folders). One branch corresponds to the public area; the other branch corresponds to the protected area. Here, too, you must store a default user for the public area and a logon for the protected area.

▶ **Self-management**
You can implement your own logon dialog for access to protected areas in the application. By doing this, you can control user access by calling a function module. To ensure that the user cannot simply enter the URL in the browser and therefore cross over to access the protected application, you must check for a successful logon on all protected pages.

Internet user    In addition to the standard SAP user, you can also create *Internet users* on the SAP Web AS. Many scenarios require the support of online users. In these applications, it makes sense for users to log on, register themselves, and have the ability to create new users from other users. Internet users are SAP users of the type *service* and are created with Transaction SU01. An alias and a small amount of personal data are maintained for an Internet user.

Authorizations are inherited from a reference user, which is also created in Transaction SU01 (type: *reference*). Reference users allow you to generate various classes of Internet users, each with different authorizations. Protected and public areas of a Web application can also be administered with Internet users. For example, you can make the start page available to a default user and then use a logon screen to change to an Internet user.

A function module, `SUSR_INTERNET_USERSWITCH`, is available to implement this function. The function module `SUSR_USER_INTERNET_CREATE` allows even external users to add users. To modify an Internet user, use the settings of service maintenance for the corresponding entry in the service data.

### 5.13.2 Enhancing the Flight Booking Portal

To implement this scenario in the flight portal, we'll use the second option: we'll partition our application (see Section 5.13.1) and continue to use the standard SAP user (only for the protected area). To begin, create two folders, *PUBLIC* and *PRIVATE*, in the BSP application.

Because the context menu does not contain an entry for creating a folder, copy the corresponding page as shown in Figure 5.89. The folder will automatically be created along with the copy.

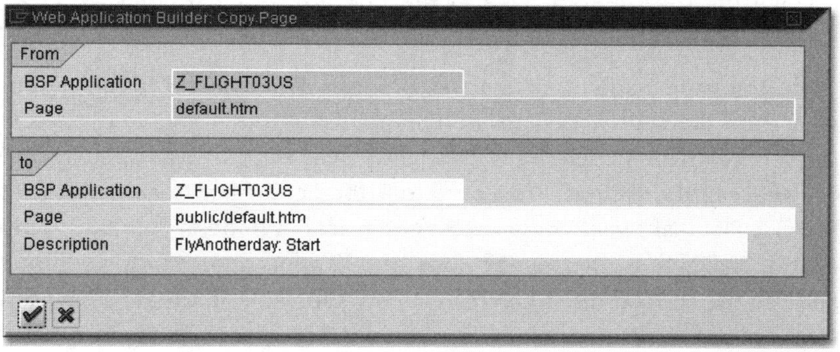

Figure 5.89 Copying a page into the PUBLIC folder

In the same manner, copy the BSP pages *default.htm*, *information.htm*, and *logout.htm* into the *PUBLIC* folders. Copy the BSP pages *book.htm* and *confirm.htm* into the *PRIVATE* folder. Save and activate the BSP application. Figure 5.90 shows the resulting object list.

Moving the BSP page affects all the defined relative paths in the BSP application. That means that all the relative references used in navigation must be checked and modified if necessary. To display the relative paths, use the convention `../` (one level above). Navigation in the `onInput-Processing` event handler of the public page *information.htm* to the protected page *book.htm* appears as follows:

```
navigation->goto_page( '../private/book.htm' ).
```

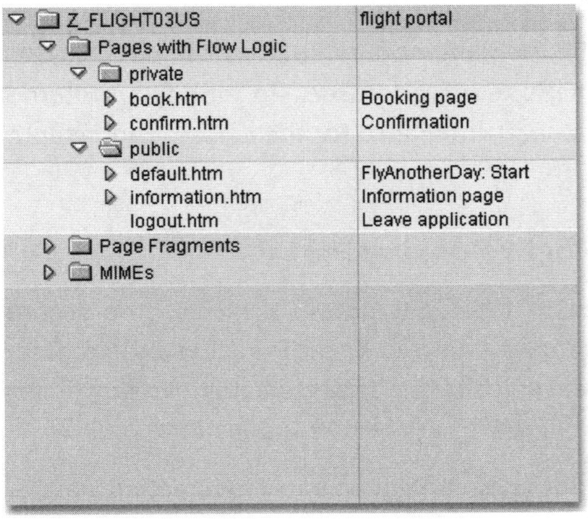

**Figure 5.90** The Object List of the partitioned BSP application

Change the default start page in the properties of BSP application Z_
FLIGHTUS03 from *default.htm* to *public/default.htm*.

**Public service** Once you have made these changes, you can define access to the various
areas. You maintain access to the BSP application that you've created in
ICF service maintenance (Transaction SICF, see Section 4.3 and Section 2.5
on the security settings). You can store the access and security policies
(Service Data tab) needed for access in the service node of your BSP application. Navigate to the service node of BSP application Z_FLIGHTUS03
and use the context menu to create a new subelement. Create a new service element, *PUBLIC*, in the dialog window that opens (see Figure 5.91).

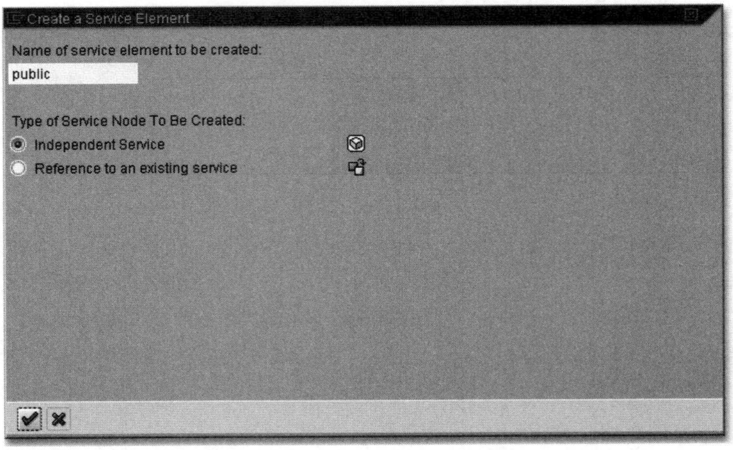

**Figure 5.91** Creating a Public service

After you confirm your entries, you arrive at Service Maintenance. To cre- **Default user** ate a public area, you must store a *default user* in the anonymous logon data. You enter client, language, and password for this special user, which is created as usual in Transaction SU01 (type: *service*).

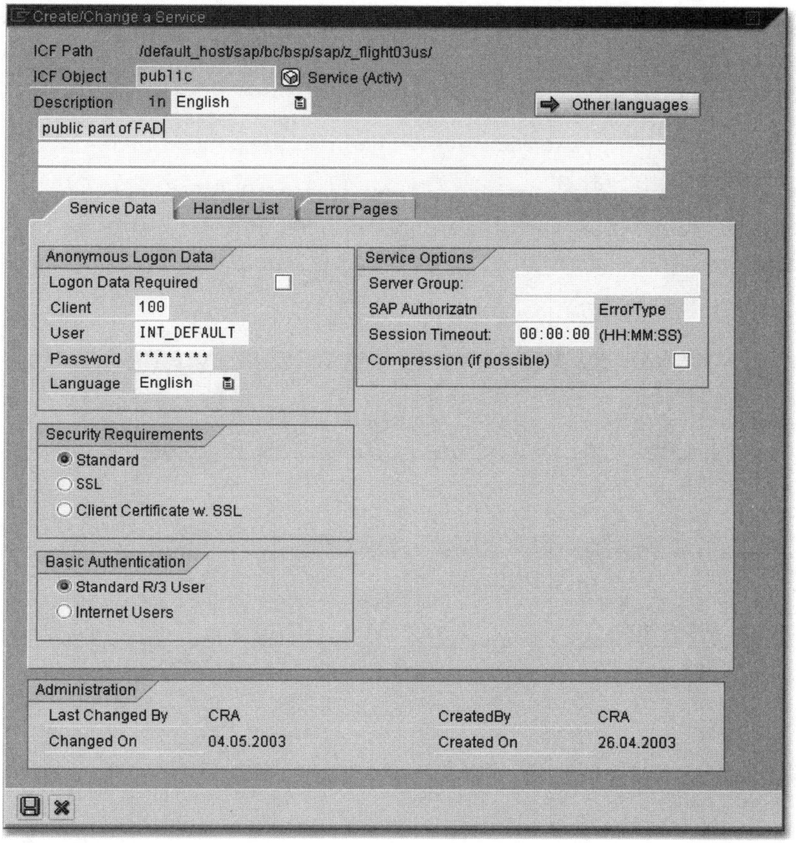

**Figure 5.92** Assigning a default user in Service Maintenance

Figure 5.92 shows the assignment of a default user, INT_DEFAULT, in the anonymous logon data. Authentication occurs as a standard SAP user (area: *Basic Authentication*). The default user has the following properties:

▶ Multiple logons are enabled

▶ Password is retained

▶ Changing to an Internet user is enabled

Note the following when you set up and use a default user for your Web application: this user is valid only for URLs that refer to this application. If the HTML pages contain references to other applications or images in other paths (such as style sheets or graphics beneath the *PUBLIC* folder in the MIME Repository), these paths must also be assigned a default user. The user does not have the required authorization to access objects outside the URL application path. In this case, the Web browser displays a pop-up window for authentication.

Save your entries and activate the service with the context menu.

**Protected service**  As we created a public service, we'll now create a *PRIVATE* service for the protected area. Maintain a description here and leave the settings unchanged: authentication as an SAP user is required to access this service (see Figure 5.93).

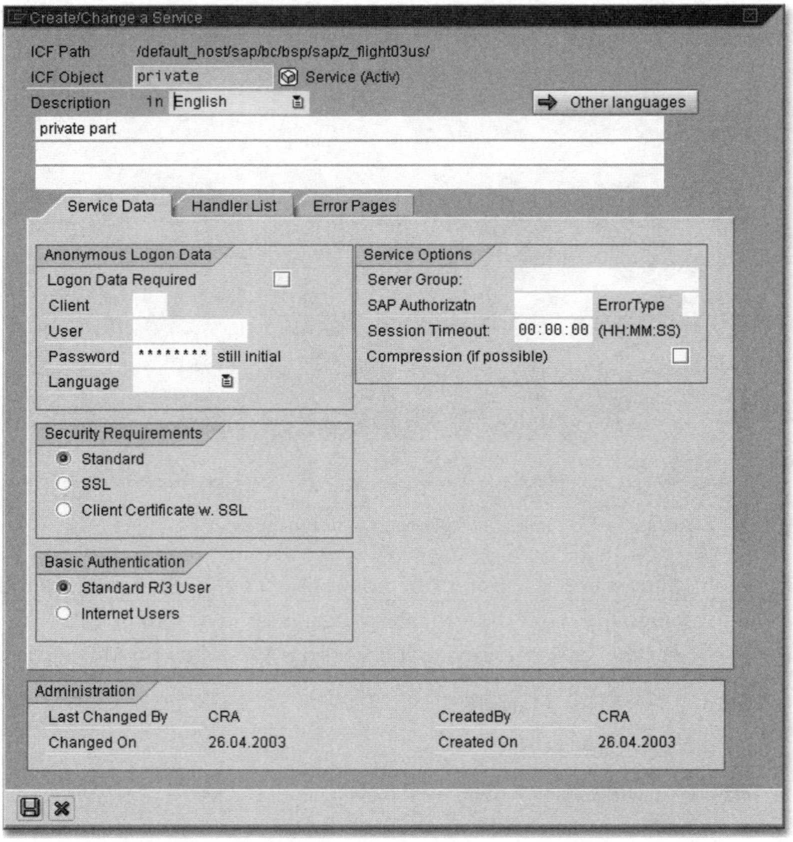

Create/Change a Service

| | |
|---|---|
| ICF Path | /default_host/sap/bc/bsp/sap/z_flight03us/ |
| ICF Object | private    Service (Activ) |
| Description | in English |

private part

Service Data | Handler List | Error Pages

Anonymous Logon Data

Logon Data Required ☐

Client

User

Password ******** still initial

Language

Service Options

Server Group:

SAP Authorizatn    ErrorType

Session Timeout: 00:00:00 (HH:MM:SS)

Compression (if possible) ☐

Security Requirements
- ◉ Standard
- ○ SSL
- ○ Client Certificate w. SSL

Basic Authentication
- ◉ Standard R/3 User
- ○ Internet Users

Administration

| | | | |
|---|---|---|---|
| Last Changed By | CRA | CreatedBy | CRA |
| Changed On | 26.04.2003 | Created On | 26.04.2003 |

**Figure 5.93** Maintaining the properties of the PRIVATE service

Then, save the entries. You'll also have to activate the new service. Two services are now created beneath the service node Z_FLIGHTUS03 in service maintenance.

In order for the MIME object to be loaded into the BSP pages without authorization, the BSP pages are stored in a new subdirectory in the *PUB-LIC* folder of the MIME directory. The ICF path to this folder is *default_host/sap/bc/bsp/sap/public*. Create a new service, *Z_FLIGHTUS*, for this service node in service maintenance and then store (again) a default user for access. You must then rework all the MIME references. For example, you must reference the CSS file as follows so that it can be found:

```
<LINK rel="stylesheet" href="../../public/Z_FLIGHTUS/z_
flight.css">
```

Now, when you close the browser and reopen it, a pop-up window for authentication opens in the background, with the default user set. Instead of seeing the personal greeting, you are now greeted by the stored name of the default user (see Figure 5.94).

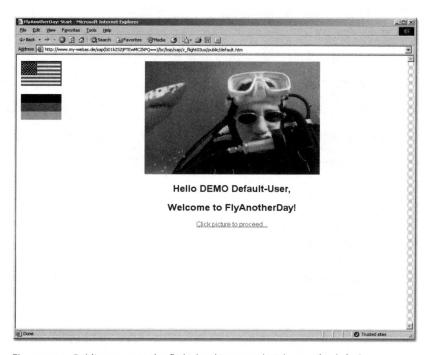

**Figure 5.94** Public access to the flight booking portal with use of a default user

If you now change to *information.htm*, you are still in the public area of the application. However, if you want to execute a booking, clicking the **Book** button puts you in the protected area (*book.htm*). A logon window for authentication opens (see Figure 5.95) because you have changed the service and a new authentication is required by the settings of the new service.

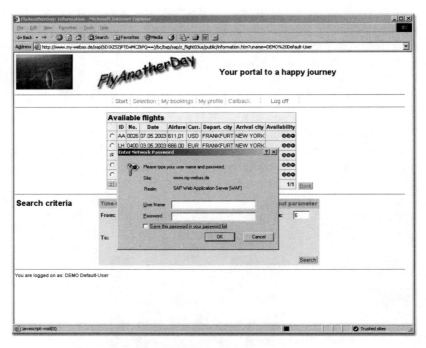

**Figure 5.95** Changing to the protected area

You can execute the booking after successful authentication (see Figure 5.96). As you can see in the footer of the BSP application, the name stored in the system under your SAP user name is now displayed. You are recognized as an authorized user. If you change back to the *PUBLIC* area, you once again function as a default user. If a BSP page from the protected area is reloaded, however, no new logon is required because the successful logon is still stored in the cache.

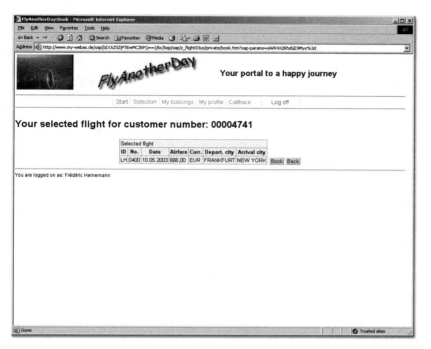

**Figure 5.96** The protected booking area

Changing from the public to the private area and vice versa requires some changes to the source code. Until now, the user name was transferred from the start page to the subsequent pages. However, in the public area, all users function under the same name (*DEMO Default User*). Accordingly, when the user moves to the protected area, the current user name is redetermined and displayed with the GET_UNAME method in the protected BSP page. In addition, the cookie that stores the table entries, Z_FLIGHTUS_IT, must now be stored with its session_id attribute as session-dependent to guarantee a unique assignment.

**Listing 5.47** Coding for a session-dependent server-side cookie

```
call method cl_bsp_server_side_cookie=>set_server_cookie
  exporting
    name                  = 'z_flight_it'
    application_name      = runtime->application_name
    application_namespace = runtime->application_name-
                            space
    username              = 'NONE'
    session_id            = runtime->session_id
```

```
data_value          = itab_result
data_name           = 'itab_result'
expiry_time_rel     = 3600.
```

## 5.14  Model View Controller Design Pattern

The *Model-View-Controller* (MVC) *Design Pattern* provides a clean way to separate presentation logic, flow control, and application logic. Section 3.3.4 explores the theory and the methodology of MVC in detail.

Working with the MVC design pattern is relatively complex and requires some time to become familiar with it. SAP has dealt with this situation. *Web Dynpro*, delivered with the SAP Web AS Release 6.30 for Java (it will also be available for ABAP in Release 6.40), abstracts application development with MVC to a graphical development environment. This function of Web Dynpro is similar to that of the screen painter (Transaction SE51) in typical Dynpro-GUI development. For developers, this means that they don't have to deal directly with the creation of the MVC framework in the following versions. For this reason, we will simply provide an overview of MVC.

**Expanding the scenario**
We will now look at working with the MVC in practice. We'll use the MVC design pattern to enhance the functions of our scenario once again. Until now, the customer (user) could find information on available flights, select a flight, and book a flight. Users who weren't logged on, or who didn't have a customer number, must log on or register to book a flight. Users should now also be given access to information on flights, which they have booked, and on their personal profiles.

### 5.14.1  Creating the Controller

**Controller**
The *controller* is the central component of the MVC design pattern. It is responsible for the flow control of the BSP application. Because it has this property, it controls the views and model classes. When users select the link to **My bookings**, the appropriate controller should be called. Therefore, we will first create a main controller. A main controller can call subcontrollers, and thereby reach parameters, events, and so on. A main controller consists of a controller object, which determines the properties, and a controller class. The class is derived from the `CL_BSP_CONTROLLER2` class, which is inherited from the `CL_BSP_CONTROLLER` class.

If possible, create the controller with forward navigation from the properties page of the controller object so that the inheritance is automatically and correctly set.

In the object list, select our BSP application, Z_FLIGHTUS03 with the right mouse button and create a new controller with the context menu as shown in Figure 5.97.

**Controller object**

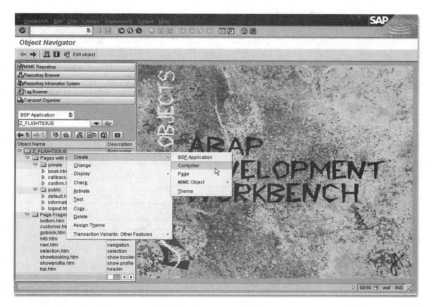

**Figure 5.97** Creating a Controller object

As discussed in Section 5.1, our main controller is named *mybooking.do*. The extension *.do* is already displayed. Enter the same text as shown in Figure 5.98.

| Web Application Builder: Create Contoller | |
|---|---|
| BSP Application | Z_FLIGHT03US |
| Controller | private/mybookings.do |
| Description | Controller: Link "My bookings" |

**Figure 5.98** Naming a Controller object

The properties page of the controller object opens: see Figure 5.99. The most important setting is for the corresponding controller class. Enter Z_CL_C_FLIGHT_BOOK_US in the **Controller Class** field. The other settings are similar to those of the BSP pages with flow logic; however, you don't have to deal with them right now.

**Controller class**

To maintain a good overview, we recommend that you assign unique names to the controller and the model classes. Accordingly, the names of controller classes begin with Z_CL_C_ and the names of model classes begin with Z_CL_M_ in our scenario.

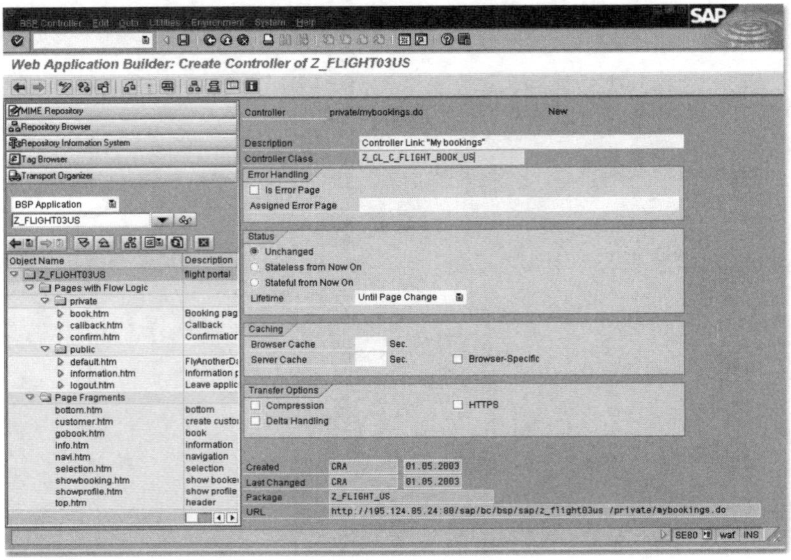

**Figure 5.99** The Properties page of the Controller object

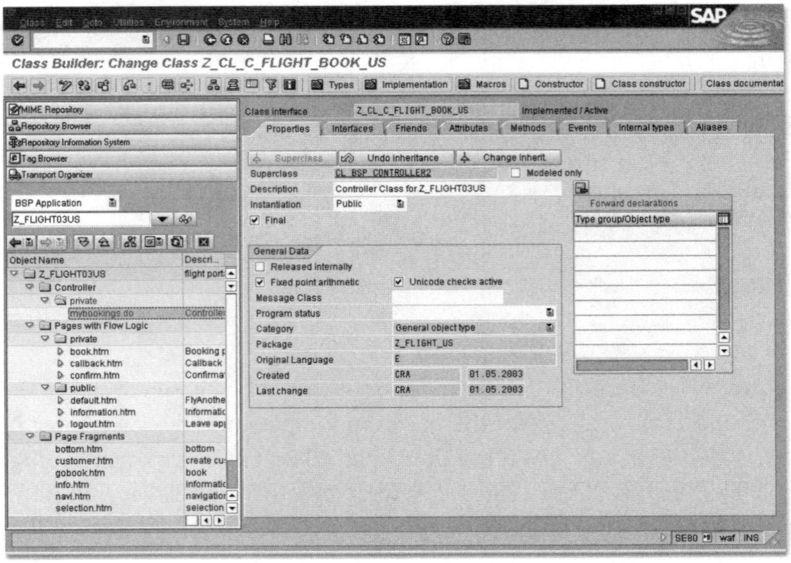

**Figure 5.100** The Properties tab of the Controller class

Use forward navigation to create a new class with the name that you just entered. After a security prompt, a question about the requested package, and the following assignment to a transport request, you arrive at the Class Builder. Compare the Properties page with Figure 5.100. The CL_BSP_CONTROLLER2 class was already entered automatically as the superclass.

Activate the class and return to the controller object. Activate the controller. Note the new directory in the object list.

The .do extension applies to all controllers. It can be called with a URL directly from the client browser. In the next step, you can modify page fragment *navi.htm*. The line with the **My bookings** link for navigation to the *mybookings.do* controller should appear as it does in Listing 5.48:

**Maintaining the Navigation link**

**Listing 5.48** Coding in navi.htm to call the Controller

```
<%-- My bookings --%>
<TD class="navi" valign="bottom">
  <A href="../private/mybookings.do" class="grau"><%=
     otr(Z_FLIGHTUS/MYBOOK) %></A>
</TD>
```

## 5.14.2 Processing Flow

The controller is responsible for the flow control of a BSP page; methods establish the control.

**Comparing events**

The methods are partially comparable to the event times in the processing flow of a BSP page with flow logic. Let's look at some of the controller's methods used or required here:

▶ DO_INIT
This method is comparable to the onCreate event handler. It's called when generating the controller instance. Here you can create a model class.

▶ DO_INITATTRIBUTES
This method is comparable to the BSP event handler onInititialization.

▶ DO_REQUEST
This method controls the following specialized methods for input processing:

- ▶ DO_HANDLE_DATA

  This method ensures that the model class is populated in the context of data binding. It transfers data from form fields and messages for the global `messages` object.

- ▶ DO_HANDLE_EVENT

  This method outputs the GLOBAL_EVENT parameter, and when events are triggered by BSP elements, it populates the HTMLB `event` object—as long as the element ID of the element is set.

- ▶ DO_FINISH_INPUT

  With the assistance of the GLOBAL_EVENT parameter, this method can react to events. It is the last method of input processing.

The event times of BSP pages with flow logic are comparable; BSP pages call (in order): `onRequest`, `onInputProcessing`, `onLayout`, and `onManipulation`.

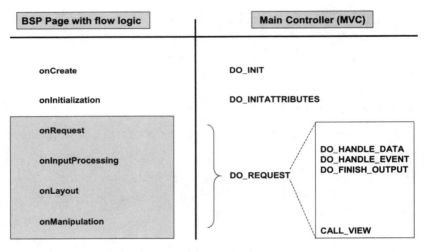

**Figure 5.101** Comparison of Event Handler Methods

## Input Processing

Incoming requests from client browsers are redirected to the main controller directly with a URL call. In this case, the URL call is the link *mybookings.do*. After processing DO_INIT and DO_INITATTRIBUTE here, the central DO_REQUEST method is called. This method redirects the incoming data to the subcontrollers.

The service function `DISPATCH_INPUT` handles this task. It reads the data from the form fields of the request object and redirects them to the subcontroller that was addressed. Addressing occurs with a prefix in the form fields of the view. For BSP elements, such as the BSP extension HTMLB, the prefix is generated automatically. When using traditional HTML tags, however, we must determine the prefix ourselves. Here we can use a service method[6], `GET_ID`, which provides the prefix.

Dispatching with a prefix

Data intended for the main controller itself is processed within the `DO_REQUEST` method by the `DO_HANDLE_DATA`, `DO_HANDLE_EVENT`, and `DO_FINISH_INPUT` methods noted above. Subcontrollers also process the data assigned to them by implementing these methods.

### Output Processing

One or more views are generated and output in the context of output processing—with the `CALL_VIEW` function. Controllers can also be set to an inactive status, or new controllers can be generated.

### 5.14.3 Creating a View

In this step, we'll create the view to display the booking data and supply it with a basic framework. In the SAP Web AS, call the context menu of the BSP application `ZFLIGHT03US` and select **Create Page**. Next, enter a name and a description as shown in Figure 5.102. Enter "view" as the page type.

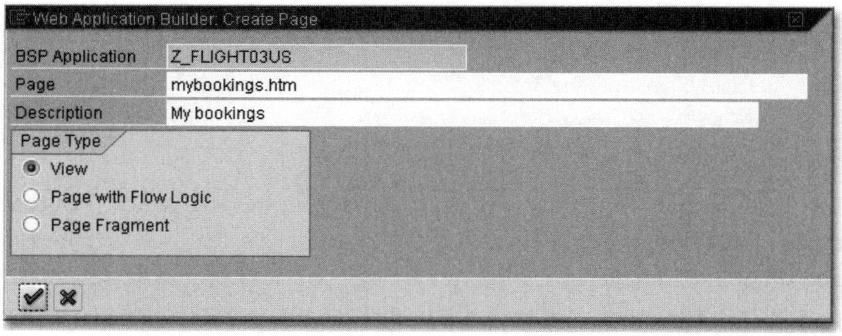

**Figure 5.102** Creating the mybookings.htm view

---

6  You can use these methods in the derived class but not overwrite them.

The basic framework is the same as it was for the *information.htm* page, so you can simply copy and modify the coding of that page. Instead of the page fragments *selection.htm* and *info.htm*, first enter any text for testing. The layout portion of the view should appear as it does in Listing 5.49.

**Listing 5.49** The basic framework of the mybookings.htm view

```
<%@page language="abap" %>
<%@extension name="htmlb" prefix="htmlb" %>
<htmlb:content design    = "CLASSIC"
               themeRoot = "../../public/Z_FLIGHTUS" >
  <htmlb:document>
    <htmlb:documentHead title="FlyAnotherDay: <%= otr(Z_
    FLIGHT/mybook) %>" >
      <htmlb:headInclude/>
      <link rel="stylesheet" href="z_flight.css">
    </htmlb:documentHead>
    <htmlb:documentBody>
      <htmlb:form id     = "myform"
                  method = "post" >
        <%-- Include header fragment   --%>
        <%@include file="top.htm" %>
        <%-- Include navigation fragment   --%>
        <%@include file="navi.htm" %>
        My first View
        <%-- Include footer fragment   --%>
        <%@include file="bottom.htm" %>
      </htmlb:form>
    </htmlb:documentBody>
  </htmlb:document>
</htmlb:content>
```

**Page attribute**  The only thing missing now is the page attribute, uname, which is output in the footer fragment *bottom.htm*. You can define it now. As noted in Section 3.3, you have two ways of marking the parameter as an automatic page attribute. The controller will populate it later, so the characteristic is not required here.

For the first time, the difference between the MVC design pattern and BSP pages with flow logic becomes clear. Using the MVC, the controllers "drive" the application; with typical BSP pages, the pages themselves determine the flow, so they have control and populate the parameters.

Save and activate the view.

## 5.14.4 Calling the View

Now we'll take a look at calling the presentation logic, the views. The appropriate method is DO_REQUEST. Here we redefine the method inherited from the CL_BSP_CONTROLLER2 class. On the methods page, check the DO_REQUEST method of Z_CL_C_FLIGHT_BOOK_US class and select the redefine icon from the application toolbar (see Figure 5.103).

CALL_VIEW

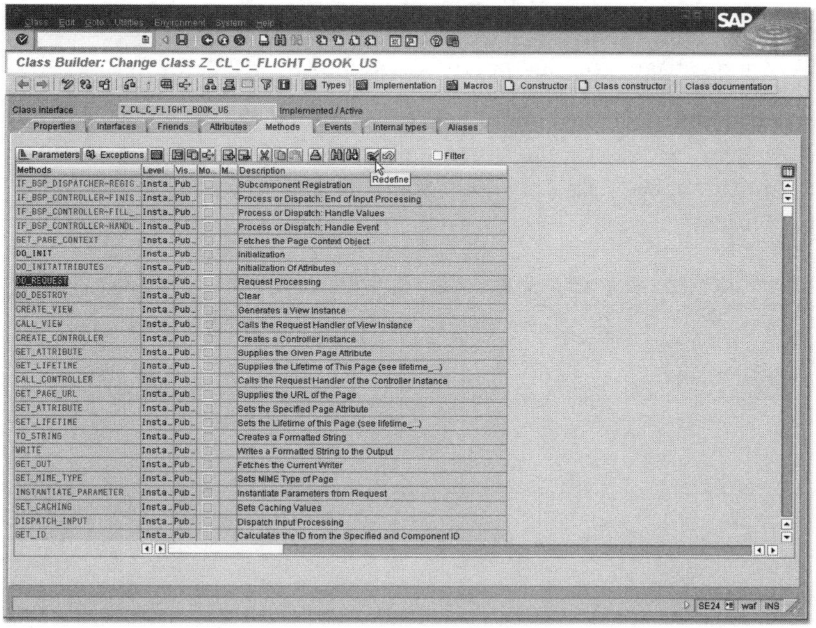

**Figure 5.103** Redefinition of the DO_REQUEST method

Now we can overwrite the method. Fill it as shown in the following.

```
* Data declaration
  data: l_view type ref to if_bsp_page.
```

Data declaration

The data declaration occurs first. Here we declare a reference to the IF_ BSP_PAGE interface. You can access the information of a Business Server Page, such as the name of the BSP, its lifetime, and so on. Then, we generate the object and assign it to a view that is yet to be written.

```
* Instantiation
  l_view = create_view( view_name = 'mybookings.htm' ).
```

Instantiation

We also want to give a primary page attribute to the view directly. In the first step, we populate the uname parameter. To do so, we first turn to the sy-uname system parameter.

**Assigning attributes**

```
* Setting the attribute
  l_view->set_attribute( name = 'uname' value = sy-uname ).
```

Next, we call the view.

**Calling the View**

```
* Calling the View
  call_view( l_view ).
```

Save and activate the method.

You can also generate simple pages by creating the HTML data stream directly in the DO_REQUEST method. In this case, the data declaration, instantiation, and call of the view are unnecessary. Try the coding in Listing 5.50:

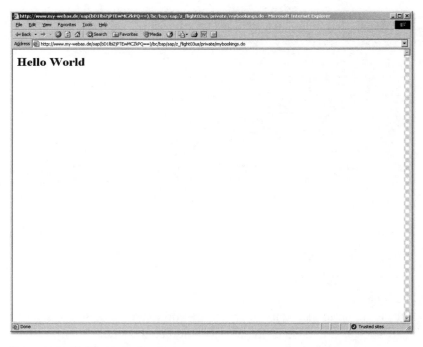

**Figure 5.104** The first call of a view

**Listing 5.50** A Simple HTML data stream in the Controller

```
METHOD do_request.
  write( '<HTML><BODY><H1>' ).
  write( 'Hello World' ).
  write( '</H1></BODY></HTML>' ).
ENDMETHOD.
```

Call the link to **My bookings** in the Web application and compare the results with Figure 5.104.

Because there's not much to see yet, we'll go another step: the user name should be transferred instead of the system user name. Here, we'll need to enhance our application.

### 5.14.5 Creating a Model Class

So far, our MVC has been more of a VC. Next, we'll determine the name in a manner similar to that of the application class method GET_UNAME.

**From VC to MVC**

Here, you do not use the method of the application class. Even though doing so is technically possible, it contradicts the principle of the MVC design pattern.

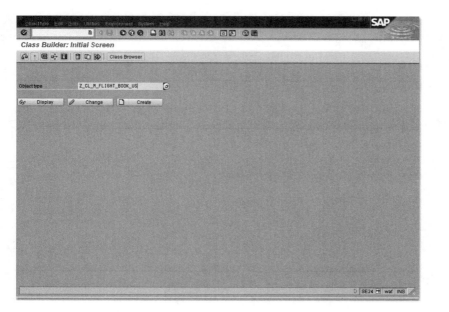

**Figure 5.105** Creating the model class Z_CL_M_FLIGHT_BOOK_US

Go to the Class Builder initial screen and create the model class `Z_CL_M_FLIGHT_BOOK_US` as shown in Figure 5.105.

Confirm the query. In the dialog window that opens next, enter class `CL_BSP_MODEL` as a superclass (inherits from) and enter a description (see Figure 5.106).

| | |
|---|---|
| Create Class Z_CL_M_FLIGHT_BOOK_US | |
| Class | Z_CL_M_FLIGHT_BOOK_US |
| Superclass | CL_BSP_MODEL |
| Description | Model for Z_FLIGHT03US |
| Instantiation | Public |

Class Type
- ● Usual ABAP Class
- ○ Exception Class
- ○ Persistent class

☑ Final
☐ Only modeled

✔ Save ✖

**Figure 5.106** The dialog window for creating the Model class

If you do not see the line "inherits from," display it by clicking on the icon in the upper right.

Save your entries and send the package assignment and a transport request.

**The GET_USER-NAME method**

Now you can create the `GET_USERNAME` method, which should be *public* and of type "instance method." You can take the coding from Listing 5.51, or the application class method `GET_USERNAME`.

**Listing 5.51** The GET_USERNAME method

```
METHOD get_username.
* Local data object
  DATA: lv_persnumber TYPE ad_persnum,
        lv_name_first TYPE ad_namefir,
        lv_name_last  TYPE ad_namelas.
* Determine the personnel number from the logon name
  SELECT single persnumber
```

```
           from    usr21
           into    lv_persnumber
           where   bname = sy-uname.
   IF sy-subrc = 0.
* Determine the complete user name (first and last name)
     SELECT single name_first name_last
             from    adrp
             into    (lv_name_first, lv_name_last)
             where   persnumber = lv_persnumber.
     IF sy-subrc = 0.
* Concatenate the name
        CONCATENATE lv_name_first lv_name_last into user-
                    name
                    SEPARATED BY space.
     ENDIF.
   ENDIF.
   IF username IS INITIAL.
     username = sy-uname.
   ENDIF.
ENDMETHOD.
```

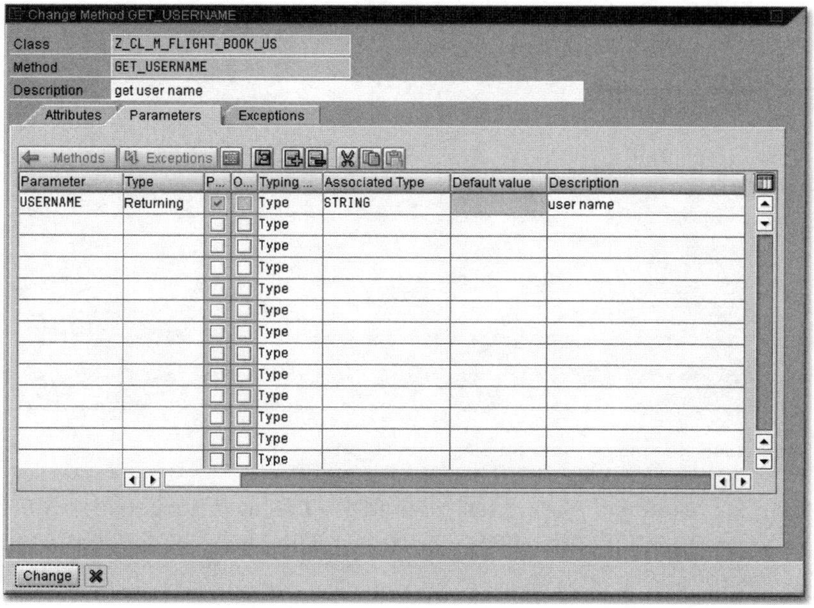

**Figure 5.107** Returning parameter username of the GET_USERNAME method

The only thing missing now is the returning parameter `username`. Go to method definition and create the parameter shown in Figure 5.107 as a `returning` parameter.

Click on the **Change** button to confirm the entry and activate the class with all its component objects. Now we can use the model class that we have generated successfully.

### 5.14.6 Calling the Model Class

You call the model class in the controller, so we'll go to the controller class `Z_CL_C_FLIGHT_BOOK_US`. We'll save the name as a member attribute. From the menu, select **GoTo Class Definition** and create an attribute named M_USERNAME in the **Attributes** tab. The attribute should be of type `STRING` and be *protected* (see Figure 5.108).

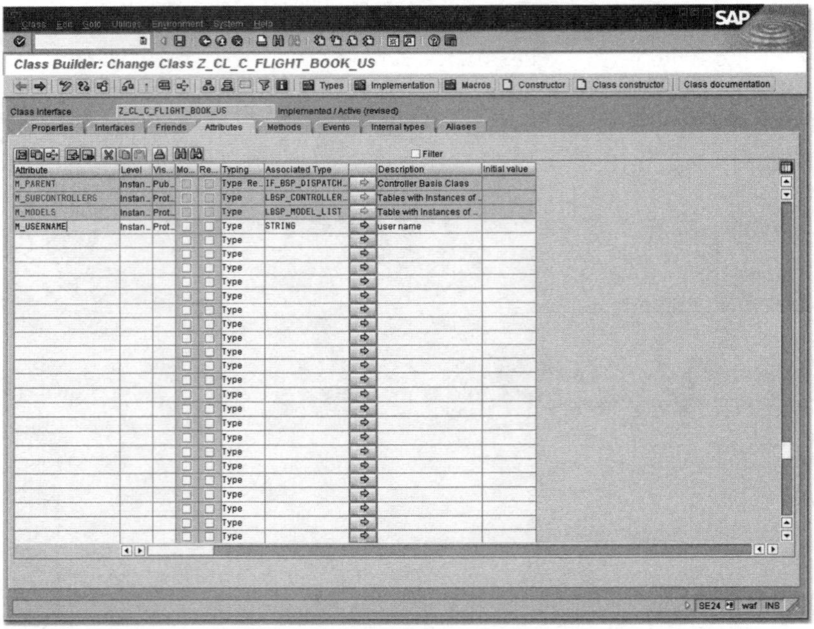

**Figure 5.108** The member attribute M_USERNAME

Next, we redefine the `DO_INIT` method. As already described, this is the proper method for binding the model class. Fill the method with the following code.

```
METHOD do_init.
*Data declaration
  DATA: model TYPE REF TO z_cl_m_flight_book_US.
```

After the data declaration, in which a reference to our model class is declared, the reference object is generated and undergoes instantiation. The model is also directly assigned a `model_id`, "mf."

```
* create and register model object
  model ?= create_model( class_name = 'Z_CL_M_FLIGHT_
                                       BOOK_US'
                         model_id   = 'mf' ).
```

Now we can use the GET_USERNAME method previously written in the model class. The result is stored in the member attribute M_USERNAME and is then available for use.

```
  CALL METHOD model->get_username
    RECEIVING
      username = m_username.
ENDMETHOD.
```

Next we can modify the DO_REQUEST method. In the following line, replace `sy-uname` with `m_username`.

```
* Setting the attribute
  l_view->set_attribute( name = 'uname'
                         value = m_username ).
```

Save and activate the class and then test the result in the browser.

If you don't see the result that you want, that is, the full name of the SAP user, close the browser and then reopen it.

### 5.14.7 Enhancing the Scenario

Next, we enhance the model class so that it displays a list of the booked flights in the view. We first need to modify the view by adding an additional page fragment to it. The new fragment is very similar to *info.htm*. You can copy *info.htm* and create it as *showbooking.htm*. But you must remember that the booking header and the tableView attribute, selectionMode, are removed from the coding. You also have to modify the title of the `tableView` and the `tableViewColumn` elements. The coding should appear as it does in Listing 5.52.

**Returning the booked flights**

**Listing 5.52** The coding of page fragment showbooking.htm

```
<%@extension name="htmlb" prefix="htmlb" %>
<htmlb:gridLayout id         = "outer"
                  columnSize = "1"
                  rowSize    = "1"
                  width      = "100%" >
  <htmlb:gridLayoutCell columnIndex          = "1"
                        rowIndex             = "1"
                        horizontalAlignment = "CENTER" >
    <htmlb:gridLayout id         = "inner"
                      columnSize = "2"
                      rowSize    = "1"
                      cellSpacing = "5" >
      <htmlb:gridLayoutCell columnIndex = "1"
                            rowIndex    = "1" >
        <htmlb:tableView id             = "flight_
                                          table"
                         table          = "<%= itab_
                                           result %>"
                         emptyTableText = "<%= otr(Z_
FLIGHT/empty_table) %>"
                         headerText     = "<%= otr(Z_
FLIGHT/MYBOOK) %>"
                         headerVisible   = "TRUE"
                         fillUpEmptyRows = "FALSE"
                         visibleRowCount = "6"
                         navigationMode  = "BYPAGE"
                         footerVisible   = "TRUE" >
          <htmlb:tableViewColumns>
            <htmlb:tableViewColumn columnName="CARRID" >
            </htmlb:tableViewColumn>
            <htmlb:tableViewColumn columnName="CONNID" >
            </htmlb:tableViewColumn>
            <htmlb:tableViewColumn columnName="FLDATE" >
            </htmlb:tableViewColumn>
            <htmlb:tableViewColumn columnName="BOOKID" >
            </htmlb:tableViewColumn>
            <htmlb:tableViewColumn columnName="CUST-
                                              TYPE" >
            </htmlb:tableViewColumn>
            <htmlb:tableViewColumn columnName="SMOKER" >
```

```
                    </htmlb:tableViewColumn>
                    <htmlb:tableViewColumn columnName="INVOICE"
>

                    </htmlb:tableViewColumn>
                    <htmlb:tableViewColumn columnName="CLASS" >
                    </htmlb:tableViewColumn>
                    <htmlb:tableViewColumn columnName="LOCCU-
                                                          RAM" >
                    </htmlb:tableViewColumn>
                    <htmlb:tableViewColumn columnName="LOCCUR-
                                                          KEY" >
                    </htmlb:tableViewColumn>
                    <htmlb:tableViewColumn columnName="ORDER_
                                                          DATE" >
                    </htmlb:tableViewColumn>
                    <htmlb:tableViewColumn columnName="COUNTER"
>

                    </htmlb:tableViewColumn>
                    <htmlb:tableViewColumn columnName="AGENCY-
                                                          NUM" >
                    </htmlb:tableViewColumn>
                    <htmlb:tableViewColumn columnName="PASS-
                                                          NAME" >
                    </htmlb:tableViewColumn>
                    <htmlb:tableViewColumn columnName="PASS-
                                                          FORM" >
                    </htmlb:tableViewColumn>
                  </htmlb:tableViewColumns>
                </htmlb:tableView>
            </htmlb:gridLayoutCell>
            <htmlb:gridLayoutCell columnIndex       = "2"
                                  rowIndex          = "1"
                                  verticalAlignment = "BOT-
                                                       TOM" >
        </htmlb:gridLayoutCell>
      </htmlb:gridLayout>
  </htmlb:gridLayoutCell>
</htmlb:gridLayout>
```

Now, the internal table with the flight data must be declared in the page fragment *mybooking.htm* as a page attribute of type ZBOOKED_FAD and the page fragment included. You must create this table type in the Data

Dictionary with a reference to the structure SBOOK. That closes the portion of the presentation logic. Now you only have to fill the page attribute. The page attribute is controlled in the controller class Z_CL_C_FLIGHT_BOOK_US by executing the data selection in the model class Z_CL_M_FLIGHT_BOOK_US.

**The GET_MYFLIGHTS method** We first create the GET_MYFLIGHTS method in the model class—a process analogous to creating the GET_USERNAME method. The method is to return the booked flights to the SAP user in a returning parameter. First, create a method parameter named r_myflights, which refers to the type of the flight table, ZBOOKED_FAD. Finally, we must implement the actual data retrieval. You can take the coding from Listing 5.53 and then insert it into the method.

**Listing 5.53** The coding of the GET_MYFLIGHTS model class method

```
METHOD get_myflights.
   DATA: userid TYPE s_customer,
         myflights TYPE TABLE OF zbooked_fad.
*  Retrieving the user ID
   SELECT SINGLE id
       FROM    zflight_customer
       INTO    userid
       WHERE   username EQ sy-uname.
*  Retrieving the booked flights
   SELECT *
           FROM sbook
           INTO TABLE r_myflights
           WHERE customid = userid.
ENDMETHOD.
```

Now, the work on the model class is finished, so we'll return to the controller Z_CL_C_FLIGHT_BOOK_US. The implementation here is also analogous to the GET_USERNAME method. Create a member attribute, m_flights, of type ZBOOKED_FAD and insert the following command into the DO_INIT method after the method for determining the user name:

```
m_flights = model->get_myflights( ).
```

Then, we must modify the coding of the DO_REQUEST method. The method should appear as it does in Listing 5.54.

**Listing 5.54** The enhanced DO_REQUEST method of the Controller class

```
METHOD do_request.
* Data declaration
  DATA: l_view TYPE REF TO if_bsp_page.
* Instantiation
  l_view = create_view( view_name = 'mybookings.htm' ).
* Setting the attribute
  l_view->set_attribute( name = 'uname'
                               value = m_username ).
  l_view->set_attribute( name = 'itab_result'
                               value = m_flights  ).
* Calling the view
  call_view( l_view ).
ENDMETHOD.
```

Then, check the results in the Web browser (see Figure 5.109).

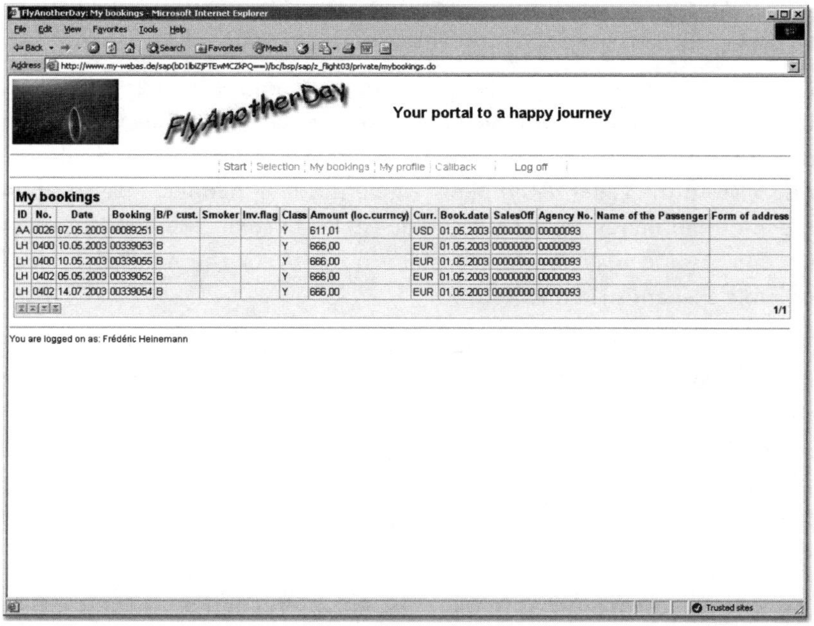

**Figure 5.109** The results list of booked flights

### 5.14.8 Additional Functions

You can enhance the scenario as you want. For example, you can set the My profile function to look like My bookings. You can use a form with the data for the recall to realize the page recall with a composite element, and you can enhance My bookings with additional selection criteria. In any case, most of the enhancement is analogous to previous functions; only the design of data retrieval differs.

You can then compare your own implementation of these missing functions with the complete application, Z_FLIGHT03US, which you can download from the SAP PRESS Web site.

## 5.15  Request Handler

So far, our programming has used the standard request handler as delivered to process BSP applications. The handler is named CL_HTTP_EXT_BSP and is listed in the ICF service path *default_host/sap/bc/bsp* in the list of handlers. The handler represents exactly the method called at an incoming request from the ICF controller.

Of course, you can also implement your own request handler based on the ICF. This handler can manage a wide variety of tasks, namely, it can display information, accept complete queries, process them, and return a response to the caller. A simple example is a PDF handler—based upon the information transferred in the request, it can create invoices or similar documents and make them available on the Web. The number of conceivable scenarios is unlimited.

The following section shows how you can implement your own request handler. You must implement the IF_HTTP_EXTENSION interface to get the request handler. The interface contains a series of attributes and a method named HANDLE_REQUEST (see Figure 5.110). The FLOW_RC attribute handles the flow control of any subsequent request handlers, and the LIFETIME_RC attribute regulates the lifetime of an instance of the request handler.

Proper implementation of the HANDLE_REQUEST method is sufficient to create your own request handler. By implementing the method, you set how an incoming request is processed and how a possible response can appear. A reference to the IF_HTTP_SERVER interface is available as a parameter of the method. The interface enables the handler to access the request and to write an answer in the response.

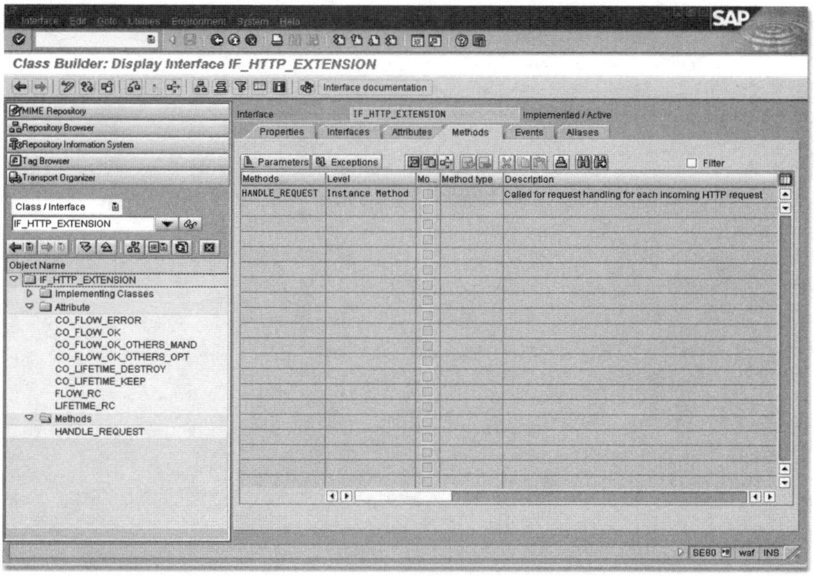

**Figure 5.110** The IF_HTTP_EXTENSION interface

To create the request handler, you must first create a specific class (in the Class Builder) to implement the IF_HTTP_EXTENSION interface. For this example, create a class named Z_CL_HTTP_MY_US, assign the IF_HTTP_EXTENSION interface (as shown in Figure 5.111), and then activate the class.

Next, open the method folder in the object list and mark the HANDLE_REQUEST method, which you then implement with forward navigation. Select "Yes" in the security query that appears (see Figure 5.112).

Now you can start implementing the source code. For this example, the request handler should format the request header data of the client, which it has received, as an HTML stream. Of course, more complicated functions are indeed conceivable here.

The GET_HEADER_FIELDS method handles reading of the header fields from the request. A valid HTML document is built successively from this name/value information and is stored in my_response. The string that has been generated in this manner is then transferred to the response object with the SET_CDATA method. The content type of the data stream is now set as "HTML" to inform the client (Web browser) of the type of response.

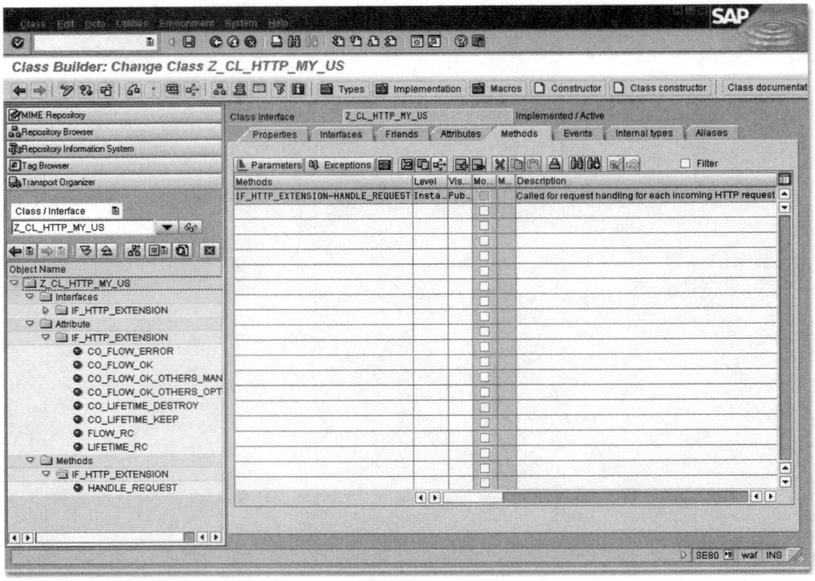

**Figure 5.111** Assigning the IF_HTTP_EXTENSION interface

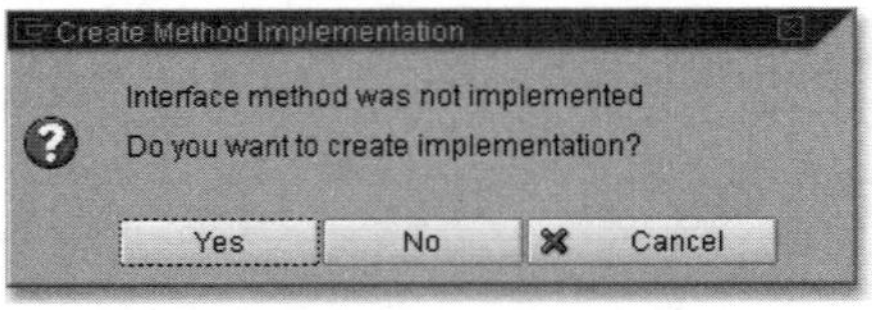

**Figure 5.112** Confirming the security query

Finally, setting the FLOW_RC attribute for flow control signals to the IFC controller that the request is processed successfully and the response is to be returned to the client. Calling additional request handlers is not permitted (CO_FLOW_OK). Listing 5.55 shows the complete coding of the method:

**Listing 5.55** The source code of the HANDLE_REQUEST method

```
METHOD if_http_extension~handle_request .
  DATA: my_response TYPE string,
        itab_header_fields TYPE tihttpnvp,
        wa_header_fields TYPE ihttpnvp.
* Reading the headers
  server->request->get_header_fields( CHANGING fields =
  itab_header_fields ).
* First part
```

```
CONCATENATE
  '<HTML>'
  '<BODY>'
  '<TABLE>'
INTO my_response.
* Second part
LOOP AT itab_header_fields INTO wa_header_fields.
  CONCATENATE
    my_response
    '<TR><TD>'
    wa_header_fields-name
    '</TD><TD>'
    wa_header_fields-value
    '</TD></TR>'
  INTO my_response.
ENDLOOP.
* Third part
CONCATENATE
  my_response
  '<H2>DEMO: Own Requesthandler</H2>'
  '</BODY>'
  '</HTML>'
INTO my_response.
* Response:setting the type
server->response->set_header_field(
  name  = 'Content-Type'
  value = 'text/html' ).
* Response: writing
server->response->set_cdata( data = my_response ).
* Flow control
if_http_extension~flow_rc = if_http_extension=>co_
flow_ok.
ENDMETHOD.
```

To test the event handler that you have created, generate a service entry in the ICF service tree (Transaction SICF: see Section 4.3). The service node `zmy_handler` was generated in the ICF path *default_host/sap* for this example. Enter the handler that you created in the request handler table and save your entries. Don't forget to activate the service that you created. If you now enter the URL of the service in the Web browser, the handler that you created is executed. Figure 5.113 shows the results.

DEMO: Own Requesthandler

| ~request_line | GET /sap(bD1lbiZjPTEwMCZkPQ==)/bc/zmy_handler_us HTTP/1.1 |
| ~request_method | GET |
| ~request_uri | /sap(bD1lbiZjPTEwMCZkPQ==)/bc/zmy_handler_us |
| ~path | /sap(bD1lbiZjPTEwMCZkPQ==)/bc/zmy_handler_us |
| ~path_translated | /sap/bc/zmy_handler_us |
| ~server_protocol | HTTP/1.1 |
| accept | image/gif, image/x-xbitmap, image/jpeg, image/pjpeg, application/vnd.ms-powerpoint, application/vnd.ms-excel, application/msword, application/x-shockwave-flash, */* |
| accept-encoding | gzip, deflate |
| user-agent | Mozilla/4.0 (compatible; MSIE 6.0; Windows NT 5.0; MyIE2; .NET CLR 1.0.3705) |
| host | www.my-webas.de |
| ~server_name | www.my-webas.de |
| connection | Keep-Alive |
| cookie | sap-usercontext=sap-language=en |
| ~remote_addr | 217.234.182.67 |
| ~script_name | /sap/bc/zmy_handler_us |
| ~path_info | |
| ~script_name_expanded | /sap/bc/zmy_handler_us |
| ~path_info_expanded | |
| ~path_translated_expanded | /sap/bc/zmy_handler_us |

**Figure 5.113** Calling the generated request handler

## 5.16 SAP Web Application Server as Client

As noted in Chapter 2, the SAP Web Application Server can fulfill the roles of both a server and a client. In this section, we'll show you how to use the Internet Communication Framework (ICF) so that the SAP Web AS functions as a client. As a simple example, we'll generate an HTTP client that displays a Web page of the server: *www.sap-was.com*.

The methods needed for implementation are in class CL_HTTP_CLIENT, which implements the IF_HTTP_CLIENT interface. The call can occur from an ABAP program or from a BSP application. We'll create a new BSP application named Z_CLIENT_DEMO and implement the client function in the onInitialization event handler of BSP page *default.htm*.

First, we perform the required data declaration. The HTTP client to be generated, LC_CLIENT, references the IF_HTTP_CLIENT interface.

```
DATA: lc_client   TYPE REF TO if_http_client,
      lv_host     TYPE string,
      lv_path     TYPE string,
      lv_url      TYPE string,
      lv_code     TYPE sy-subrc,
      lv_message  TYPE string.
```

A series of link information is now set, including the page to be displayed in the PATH parameter.

```
lv_url = 'http://www.sap-was.de'.
lv_path = '/client-test.htm'.
lv_host = 'www.sap-was.de'.
```

An HTTP client is to be created. We use the CREATE method, which requires the host as a parameter (as a minimum). The generated instance is stored in LC_CLIENT. As an option, you can also transfer the port (Service), the proxy settings (PROXY_HOST and PROXY_Service), the protocol (SCHEME, Value 1 = HTTP, Value 2 = HTTPS), and an SSL identity. Alternatively, you can use the CREATE_BY_URL and CREATE_BY_DES-TINATION methods.

```
CALL METHOD cl_http_client=>create
    EXPORTING
      host                = lv_host
*       Service           =
*       PROXY HOST        =
*       PROXY Service     =
*       SCHEME            = SCHEMETYPE_HTTP
*       SSL_ID            =
    IMPORTING
      client              = lc_client
*   EXCEPTIONS
*       ARGUMENT NOT FOUND = 1
*       PLUGIN NOT ACTIVE  = 2
*       INTERNAL ERROR     = 3
*       others             = 4.
```

All the methods introduced here react to errors with exceptions. You can also use the GET_LAST_ERROR method to query a return value and a corresponding error text.

```
IF sy-subrc <> 0.
  CALL METHOD lc_client->get_last_error
    IMPORTING
      code    = lv_code
      MESSAGE = lv_message.
ENDIF.
```

Once the HTTP client has been generated successfully, you can access all the data (request, response, header fields, and so on) with the `LC_CLI-ENT` object. You can now set additional header fields for the request to specify your request further. In the following example, the requested path must be set explicitly:

```
lc_client->request->set_header_field( name  = '~request_
uri' value = lv_path ).
```

Afterward, the actual request can be transmitted to the host:

```
CALL METHOD lc_client->send( ).
```

The host's response is received with:

```
CALL METHOD lc_client->receive( ).
```

The response is placed into a character-type page attribute, content, with the `GET_CDATA` method:

```
content = lc_client->response->get_cdata( ).
```

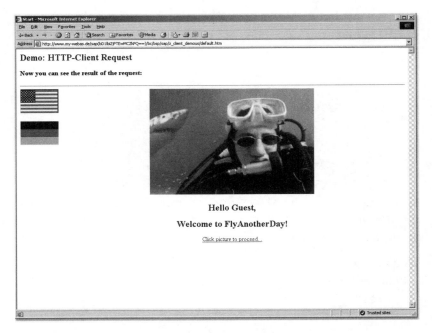

**Figure 5.114** The result of the HTTP client query in the Web browser

The contents of the page attribute are then output to the layout with the print directive. The HTTP connection is then closed:

```
CALL METHOD lc_client->close( ).
```

When you test the application, a request is transmitted to the server. The server's response is output in the layout and presented as it appears in Figure 5.114.

At first glance, the result of the method described is reminiscent of entering a URL in the Web browser. However, when you enter a URL in the browser, the browser displays the results of the request. If you look closely, you'll see that in this example, the URL is the same URL used in our example, Z_CLIENT_DEMO. The displayed page is the layout that was received by the transmitted request. Here, the server executes the request in its role as an HTTP client and displays the layout.

# Appendix

# A   Reference: Web Development on the SAP Web Application Server

In this appendix, you will find the most important classes and interfaces for developing BSP applications, an overview of the BSP elements, the supported MIME types, the BSP directives, and notes on logging onto the Internet Communication Manager (ICM). The information in this appendix is based primarily on the online documentation. When it became apparent at the time of printing that the online documentation was not complete, new methods, attributes, and constants were added.

## A.1   The HTTP Interface of the ICF

The following sections provide a more detailed description of the main interfaces in the ICF (see Figure A.1). The focus here is on describing the interfaces required for processing HTTP requests/responses.

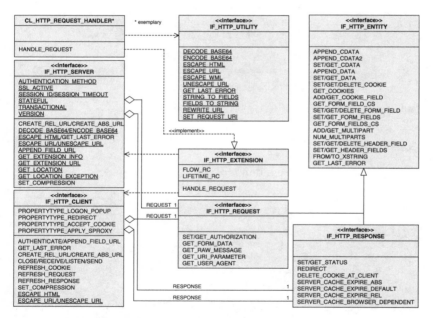

**Figure A.1**  The ICF class model (UML notation)

### A.1.1   The IF_HTTP_EXTENSION Interface

The IF_HTTP_EXTENSION interface should be implemented by all request handlers processing incoming requests. The only method of this interface is HANDLE_REQUEST. Implementing this method ensures clearly defined interaction between the ICF and HTTP request handlers, regardless of the task of the corresponding HTTP request handler.

This method is called by the ICF controller when there is an incoming request. A reference is transferred to the IF_HTTP_SERVER interface as an argument, which enables the HTTP request handler to work with the request and response data. After processing the request, the HTTP request handler returns control back to the ICF controller. Here, two attributes of the HTTP request handler manage the control flow[1] for possible subsequent request handlers; they also control the life cycle of the request handler's instance.

## Attributes

The following attributes are available:

| Name | Meaning |
|------|---------|
| FLOW_RC | This attribute is used to control any subsequent HTTP request handler and it is also used to track error information. This attribute can accept the CO_FLOW_* constants. |
| LIFETIME_RC | This attribute is used to control the lifetime of the HTTP request handler instance. This attribute can accept the CO_LIFETIME_* constants. |

**Table A.1** Attributes of the IF_HTTP_EXTENSION interface

## Constants

The following constants are defined:

| Name | Meaning |
|------|---------|
| CO_FLOW_OK | This constant signals to the HTTP request handler that it is processing the request successfully. No further registered HTTP request handlers matching the request URL may be called. The ICF controller must return the response to the client immediately. (This is the default). |
| CO_FLOW_ERROR | This constant signals to the HTTP request handler that it has processed the request and an error has occurred. No further registered HTTP request handlers matching the request URL may be called. The ICF controller must return the response to the client immediately. This return code signals serious errors that automatically close the session if working in stateful mode. |

**Table A.2** Constants of the IF_HTTP_EXTENSION interface

---

1   There can be more than one request handler available for a service (Transaction SICF).

| Name | Meaning |
|------|---------|
| CO_FLOW_OK_ OTHERS_ OPT | This constant signals to the HTTP request handler that it has processed the request successfully. It also permits other HTTP request handlers matching the request URL to be called before the response is returned to the client. |
| CO_FLOW_OK_ OTHERS_ MAND | This constant signals to the HTTP request handler that it is processing the request successfully. However, at least one further HTTP request handler must have successfully processed the request before the response is returned to the client. A typical example of how this return code is used is as an HTTP request handler for authentication. |
| CO_LIFETIME_ KEEP | This instance of the HTTP request handler should be retained for subsequent requests in the same session. Data in instance attributes of the implementation class are therefore retained across multiple requests and can be used for local caching and optimization or status handling (This is the default setting for all HTTP request handlers in stateful mode). |
| CO_LIFETIME_ DESTROY | This instance of the HTTP request handler is destroyed after processing the request. A new instance of this HTTP request handler is generated in case stateful mode is being used. For this reason, local instance data is lost. |

**Table A.2**  Constants of the IF_HTTP_EXTENSION interface (Cont.)

## Method

The following method is available:

| Name | Meaning |
|------|---------|
| HANDLE_REQUEST | This method must be implemented by all HTTP request handlers in the ICF. It contains the current code for request processing. It is called for each incoming request if the HTTP request handler is registered for the relevant request URL (or a prefix). |

**Table A.3**  The method of the IF_HTTP_EXTENSION interface

## A.1.2   The IF_HTTP_SERVER Interface

The IF_HTTP_SERVER interface is implemented by the CL_HTTP_SERVER class. For each incoming request, this class is used to create a server control block (instance). The object created in this way provides access to the request and response data structures using interface references.

## Attributes

The following attributes are defined:

| Name | Meaning |
|---|---|
| CO_COMPRESSION_IN_ALL_CASES | Compression for all documents |
| VERSION | Version of the ICF |
| REQUEST | Interface reference to the request object |
| RESPONSE | Interface reference to the response object |
| SESSION_ID | ID of the HTTP session (automatically generated) |
| EXTERNAL_SESSION_ID | External session-ID |
| SESSION_TIMEOUT | Session timeout |
| VERSION | Version of the ICF implementation |
| AUTHENTICATION_METHOD | Specifies the logon procedure being used. The attribute can adopt the AUTHMETHOD_* values described in the *Constants* section. |
| STATEFUL | Defines whether the SAP session is retained after a request (CO_ENABLED, stateful mode) or is closed (CO_DISABLED, stateless mode). The default is stateless. |
| TRANSACTIONAL | Specifies that an application is transactional. Therefore, depending on the return code of the last HTTP request handler called, either a commit (return codes CO_FLOW_OK and CO_FLOW_OK_OTHERS_OPT) or a rollback (return codes CO_FLOW_ERROR and CO_FLOW_OK_OTHERS_MAND) is executed. If the flag is not set, the application needs to place the commit in the correct place itself; otherwise the ICF carries out an implicit rollback. TRANSACTIONAL can adopt the CO_DISABLED (default) and CO_ENABLED values. |
| SSL_ACTIVE | Checks whether HTTPS is activated. |

**Table A.4** Attributes of the IF_HTTP_SERVER interface

## Constants

The following constants are defined:

| Name | Meaning |
|---|---|
| CO_DISABLED | Not active (default) |

**Table A.5** Constants of the IF_HTTP_SERVER interface

| Name | Meaning |
|---|---|
| CO_ENABLED | Active |
| CO_COMPRESS_BASED_ON_MIME_TYPE | Compression depending on MIME type |
| AUTHMETHOD_NONE | No logon |
| AUTHMETHOD_BASIC | HTTP basic authentication |
| AUTHMETHOD_SSO | Authentication via Mysapsso2 cookie |
| AUTHMETHOD_SAP | SAP logon procedure |
| AUTHMETHOD_Service | Service logon procedure |
| AUTHMETHOD_FIELD | Logon via form fields |
| AUTHMETHOD_CERTIFICATE | Logon via X.509 certificate |

**Table A.5** Constants of the IF_HTTP_SERVER interface (Cont.)

## Methods

The methods ESCAPE_URL, UNESCAPE_URL, ESCAPE_HTML, DECODE_BASE64, ENCODE_BASE64, and GET_LAST_ERROR are auxiliary methods and are both part of the IF_HTTP_SERVER interface and the IF_HTTP_UTILITY interface.

We recommend using the methods from the IF_HTTP_UTILITY interface.

The following methods are defined:

| Name | Meaning |
|---|---|
| CREATE_ABS_URL | Generates the string representation of an absolute URL, either based on the supplied arguments (such as protocol, server, port, path, query string) or the values indirectly defined by the current request (e.g., the server and port for a current request are always known). The resultant URL can be used in HTML pages to reference the current session and thus link various dialog steps in the system with the same session. |
| CREATE_REL_URL | Operates as does CREATE_ABS_URL; however, it generates a relative URL (i.e., no protocol, server, or port can be specified). |

**Table A.6** Methods of the IF_HTTP_SERVER interface

| Name | Meaning |
|------|---------|
| ESCAPE_URL | Generates a string conforming to the URL from a string. In this case, all URL control marks are replaced with "%xx". "xx" stands for the hexadecimal value of the character. |
| UNESCAPE_URL | This is the counterpart to ESCAPE_URL. A URL-compliant string is converted to a string without a hexadecimal view. |
| GET_EXTENSION_URL | Returns the URLs for which the given HTTP-request handler is stored in the associated services. |
| GET_EXTENSION_INFO | Returns the protocol, the hostname, the port, and the URL for an HTTP extension. |
| ESCAPE_HTML | Generates a string conforming to the HTML from a string. In this process, all letters that can be interpreted as an HTML control sequence, e.g., the start and end tags ($<$ becomes ;lt and $>$ becomes ;gt) are converted. |
| DECODE_BASE64 | A Base64-coded[2] string is converted back to byte format. |
| ENCODE_BASE64 | A string is converted into the Base64 format. |
| GET_LAST_ERROR | Returns the last known error code. |
| GET_LOCATION | Delivers the host and port for the SAP Web AS in the customer domain. |
| GET_LOCATION_EXCEPTION | Delivers the host and port from an exception table. |
| SET_COMPRESSION | Activation/deactivation of compression. |
| SET_SESSION_STATEFUL | Activation/deactivation of stateful sessions. |
| SET_SESSION_STATEFUL_VIA_URL | Activation/deactivation of stateful sessions via URL rewriting. |

**Table A.6** Methods of the IF_HTTP_SERVER interface (Cont.)

---

2 Base64-coding is a process for coding any binary data into printable characters. This way binary data can also be transferred with character-based protocols. In Base64-coding, each byte is converted into a string of printable characters (the set contains 64 characters).

## A.1.3    The IF_HTTP_CLIENT Interface

The `IF_HTTP_CLIENT` interface is implemented by the class `CL_HTTP_CLIENT`. For each outgoing request, this class is used to create a client control block. The object created provides access to the request and response data structures using interface references.

### Attributes

The `PROPERTYTYPE_*` attributes can adopt the values `CO_DISABLED`, `CO_EVENT`, `CO_PROMPT`, and `CO_ENABLED`.

The following attributes are defined:

| Name | Meaning |
|---|---|
| REQUEST | Interface reference to the request object |
| RESPONSE | Interface reference to the response object |
| PROPERTYTYPE_LOGON_POPUP | Display of the logon screen (default: CO_ENABLED) |
| PROPERTYTYPE_REDIRECT | Redirect of documents (default: CO_ENABLED) |
| PROPERTYTYPE_ACCEPT_COOKIE | Transfer of the cookie fields from response (default: CO_DISABLED) |
| PROPERTYTYPE_APPLY_SPROXY | Evaluation of the system proxy configuration |

**Table A.7**  Attributes of the IF_HTTP_CLIENT interface

### Constants

The following constants are defined:

| Name | Meaning |
|---|---|
| VERSION | Version of the HTTP client (user agent) |
| CO_DISABLED | Inactive |
| CO_EVENT | Cookie handling: An event handler programmed specifically for the purpose should be used to control it. The event EVENTKIND_HANDLE_COOKIE is triggered each time a cookie is set. The application must then be programmed so that the cookies are accepted or declined as preferred. |

**Table A.8**  Constants of the IF_HTTP_CLIENT interface

| Name | Meaning |
|------|---------|
| CO_PROMPT | Cookie handling: The Web browser prompt pop-up should appear, which asks whether cookies are to be accepted. |
| CO_ENABLED | Active |
| CO_TIMEOUT_DEFAULT | Time-out default value (instance timeout) |
| CO_TIMEOUT_INFINITE | No timeout |
| CO_COMPRESS_BASED_ON_MIME_TYPE | Compression only for defined MIME types |
| CO_COMPRESS_IN_ALL_CASES | Compression of all documents |
| CO_COMPRESS_NONE | No compression |

**Table A.8** Constants of the IF_HTTP_CLIENT interface (Cont.)

## Methods

The methods ESCAPE_URL, UNESCAPE_URL, ESCAPE_HTML, DECODE_BASE64, ENCODE_BASE64, and GET_LAST_ERROR are auxiliary methods and are both part of the interface IF_HTTP_CLIENT and the interface IF_HTTP_UTILITY. We recommend using the methods from the interface IF_HTTP_UTILITY.

The following methods are defined:

| Name | Meaning |
|------|---------|
| ESCAPE_HTML | Generates a string conforming to the HTML from a string. In this process, all letters that can be interpreted as an HTML control sequence, e.g., the start and end tags (< becomes ;lt and > becomes ;gt) are converted. |
| ESCAPE_URL | Generates a string conforming to the URL from a string. In this case, all URL control marks are replaced with "%xx". "xx" stands for the hexadecimal value of the character. |
| UNESCAPE_URL | This is the counterpart to ESCAPE_URL. A URL-compliant string is converted to a string without a hexadecimal view. |
| AUTHENTICATE | Carries out the authentication on the HTTP server. If this is an SAP system, it creates an SAP logon screen, and by running AUTHENTICATE, the user, password, client, and language are entered. The authentication is typically carried out as specified by the relevant HTTP server. |

**Table A.9** Methods of the IF_HTTP_CLIENT interface

| Name | Meaning |
|------|---------|
| APPEND_FIELD_URL | Appends the given name/value pair to the supplied URL as a query string. Name and value are automatically URL-escaped. |
| CREATE_ABS_URL | Absolute URL, either based on the supplied arguments (such as protocol, server, port, path, query string) or the values indirectly defined by the current request (e.g., the server and port for a current request are always known). The resultant URL can be used in HTML pages to reference the current session and thus link various dialog steps in the system with the same session. |
| CREATE_REL_URL | Operates as does CREATE_ABS_URL; however, it generates a relative URL (i.e., no protocol, server, or port can be specified). |
| CLOSE | Closes the HTTP connection. This method is called if the HTTP connection, i.e., the client control block, is no longer required. |
| RECEIVE | Fills the response into the RESPONSE structure. This method must be called for each HTTP request so that the data obtained can be processed further. |
| GET_LAST_ERROR | Returns the last known error code. |
| LISTEN | The method RECEIVE can only be called if multiple requests have been sent in parallel; and if a response is received, the request to which it relates is determined. |
| SEND | If the REQUEST attribute is filled with the request data, the HTTP request can be sent to the HTTP server by calling the method SEND. The method converts the data into an HTTP data flow and sends it to the server. The method is supplied to the timeout for the time to wait for the response in seconds. The constants CO_TIMEOUT_DEFAULT and CO_TIMEOUT_INFINITE can also be used here. |
| REFRESH_COOKIE | Resets the cookie object (the object still exists, but no longer has any content). |
| REFRESH_REQUEST | Resets the request object. |
| REFRESH_RESPONSE | Resets the response object. |
| SET_COMPRESSION | Activation/deactivation of the compression using the CO_COMPRESS_* constants. |

**Table A.9** Methods of the IF_HTTP_CLIENT interface (Cont.)

## A.1.4 The IF_HTTP_ENTITY Interface

The IF_HTTP_ENTITY interface provides a series of methods for editing request/response data. This interface forms the basis for the interfaces

IF_HTTP_REQUEST and IF_HTTP_RESPONSE and is implemented by the class CL_HTTP_ENTITY.

### Attributes

This interface does not contain any attributes.

### Constants

The available constants of the interface IF_HTTP_ENTITY determine the way in which text is handled or output.

Text should typically be output in the same way as it was specified. In this case, the constant CO_ENCODING_RAW is available. If text is to be used in a URL, however, it must have a specific coding (URL-coded). In this instance, the constant CO_ENCODING_URL is used. If a text is to appear in an HTML page as it is specified, characters with special characters in HTML (such as "<") must be replaced by their HTML-coded counterpart ("&lt") (CO_ENCODING_HTML). For WML coding, the constant CO_ENCODING_WML is available.

These coding types can also be used for output in BSP pages (e.g., <%html= mystring %>). The specifications are html, url, and raw. The WML coding is run if html is specified as the coding, but the page is a MIME type of WML document. The constants' parameters of the method APPEND_CDATA2 are also for defining the text coding.

The following constants are defined:

| Name | Meaning |
| --- | --- |
| CO_ENCODING_RAW | Encoding constant (output format) |
| CO_ENCODING_URL | Encoding constant (conforming to the URL) |
| CO_ENCODING_HTML | Encoding constant (conforming to HTML) |
| CO_ENCODING_WML | Encoding constant (conforming to WML) |

**Table A.10** Constants of the IF_HTTP_ENTITY interface

### Methods for processing HTTP header fields

HTTP Header  Using the methods available here, the HTTP request handler has access and manipulation options relating to the HTTP header. The HTTP header contains all the fields (in the form of name/value pairs) defined in the HTTP-1.1 specification.

A modification of the request header may be required, for example, if acting as an HTTP client, or additional information is added to a request and needs to be written back.

The fields in the HTTP header can be addressed using their case-insensitive designations (e.g., "content-type" for the content type attribute of the HTTP header).

In addition to these fields, there are some fields that are not pure field attributes of the HTTP header, but fields that can be derived from the HTTP request line. These fields are known as *pseudo header fields*. A typical example is the query string part of a URL or the method of the request (e.g., GET or POST). In order to distinguish pseudo header fields from true header fields, the pseudo header fields are distinguished with a ~ (tilde) character (e.g., ~ query_string).

**Pseudo Header**

You will find an overview of the supported HTTP header fields in the IF_ HTTP_HEADER_FIELDS interface in Section A.1.9. The pseudo header fields are described in the IF_HTTP_HEADER_FIELDS_SAP interface in Section A.1.10.

The following methods are available for processing header fields:

| Name | Meaning |
| --- | --- |
| GET_HEADER_FIELD | Returns the value of the specified (pseudo) HTTP header field (case-insensitive). |
| GET_HEADER_FIELDS | Returns a table of all (pseudo) HTTP header fields as name/value pairs. |
| DELETE_HEADER_FIELD | Removes the specified header field from the list of header fields. |
| SET_HEADER_FIELD | Sets the specified (pseudo) header field (case-insensitive) to the given value. |
| SET_HEADER_FIELDS | Sets all (pseudo) HTTP header fields of the request object to the values stored in the name/value table. |

**Table A.11** The methods for processing HTTP header fields in the IF_HTTP_ENTITY interface

### Methods for processing HTML form fields

Using these methods, the HTTP request handler has access to transferred form fields. The HTTP request handler is encapsulated in the same way as these fields occur in a request. This means that an HTML page can transfer the form fields both in the URL and query string (HTTP method GET) or in the HTTP body (HTTP method POST; multipart also possible).

The following methods are defined:

| Name | Meaning |
| --- | --- |
| GET_FORM_FIELD | Returns the value of the specified HTML form field (case-insensitive). |
| GET_FORM_FIELDS | Returns a table of all name/value pairs from the HTML form fields (case-insensitive). |
| GET_FORM_FIELD_CS | Returns the value of the specified HTML form field (case-sensitive). |
| GET_FORM_FIELDS_CS | Returns a table of all name/value pairs from the HTML form fields (case-sensitive). |
| DELETE_FORM_FIELD | Removes the specified form field. |
| SET_FORM_FIELD | Sets the specified HTML form field (case-insensitive) to the given value. |
| SET_FORM_FIELDS | Sets all HTML form fields of the request object to the specified values. |

**Table A.12** The methods for processing HTML form fields in the IF_HTTP_ENTITY interface

### Methods for Processing Cookies

There are methods available that the HTTP request handler can use to access cookies sent using the HTTP request. These methods can be used to define new cookies (e.g., in the HTTP client role), or to change the cookies already defined (e.g., writing back data of the request in the HTTP server role).

The following methods are defined:

| Name | Meaning |
| --- | --- |
| ADD_COOKIE_FIELD | Sets the specified subfield of the given cookie. |
| GET_COOKIE_FIELD | Returns the specified subfield of the given cookie. |
| GET_COOKIE | Returns the value of the specified cookie (case-insensitive). |
| GET_COOKIES | Returns a list of all cookies. |

**Table A.13** The methods for processing cookies in the IF_HTTP_ENTITY interface

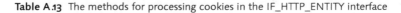

| Name | Meaning |
|---|---|
| DELETE_COOKIE | Deletes the specified cookie from the list of all cookies. |
| SET_COOKIE | Sets the value of the specified cookie (case-insensitive). |

**Table A.13** The methods for processing cookies in the IF_HTTP_ENTITY interface (Cont.)

The SET_COOKIE method can be used to store cookies. The possible import parameters are defined in the following table:

| Name | Meaning |
|---|---|
| NAME | Name of the cookie |
| VALUE | Value of the cookie |
| PATH | Specifies the path attributes for a given cookie. If no value has been specified, the path of the page that generated the cookie is used. |
| DOMAIN | Specifies the domain attributes for a given cookie. If no value has been specified, the hostname of the server that generated the cookie response is used. |
| EXPIRES | Specifies the timestamp (date and time) at which the life cycle of the cookie ends. Once the life cycle of the cookie has expired, it is no longer stored and no longer returned. <br><br>The timestamp has the following format: <br><br>`Wdy, DD-Mon-YY HH:MM:SS GMT` <br><br>Example: <br><br>`Tue, 12 Nov 2002 12:45:26 GMT` <br><br>If no date has been set, the cookie is stored as a session cookie. Otherwise, it is stored on the hard disk (persistent). |
| SECURE | Determines whether the cookie can be transferred only via secure (HTTPS, value = 1) or via non-secure connections (HTTP, value = 0). |

**Table A.14** Parameters of the SET_COOKIE method

## Methods for Processing HTTP Body Data

The following methods are defined:

| Name | Meaning |
|---|---|
| APPEND_CDATA | Appends the given character string (RAW format) to the body of the HTTP unit. |

**Table A.15** The methods for processing HTTP body data in the IF_HTTP_ENTITY interface

| Name | Meaning |
|------|---------|
| APPEND_CDATA2 | Appends the given character string to the body of the HTTP unit. Unlike APPEND_CDATA, the coding of the string (CO_ENCODING_* constants) can be included in this case. |
| APPEND_DATA | Appends the given binary string to the body of the HTTP unit. |
| GET_CDATA | Returns the data of the body of the HTTP unit as a character string. This is useful if the content type of the document is text/html or text/xml and access is required to the unprocessed data, for example. |
| GET_DATA | Returns the data of the body of the HTTP unit as a binary string. |
| SET_CDATA | Allocates the content of the HTTP unit body to the given character string. |
| SET_DATA | Allocates the content of the HTTP unit body with the given binary string. |
| FROM_XSTRING | Instantiates the HTTP unit using the given XSTRING. |
| TO_XSTRING | Reverse function of FROM_XSTRING: converts an HTTP unit into an XSTRING. |
| GET_LAST_ERROR | Returns the last known error code. |

**Table A.15** The methods for processing HTTP body data in the IF_HTTP_ENTITY interface (Cont.)

## Methods for Processing HTTP Multipart Data

HTTP requests can keep their data not only in a single body component, but in different segments, known as *multiparts (data with multiple parts)*. An example of multiparts is the file upload from an HTML document. The multiparts are formed by a separate HTTP (sub-) header and (sub-) body. The table below contains an overview of the available methods that permit navigation in the multipart segments:

| Name | Meaning |
|------|---------|
| ADD_MULTIPART | Adds a multipart segment to the body of the HTTP unit. |
| GET_MULTIPART | Returns the multipart segment specified by an index. |
| NUM_MULTIPARTS | Returns the number of multipart segments of the request object. |

**Table A.16** The methods for processing HTTP multipart data in the IF_HTTP_ENTITY interface

## A.1.5 The IF_HTTP_REQUEST Interface

The IF_HTTP_REQUEST interface can be accessed by an HTTP request handler via the attribute REQUEST. It provides methods in order to be able to process the data of a request. The methods are implemented by the CL_HTTP_REQUEST class. The interface expands the IF_HTTP_ENTITY interface.

**Attributes**

No attributes are defined.

**Constants**

No constants are defined.

**Methods**

The following methods are defined:

| Name | Meaning |
| --- | --- |
| GET_AUTHORIZATION | Delivers information from the authorization header field. |
| SET_AUTHORIZATION | Sets the authorization header field of this request. |
| GET_FORM_DATA | Delivers form data in a complex data structure. |
| GET_RAW_MESSAGE | Delivers the full HTTP message. |
| GET_URI_PARAMETER | Delivers the value of the requested URI parameter. |
| GET_USER_AGENT | Delivers user agent information from the request. |

**Table A.17** Methods of the IF_HTTP_REQUEST interface

## A.1.6 The IF_HTTP_RESPONSE Interface

The IF_HTTP_RESPONSE interface can be accessed by an HTTP request handler via the attribute RESPONSE. It provides methods in order to be able to access the data of a response. The methods are implemented by the CL_HTTP_RESPONSE class. This interface expands the IF_HTTP_ENTITY interface.

**Attributes**

No attributes are defined.

## Constants

No constants are defined.

## Methods

The following methods are defined:

| Name | Meaning |
|------|---------|
| GET_RAW_MESSAGE | Delivers the full HTTP message. |
| GET_STATUS | Gets the current HTTP status code set. |
| SET_STATUS | Sets the given HTTP status code. |
| DELETE_COOKIE_AT_CLIENT | Deletes the given cookie on the client side. |
| REDIRECT | Executes a redirect to the given URL. |
| SERVER_CACHE_EXPIRE_ABS | Sets the expiry date for the ICM server cache (ISC). An absolute time is specified, after which the page held in the cache is invalid. |
| SERVER_CACHE_EXPIRE_DEFAULT | Activates the ISC using the default expiry setting. |
| SERVER_CACHE_EXPIRE_REL | Sets the expiry date for the ISC relatively in seconds. |
| SERVER_CACHE_BROWSER_DEPENDENT | Sets the indicator for browser-specific HTML in the ISC. The request is only met from the cache if the request comes from the correct browser type. |

Table A.18  Methods of the IF_HTTP_RESPONSE interface

### A.1.7  The IF_HTTP_UTILITY Interface

The IF_HTTP_UTILITY interface provides methods for general HTTP processing. The implementation is carried out via the CL_HTTP_UTILITY class.

## Attributes

No attributes are defined.

## Constants

No constants are defined.

## Methods

The following methods are defined:

| Name | Meaning |
|------|---------|
| DECODE_BASE64 | A Base64-encoded[3] string is reconverted into byte format. |
| ENCODE_BASE64 | A string is converted into the BASE 64 format. |
| ESCAPE_HTML | Generates a string conforming to the HTML from a string. In this process all letters that can be interpreted as an HTML control sequence, e.g. the start and end tags (< becomes ;lt and > becomes ;gt) are converted. |
| ESCAPE_URL | Generates a string conforming to the URL from a string. In this case, all URL control marks are replaced with "%xx". "xx" stands for the hexadecimal value of the character. |
| ESCAPE_WML | Generates a string conforming to the WML from a string. |
| UNESCAPE_URL | This is the counterpart to ESCAPE_URL. A string conforming to the URL becomes a regular string, i.e. without hexadecimal representation. |
| GET_LAST_ERROR | Returns the last known error code. |
| STRING_TO_FIELDS | Decodes a query string into a list of fields.. |
| FIELDS_TO_STRING | Encodes a list of fields into a query string. |
| REWRITE_URL | Formats a URL with URI parameters. |
| SET_REQUEST_URI | Sets the request URI.. |

**Table A.19** The Methods of the IF_HTTP_UTILITY Interface

## A.1.8 The IF_HTTP_STATUS Interface

The IF_HTTP_STATUS interface contains all HTTP server response codes in the form of attributes.

---

3 Base64-coding is a process for coding any binary data into printable characters. This way binary data can also be transferred with character-based protocols. In Base64-coding, each byte is converted into a string of printable characters (the set contains 64 characters).

## Attributes

The following attributes are defined:

| Name | Meaning |
|------|---------|
| REASON_100 | Continue |
| REASON_101 | Switching Protocols |
| REASON_200 | OK |
| REASON_201 | Created |
| REASON_202 | Accepted |
| REASON_203 | Non-Authoritative Information |
| REASON_204 | No Content |
| REASON_205 | Reset Content |
| REASON_206 | Partial Content |
| REASON_300 | Multiple Choices |
| REASON_301 | Moved Permanently |
| REASON_302 | Found |
| REASON_303 | See Other |
| REASON_304 | Not Modified |
| REASON_305 | Use Proxy |
| REASON_307 | Temporary Redirect |
| REASON_400 | Bad Request |
| REASON_401 | Unauthorized |
| REASON_402 | Payment Required |
| REASON_403 | Forbidden |
| REASON_404 | Not Found |
| REASON_405 | Method Not Allowed |
| REASON_406 | Not Acceptable |
| REASON_407 | Proxy Authentication Required |
| REASON_408 | Request Timeout |

**Table A.20** Attributes of the IF_HTTP_STATUS interface

| Name | Meaning |
| --- | --- |
| REASON_409 | Conflict |
| REASON_410 | Gone |
| REASON_411 | Length Required |
| REASON_412 | Precondition Failed |
| REASON_413 | Request Entity Too Large |
| REASON_414 | Request-URI Too Long |
| REASON_415 | Unsupported Media Type |
| REASON_416 | Requested Range Not Satisfiable |
| REASON_417 | Expectation Failed |
| REASON_500 | Internal Server Error |
| REASON_501 | Not Implemented |
| REASON_502 | Bad Gateway |
| REASON_503 | Service Unavailable |
| REASON_504 | Gateway Timeout |
| REASON_505 | HTTP Version Not Supported |

**Table A.20** Attributes of the IF_HTTP_STATUS interface (Cont.)

## Constants

No constants are defined.

## Methods

No methods are defined.

### A.1.9 The IF_HTTP_HEADER_FIELDS Interface

The IF_HTTP_HEADER_FIELDS interface contains all supported HTTP header fields in the form of attributes.

## Attributes

The following attributes are defined:

| Name | Meaning |
| --- | --- |
| ACCEPT | Media types accepted by the client (e.g., text/*) |
| ACCEPT_CHARSET | Character set preferred by the client (e.g., ISO-8859-7) |
| ACCEPT_ENCODING | Coding mechanisms accepted by the client (e.g., gzip) |
| ACCEPT_LANGUAGE | The language preferred by the client (e.g., en) |
| ACCEPT_RANGES | Specifies the acceptance of range requests for a URL (e.g., bytes or none) |
| AGE | Age of the document in seconds |
| ALLOW | List of methods permitted for a URL (e.g., GET or head) |
| AUTHORIZATION | Authorization schema (e.g., BASIC) |
| CACHE_CONTROL | Specification of cache request directives (e.g., no-cache) |
| CONNECTION | Requested operation for connection (e.g., close) |
| CONTENT_ENCODING | Coding schema for the body (e.g., gzip) |
| CONTENT_ LANGUAGE | Language |
| CONTENT_LENGTH | Length of the data in bytes |
| CONTENT_LOCATION | URL (absolute or relative) of an entity if a document has multiple entities accessible via different positions |
| CONTENT_MD5 | Provides an MD5 digest of an entity (identity check) |
| CONTENT_RANGE | Insert position for partial bodies |
| CONTENT_TYPE | Media and subtype of a body (e.g., text/html) |
| DATE | Date (e.g., according to RFC 1123) |
| ETAG | Entity tag (identifier) for a server resource |
| EXPECT | Expectations of the client |
| EXPIRES | Change or valid date |
| FROM | E-mail address of the client user |
| HOST | Host name and port number of the host |
| IF_MATCH | Entity request for matching entity tags |

**Table A.21** Attributes of the IF_HTTP_HEADER_FIELDS interface

| Name | Meaning |
|------|---------|
| IF_MODIFIED_SINCE | Date condition |
| IF_NONE_MATCH | Entity request for non-matching entity tags |
| IF_RANGE | Entity request for missing part of an entity if it has been changed |
| IF_UNMODIFIED_ SINCE | Date condition |
| LAST_MODIFIED | Last change of a URL |
| LOCATION | New position of a document |
| MAX_FORWARDS | Maximum number of proxies or gateways |
| PRAGMA | Specifies directives for proxy and gateway systems |
| PROXY_ AUTHENTICATE | Authentication scheme |
| PROXY_ AUTHORIZATION | Identification of clients with proxies |
| RANGE | Partial areas requested by the document |
| REFERER | Source of a link |
| RETRY_AFTER | Specifies a time/date at which a server can process requests |
| SERVER | Name and version of the server |
| TE | Accepted transfer codings |
| TRAILER | List with transfer coded headers |
| TRANSFER_ ENCODING | Transfer coding (e.g., chunked) |
| UPGRADE | Additional supported protocols of the client |
| USER_AGENT | Identification data of the client program (e.g., Mozilla 3.0b) |
| VARY | Source of the entity |
| VIA | List of proxy servers (trace) |
| WARNING | Additional information on the status code |
| WWW_ AUTHENTICATE | Authentication schema and authentication area |

**Table A.21** Attributes of the IF_HTTP_HEADER_FIELDS interface (Cont.)

## Constants

No constants are defined.

## Methods

No methods are defined.

### A.1.10 The IF_HTTP_HEADER_FIELDS_SAP Interface

The IF_HTTP_HEADER_FIELDS_SAP interface contains all of SAP's additional HTTP header fields in the form of attributes. These fields can only be used in the HTTP request object and can be called there using the method IF_HTTP_REQUEST~GET_HEADER_FIELD. The fields contain server-specific environment information derived directly or indirectly from the HTTP request, but are not covered there using the standard HTTP header fields (pseudo headers). The header fields are case-insensitive and start with the reserved character "~" (tilde) to distinguish them from the standard header fields.

## Attributes

The following attributes are defined:

| Name/Pseudo Header | Meaning |
| --- | --- |
| CONTENT_DATA<br>~content_data | The body of the multipart segment is returned here. |
| CONTENT_DISPOSI-<br>TION<br>~content_disposi-<br>tion | This field contains the content disposition of a multipart segment (name, type, file name).<br>The value should not be changed. A request is possible via the method GET_HEADER_FIELD of the interface IF_HTTP_ENTITY. |
| CONTENT_FILENAME<br>~content_filename | The name of the file is returned during file upload from HTML forms, or in the file selection dialog box (multipart entities).<br>The value should not be changed. A request is possible via the method GET_HEADER_FIELD of the interface IF_HTTP_ENTITY. |

**Table A.22** Attributes of the IF_HTTP_HEADER_FIELDS_SAP interface

| Name/Pseudo Header | Meaning |
|---|---|
| CONTENT_NAME<br>~content_name | This field contains the name of the input field from HTML forms, whose value can be determined via ~content_ data of the same entity (multipart entities).<br><br>The value should not be changed. A request is possible via the method GET_HEADER_FIELD of the interface IF_ HTTP_ENTITY. |
| PATH<br>~path | The URL-coded path name from the request URL (without the query string) is returned.<br><br>▶ From the request URL /sap(bdK1qZ==)/bc/bsp/ sap/xyz/default.htm?name=hans&loc=lon- don, e.g., sap/bc/bsp/sap/xyz/default.htm is returned. |
| PATH_INFO<br>~path_info | This field contains the URL-coded part of the URL (suffix) given after the part of the URL (prefix) executed by the request handler. If an alias is defined and is a (sub-)compo- nent of this prefix, the suffix will be returned after the alias.<br><br>▶ If the request handler is registered under the URL /sap/bc/bsp, the value /sap/xyz/default.htm is returned for the request URL /sap/bc/bsp/sap/xyz/ default.htm.<br><br>▶ If an alias is also created, e.g. myalias, pointing to /sap/bc/bsp/sap and access is made in the request via this alias, in other words /myalias/xyz/ default.htm, /xyz/default.htm is returned. |
| PATH_INFO_<br>EXPANDED<br>~path_info_<br>expanded | This field contains the URL-coded part of the URL (suffix) given after the part of the URL (prefix) executed by the request handler. If an alias is defined and is a (sub-)compo- nent of this prefix, it will be resolved.<br><br>▶ If the request handler is registered under the URL /sap/bc/bsp, the value /sap/xyz/default.htm is returned for the request URL /sap/bc/bsp/sap/xyz/ default.htm.<br><br>▶ If an alias is also created, e.g. myalias, pointing to /sap/bc/bsp/sap, and access is made in the request via this alias, in other words /myalias/xyz/ default.htm,<br>/sap/xyz/default.htm is returned. |

**Table A.22** Attributes of the IF_HTTP_HEADER_FIELDS_SAP interface (Cont.)

| Name/Pseudo Header | Meaning |
|---|---|
| PATH_TRANSLATED<br>~path_translated | The URL-uncoded path name from the request URL (without the query string) is returned.<br>▶ From the request URL /sap(bdK1qZ==)/bc/bsp/sap/xyz/default.htm?name=hans&loc=london, sap/bc/bsp/sap/xyz/default.htm is returned.<br>~path_translated = ~script_name +<br>~path_info |
| PATH_TRANSLATED_<br>EXPANDED<br>~path_translated_<br>expanded | This field contains the URL-uncoded part of the URL (suffix) given after the part of the URL (prefix) executed by the request handler. If an alias is defined and is a (sub-)component of this prefix, it will be resolved.<br>▶ If the request handler is registered under the URL /sap/bc/bsp, the value /sap/xyz/default.htm is returned for the request URL /sap/bc/bsp/sap/xyz/default.htm.<br>▶ If an alias is also created, e.g. myalias, pointing to /sap/bc/bsp/sap and access is made in the request via this alias, in other words /myalias/xyz/default.htm, /sap/xyz/default.htm is returned.<br>~path_translated_expanded = ~script_name_expanded +<br>~path_info_expanded |
| QUERY_STRING<br>~query_string | This field contains the URL-coded query string from the request URI of an HTTP request, i.e., the partial string after the first question mark.<br>▶ From the URL http://my-webas.de:8080/sap/bc/xyz/default.htm?name=hans&loc=london, name=hans&loc=london is returned.<br>The individual form fields should be manipulated to change a query string. The method SET_FORMFIELD or SET_FORMFIELDS of the interface IF_HTTP_ENTITY is available for this purpose. |
| REMOTE_ADDR<br>~remote_addr | The IP address of the HTTP client is determined if the server is accessed without HTTP proxy, otherwise the IP address of the last proxy in the proxy chain before the server is determined. |
| REQUEST_LINE<br>~request_line | This field returns the complete HTTP request line.<br>Example:<br>GET /sap/bc/xyz/default.htm?param=6 HTTP/1.1 |
| REQUEST_METHOD<br>~request_method | The HTTP method is determined from the HTTP request line of the request, e.g., GET or POST. |

**Table A.22** Attributes of the IF_HTTP_HEADER_FIELDS_SAP interface (Cont.)

| Name/Pseudo Header | Meaning |
|---|---|
| REQUEST_URI<br>~request_uri | The complete URI is determined from the HTTP request line of the request.<br>▶ From the request URL GET /sap/bc/xyz/default.htm?param=6HTTP/1.1 wird /sap/bc/xyz/default.htm?param=6 is returned. |
| RESPONSE_LINE<br>~response_line | This field contains the complete HTTP response line (status line) of a received HTTP response:<br>HTTP/1.1 200 OK |
| SCRIPT_NAME<br>~script_name | This field contains the part of the URL (prefix) that has resulted in the HTTP request handler being executed. Any alias names are not resolved.<br>▶ If the request handler is registered under the URL /sap/bc/bsp, the value /sap/bc/bsp is returned for the request URL /sap/bc/bsp/sap/xyz/default.htm.<br>▶ If an alias is also created, e.g., myalias, pointing to /sap/bc/bsp and access is made in the request via this alias, in other words /myalias/sap/xyz/default.htm, /myalias is returned. |
| SCRIPT_NAME_<br>EXPANDED<br>~script_name_<br>expanded | This field contains the part of the URL (prefix) that has resulted in the HTTP request handler being executed. Any alias names are resolved (expanded).<br>▶ If the request handler is registered under the URL /sap/bc/bsp, the value /sap/bc/bsp is returned for the request URL /sap/bc/bsp/sap/xyz/default.htm.<br>▶ If an alias is also created, e.g., myalias, pointing to /sap/bc/bsp and access is made in the request via this alias, in other words /myalias/sap/xyz/default.htm, /sap/bc/bsp is returned. |
| SERVER_NAME<br>~server_name | This field contains the name of the server that received the request. |
| SERVER_PORT<br>~server_port | This field contains the port number via which the request was received. |
| SERVER_PROTOCOL<br>~server_protocol | This field contains the protocol from the HTTP request line, e.g., HTTP/1.0 or HTTP/1.1. |
| STATUS_CODE<br>~status_code | In the case of an HTTP response (client), contains the HTTP status code, e.g., 401 for Not found.<br>The method SET_STATUS of the interface IF_HTTP_RESPONSE should be used to set a status. |

**Table A.22** Attributes of the IF_HTTP_HEADER_FIELDS_SAP interface (Cont.)

| Name/Pseudo Header | Meaning |
|---|---|
| STATUS_REASON<br>~status_reason | In the case of an HTTP response (client), contains the descriptive text of the HTTP status code, e.g., `Not found` for the status code 401.<br>The method `SET_STATUS` of the interface `IF_HTTP_RESPONSE` should be used to set a status. |
| URI_SCHEME<br>~uri_scheme | This field contains the string at the beginning of the URL in front of `://`. This is typically the URI schema, i.e., the protocol.<br>▶ For the URL `http://www.my-webas.de`, `http` is returned, for example.<br>A check for `https` should be carried out using the attribute `SSL_ACTIVE` of the interface `IF_HTTP_SERVER`. |

**Table A.22** Attributes of the IF_HTTP_HEADER_FIELDS_SAP interface (Cont.)

### Constants

No constants are defined.

### Methods

No methods are defined.

## A.1.11 The IF_HTTP_FORM_FIELDS_SAP Interface

The `IF_HTTP_FORM_FIELDS_SAP` interface contains all of SAP's own HTML form fields in the form of attributes.

### Attributes

The following attributes are defined:

| Name | Meaning | String constant (form field name) |
|---|---|---|
| SAP_CLIENT | Client for logon | *sap-client* |
| SAP_EXITURL | BSP: Exit URL | *sap-exiturl* |
| SAP_LANGUAGE | Language for logon (ISO) | *sap-language* |
| SAP_PASSWORD | Password for logon | *sap-password* |
| SAP_PROFILE | Activate profiling | *sap-profile* |

**Table A.23** Attributes of the IF_HTTP_FORM_FIELDS_SAP interface

| Name | Meaning | String constant (form field name) |
|------|---------|-----------------------------------|
| SAP_SESSIONCMD | BSP: Session command | *sap-sessioncmd* |
| SAP_SYSCMD | BSP: System command | *sap-syscmd* |
| SAP_THEME | BSP: Theme | *sap-theme* |
| SAP_TRACE | Activate tracing | *sap-trace* |
| SAP_USER | User for logon | *sap-user* |

**Table A.23** Attributes of the IF_HTTP_FORM_FIELDS_SAP interface (Cont.)

## Constants

No constants are defined.

## Methods

No methods are defined.

### A.1.12   The IF_HTTP_PROXY_CONFIG Interface

The IF_HTTP_PROXY_CONFIG interface provides a method for determining proxy settings. It is implemented by the CL_HTTP_PROXY_CONFIG class.

## Attributes

No attributes are defined.

## Constants

No constants are defined.

## Methods

The following method is defined:

| Name | Meaning |
|------|---------|
| GET_PROXY_INFO | Determines the proxy settings for HTTP requests. |

**Table A.24** Method of the IF_HTTP_PROXY_CONFIG interface

## A.2 Interfaces and Classes for BSP Development

The following section provides a description of selected important interfaces and classes for BSP development.

### A.2.1 The IF_BSP_APPLICATION Interface

The IF_BSP_APPLICATION interface provides methods that a BSP application can use to query and manipulate information via its runtime environment (e.g., session timeout, current URL for the BSP application, status mode, etc.). The interface is implemented by the CL_BSP_APPLICATION class. Because this information can be useful for any BSP application, we recommend that you base your own BSP application classes on it.

**Attributes**

No attributes are defined.

**Constants**

No constants are defined.

**Methods**

The following methods are defined:

| Name | Meaning |
| --- | --- |
| GET_APPLICATION_NAME | Returns the name of the BSP application. |
| GET_APPLICATION_NAMESPACE | Returns the name range of the BSP application. For BSP applications without explicit name range specifications, this is the SAP name range, i.e., "sap" is returned. |
| GET_APPLICATION_START_PAGE | Returns the start page of the associated BSP application. If no start page has been defined, "default.htm" is returned. |
| GET_APPLICATION_THEME | Supplies the name of the BSP application theme. If no theme has been assigned to the BSP application, an empty string is delivered (default theme). |
| GET_APPLICATION_URL | Returns the relative URL of the BSP application. |
| GET_REQUEST | Delivers an interface reference for the current HTTP request object. |

**Table A.25** Methods of the IF_BSP_APPLICATION interface

| Name | Meaning |
|------|---------|
| GET_RESPONSE | Delivers an interface reference for the current HTTP response object. |
| GET_RUNTIME | Delivers an interface reference for the current BSP runtime object. |
| GET_TIMEOUT | Returns the time-out value set in the transaction SICF for a stateful BSP application. If no other requests are received within this value, the BSP application currently running will be closed. |
| SET_TIMEOUT | Sets the time-out value for a BSP application. |
| IS_STATEFUL | Is the BSP application stateful? |
| SET_STATEFUL | The BSP application is changed to stateful mode. |
| IS_STATELESS | Is the BSP application stateless? |
| SET_STATELESS | The BSP application is changed to stateless mode. |

**Table A.25** Methods of the IF_BSP_APPLICATION interface (Cont.)

## A.2.2 The IF_BSP_APPLICATION_EVENTS Interface

The IF_BSP_APPLICATION_EVENTS interface provides a range of application events (callup points) in the form of methods. At these callup points, separate functionality can be stored, such as authorization checks or data acquisition, or restore functions. In order to be able to use these application events or callup points, the application class of this interface must be implemented.

**Attributes**

No attributes are defined.

**Constants**

No constants are defined.

**Methods**

The following methods[4] are defined:

---

4  When using the methods, you should also consider the BSP control-flow concept (see Section 3.3.3).

| Name | Meaning |
|---|---|
| ON_START | Called by the BSP runtime if the associated BSP application has been started for the first time. |
| ON_STOP | Called by the BSP runtime if the associated BSP application is explicitly closed (i.e., not by a timeout). |
| ON_REQUEST | Called by the BSP runtime for each incoming request to a BSP, before the BSP receives control (in the OnRequest event handler). |
| ON_RESPONSE | Called by the BSP runtime for each outgoing response of a BSP after the BSP has been edited (after the OnManipulation event handler). |

**Table A.26** Methods of the IF_BSP_APPLICATION_EVENTS interface

### A.2.3 The IF_BSP_NAVIGATION Interface

The IF_BSP_NAVIGATION interface is used primarily to define transfers (navigation) between BSP pages and the transfer of parameters to follow-on pages. This interface is implemented by the CL_BSP_NAVIGATION class. An instance of this class is available as a global runtime object in a series of event handlers.

**Attributes**

No attributes are defined.

**Constants**

No constants are defined.

**Methods**

The following methods are defined:

| Name | Meaning |
|---|---|
| CALL_APPLICATION | Used to call an external application (addressed via URL) which can then be accessed by the HTTP redirect mechanism. In order to be able to return from the external application back to the calling application, the following must occur: <br> 1. This method must be implemented appropriately. <br> 2. The return address must be transferred. |

**Table A.27** Methods of the IF_BSP_NAVIGATION interface

| Name | Meaning |
|---|---|
| | The default return URL is the calling page. Alternatively, a parameter containing the return address can be transferred. By default, the name of this parameter is *sap-exiturl*. This parameter can be used to call BSP applications easily from one another. An optional event ID can be generated on the return and processed in the OnInputProcessing event handler of the calling BSP. The actual navigation is only executed once the relevant event handler is exited. |
| ENCODE_PARAMETERS | Specifies the coding of the transfer parameter ; it has been defined using the method set_parameter. There are two coding options:<br><br>1. Uncoded, i.e., in plain text as name/value pairs in the query string of the URL<br><br>2. Coded, i.e., Base64-coded (default) as the value of the URL parameter *sap-params* |
| EXIT | Closes the current BSP application, regardless of whether this application is functioning as stateful or stateless. If the IF_BSP_APPLICATION_EVENTS interface has been implemented by the application class, the event handler ON_STOP is executed. In addition, an exit URL can be specified to navigate to any "end page" or URL via HTTP redirect. The actual navigation (when an exit URL is specified) is only executed once the relevant event handler is exited. |
| GET_PARAMETER | Returns the value of the requested parameter from the navigation object as a string. |
| HAS_PARAMETERS | Determines whether parameters for the current navigation object have been set. (0: no, 1: yes) |
| SET_PARAMETER | Sets a parameter for transfer to the follow-on page. The name of the parameter is typically covered by an auto page attribute of the follow-on page. Otherwise, the parameter can be read using the request object and the method IF_HTTP_REQUEST~GET_FORM_FIELD in the follow-on page. The value of the parameter is not required if a form field of the same name is sent in the current request. |

**Table A.27** Methods of the IF_BSP_NAVIGATION interface (Cont.)

| Name | Meaning |
|---|---|
| GOTO_PAGE | This method triggers the navigation to the specified absolute or relative URL respectively. The navigation is done via a redirect (HTTP method GET)[5]. You can transfer parameters to the subsequent page via the SET_PARAMETER method (particularly to fill auto-page attributes). For a redirect, however there is a data restriction of approximately 1 KB for parameters to be transferred. For larger forms, the method USE_AUTO_SUBMIT_FORM should therefore be used (see description below) that transfers the form fields using POST. <br><br> Comment: <br> The actual navigation is only executed once the relevant event handler is exited. |
| GOTO_PAGE_CS | Triggers navigation to the specified absolute or relative URL (case-sensitive). <br><br> Comment: <br> The actual navigation is only executed once the relevant event handler is exited. |
| NEXT_PAGE | Determines the follow-on page by specifying a page outbox defined in the Navigation Modeler. <br><br> The actual navigation is only executed once the relevant event handler is exited. |
| USE_AUTO_SUBMIT_FORM | Used to transfer forms to the follow-on page. The HTTP method POST is used instead of a redirect (HTTP method GET). Therefore, the data volume limit with query string parameters (in the case of a redirect—only around 1 KB) can be circumvented. The parameters to be transferred are integrated into the form as hidden fields in this process, and the form is automatically returned to the follow-on page directly after it has been received in the browser (auto-submit). Auto-submit forms can result in problems in the browser history (Back button in the browser is not working) and cannot be used with WAP devices. As an option, a target frame can be specified for the follow-on page. The actual navigation is carried out using the then call of GOTO_PAGE or NEXT_PAGE. |
| USE_ABSOLUT_URL | Signals to the navigation object to use a relative URL and not an absolute one. |

**Table A.27** Methods of the IF_BSP_NAVIGATION interface (Cont.)

---

5 This does also not depend on the HTML form-tag settings (Attribute method).

| Name | Meaning |
|---|---|
| RESPONSE_COMPLETE | Signals to the BSP runtime that after returning to the BSP event handler where it was called, no further event handlers/sections are to be addressed. The HTTP response is already fully generated at this point and must be returned to the client or browser. This method is usually called in the OnRequest or OnInitialization section of a BSP if the HTTP response is generated in a different way than with the OnLayout section (e.g., MIME object from the database or generated XML output) and is to be written directly to the HTTP response object. In these cases, calling the OnLayout section would append slightly undesirable outputs to the response (e.g., spaces that are critical in binary documents). |

**Table A.27**  Methods of the IF_BSP_NAVIGATION interface (Cont.)

## A.2.4  The IF_BSP_RUNTIME Interface

The IF_BSP_RUNTIME interface permits access to information from the current runtime environment of a BSP application. The interface is implemented by the CL_BSP_RUNTIME class (BSP runtime).

**Attributes**

The following attributes are defined:

| Name | Meaning |
|---|---|
| APPLICATION_NAME | Contains the name of the BSP application. |
| APPLICATION_ NAMESPACE | Saves the name range of a BSP application (if defined); otherwise, the value "sap" is set. |
| APPLICATION_THEME | Saves the theme used for the BSP application. |
| APPLICATION_URL | Saves the URL prefix of the BSP application. |
| DDIC_UTILS | Delivers an interface reference to available dictionary services (IF_BSP_SERVICES). |
| KEEP_CONTEXT | Contains the mode of the BSP application: 0 for stateful, 1 for stateless. |
| PAGE_NAME | Stores the name of the BSP. |
| PAGE_URL | Stores the URL prefix of the BSP. |
| RUNTIME_URL | Stores the URL prefix of the BSP runtime (path to the request handler). |

**Table A.28**  Attributes of the IF_BSP_RUNTIME interface

| Name | Meaning |
|------|---------|
| SERVER | Delivers an interface reference to the HTTP server (IF_HTTP_SERVER). |
| SESSION_MANAGER | Delivers an interface reference to the Workplace Session Manager (IF_BSP_SESSMAN). |
| CLIENT_INFO | Delivers an interface reference to the device properties of the client, e.g., browser properties (IF_CLIENT_INFO). |
| SESSION_ID | Contains the BSP session ID identifying a unique user session. The value of this attribute only changes if the browser is closed and reopened. |

**Table A.28** Attributes of the IF_BSP_RUNTIME interface (Cont.)

## Constants

No constants are defined.

## Methods

The following methods are defined:

| Name | Meaning |
|------|---------|
| CONSTRUCT_BSP_URL | This method constructs a server-local, absolute URL (HTTP or HTTPS) for a BSP application or BSP. Comment: This method can be expensive in terms of runtime (several milliseconds) and should not be called unnecessarily often. Alternatively, the access to the instance attribute RUNTIME_URL, APPLICATION_URL or PAGE_URL can be used. |
| GET_OTR_TEXT | The OTR text stored for a transferred alias (including name range details) in the current language is returned. If the alias is not known, an empty string is returned. If there is no text for the alias in the current language, the secondary language will be used. |
| WITH_ACCESSIBILITY | There is a prompt as to whether support for *Accessibility*[6] is activated in the BSP runtime. |

**Table A.29** Methods of the IF_BSP_RUNTIME interface

---

6 The U.S. Accessibility Policy (Section 508) is supposed to enable people with a sight handicap to use software interfaces without any problem. Usually all texts that appear on screen are read out using an external tool, i.e., a screen reader. This implies that all interface elements, even icons, pushbuttons, etc., contain texts or quick infos.

## A.2.5 The IF_BSP_PAGE Interface

The `IF_BSP_PAGE` interface permits access to all relevant information in a BSP. The interface is implemented by the class `CL_BSP_PAGE`, which is the basic class of all BSPs.

### Attributes

The following attribute is defined:

| Name | Meaning |
|------|---------|
| MESSAGES | Delivers a reference to the messages for this BSP (CL_BSB_MES-SAGES). |

**Table A.30** The attribute of the IF_BSP_PAGE interface

### Constants

The following constants are defined:

| Name | Meaning |
|------|---------|
| CO_FORMAT_NONE | formatted output: none (default) |
| CO_FORMAT_LONG | formatted output: long |
| CO_FORMAT_SHORT | formatted output: short |
| CO_FORMAT_LOWER | formatted output: lowercase letters |
| CO_FORMAT_UPPER | formatted output: uppercase letters |
| CO_FORMAT_CURRENCY | formatted output: currency |
| LIFETIME_PAGE | The page is valid until the user explicitly navigates from this page. |
| LIFETIME_REQUEST | The page is only valid for this HTTP request. |
| LIFETIME_SESSION | The page is valid for the entire session (only with stateful BSP applications). |

**Table A.31** Constants of the IF_BSP_PAGE interface

## Methods

The following methods are defined:

| Name | Meaning |
| --- | --- |
| GET_APPLICATION | Returns a reference to the application object of this BSP. (CL_BSP_APPLICATION) or if not present, a zero reference is returned. |
| GET_APPLICATION_ NAME | Delivers the name of the BSP application. |
| GET_APPLICATION_ NAMESPACE | Returns the name range of the BSP application. If no range is defined, "sap" is returned. |
| GET_APPLICATION_ START_PAGE | Determines the start page of the associated BSP application, as defined in the development environment. If no page has been defined, "default.htm" is returned. |
| GET_APPLICATION_ THEME | Determines the theme being used for the BSP application. If no theme has been defined, the default theme (SAP_DEFAULT) is returned. |
| GET_APPLICATION_URL | Returns the relative URL of the BSP application. |
| GET_ATTRIBUTE | Delivers the page of the requested page attribute (case-insensitive). As there may be attributes of any type, the return value cannot be a specific type and must be linked according to the type when called. |
| SET_ATTRIBUTE | Sets the value of a page attribute. Only existing attributes can be changed. |
| GET_LIFETIME | Delivers the current setting for the life cycle of this BSP (see LIFETIME* constants). With stateless applications, LIFETIME_REQUEST is always returned. |
| SET_LIFETIME | Sets the setting for the life cycle of this BSP (see LIFETIME* constants). Comment: With stateless applications, this setting has no effect. With stateful applications, however, a page with the status LIFETIME_REQUEST can be "triggered" from this context, for example. |
| GET_PAGE_NAME | Delivers the name of the BSP. |
| GET_PAGE_URL | Delivers the server-local (relative) URL of the BSP. |
| GET_REQUEST | Delivers an interface reference of the current HTTP request object (IF_HTTP_REQUEST). |

**Table A.32** Methods of the IF_BSP_PAGE interface

| Name | Meaning |
|------|---------|
| GET_RESPONSE | Delivers an interface reference of the current HTTP response object (IF_HTTP_RESPONSE). |
| GET_RUNTIME | Delivers an interface reference of the current BSP runtime object (IF_BSP_RUNTIME). |
| SERIALIZE | After the layout event handler has been run, this method can be used to write the contents of the BSP to a string (serialization). The call is usually carried out in the OnManipulation event of the BSP if the output generated is to be processed further. If this method has been used, the HTTP response is not automatically sent to the client. This should then be done via IF_HTTP_RESPONSE~SET_CDATA and the HTTP response object, for example. |
| TO_STRING | The value of a scalable ABAP variable of any type if prepared as a string. Parameters such as formatting (CO_FORMAT_* constants), output length, number of decimal places, and reference value (e.g., currency) are available for this purpose. The string generated in this way is suitable for output in a BSP, for example, using the <%= ... %> directive. |
| WRITE | The value of a scalable ABAP variable of any type is output to the current "write position" in the BSP as a string. Various formatting options are available (see the TO_STRING method). |

**Table A.32** Methods of the IF_BSP_PAGE interface (Cont.)

## A.2.6 The IF_BSP_PAGE_CONTEXT Interface

The IF_BSP_PAGE_CONTEXT interface forms a framework around a BSP and is based on the page context object (PAGE_CONTEXT). This interface is implemented by the CL_BSP_PAGE_CONTEXT class. The methods of the interface are used with BSP extensions or elements.

### Attributes

No attributes are defined.

### Constants

No constants are defined.

**Methods**

The following methods are defined:

| Name | Meaning |
|------|---------|
| DELTA_HANDLING_BEGIN | HTML demarcation limit (beginning). |
| DELTA_HANDLING_END | HTML demarcation limit (end). |
| ELEMENT_AT_TOP_OF_STACK | Returns the top element on the stack. |
| ELEMENT_PROCESS | Processes other BSP elements dynamically. This method can be used, for example, when creating composite elements. |
| ELEMENT_STACK_DUMP | Returns a list of all elements on the stack. |
| GET_ABSOLUTE_ID | Returns a complete ID. |
| GET_MODEL | Returns a reference to the binding interface. |
| GET_OUT | Returns the current active writer on the stack. |
| GET_RUNTIME | Returns the runtime object. |
| GET_NAVIGATION | Returns the navigation object. |
| GET_REQUEST | Returns the request object. |
| GET_RESPONSE | Returns the response object. |
| GET_PAGE | Returns the page object. |
| POP_WRITER | Takes the first writer from the stack and returns it. |
| PUSH_WRITER | Sets a new writer on the stack and returns it as a response. |
| RELEASE | The destructor is called from the BSP factory. |

**Table A.33** Methods of the IF_BSP_PAGE_CONTEXT interface

### A.2.7 The IF_BSP_ServiceS Interface

The IF_BSP_ServiceS interface provides various dictionary services and is implemented by the CL_BSP_SERVICES class.

**Attributes**

No attributes are defined.

## Constants

The following constants are defined:

| Name | Meaning | Initial value |
|------|---------|---------------|
| SORT_BY_KEY | Sort by key column | BY_KEY |
| SORT_BY_VALUE | Sort by value column | BY_VALUE |
| NO_SORT | No sorting | NONE |

**Table A.34** Constants of the IF_BSP_ServiceS interface

## Methods

The following methods are defined:

| Name | Meaning |
|------|---------|
| GET_FIELD_LABEL | Delivers the field description for a data object. |
| GET_QUICKINFO | Returns the short description for a data object. |
| GET_SIMPLE_HELPVALUES | Generates a list of values from a simple search tool. This functionality is built on the **F4** values tool in the SAP system. |
| GET_HISTORY_ID | Returns a global history ID. |
| GET_DAY_COLLECTION | Determines the name and short description of all days. |
| GET_MONTH_COLLECTION | Determines the name and short description of all months. |
| GET_TABL_INFO | Returns type information and texts for a table. |
| GET_LOCAL_HISTORY_ID | Returns an application-local history ID. |

**Table A.35** Methods of the IF_BSP_ServiceS interface

## A.2.8 The CL_BSP_MESSAGES Class

The CL_BSP_MESSAGES class is used to track messages (error and information messages) for a BSP. To track messages, there is an instance of this class for each BSP, containing the current messages for this class. The lifetime of the instance is limited to an HTTP request/response cycle. These messages are accessed from a BSP, or from the event handlers via the global runtime object PAGE (PAGE->MESSAGES), or via the self-reference in the form ME->IF_BSP_PAGE~MESSAGES (see also the interface IF_BSP_

`PAGE`). Each individual message can be identified by a condition used as a key for the message.

**Attributes**

No public attributes are defined.

**Constants**

The following constants are defined:

| Name | Meaning | Value |
|------|---------|-------|
| `CO_SEVERITY_FATAL_ ERROR` | Error level of a message: Fatal Error | 1 |
| `CO_SEVERITY_ERROR` | Error level of a message: Error | 2 |
| `CO_SEVERITY_ WARNING` | Error level of a message: Warning | 3 |
| `CO_SEVERITY_INFO` | Error level of a message: Information | 4 |
| `CO_SEVERITY_SUCCESS` | Error level of a message: Success Message | 5 |

**Table A.36** Constants of the CL_BSP_ MESSAGES class

**Methods**

The following methods are defined:

| Name | Meaning |
|------|---------|
| `ADD_MESSAGE` | A message is entered under the given condition in the list of messsages. If a message already exists under this condition, it is overwritten. In addition, the text of the message (also OTR alias possible) and the error level (CO_SEVERITY_* constants) are entered. |
| `ADD_MESSAGE2` | Same as ADD_MESSAGE, except that in this case, an optional message type (`sy-msgty`) can also be specified. |
| `ADD_MESSAGE_FROM_ T100` | A message from the message table (T100) is added here. |
| `ADD_MESSAGE_FROM_ EXCEPTION` | Creates a message from an exception. |
| `GET_MESSAGE` | Condition, message ,and error level are returned from the message list at a given index. If there is no message for the index, the error level receives the value 0. |

**Table A.37** Methods of the CL_BSP_ MESSAGES class

| Name | Meaning |
|---|---|
| NUM_MESSAGES | Returns the number of messages generated using ADD_MESSAGE. |
| DELETE_MESSAGE | Deletes messages with a specific condition. |
| MERGE_MESSAGE | Merges messages with (added to) another message instance. |
| MODIFY_MESSAGE | Changes a message. |
| RESET | Deletes all messages. |
| ASSERT | Delivers the index of the message for a given condition. If there is no message for this condition, 0 is returned. |
| ASSERT_SEVERITY | Returns the severity of the message (CO_SEVERITY_* constants) for a given condition. If nothing is found for this condition, 0 is returned. |
| ASSERT_MESSAGE | Delivers a message for a given condition or an empty string; if no message is available under this condition. |

**Table A.37** Methods of the CL_BSP_ MESSAGES class (Cont.)

## A.2.9 The CL_BSP_GET_TEXT_BY_ALIAS Class

The CL_BSP_GET_TEXT_BY_ALIAS class contains a method for pulling OTR alias texts.

### Attributes

No public attributes are defined.

### Constants

No constants are defined.

### Method

The following method is defined:

| Name | Meaning |
|---|---|
| GET_TEXT | The text in the relevant language is returned for an OTR alias.<br><br>Comment:<br>Unlike the method IF_BSP_RUNTIME~GET_OTR_TEXT, here, the language is an import parameter of the method. |

**Table A.38** The method of the CL_BSP_GET_TEXT_BY_ALIAS class

## A.2.10 The CL_BSP_CONTROLLER2 Class

The CL_BSP_CONTROLLER2 class delivers various attributes and methods that are important for the developer, in connection with the Model View Controller (MVC) Design Pattern. This class implements the interfaces IF_BSP_CONTROLLER and IF_BSP_DISPATCHER and is derived from the CL_BSP_CONTROLLER class.

### Attributes

The following attributes are defined:

| Name | Meaning |
|---|---|
| COMPONENT_ID | Component identification |
| ADAPTER | Reference for the adapter |
| REQUEST | Request object |
| RESPONSE | Response object |
| RUNTIME | Runtime object |
| NAVIGATION | Navigation object |
| SERVER | Server object |
| CONTROLLER_NAME | Name of the controller |
| APPLICATION_NAME | Name of the application |
| APPLICATION_ NAMESPACE | Application name range |
| APPLICATION | Application object |
| MESSAGES | Messages |
| M_PARENT | Controller basis class |

**Table A.39**  Attributes of the CL_BSP_CONTROLLER2 class

### Constants

No relevant constants are defined.

## Methods

The following methods are defined:

| Name | Meaning |
| --- | --- |
| DO_INIT | Used as a constructor for the controller and therefore for initializing the attributes. |
| DO_INITATTRIBUTES | Used to read the parameters from the request. The parameters could also be read using DO_REQUEST, however, if the controller determines a component, or has been called by a goto or call tag, other attributes can be set after DO_INITATTRIBUTES. Initializations that are required for each request can also be carried out. |
| DO_REQUEST | Processes the request and then branches to a view. This method must be overwritten. |
| DO_DESTROY | Represents the destructor called if the instance is deleted. If the instance is destroyed by deleting the work process (e.g., in a timeout), the method is not called. |
| CREATE_VIEW | Creates a view instance. |
| CALL_VIEW | Calls the request handler of the view instance. |
| CREATE_CONTROLLER | Creates a controller instance. |
| CALL_CONTROLLER | Calls the request handler of the controller instance. |
| GET_PAGE_CONTEXT | Returns the page context object. |
| GET_ATTRIBUTE | Returns the specified page attribute. |
| SET_ATTRIBUTE | Sets the specified page attribute if none exists (not possible to create a new one). |
| GET_LIFETIME | Returns the lifetime of the page. |
| SET_LIFETIME | Defines the lifetime of the page. |
| GET_PAGE_URL | Returns the URL of the page. |
| TO_STRING | Creates a formatted string. |
| WRITE | Writes a formatted string to the output. |
| GET_OUT | Retrieves the current writer. |
| SET_MIME_TYPE | Specifies the MIME type of the page. |
| SET_CACHING | Specifies the caching behavior. |

**Table A.40** Methods of the CL_BSP_CONTROLLER2 class

| Name | Meaning |
|------|---------|
| INSTANTIATE_PARAMETER | The parameters from the request are instanced. |
| REGISTER | Registers subcomponents. |
| FINISH_INPUT_PROCESSING | The input processing is ended. |
| FILL_VALUES | The values are handled. |
| HANDLE_EVENT | The event is handled. |
| CREATE_CONTROLLER | Generates a controller instance. |
| DISPATCH_INPUT | Carries out the input processing. |
| GET_ID | Determines the ID from the specified and the component ID. |
| SET_MODEL | Generates and registers a model instance. |
| GET_MODEL | Returns a model instance. |
| CREATE_MODEL | Generates and registers a model instance. |
| GET_CONTROLLER | Returns the subcontroller. |
| DELETE_MODEL | Deletes the model instance. |
| FILL_MODEL_DATA | Fills the model data. |
| DELETE_CONTROLLER | Deletes the subcontroller. |
| IS_TOPLEVEL | Checks whether the controller is the top-level controller. |
| CONTROLLER_SET_ACTIVE | Sets a controller to "active" or "inactive." |

**Table A.40** Methods of the CL_BSP_CONTROLLER2 class (Cont.)

## A.2.11 The CL_BSP_SERVER_SIDE_COOKIE Class

The CL_BSP_SERVER_SIDE_COOKIE class provides methods for setting, reading, deleting, and managing server-side cookies. The cookies are stored in the database (cluster table SSCOOKIE) and can be used as a field, structure, or internal table. There are no size restrictions.

The SAP Web Application Server contains two ABAP reports for managing cookies. The first report is the BSP_SHOW_SERVER_COOKIES report, which provides an overview of all cookies set on the system. The second report is the BSP_CLEAN_UP_SERVER_COOKIES report, which removes all expired cookies from the system that have been executed on the exact day that was previously specified. We recommend that this report be scheduled as a regularly run background job to reduce the workload on the cookie table.

## Attributes

No public attributes are defined.

## Constants

The following constants are defined:

| Name | Meaning | Value |
|---|---|---|
| CC_OK | The action was successful. | 0 |
| CC_WRONG_DATA_OBJECT | The data object of the cookie being read does not match the data object of the set cookie. | 1 |
| CC_PARAMETER_MISSING | Indicates that call parameters are missing. | 2 |
| CC_NOT_EXISTS | The cookie does not exist. | 4 |

**Table A.41** Constants of the CL_BSP_SERVER_SIDE_COOKIE class

## Methods

The following methods are defined:

| Name | Meaning |
|---|---|
| GET_SERVER_COOKIE | Reads a cookie from the database. The following should be passed on: the name of the cookie, the name of the BSP application, the name range of the BSP application, the name of the user, the session ID, and the data object name. The validity data of the cookie (date, time) and the actual data object content are returned. |

**Table A.42** Methods of the CL_BSP_SERVER_SIDE_COOKIE class

| Name | Meaning |
| --- | --- |
| SET_SERVER_COOKIE | Writes a cookie to the database. The following should be passed on: the name of the cookie, the name of the BSP application, the name range of the BSP application, the name of the user, the session ID, the data object name, and the data object content. As an option, the validity data of the cookie is transferred; once in absolute sizes (date, time in seconds) and once in relative sizes (starting from the time it was created). If no value has been set for the expiry time, default values are set. For the absolute time, "23:59" should be set, and for the relative time,"3600" (seconds) should be set. |
| DELETE_SERVER_COOKIE | Deletes a server-side cookie. To do this, the name of the cookie, the name of the BSP application, the name range of the BSP application, the name of the user, and the session ID must be transferred as import parameters. |
| GET_LAST_ERROR | Returns a return code (CC_* constants) for the methods GET_SERVER_COOKIE and SET_SERVER_COOKIE. |
| GET_LAST_ERROR_NAME | Returns a description text in the event of an error. |
| GET_SERVER_COOKIE_INFO | Delivers a list with information on the cookies stored on the server (including validity data). As an option, the list can be restricted to a specific cookie name, a BSP application, a name range of the BSP application, a user name, or a session ID. |

**Table A.42** Methods of the CL_BSP_SERVER_SIDE_COOKIE class

## A.2.12 The CL_BSP_MIMES Class

The CL_BSP_MIMES class allows access to the SAP icons stored in the *public* directory of the MIME repository.

**Attributes**

No public attributes are defined.

**Constants**

No constants are defined.

## Methods

The following methods are defined:

| Name | Meaning |
| --- | --- |
| SAP_ICON | Returns the URL for a SAP icon from the MIME repository. |
| SAP_ICON_TEXT | Returns the description for a SAP icon. |

### A.2.13 The IF_CLIENT_INFO Interface

The IF_CLIENT_INFO interface provides various methods that consider the different display options of Web applications on different browsers and other specific properties of mobile devices. This interface is implemented by the CL_CLIENT_INFO class.

## Attributes

No public attributes are defined.

## Constants

No constants are defined.

## Methods

For each method, there is also a specification of which content type is relevant, that is, the markup language to which the device property in question relates. The following methods are defined:

| Name | Meaning | Content Type |
| --- | --- | --- |
| GET_ACCEPT | Corresponds to the HTTP request header accept. | HTML/WML |
| GET_ALERTING_SUPPORTED | Describes whether the device supports messages, e.g., via SMS. | HTML/WML |
| GET_ANCHOR_SUPPORTED | Describes whether the tag <anchor> is supported. | WML |
| GET_ANCHOR_PREV_ SUPPORTED | Describes whether the tag <anchor> can be used to execute a back action. | WML |

**Table A.43** Methods of the IF_CLIENT_INFO interface

| Name | Meaning | Content Type |
|---|---|---|
| GET_APP_LINKS_ SUPPORTED | Describes whether a local application can be called on the device using a special link. | HTML |
| GET_APP_LINK_TYPES | Describes which types of application links are supported. | HTML |
| GET_BACK_HARD_WIRED | Describes whether the back function can be executed via a fixed key without a corresponding tag. | WML |
| GET_BACK_LABEL | Describes whether a label attribute needs to be specified in the tag `<do type=prev>` to display the label. | WML |
| GET_BACK_TO_ANY_URL_ SUPPORTED | Describes whether the tag `<do type="prev">` can be run on any Web address. | WML |
| GET_BIG_SUPPORTED | Describes whether text can be formatted as large text. | WML |
| GET_BOLD_SUPPORTED | Describes whether text can be formatted as bold text. | WML |
| GET_BREAKING_SPACE | Delivers the smallest string character for a space. | HTML/WML |
| GET_BROWSER_CATEGORY | Delivers the category of the browser. | HTML/WML |
| GET_BROWSER_NAME | Delivers the name of the browser. | HTML/WML |
| GET_BROWSER_OS | Delivers the operating system on the device. | HTML/WML |
| GET_BROWSER_VERSION | Delivers the browser version. | HTML/WML |
| GET_CACHE_ENABLED_ BY_DEFAULT | Describes whether the browser cache is activated by default. | HTML/WML |
| GET_CERTIFICATES_ SUPPORTED | Describes whether the device supports client certificates. | HTML/WML |
| GET_CHAR_HEIGHT | Delivers the screen height in lines. | HTML/WML |
| GET_CHAR_WIDTH | Delivers the screen width in characters. | HTML/WML |

**Table A.43** Methods of the IF_CLIENT_INFO interface (Cont.)

| Name | Meaning | Content Type |
|---|---|---|
| GET_COLOR_DEPTH | Delivers the color depth, e.g., 256 colors. | HTML |
| GET_COLOR_SUPPORTED | Describes whether a device has a color screen. | HTML |
| GET_CONTENT_TYPE | Delivers the content type, e.g., HTML or WML. | HTML/WML |
| GET_CONTENT_TYPE_VERSION | Delivers the version of the content type, such as "3.2" for HTML 3.2 or "1.1" for WML 1.1. | HTML/WML |
| GET_COOKIES_SUPPORTED | Describes whether the browser supports cookies. | HTML/WML |
| GET_CSS_SUPPORTED | Describes whether the browser supports CSS. | HTML |
| GET_CSS_VERSION | Delivers the CSS version. | HTML |
| GET_DEFAULT_ACTION_DESIGN | Delivers the preferred design for interface elements for displaying actions. | WML |
| GET_DEFAULT_BLOCK_SEPARATOR | Delivers the preferred character string for separating paragraphs. | HTML/WML |
| GET_DEFAULT_BULLET | Delivers the preferred symbol for identifying bullet points. | WML |
| GET_DEFAULT_FORM_STYLE | Delivers the preferred display type for input masks. | WML |
| GET_DEFAULT_MENU_STYLE | Delivers the preferred display type for menus. | WML |
| GET_DEVICE_CATEGORY | Delivers the category of the device. | HTML/WML |
| GET_DEVICE_NAME | Delivers the name of the device. Unique designation of a record of device properties. | HTML/WML |
| GET_DOM_SUPPORTED | Describes whether the browser supports the DOM (Document Object Model). | HTML |
| GET_DOM_VERSION | Delivers the supported DOM version. | HTML |

**Table A.43** Methods of the IF_CLIENT_INFO interface (Cont.)

| Name | Meaning | Content Type |
|------|---------|--------------|
| GET_EMPHASIZED_ SUPPORTED | Describes whether text can be formatted as emphasized text. | WML |
| GET_EMULATOR | Describes whether the device is evaluated as an emulator. | HTML/WML |
| GET_FIELDSET_LAYOUT | Describes how multiple related input fields are arranged using the `<fieldset>` tag. | WML |
| GET_FIELDSET_TITLE_ VISIBLE | Describes whether the `title` attribute of the `<fieldset>` tag is used as a title. | WML |
| GET_FONT_PROPORTIONAL | Describes whether the default font of the device is a proportional font. | HTML/WML |
| GET_FORM_FACTOR | Delivers the form factor of the device. | HTML/WML |
| GET_FORM_MENU_ SUPPORTED | Describes whether input masks with a preceding menu are supported. | WML |
| GET_FRAMES_SUPPORTED | Describes whether the browser supports frames. | HTML |
| GET_GRAY_LEVEL | Delivers the number of gray tones in grayscale images. | HTML/WML |
| GET_HORZ_SCROLLING_ SUPPORTED | Describes whether the device is available via a horizontal rollbar. | HTML/WML |
| GET_HREF_WITH_PARAMS_ SUPPORTED | Describes whether an HREF attribute can be contained within a URL parameter. | WML |
| GET_HTTP_GET_ SUPPORTED | Describes whether HTTP GET is supported. | WML |
| GET_HTTP_POST_ SUPPORTED | Describes whether HTTP POST is supported. | WML |
| GET_IMAGE_ALIGNMENT_ SUPPORTED | Describes whether a graphic can be left-justified, right-justified, or centered. | WML |
| GET_IMAGE_LINKS_ SUPPORTED | Describes whether a graphic can be used as a link. | HTML/WML |

**Table A.43** Methods of the IF_CLIENT_INFO interface (Cont.)

| Name | Meaning | Content Type |
|------|---------|--------------|
| GET_IMAGE_SIZE_MAX | Delivers the maximum memory size of a graphic. | WML |
| GET_INPUT_FORMAT_DATE | Delivers the formatting character string used to check the data input for date values. | WML |
| GET_INPUT_FORMAT_ NUMERIC | Delivers the character string used to check the data input for numeric values. | WML |
| GET_INPUT_METHOD_ HAND_WRITING | Describes whether the device supports input via handwriting recognition. | HTML/WML |
| GET_INPUT_METHOD_ KEYBOARD | Describes whether the device supports input via a keyboard. | HTML/WML |
| GET_INPUT_METHOD_ KEYPAD | Describes whether the device supports input via telephone keypad. | HTML/WML |
| GET_INPUT_METHOD_ KEYPAD_INTELL | Describes whether the device supports input via T9 text input or similar. | HTML/WML |
| GET_INPUT_METHOD_ VOICE | Describes whether the device supports voice input for data in the browser. | HTML/WML |
| GET_INPUT_SHOWN_ WITH_CAPTION | Describes whether the browser uses the `title` attribute of the `<input>` tag as a title. | WML |
| GET_ITALIC_SUPPORTED | Describes whether text can be formatted as italic text. | WML |
| GET_JAVA_SUPPORTED | Describes whether the device supports the Java programming language. | HTML |
| GET_JAVA_VERSION | Delivers the supported Java version. | HTML |
| GET_LINKS_SEPARATED | Describes whether two consecutive links are clearly separated. | WML |
| GET_LINK_DECORATION | Delivers the border character automatically inserted by the device around the link text, e.g., [ ] or < >. | WML |

**Table A.43** Methods of the IF_CLIENT_INFO interface (Cont.)

| Name | Meaning | Content Type |
|------|---------|--------------|
| GET_LINK_TEXT_WIDTH | Delivers the maximum number of characters a link can have to fit onto a line. | WML |
| GET_LOCAL_IMAGES_SUPPORTED | Describes whether the device supports graphics or symbols located locally on the device. | HTML/WML |
| GET_LOCAL_VARIABLES_SUPPORTED | Describes whether the browser supports local variables. | WML |
| GET_MARQUEE_LINK_SUPPORTED | Describes whether an excessively long link can be displayed in a line, e.g., as running text. | WML |
| GET_MARQUEE_TEXT_SUPPORTED | Describes whether an excessively long text can be displayed in a line, e.g. as running text. | WML |
| GET_MAX_LINK_LENGTH | Delivers the maximum size of the HREF attribute of a link. | HTML/WML |
| GET_MEDIA_FORMATS | Delivers the listing of supported multimedia formats, e.g., .agif (for animated .gif format), .gif, .jpg, .png, .wbmp. | HTML/WML |
| GET_MEMORY | Delivers the maximum main memory capacity of the device. | HTML |
| GET_MODEL | Delivers the name of the device type. | HTML/WML |
| GET_NBSP_SUPPORTED | Describes whether the device supports non-wrapping characters. | WML |
| GET_NESTED_TABLES_SUPPORTED | Describes whether the browser supports nested tables. | HTML |
| GET_NEWLINE_AFTER_IMAGE | Describes whether a line break is automatically inserted after an `<img>` tag. | WML |
| GET_NEWLINE_AFTER_INPUT | Describes whether a line break is inserted after an `<input>` tag with a specific mobile device. | WML |
| GET_NEWLINE_AFTER_LINK | Describes whether a line break is automatically inserted after a link. | WML |

**Table A.43** Methods of the IF_CLIENT_INFO interface (Cont.)

| Name | Meaning | Content Type |
|------|---------|--------------|
| GET_NEWLINE_AFTER_<br>SELECT | Describes whether a line break is automatically inserted after a `<select>` tag. | WML |
| GET_NEWLINE_BEFORE_<br>IMAGE | Describes whether a line break is automatically inserted before an `<img>` tag. | WML |
| GET_NEWLINE_BEFORE_<br>INPUT | Describes whether a line break is automatically inserted before an `<input>` tag. | WML |
| GET_NEWLINE_BEFORE_<br>LINK | Describes whether a line break is automatically inserted before a link. | WML |
| GET_NEWLINE_BEFORE_<br>SELECT | Describes whether a line break is inserted before a `<select>` tag. | WML |
| GET_NEWLINE_BETWEEN_<br>IMAGES | Describes whether a line break is automatically inserted between `<image>` tags. | WML |
| GET_NEWLINE_BETWEEN_<br>LINKS | Describes whether a line break is automatically inserted between two links. | WML |
| GET_NEWLINE_BETW_<br>LINK_AND_TAG | Describes whether a line break is automatically inserted between a link and a tag. | WML |
| GET_OFFLINE_BROWSING_<br>SUPPORTED | Describes whether the browser supports the scrolling of locally saved (cached) pages offline. | HTML |
| GET_OFFLINE_FORMS_<br>SUPPORTED | Describes whether the browser supports the offline completion of input forms on the device. | HTML |
| GET_PAGE_SIZE_MAX | Delivers the maximum size of a page that can be processed on the device. | HTML/WML |
| GET_PIXEL_HEIGHT | Delivers the height of the screen in pixels. | HTML/WML |
| GET_PIXEL_WIDTH | Delivers the width of the screen in pixels. | HTML/WML |
| GET_REDIR_ABSOLUTE_<br>SUPPORTED | Describes whether the browser supports forwarding to an absolute URL address. | HTML/WML |

**Table A.43** Methods of the IF_CLIENT_INFO interface (Cont.)

| Name | Meaning | Content Type |
|---|---|---|
| GET_REDIR_RELATIVE_SUPPORTED | Describes whether the browser supports forwarding to a relative URL address. | HTML/WML |
| GET_SCRIPT_SUPPORTED | Describes whether the browser supports scripting. | HTML/WML |
| GET_SCRIPT_VERSION | Delivers the supported script version. | HTML/WML |
| GET_SECURE_PROTOCOLS_SUPPORTED | Describes whether the browser supports SSL (Secure Sockets Layer) or WTLS (Wireless Transport Layer Security). | HTML/WML |
| GET_SECURE_PROTOCOLS_NAMES | Delivers the name of the supported security protocols. The names are separated by semicolons. | HTML/WML |
| GET_SELECTION_MENU_SUPPORTED | Describes whether the menu formatting type selectionList (numbered list) is supported. | WML |
| GET_SETVAR_ON_EVENT_SUPPORTED | Describes whether the `<set-var>` tag may be used within the event handler `<onevent type="onenterforward">`. | WML |
| GET_SKIPPING_TO_INPUT | Describes whether the browser automatically goes to the first `<input>` tag on a mobile device and displays a screen extract around this `<input>` tag. | WML |
| GET_SMALL_SUPPORTED | Describes whether text can be formatted as small text. | WML |
| GET_SOFTKEY_NUM | Delivers the number of softkeys supported by the device. | WML |
| GET_SOFTKEY_STYLE1 | Describes how softkey 1 is displayed on the screen. | WML |
| GET_SOFTKEY_STYLE2 | Describes how softkey 2 is displayed on the screen. | WML |
| GET_SOFTKEY_TITLE_WIDTH | Delivers the number of characters displayed for a softkey title. | WML |
| GET_SOUND_SUPPORTED | Describes whether the device can play audio. | HTML |

Table A.43 Methods of the IF_CLIENT_INFO interface (Cont.)

| Name | Meaning | Content Type |
|---|---|---|
| GET_STRONG_SUPPORTED | Describes whether text can be emphasized using the `<strong>` tag. | WML |
| GET_SUBMIT_ONEVENT_SUPPORTED | Describes whether "Submit" is supported within the event handler `<onevent type="onenterforward">`. | HTML/WML |
| GET_SUB_CATEGORY | Used for further subdivision of devices. | HTML/WML |
| GET_TABLE_HAS_BORDERS | Describes whether tables are displayed with gridlines. | HTML/WML |
| GET_TABLE_SUPPORTED | Describes whether the browser supports multi-column tables. | HTML/WML |
| GET_TELEPHONY_LINKS_SUPPORTED | Describes whether a telephone number can be dialed directly via a link. | HTML/WML |
| GET_TEXT_ALIGNMENT_SUPPORTED | Describes whether text can be left-justified, right-justified, or centered within a paragraph. | WML |
| GET_TEXT_STYLES_SUPPORTED | Describes whether the browser can format text, e.g., using tags `<b>`, `<small>` etc. | WML |
| GET_TITLE_SUPPORTED | Describes whether a title is visibly displayed at the top of the screen using the `title` property of the WML tag `<card>`. | WML |
| GET_TITLE_WIDTH | Delivers the maximum number of characters in the title. | HTML/WML |
| GET_UNDERLINE_SUPPORTED | Describes whether text can be formatted as underlined text. | WML |
| GET_USER_AGENT | Corresponds to the HTTP request header `User-Agent`. | HTML/WML |
| GET_VARS_ACROSS_CARD_SUPPORTED | Describes whether browser variables transferred to a card can also be used for other cards. | WML |
| GET_VENDOR | Delivers the name of the device manufacturer. | HTML/WML |

**Table A.43** Methods of the IF_CLIENT_INFO interface (Cont.)

| Name | Meaning | Content Type |
| --- | --- | --- |
| GET_XSL_SUPPORTED | Describes whether the browser supports XSL. | HTML |
| GET_XSL_VERSION | Delivers the supported XSL version. | HTML |

**Table A.43** Methods of the IF_CLIENT_INFO interface (Cont.)

## A.2.14 The CL_HTMLB_MANAGER Class

The CL_HTMLB_MANAGER class is used to manage HTMLB extensions.

### Attributes

The following attribute is defined:

| Name | Meaning |
| --- | --- |
| EVENTS_DICTIONARY | A table with HTMLB events. |

**Table A.44** Attribute of the CL_HTMLB_MANAGER class

### Constants

The following constants are defined:

| Name | Meaning |
| --- | --- |
| EVENT_ID | The Event-ID (htmlb) |
| BROWSER_NN4 | Browser constant (Mozilla) |
| BROWSER_NN6 | Browser constant (Mozilla) |
| BROWSER_IE4 | Browser constant (Internet Explorer) |
| BROWSER_IE5 | Browser constant (Internet Explorer) |
| BROWSER_IE6 | Browser constant (Internet Explorer) |
| BROWSER_DEFAULT | Browser constant (Default) |

**Table A.45** Constants of the IF_HTMLB_MANAGER interface

## Methods

The following methods are defined:

| Name | Meaning |
| --- | --- |
| GET_EVENT | Returns a CL_HTMLB_EVENT. |
| GET_CELL_ID | Returns the identification of a TableView cell. |
| DISPATCH_EVENT | Distributes an event to IF_HTMLB_EVENT. |
| GET_DATA | Returns the request data. |
| GET_BROWSER_ID | Returns a browser identifier. |
| GET_MIME_PATH | Returns the MIME path. |
| GET_JAVASCRIPT_URL | Determines a browser-dependent JavaScript URL. |
| GET_STYLESHEET_URL | Determines a browser-dependent CSS URL. |
| GET_JAVASCRIPT_FUNCTION_NAME | Returns a JavaScript function name. |
| GET_TABLE_CELL | Returns a TableView cell. |
| RENDER_EVENT_CALL | Writes an event to the HTML code. |
| CHECK_TABLEVIEW_ALL_ROWS | Checks all lines of a TableView. |
| CHECK_TABLEVIEW_ROW | Checks one line of a TableView. |
| GET_EVENT_EX | Returns an event of type IF_HTMLB_DATA. |
| DISPATCH_EVENT_EX | Dispatches an event. |
| CHECK_AND_INITIALISE_EVENT | Checks and initializes an event. |
| GET_CHECK_TABLEVIEW_ALL_ROWS | Checks all rows in a TableView. |
| BUILD_EVENT_KEY | Creates an event identifier (taglib + tag + event + event-defined). |
| RENDER_EVENT_TABLEVIEW_CELL | Writes an event to the HTML code (TableView). |
| GET_TABLE_CELL_VALUE | Returns the value of a TableView cell. |

**Table A.46** Methods of the CL_HTMLB_MANAGER class

| Name | Meaning |
|---|---|
| GET_FILTER_ROW_VALUE | Returns the value of the filter for a row. |
| GET_SCRIPT_NAME_ONCLIENTROWSEL | Determines the name of the client-side event with a row selection. |

**Table A.46** Methods of the CL_HTMLB_MANAGER class (Cont.)

## A.2.15 The CL_HTMLB_EVENT Class

The CL_HTMLB_EVENT class is used for event handling of HTMLB elements (Basis class) and implements the IF_HTMLB_DATA interface.

### Attributes

The following attributes are defined:

| Name | Meaning |
|---|---|
| EVENT_CLASS | Event class |
| EVENT_SERVER_NAME | Name of the server event |
| EVENT_ID | Event identifier |
| EVENT_NAME | Name of the event |
| EVENT_TYPE | Type of the event |
| EVENT_DEFINED | Specifies whether an event has been defined |
| EVENT_INTERCEPT_DEPTH | Event intercept depth |

**Table A.47** Attributes of the CL_HTMLB_EVENT class

### Constants

No constants are defined.

### Methods

The following methods are defined:

| Name | Meaning |
|---|---|
| RESTORE_FROM_REQUEST | Restores the input from the request. |

**Table A.48** Methods of the CL_HTMLB_EVENT class

| Name | Meaning |
|------|---------|
| `EVENT_INITIALIZE` | Initializes an event. |
| `EVENT_SET_ PARAMETERS` | Sets the parameters of an event. |
| `EVENT_DISPATCH` | Calls an event. |

**Table A.48** Methods of the CL_HTMLB_EVENT class (Cont.)

## A.3 BSP Extensions

BSP extensions are a powerful tool for developing Web applications. Some BSP extensions are already included with the standard SAP Web AS environment. These BSP extensions include:

▶ **HTMLB Extension**
This extension maps HTML business to BSP and replaces a variety of HTML elements. The various BSP elements of the extension permit convenient access and offer an expanded range of functions of the standard tags.

▶ **XHTMLB Extension**
This extension is an expanded HTML Business Library for BSP. It includes toolbars, pushbutton groups, and tabs.

▶ **Benchmark Extension**
The use of BSP elements of this extension permits benchmark evaluations, that is, calculations on the processing time of body elements.

▶ **BTF-Extension**
This extension contains a BSP element that is used by an editor to create a WYSIWYG[7] and source view for BTF documents. The BSP application `BTF_EXT_DEMO` shows the options of this extension.

▶ **Graphics Extension**
The BSP elements of this extension permit the display of graphical objects (e.g., charts, cards, etc.) in BSP applications on the basis of the *SAP Internet Graphics Servers* (*SAP IGS*).

This section introduces you to the various BSP elements of the HTMLB extension. These elements are ideally suited for use with complex tables, tabs, and dynamic menus. The BSP applications `HTMLB_SAMPLES` and `SBSPEXT_HTMLB` provide a good overview of the various parameters and

**HTMLB Extension**

---

7  WYSIWYG is only available in Internet Explorer version 5.5 or higher. Other browsers only support the source view.

uses of BSP elements[8]. The BSP elements of this extension are introduced briefly in the following sections.

▶ `breadCrumb/breadCrumbItem`
Use these BSP elements to establish navigation via the path history. For example, visited pages can be stored in a history and displayed. This list then provides simple navigation between the various objects. The individual entries correspond to mouse clicks and can be queried using an event handler. You can also define the appearance and behavior of the entries (see Figure A.2).

**Figure A.2** BSP element "breadCrumb"

▶ `button`
Use this element to create a button. The appearance and behavior can be changed. For example, a client-side event handler can be used in addition to the standard event handler. Some different versions of a button are shown in Figure A.3.

standard

disabled

Emphasized button

Small button with fixed size

**Figure A.3** BSP element "button"

▶ `chart`
Use this BSP element to create presentation graphics. A variety of diagram types can be selected for the display. The concept of data bindings is used to link the data from a table to an attribute of this element. The header line of this table must be of type `IGS_DATA` (see Figure A.4).

▶ `checkBoxGroup/checkBox`
Use this element to display check boxes in an application. A summary and layout of check boxes can be created using an additional grouping (see Figure A.5).

---

8 The images of the following BSP elements (classical design) originate from these applications.

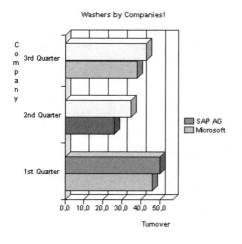

**Figure A.4** BSP element "chart"

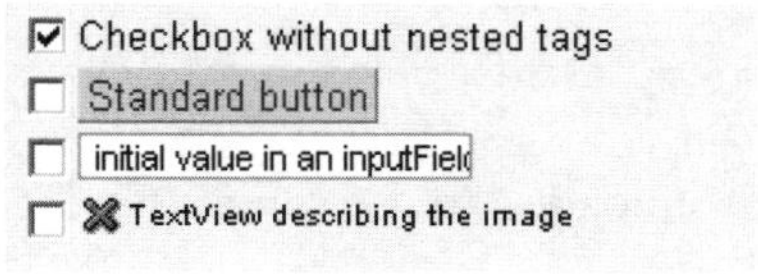

☑ Checkbox without nested tags
☐ Standard button
☐ initial value in an inputField
☐ ✖ TextView describing the image

**Figure A.5** BSP element "checkbox"

▶ `content`
This element provides a border or a container for the other BSP elements.

▶ `dateNavigator/month/week/days`
Use this element to create a calendar view. Each month is shown as a table in this process. Multiple months can be displayed at the same time. The appearance of the individual weeks and days can be specified. Several event handlers are made available, depending on whether a navigation, a month, a week, or a day has been selected (see Figure A.6).

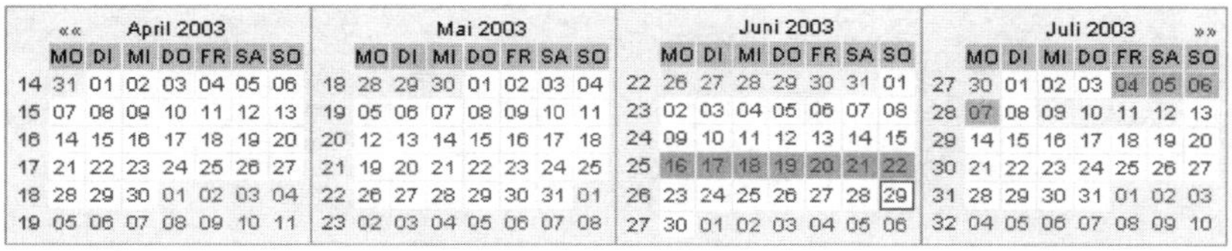

**Figure A.6** BSP element "dateNavigator"

- `document/documentHeader/headInclude/documentBody`
  Use this element to render the root element of a Web document. The header and body elements structure the document. Other elements or pure HTML can be integrated into the body section.
- `dropDownListbox/listBoxItem`
  Use this element as a replacement for the `listBox` element if very long lists are being displayed. The list entries can be generated statically or via the concept of data binding to a table. In this case, too, the standard event handler can be supplemented with a client-side handler (see Figure A.7).

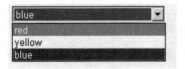

**Figure A.7** BSP element "dropDownListBox"

- `fileUpload`
  This simple element allows a file to be uploaded to the server (see Figure A.8).

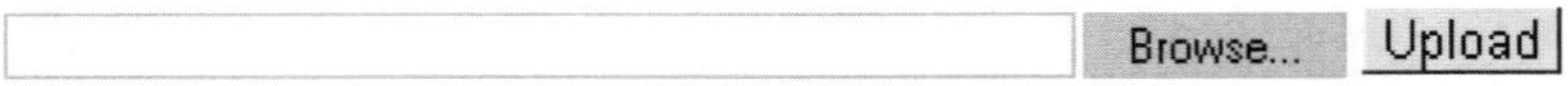

**Figure A.8** BSP element "fileUpload"

- `gridLayout/gridLayoutCell`
  Use this element to create a table-style layout of various components on a page. Each cell can accept a separate element (see Figure A.9).

| | | Image | Input Field | User defined: List Box | User defined: Check Box | Datum | Link | Link with Handler | ImageLink |
|---|---|---|---|---|---|---|---|---|---|
| | AA | | 29.06.2003 | American Airlines (0017/14.05.2003) | American Airlines (0017/14.05.2003) | 14.05.2003 | American Airlines | American Airlines | |
| | AA | | 29.06.2003 | American Airlines (0017/11.06.2003) | American Airlines (0017/11.06.2003) | 11.06.2003 | American Airlines | American Airlines | |
| | AA | | 29.06.2003 | American Airlines (0017/) | American Airlines (0017/) | | American Airlines | American Airlines | |
| | AA | | 29.06.2003 | American Airlines (0017/06.08.2003) | American Airlines (0017/06.08.2003) | 06.08.2003 | American Airlines | American Airlines | |
| | AA | | 29.06.2003 | American Airlines (0017/03.09.2003) | American Airlines (0017/03.09.2003) | 03.09.2003 | American Airlines | American Airlines | |
| | AA | | 29.06.2003 | American Airlines (0017/01.10.2003) | American Airlines (0017/01.10.2003) | 01.10.2003 | American Airlines | American Airlines | |
| | AA | | 29.06.2003 | American Airlines (0017/29.10.2003) | American Airlines (0017/29.10.2003) | 29.10.2003 | American Airlines | American Airlines | |
| | AA | | 29.06.2003 | American Airlines (0017/26.11.2003) | American Airlines (0017/26.11.2003) | 26.11.2003 | American Airlines | American Airlines | |

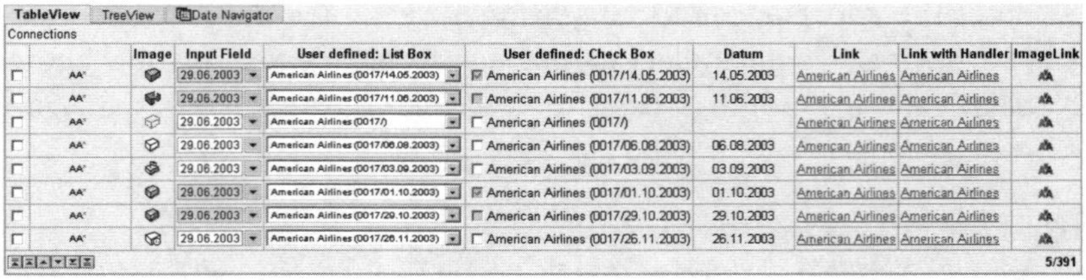

**Figure A.9** BSP element "gridLayout"

► group/groupHeader/groupBody

Use this element to group related elements. A border is drawn around the embedded elements (see Figure A.10).

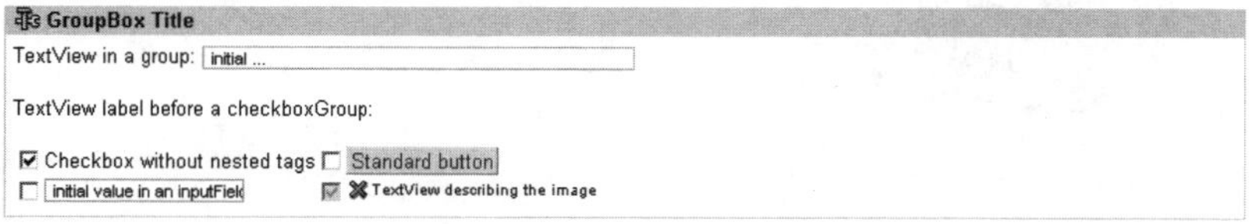

**GroupBox Title**

TextView in a group: [ initial ... ]

TextView label before a checkboxGroup:

☑ Checkbox without nested tags ☐ Standard button
☐ initial value in an inputFiek ☑ ✗ TextView describing the image

**Figure A.10** BSP element "group"

► image

This element allows the embedding of a MIME object referenced by a URL.

► inputField/label

The combination of both elements allows labeled, single-line input fields to be created. The accepted content type of the field is determined by an associated data object (data binding). All generic data objects are supported and only these objects are accepted as inputs (see Figure A.11).

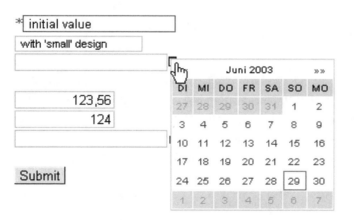

**Figure A.11** BSP element "inputField"

► itemList/listItem

Use this element to create a bulleted list. The bullet point character can be displayed as a number or a symbol. In addition to plain text, more complex elements can also be displayed in the list (see Figure A.12).

- **native HTML**
- textView Item
- Button2

**Figure A.12** BSP element "itemList"

▶ `link`
Use this element to display a hyperlink. The element may contain other elements or pure HTML.

▶ `listBox/listBoxItem`
Use this element to create a selection list with multiple selection options. The list entries can be generated statically or via the concept of data binding to a table (see Figure A.13).

| red | | Multiple selections |
|-----|---|---------------------|
| orange | | k2 |
| yellow | | k4 |
| green | | k6 |

Update

**Figure A.13** BSP element "listBox"

▶ `page`
Use this element to define a document structure. This element represents a complete HTML page. The internal element structure may consist of embedded elements and pure HTML.

▶ `radioButtonGroup/radioButton`
Use these elements to create groups of radio buttons (see Figure A.14).

| ○ red | ⦿ orange | ○ yellow |
|-------|-----------|----------|
| | *orange* | |
| ○ green | ○ blue | ○ violet |

**Figure A.14** BSP element "radioButtonGroup"

▶ `tableView/tableViewColumn/tableViewColumns`
Use these elements to enable the definition and visualization of complex tables. The data is displayed using the data-binding concept. The

visible line areas can be limited and the title bar, column headings, and footer can be defined. With the appropriate activation, pushbuttons can also be displayed to enable navigation in the table (see Figure A.15).

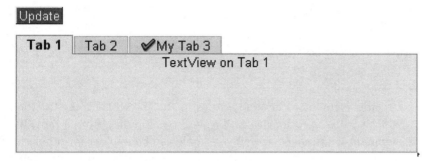

**Figure A.15** BSP element "tableView"

▶ `tabStrip/tabStripHeader/tabStripBody/tabStripItem`
Use these elements to create tabs (card index tabs). Each element consists of one or more tabs. These tabs allow users to switch quickly between different views. The tab names are always visible. For each tab, a separate content area can be defined. This content area is only visible if the corresponding tab has been selected (see Figure A.16).

**Figure A.16** BSP element "tabStrip"

▶ `textEdit`
Use this element to define and display a multi-line text element.

▶ `textView`
This element is a text block.

▶ `tray/trayBody`
Use this element to define a border around any embedded element. Three different buttons are provided in the title bar for the element. These buttons affect the visibility of the framing element and are assigned the relevant event handlers. The first pushbutton allows users

to change to an edit mode, the second button allows the content to be expanded and compressed, and the third button closes the tray (see Figure A.17).

**Figure A.17** BSP element "tray"

▶ `tree/treeNode`
Use this element to arrange entries in the form of a tree structure, which can be used for navigation purposes. Starting from a root, the elements are arranged as nodes. A node can be a folder for other elements or a page. The page ultimately represents the information being displayed in the form of text or a link. Opening a folder corresponds to expanding the underlying sub-tree. This change of status is carried out on the client side (see Figure A.18).

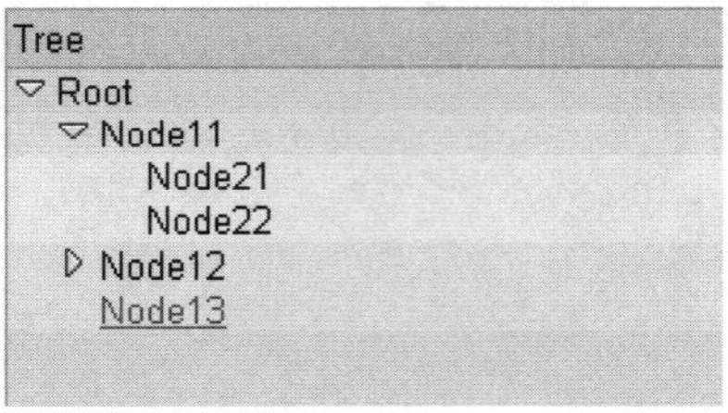

**Figure A.18** BSP element "tree"

## A.4    Supported MIMEs

The SAP Web AS supports a variety of MIME categories. The MIMEs are assigned to a main category and a subcategory in this process. The main categories include text, graphic, audio, video, and applications. The subcategory specifies the exact type of the main category in more detail. The MIMEs are imported using the MIME browser that then stores the objects in the MIME Repository. The following table provides information on which MIMEs are directly supported.

| Main/Subcategory | File extension | Meaning |
|---|---|---|
| text/css | .css | CSS file |
| text/html | .htm, .html | HTML file |
| text/javascript | js | JavaScript file |
| text/plain | .txt, .c, .cc, .g, .h, .hh, .m, .f90 | Text file |
| text/richtext | .rtx | MIME rich text |
| text/xml | .xml | XML file |
| image/gif | .gif | GIF graphic |
| image/gif | .ief | Image Exchange Format |
| image/jpeg | .jpeg, .jpg , .jpe | JPEG graphic |
| image/x-rgb | .rgb | RGB graphic |
| image/x-windowdump | .xwd | X-Windows dump |
| image/tiff | .tiff, .tif | TIFF graphic |
| image/bmp | .bmp | Icon |
| image/ico | .ico | Windows icon |
| audio/basic | .au, .snd | AU and SND sound files |
| audio/x-aiff | .aif, .aiff, .aifc | AIFF sound files |
| audio/x-midi | .midi, .mid | MIDI files |
| audio/x-pn-realaudio | .ram, .ra | RealAudio files |
| audio/x-pn-realaudio-plugin | .rpm | RealAudio plug-in files |
| video/mpeg | .mpeg, .mpg, .mpe | MPEG video |
| video/x-msvideo | .avi | Microsoft AVI video |
| video/x-sgi-movie | .movie | Microsoft SGI video |
| video/quicktime | .qt, .mov | Quicktime video |
| application/acad (NCSA) | .dwg | AutoCAD files |
| application/dxf (CERN) | .dxf | AutoCAD files |
| application/mif | .mif | Maker Interchange Format (Adobe FrameMaker) |
| application/msword | .doc, .dot | Microsoft Word files |
| application/mspowerpoint | .ppt, .ppz, .pps, .pot | Microsoft PowerPoint files |

**Table A.49** Supported MIME types

| Main/Subcategory | File extension | Meaning |
| --- | --- | --- |
| application/msexcel | .xls, .xla | Microsoft Excel files |
| application/mshelp | .hlp, .chm | Microsoft Windows Help files |
| application/octet-stream | .com, .exe, .bin, .dll, .class | Executable files or program code files |
| application/pdf | .pdf | PDF files (Adobe Acrobat Exchange/Reader) |
| application/postscript | .ai, .eps, .ps | PostScript files (Adobe) |
| application/rtf | .rtf | RTF files (Microsoft) |

**Table A.49** Supported MIME types (Cont.)

## A.5 BSP Directives

The following list of BSP directives can be used in developing BSP pages.

| BSP Directive | Example | Meaning |
| --- | --- | --- |
| `<%@extension%>` | `<%@extension name="htmlb" pre-fix="htmlb" %>` | Include BSP extension |
| `<%@page%>` | `<%@page language="abap" %>` | Specify the script language |
| `<%@include%>` | `<%@include file="frag.htm" %>` | Include page fragments |
| `<% %>` | `<% loop at itab into wa. %>` | Script tag |
| `<%-- --%>` | `<%-- comment --%>` | BSP comment |
| `<%= %>` | `<%= Variable %>` | Print tag for output |
| `<%=otr()%>` | `<%=otr(package/alias)%>` | OTR short text |
| `<otr></otr>` | `<otr> Text </otr>` | OTR long text |
| `<%# %>` | not documented | Not documented |

**Table A.50** Available BSP directives

## A.6 Logging onto the ICM

Logging can be explicitly configured using the profile parameter *icm/HTTP/logging_<xx>* ("xx" stands for a two-digit number here). To configure logging, at least two mandatory parameters must be defined:

► **URL Prefix** (*PREFIX*)

This prefix determines which requests are recorded on the ICM. The value "/" is used to log all requests.

► **Name of the Log file** (*LOGFILE*)

The name of the log file written to the application server file system is specified here. The name consists of a combination of characters and permanently defined placeholders, which are described in the following table.

| Placeholder | Meaning |
| --- | --- |
| %d | Day of the month (1–31) |
| %m | Month of the year (1–12) |
| %y | 4-figure year in the format YYYY |
| %h | Hour (0–23) |
| %t | Minute (0–59) |
| %s | Second (0–59) |
| %% | '%' character |

**Table A.51** Placeholders for naming a log file

An example of a log file is:

```
LOGFILE=my_logfile_%d-%m-%y
```

This results in the following name for the log file:

```
my_logfile_17-07-2002
```

The logging profile parameter also provides a range of optional parameters:

► **Format of the Log file** (*LOGFORMAT*)

The log format, that is, the content of the log file, can also be defined. In order to track the different requirements, there is a range of placeholders available that can be individually combined. These placeholders are listed in the following table:

| Placeholder | Meaning |
| --- | --- |
| %b | Length of the response in bytes |
| %h | Name of the remote computer |
| %H | Name of the local computer |

**Table A.52** Placeholders for the structure of the log format

| Placeholder | Meaning |
|---|---|
| %S | Local port name/service |
| %a | IP address of the remote computer |
| %u | User name of a basic authentication |
| %t | Time specification in CLF format: [11/Jan/2002:12:45:00 +0100] |
| %T | Duration of a request in seconds |
| %r | The first line of an HTTP request: e.g., GET /demo HTTP/1.0 |
| %f | Name of the requested object without form fields |
| %U | Total URI of a request (with form fields) |
| %s | OK code of the response |
| %v | Name of the virtual computer |
| %V | Name of the virtual server |
| %{name}i | Name of a request header field, e.g., %{user-agent}i |
| %{name}o | Name of a response header field, e.g., %{server}o |
| %{cookie}c | Output of a request cookie |

**Table A.52** Placeholders for the structure of the log format (Cont.)

The standard log format of the ICM, if no log format has been specified, is the *CLF* (*Common Logfile Format*). This format is very commonly used and has the following structure:

```
192.168.74.99–[17/Jul/2002:22:00:02 +0100] "GET /test/
start HTTP/1.0" 200 128
```

For the CLF, this produces the following structure:

```
LOGFORMAT=%h %l %u %t "r" %s %b
```

▶ **Size of the Log file** (*MAXSIZE*)
This parameter specifies the maximum size of the log file in kilobytes. If this size is exceeded, a new log file is created. The new log file has a unique name (if the time is part of the name), or is assigned a suitable consecutive number at the end of the file (_<xx>).

▶ **Time limit of a log file** (*SWITCHF*)
You can create a new log file at various points in time.

  ▶ Hour (at each change of hour)

  ▶ Day (at each change of day)

  ▶ Month (at each change of month)

▶ **Update type of a log file** (*FILEWRAP*)

If this parameter is set ("on"), the existing log file is deleted and created anew when a size limit is reached (*MAXSIZE*), or a time limit is exceeded (*SWITCHF*). This means there is never more than one log file on the system.

# B  Glossary

The glossary defines a number of important terms used in this book from the world of SAP.

**ABAP:** Advanced Business Application Programming. Programming language of SAP.

**ABAP Dictionary:** Central storage for all system data and data structures in the R/3 system.

**ABAP Editor:** The ABAP Editor can be used to develop and maintain ABAP programs.

**ABAP Interpreter:** Evaluates the instructions of the ABAP program during the runtime.

**Application Server:** Server (from a software point of view) providing a range of services for operating the R/3 system. Typically, the terms → *Instance* and *Application server* are used interchangeably in the SAP environment.

**Application Toolbar:** The application toolbar contains pushbuttons providing the user with fast access to application-specific functions. It is located on the graphical user interface (GUI) underneath the title bar.

**Authorization:** Permission to carry out a specific action in the SAP system.

**Backend System:** Standalone data-processing system with separate database (e.g., mySAP Business Suite component systems).

**BAPI:** Business Application Programming Interface. Functional interfaces using the business methods of the business objects.

**BOR:** Business Object Repository. Directory of all business object types.

**Browser:** → Web browser.

**Buffer:** Area in the main storage of an instance where data often required by the applications is temporarily stored.

**Business Connector:** Software component for exchanging XML messages between different systems.

**Business Framework:** The SAP Business Framework allows customers and partners to link their own components into SAP systems.

**Business Object:** Abstract programming-based display of actual business objects.

**Change Request:** Also Transport request. Information carrier in the Transport Organizer for entering, managing, transporting changes to repository objects, and customizing settings.

**Class Builder:** Tool for creating and maintaining global ABAP classes and interfaces.

**Client:** Software component utilizing the services of a server (software point of view).

**Client:** A commercial, organizational and data-based enclosed unit within a SAP system.

**Command Field:** Element of the system function bar for entering commands, for example, transaction codes.

**Communications Interface:** Interface for exchanging data between programs according to specified protocols.

**CSS:** Cascading Style Sheets. Enhancement for the flexible layout of HTML pages and the one-off definition of frequently used formatting specifications and fonts.

**Customizing:** Configurations that are required to be carried out during a system installation, for example, to modify the supplied neutral functionality to the specific business requirements of a company.

**Data Dictionary:** → ABAP Dictionary.

**Database Interface:** Component of a work process linking it to the database. It converts Open SQL into the database SQL and permits communication with the database.

**Database Server:** Server where the database is installed.

**Data Element:** Object of the ABAP Dictionary. Describes the business significance of a table field and specifies key words, headings, a documentation text, and a domain.

**Debugger:** Tool in ABAP Workbench for detecting errors in ABAP programs and rectifying them.

**Developer Key:** Required in order to be able to carry out your own development work on the SAP system (also *SSCR key*).

**Development Class:** → Package.

**DIAG:** Dynamic Information and Action Gateway. Protocol for communication between the SAP GUI and the application server (also known as the *SAP GUI Protocol*).

**Dialog Process:** → Work process.

**Dictionary:** → ABAP Dictionary.

**Digital Certificate:** Digital document containing proof of identify for a user and the information required for encrypting and decrypting messages. The most common format for client certificates is the X.509 standard.

**Domain:** Object describing the technical characteristics—for example, the data type and the length—of a field.

**Drag & Drop:** Drag & Drop can be used to select objects from an area (source) with the mouse pointer, and to drag and deposit them in another area (target).

**Drag & Relate:** Browser-based navigation tool allowing data from an application to be linked to another application. This makes it possible to link both SAP applications and applications on the Web.

**Dynpro:** DYNamic PROgram. A Dynpro consists of a screen and the underlying flow logic.

**Enqueue process:** → Work process.

**Entity:** Abstract object used in data models (SERM) and typically implemented as a table or view.

**ERP:** Enterprise Resource Planning. ERP systems provide company-wide resource planning using a targeted workflow management system. ERP covers back-office systems such as production, finance, personnel, sales, and materials management systems.

**F1 Help:** Help on the field where the cursor is currently located (**F1** key).

**F4 Help:** Input tool. List of possible input values for a screen (**F4 key**).

**Firewall:** Protects a local network against unauthorized access from outside.

**Forward Navigation:** Starting the ABAP Editor by positioning the cursor on a program name in the ABAP Workbench and then double-clicking.

**Frame:** A WWW page may consist of multiple HTML pages separated by visible or invisible frames.

**Frontend:** Workstation computer.

**Function Builder:** Tool for creating and managing function modules.

**Function Module:** Program module written in ABAP developed in the → Function Builder.

**Gateway:** Interface translating a protocol into another protocol.

**HTML:** HyperText Markup Language. Contains formatting instructions (that the Web browser can interpret) and links to other documents or objects.

**HTTP:** HyperText Transfer Protocol. Protocol between the Web server and Web client.

**HTTPS:** HTTP with → SSL. Data packets transmitted via an HTTPS connection are encrypted using SSL.

**HTTP Server:** → Web server.

**IDES:** Internet Demonstration and Evaluation System. Contains sample companies providing a model for the relevant business processes in the mySAP Business Suite system.

**Instance:** Administrative unit summarizing components of a SAP system, which offers one or more services (generally dispatchers and work processes). Within an instance, the offered services are started and stopped together.

**Interface Repository:** Storage location for interface definitions, for example, for data exchange via → XML (→ also *http://ifr.sap.com*).

**ITS:** Internet Transaction Server. Interface between the component systems and the Internet. The ITS allows users on the Internet and on an intranet to communicate directly with the SAP system by starting business transac-

tions, function modules, and reports as Internet applications.

**LAN:** A Local Area Network has a limited spatial range; for example, within a company site. In contrast, Wide Area Networks (WAN) can extend across large distances.

**Master Data:** Data that remains unchanged for an extended period. It contains information that is frequently required for use in the same way.

**Metadata:** Data describing other data. Metadata are data definitions normally stored in a data dictionary.

**Mode:** Windows where an application function can be processed. The user can keep multiple modes open at any one time.

**Modification:** Customized modification to SAP repository objects.

**mySAP Business Suite:** Comprehensive solution from SAP for optimum integration of all relevant business processes via the Internet. mySAP Business Suite offers seamless, uniform integration between SAP solutions and non-SAP systems across all business processes and therefore provides a complete business environment for electronic commerce. It was previously marketed under the name of "mySAP.com".

**Native SQL:** Database-specific SQL dialect. Native SQL permits the execution of (almost) all instructions provided by the database and their SQL programming interface for the direct execution of a SQL program text. A native SQL instruction largely circumvents the database interface of R/3. There is no table logging and no synchronization with the data buffer on the application server.

**Object Navigator:** Navigation tool for managing development objects.

**Open SQL:** Instructions, originating partly from ANSI-SQL and partly from SAP itself, that provide ABAP programs with uniform access to data, regardless of the database system installed.

**Package:** Group of logically linked development objects.

**Platform:** Combination of database, operating system, and hardware.

**Plug-In:** Add-on program that expands the functionality of a software system.

**Portability:** Transportability of applications between different platforms.

**Portal:** Pages used as initial screens for Internet users; provide users with relevant information immediately and form the platform for visiting other Web sites.

**Presentation Interface:** → SAP GUI.

**Protocol:** Collection of rules for formats and types of data transfer between different computer systems.

**RDBMS:** Relational Database Management System. Record of processes that process data in the corresponding database via SQL. The data and their interrelationships are held in the form of two-dimensional tables.

**Remote System:** Remote standalone system that can be communicated with via the in-house system.

**Repository:** Central storage for all development objects of ABAP Workbench.

**RFC:** Remote Function Call. SAP interface protocol based on CPI-C, which can be used to call and execute prede-

fined functions on a remote system, or within the same system.

**Roll Area:** The roll area is a fixed memory area belonging to a work process. In the roll area, the user context is maintained.

**Runtime Environment:** Quantity of all data and programs available during the runtime.

**Runtime System:** → Runtime Environment.

**SAP Basis:** Total of processes switching between the task level (ABAP programs) and the operating system and database level.

**SAP DCOM:** Distributed Component Object Model. Standardized basis for creating and integrating distributed software components. External client applications can use DCOM as the infrastructure for their communication with SAP servers in order to access mySAP components.

**SAP Easy Access:** Navigation menu providing a user-specific entry point into the SAP system.

**SAP GUI:** The SAP Graphical User Interface is used for the R/3 system. It permits access to the applications and the data input and output.

**SAP GUI for HTML:** GUI running in the Web browser that generates HTML pages dynamically on the basis of SAP screens. Located in the ITS.

**SAP GUI for Java:** Platform-independent GUI that requires a Java environment on the PC workstation.

**SAP GUI for Windows:** GUI for 32-bit Windows workstations.

**SAP Help Portal:** Access to SAP libraries for different releases.

**SAP Library:** Extensive collection of SAP information covering the entire SAP system. The SAP library can be accessed from the SAP system via the **SAP library** Help menu options or via the application Help system.

**SAP Service Marketplace:** World-wide information and communication network from SAP.

**SAP Transaction:** → Transaction.

**SERM:** Structured Entity Relationship Model. Modeling method used to create data models with the Data Modeler.

**Server:** Software component providing a service (software-oriented view).

**Session Handling:** The session handling permits sessions to be held simultaneously, which means that the user can employ multiple browser windows concurrently without having to log on more than once.

**Single Sign-On (SSO):** Mechanism via which the user no longer needs to enter a password for each system that he or she logs onto. The user only identifies himself or herself once, and can then log onto all systems that are part of the SSO environment.

**SQL:** Structured Query Language. SQL is a largely standardized language for accessing data in relational databases.

**SSL:** Secure Sockets Layer. Protocol using powerful authentication mechanisms and encryption to protect data transferred via the Internet.

**Status Bar:** Element of the graphical user interface (GUI) located on the lower edge of a primary window that issues remote messages from the R/3 system as well as other information on the system status.

**System Function Bar:** The system function bar is located underneath the menu bar and contains buttons providing the user with access to frequently used functions such as Save, Back, Exit, and Cancel along with navigation and Help functions.

**System Landscape:** The system landscape defines the systems and clients required for the implementation and maintenance process, with their meanings, along with the transport paths between the systems.

**Tab:** Graphical control element resembling a card file tab.

**TCP/IP:** Transmission Control Protocol/Internet Protocol. Software protocol defining the communication between computers.

**Template:** Template for certain types of HTML documents that is used to standardize or to retrieve functions.

**Ticket:** Authentication used in the SAP Enterprise Portal for single sign-on (SSO). The SSO ticket is assigned to the user by the central portal server. It is then verified by the portal component systems to ensure that the user has access without having to enter his or her user ID and password more than once.

**TMS:** Transport Management System. Sum total of all tools in the R/3 system for organizing, executing, and monitoring transports between R/3 systems.

**Transaction:** Logically completed operation in the SAP system. From the user's point of view, a transaction represents a unit, for example, changing the address of a customer.

**Transaction Code:** Sequence of alpha-numeric characters naming a transaction in the R/3 system.

**Transaction Data:** Activity-related data that is short-lived and assigned to specific master data.

**Transport Organizer:** Tool for managing central and local development projects of ABAP Workbench and for customizing projects.

**URL:** Uniform Resource Locator. Address of an Internet presence, for example, *http://www.mysap.com*.

**User Context:** Data assigned to one specific user. The user context contains, for example, a user-specific area with user and authorization data.

**User Menu:** User-specific access to the SAP system ($\rightarrow$ also SAP Easy Access).

**View:** Virtual table that does not contain any data, but is an application-oriented view of one or more ABAP dictionary table(s).

**WAN:** $\rightarrow$ LAN.

**WAP:** Wireless Application Protocol. Protocol defining the transfer and display of special Internet content on devices with limited display capabilities, for example, mobile phones.

**Web Application Builder (WAB):** Tool for developing Internet applications. The Web Application Builder can be used to create all the files required to run an application on a Web browser.

**Web Browser:** Easy to operate navigation program with graphical user interface for interpreting and displaying HTML documents on the internet.

**Web Server:** Server managing connections to the Internet.

**Workbench:** Integrated development environment of the SAP system.

**Work Process:** Process that processes requests sent to the SAP system. The following work process types exist: Dialog (for executing dialog programs), update (for database changes), background (for executing background jobs), enqueue (for executing blocking operations), and spool (for print editing).

**XML:** eXtensible Markup Language. Standard language for defining individual markup languages that are intended to mark up the structured information. Just like HTML, XML is also a link-based language for Web content.

# C    Bibliography

**Sources**

- *mySAP Technology Roadmap*, Günther Färber and Julia Kirchner, Galileo Press 2003.
- *ABAP Objects: The Official Reference*, Horst Keller and Joachim Jacobitz, Galileo Press 2003
- *ABAP Objects, Introduction to Programming SAP Applications*, Horst Keller and Sascha Kruger, Pearson Education, Great Britain 2002, first published in German by SAP Press 2001.
- *WebBusiness mit SAP*, Mario Perez, Steffen Karch, SAP Press 2002.

# D   About the Authors

Frédéric Heinemann and Christian Rau work internationally as Technology Consultants and Developers at Novasoft AG, Rüsselsheim, Germany. They are primarily involved in new fields in the SAP environment, such as the SAP Web Application Server and SAP Enterprise Portals. Their vast experience enables them to provide assistance with projects on SAP products that have only just appeared in the marketplace in international customer environments.

Novasoft AG was founded in 1989 and today has a position among the leading IT consulting companies as a thoroughbred SAP consulting agency. In line with developments in the marketplace, the company focused on projects in e-commerce and e-business very early on. At the beginning of 2001, Novasoft was included in the circle of mySAP.com Alliance Partners. Over 500 highly specialized SAP consultants sustain the basic "supreme quality" principle. The range of services extends from strategic consulting and feasibility studies, to implementation, customization, project monitoring, and user training, and covers the entire SAP product range and their own development projects.

In addition to five companies in Germany, the Novasoft Group is also represented in England, Finland, Spain, Poland, Singapore, the Czech Republic, and the USA.

# Index